Radiotelegraph and Radiotelephone Codes, Prowords And Abbreviations

for the

Summerland Amateur Radio Club

What started out as a minor Project in 1987, blew out like the national debt so with all this accumulated info, it seemed worthwhile to produce the first book, here now is the enlarged Third Edition.

The sources and references have been many and varied and although the utmost care was taken, the Lists are far from complete and may contain errors.

The original Codes etc were designed principally for marine use as this was the field in which radio was initially developed. The majority retain this influence but many have been modified and modernised to cover land and air applications. Technical terms have also varied as technology has changed however most abbreviations of the computer age have been omitted. These are specialist terms of that mode, not often encountered in telegraphy.
Their number is huge and varied and computer books list them.

Specialised Codes etc are not listed, eg. Armed Services, Civil Aviation, Weather Bureau, Commercial codes etc as these run into many hundreds And are beyond our scope. There are exceptions of course, especially the Navy, where their codes etc formed part of the original listings. Obsolete and obscure codes etc are included for historical interest but are never likely to be encountered in use.

The lists are far from complete and it is requested that anyone who has information that will fill gaps or has an obscure code that could be included please send it to me so the lists can he made more complete. Please quote the reference and date with a photocopy of the list.

The Third Edition has extra material and additions to existing items, marked by an asterisk (*) in the Contents. This includes new codes from the "International Code of Signals" 1987 - 1995.

I thank everyone who has already supplied information and, in anticipation, anyone who might assist in the future. I thank particularly the US Army and Navy Historical Branches, the ITU, Geneva, Mr. Brian Kelk of Cambridge, Engl., BT Archives, Royal Signals Museum, Blandford and many Internet sources and contributors for their assistance. There are many others, both via Internet and other means have supplied or sourced information which might never have otherwise been recorded. Thanks to all of you.

73,

John Alcorn, VK2JWA, QTHR

Compiler.

Lismore,   2002.

ONLINE EDITION
November 2013.

Radiotelegraph and Radiotelephone Codes, Prowords and Abbreviations

TOF / QLF

" Well,, ... He SAID .. 'Send with the other foot' ! "   Signals, 1954

Radiotelegraph and Radiotelephone Codes, Prowords and Abbreviations

Modern Amateur Wireless Station

Hawkins Electrical Guide. No 8 — 1917

Compilation 1987 - 2013
   John Alcorn, VK2JWA

First published 1997
 by REPRINT
   33 Spring St. Lismore, NSW 2480, Australia.

For Summerland Amateur Radio Club.   Email VK2SRC@sarc.org.au
   414 Richmond Hill Rd. Richmond   Phone +61 2 66225759
   Hill, Lismore, NSW, 2480.   Web - http://www.sarc.org.au

Copyright ©   John W. Alcorn
   1997, 2013   412 Richmond   Email VK2JWA@sarc.org.au
 and Orders to -   Hill Rd   Phone +61 0401564323
   Richmond Hill,   Web - http:// http://phonetic.org.au/alphabet.htm
   NSW.
   2480. Australia

ISBN 1 86384 424 4

First Edition, April 1997.
2nd Edition, November 1997
3rd Edition, October 2002
Online Edition November 2013

Radiotelegraph and Radiotelephone Codes, Prowords and Abbreviations

CONTENTS

* Additions or Alterations.

Page					
6		Glossary of Abbreviations and Terms.			
7		Codes	ARL, PRB, RRR		
7	*	Q Code	QAA - QNZ	-	Civil Aviation
15		"	QOA - QQZ	-	Maritime Services
17		"	QRA - QZZ	-	Radio Telecommunications Service (All Services)
23	*	Z Code	ZAA - ZCZ	-	Air Traffic Control Services
26		"	ZDA - ZFZ	-	Message Procedures
28		"	ZGA - ZGZ	-	Calling Procedure
29			ZHA - ZHM	-	Interference and Delay Procedure
			ZHN - ZHZ	-	Automatic Transmission Procedure
			ZIA - ZIZ	-	Serial Numbers
			ZJA - ZJZ	-	Optical Services and Equipment
30			ZKA - ZKZ	-	Radio Guard Procedures
31			ZLA - ZLM	-	Facsimile
			ZLN - ZLZ	-	Radio Navigation and Landing Facilities
			ZMA - ZMZ	-	Direction Finding
32			ZNA - ZNZ	-	Communications Security
		"	ZOA - ZOM	-	Relay.
33			ZON - ZOZ	-	Routing Procedures Strength
			ZPA - ZPM	-	and Readability Search and
			ZPN - ZPZ	-	Rescue Procedures
34			ZQA - ZQZ	-	Take Off and Landing Instructions
			ZRA - ZRZ	-	Frequencies
35			ZSA - ZSZ	-	Air and Sea Traffic Control
		"	ZTA - ZTZ	-	Equipment
36			ZUA - ZUM	-	Miscellaneous
37			ZUN - ZUZ	-	Meteorology
			ZVA - ZVZ	-	Relay Procedure
			ZWA - ZWZ	-	Communications Exercises
			ZXA - ZXZ	-	Radiophoto and Facsimile.
38			ZYA - ZZZ	-	Reserved for National Allocations, Multiplex.
			ZZA - ZZZ	-	Communications Exercises.
39		Telegraphic Code to Insure Secrecy in the Transmission of Telegrams - 1885 - US War Dept.			
40		List of Procedures, Abbreviations, Prosigns and Priorities. British Army, 1896.			
41		Method of Coding Time, Ciphers and Cryptograms. 1896.			
42		German Regulations for the Control of Wireless Telegraphy - 1905 (Extracts)			
43		Z Codes, Original 1907 from Admiralty 'The British Signals Manual'.			
47		List of Prosigns, Abbreviations, RA-SF Codes 'Handbook for Wireless Telegraph Operators' 1908.			
48		Operator's Qualifications - British Army 1896, Ship's W/T Operator, British PO. 1908.			
49	*	List of Procedure Signs and QRA to QSJ and Abbreviations 1909. British Post Office.			
50		Machine gun fire observation semaphore signals. British Army 'Infantry Training. 1911'.			
51		Miscellaneous Procedures, WW1, British and German, 1918			
52-74	*	X Codes British Empire Forces c 1918 to c 1943+.			
74		Ground Signal Codes, The Panel Code. Referenced only, not listed.			
75		List of Military Data Transmission 'X'-Codes.			
76		Zogging. The Signalling Disc or Shutter.			
77		American - British military phraseology differences - Common usages.			
78		Radiotelegraphy and Radiotelephony Combined Abbreviations List			
105	*	Map – 1957 US Coastal Stations open for public correspondence.			
106	*	Five Letter Codes of the ITU and Cable and Wireless. 1975.			
130	*	Special Telegraphic Service Indicators for handling and charging etc. 1908 - 1996.			
132		Royal Navy Convoy Codes - WW I.			
133		Abbreviations - Phillips Press Code.			
138		ARRL - ARL Radiogram Abbreviations List. (1949).			
139	*	German Semaphore and Morse Methods and Procedures, with English Translation.			
143		Radio Signal Reporting Codes - QSA, QRK, Tone, SINFO and SINPFEMO Reports			
144	*	Phonetic Alphabets etc. (USA 1860, British, Australian, 1891-1915, R Navy 1917)			
145		" " (Brit – Aust. 1927 – 1943, USN 1913, US Army 1916, 1919)			
146		" " (USA 1922-41, Allied Forces 1943, ICAO 1947)			
147		" " (Allied Forces 1955, ICAO 1952, NATO 1956-83, IRC 1927, ITC 1932-58)			
148	*	" " (IITS 1932-75, Brit. PMG 1932, Western Union 1933, AR, Brit. 1942)			
149		" " (RSGB, British, ARRL, IBM, Afrikaans.)			
150	*	" " (Argentina, Austria, Azores, Brazil, Chinese Army.)			
151	*	" " (Czech, Croatian, Danish)			
152		" " (Dutch, Esperanto, Finnish)			
153		" " (Finnish, Flemish, French)			
154		" " (French, German - WW1, WW2, > 1993, Greek)			
155	*	" " (Hebrew, Hungarian)			

Radiotelegraph and Radiotelephone Codes, Prowords and Abbreviations

CONTENTS

156		" "	(Hungarian, Indian, Italian)
157		" "	(Italian)
158		" "	(Italian, Kenya-Tanzania)
159		" "	(Kenya, Kwanyama, Latin America)
160		" "	(Ndonga, Norwegian, Polish)
161		" "	(Polish, Portuguese)
162		" "	(Portuguese, Romanian, Rumantsch, Russian,)
163		" "	(Russian, Serbo-Croat)
164	*	" "	(Slovak, Slovenian, South. Africa, Spanish)
165		" "	(Spanish, Swahili)
166	*	" "	(Swedish, Switzerland - [French, German, Italian, Romansh])
167		" "	(Turkish, Ukrainian)
168	*	" "	(USA Police)
169	*	" "	(Japanese, 1999)
170	*	" "	(NATO Phonetics 1987 - English and French pronunciations)
171-192		International Code of Signals 1987-1995 - Extracts of new procedures, abbreviations.	
171	*	Methods of Signalling and General Instructions.	
173	*	Radiotelephony - Calling and basic procedure.	
174	*	Morse Signalling by Hand Flags or Arms.	
175	*	Procedure Signals for Voice, Telegraphy, Lights and Flags.	
178	*	Single Letter Signals for Icebreakers and Assisted Vessels.	
178	*	Distress - Vessels, Signals, Position.	
181	*	Search and Rescue - Proceeding, Position, Info, Instructions, Search, Results, Rescue, Survivors.	
186	*	Communications - Calling, Answer, Acknowledge, Cancel, Communicate, Exercise.	
188	*	International Health Regulations.	
189	*	Table of Complements.	
190	*	Request for Medical Assistance - General, Description of Patient.	
191	*	Innocent Passage and Freedom of Navigation. ICS, Supp 1995.	
192	*	USA / Russia Supplementary Signals for Naval Vessels 1969, 1999.	
193		USA Landline Numerical Code - 1857, 1859 etc. Incomplete.	
194	*	USA Railroads - Weather, Block Codes, Abbreviations. Approx 1864 - 1909.	
195		USA Police Ten-Code - Postwar - 1996.	
197		USA Police etc. 11-Codes, 12-Codes, 1996.	
198		CB Radio Operator's Ten-Code - 1996.	
199	*	CB Radio Operator's 11 - Code.	
200		CB Radio Trucker's 12 - Code - 1976.	
201		CB Radio Operator's 13 - Code - 1996.	
202	*	British Police Radio Codes. – Restricted. 1972.	
203		Standard Marine Navigational Vocabulary, 1996.	
205		Telegraph Transmission Codes, Code Chronology.	
206		Chronology Early Machine Codes and Wireless Telegraphy.	
207		Information Sought. Wireless or Radio?	
207		Morse and Other Telegraph Codes - Introduction.	
208	*	French Method of Semaphoring by Hand Flags. 1911.	
209	*	Semaphore Alphabet - (ICS 1931). Morse and Semaphore Flag Positions. RN Pasley, 1866.	
210		The US General Service Code (Myer, Army/Navy Code) 1860-1912.	
212		1912 Flag usage, USA Morse. Conventional Signs for Flag, Torch, Heliograph, Flash Lantern.	
212	*	Other US services Codes, 1909 - 1915. Fog horn, whistle, bugle, bell, Ardois, Very, Semaphore.	
213	*	Light and Sound Signals, According to Colomb's Flashing Signals System.	
215	*	Needle Telegraphs - Five, Two, Single Needle and Direct Indicating Telegraphs.	
216	*	Needle Telegraph Codes - Schilling, Gauss & Weber, Steinheil, Cooke & Wheatstone, De La Rive, Wilson.	
218		Morse - Morse, Vail, Bain, Boston Fire Dept., American, Austro-German.	
219	*	" Continental, Myer 1864-72, Myer 1912, WATCo, Phillips..	
220	*	" Buckingham, Barclay, USN Code, Anderson, Phillips American, US Navy Bugle.	
221	*	" Vietnam POW Codes, Polish Survival. – Punctuation.	
222		" International, USA (American) and Arabic Morse - 1943	
223-224		" Greek, Russian, Turkish and Japanese Morse - 1943-1997	
225		" Chinese	
227		The Heliograph. 1857 – 1995, Cairns to Coffs Harbour links.	
229	*	World Time Zones. 2001.	
230		Early Hughes, Wheatstone and Baudot Telegraph Systems.	
231	*	Addenda – Material received after printing of main text – Q, Z Codes, Abbrevs, Patriot, Israeli, Navajo Phonetics.	
235-236		Bibliography, Sources and References.	

Radiotelegraph and Radiotelephone Codes, Prowords and Abbreviations

Glossary of Abbreviations and Terms

AA	Australian Army.
ACP-###	Allied Communications Publication. Issue No. ###.
AIF	Australian Imperial Forces. 1st. = WW1, 2nd. = WW2.
AM	Air Ministry. UK administration of RAF and air affairs etc.
AR	Amateur Radio. Organisations and operators. AR - Amateur Radio magazine Aust.
ARRL	Amateur Radio Relay League. Amateur Radio organisation in the USA.
AUST	Australia, Australian. Forces, Services and Agencies etc.
BAMS	Broadcast to Allied Merchant Ships – WW2 shipping info / directions. Not replied to.
BR	British Railways, all companies etc. Esp 19th Century +.
BT	British Telecom, its archives.
CAP	Civil Air Patrol. USA air emergency organisation.
CCITT	International Telegraph and Telephone Consultative Committee.
CT#	Complements Table # - Suffixes to ICS '87 codes, # series number.
C&W	Cable and Wireless - Large International US-Atlantic telegraph company.
GER	German. Forces and Agencies etc.
GPO	General Post Office. (US - Govt. Printing Office)
HMS	His / Her Majesty's Ship. British Royal Navy ship.
HMSO	His / Her Majesty's Stationary Office. UK Govt. Publications etc.
IARU	International Amateur Radio Union.
ICAO	International Civil Aviation Organisation.
ICS	International Code of Signals book. 1912, 1915, 1931 (1950 Supp.), 1987 (1995 Supp.).
ICSLS	International Convention for the Safety of Life at Sea.
IFF	"Identification Friend or Foe" Aircraft ID, WW2 radio R3002 for 'friendly a/c'.
IITS Art. 40	Instructions for the International Telephone Service, Article 40.
IMCO	Inter-Governmental Maritime Consultative Organisation.
IMO	International Maritime Organisation.
IRC	International Radiotelegraph Convention.
IRU	International Radio Union.
ITU	International Telegraphic / Telecommunications Union.
IWTC	International Wireless Telegraph Convention 1906, Berlin.
JARL	Japanese Amateur Radio League.
L&NWR	London & North Western Railway.
Met.	Meteorological.
MM#	Morsum Magnificat - Morse enthusiasts magazine, UK, Issue #.
NATO	North Atlantic Treaty Organisation.
NSW	New South Wales. State in Eastern Australia.
OHMS	On His / Her Majesty's Service.
PMG	Postmaster General's Dept.
QLD	Queensland. NE Australian state.
RACES	Radio Amateur Civil Emergency Service. ARRL emergency service.
RAF	Royal Air Force, Britain.
RCAF	Royal Canadian Air Force.
RN	Royal Navy, Britain.
RSGB	Radio Society of Great Britain. Amateur Radio organisation in the UK.
RTG	Radio Track Guide.(used in Q Codes)
S/I	Special Installation (used in Q Codes) UK imported (US) equipment.
SOE	Special Operations Executive. British agents etc. in occupied Europe WW2.
UK	United Kingdom of Great Britain etc. Services and Agencies etc.
US, USA	United States (of America), Armed and Government services etc.
USN	United States Navy.
USSC	United States Signal Corps.
VDC	Volunteer Defence Corps. Australian home guard forces, WW2.
WA	Western Australia. A state of Australia.
WATCo.	Western Australian Telegraph Co. (Ref. MM56)
WIA	Wireless Institute of Australia. Amateur Radio society, formed 1910.
WICEN	Wireless Institute Civil Emergency Network. Aust AR emergency service.
WWI, WW1	The First World War, the Great War, 1914 - 1918.
WWII, WW2	The Second World War, 1939 - 1945.

Radiotelegraph and Radiotelephone Codes, Prowords and Abbreviations

List of Radiotelegraph 'Q' and 'Z' Codes

Key to date of changes noted and references, NOT part of the Code Indicator.
*1912 $1924 #1933 %1938 ¶1943 ?1960 +1972 @1985 &1987 1990   ~ ARRL Codes » C&W

Q Codes etc. become a QUESTION when followed by the Question Mark (?).

CODE	QUESTION	ANSWER or NOTICE
ARL ~	Do you have the ARRL abbreviations list ?	I have ARRL-Numbered Radiogram list. Ready.
PRB *	Will I use the International Signal Code ?	Use International Signal Code.
RRR		Have been ordered to stop by surface raider.
QAA - QNZ	Allocated for Civil Aviation use.	
QAA ¶	At what time do you expect to arrive at ... ?	I expect to arrive at ... at ...
QAB	May I have clearance from.......to......... ?	UR cleared for............ by........from......to........
QAB ¶	Are you making for ... ?	Make / I am making for ...
QAC ¶	Are you returning to ... ?	Return / I am returning to ...
QAD ¶	At what time did you leave ... ?	I left ... at ...
QAE ¶	Have you news of ... (c/s) ?	I have no news of .... (c/s)
QAF	Advise where you are at .... / over	I am / was at ..... hrs height.
QAF ¶	At what time did you pass ... ?	I passed ... at ... (time)
QAG	Arrange flight to be over........at...........	Will arrange flight to be over .... at ....
QAH	What is your height above .... What	I am at ...... height above ....
QAI	is the essential A/C traffic ? Shall I	The essential A/C traffic is ....
QAJ ¶	take steps to search for an aircraft (or ...) in my vicinity ?	Search for an aircraft (or...) in your vicinity.
QAK	Is there any risk of collision ?	There is risk of collision.
QAL	Are you/r A/C landing/ed at .... ?	I am / A/C has landing/ed at ....
QAM	What is met info for .... ?	Met info for .... at .... is ....
QAN	What is surface wind speed at .... ?	Surface wind dir and speed at .... is ....
QAO	Wind speed & TRUE dir at ...... levels ....?	Wind speed & TRUE dir at ..... levels ...... is.
QAP	Please listen for .... on	I am listening for .... on ....
QAP ¶	Must I listen for you (on ... Kc/s) ?	Continue to listen for me (on ...Kc/s).
QAQ	Am I near a Prohibited Area?	You are near/flying over a Prohibited Area..
QAR	May I stop listening on freq ...... for .... ?	You may stop listening on ...... for ..... min.
QAS ¶		You are flying over a forbidden zone (or f. z. of ...) Lister
QAT ¶	Shall I continue to send ?	before sending, you are interfering/sending over ... I am
QAU	Where may I jettison fuel ?	about to jettison fuel.
QAV	Can you home on my signal / DF?	I am flying on (...stn) my homer / DF.
QAW		About to do overshoot procedure.
QAW ¶		The Beam Approach (BABS) installation is out of action.
QAX	Have you ...... aboard for a telegram ?	Yes I have .... aboard for a telegram.
QAY	Advise when you pass bearing .... deg. .....?	Passed bearing .... deg at .... to heading at ....
QAZ	Have you comms problem from storm?	I have comms problems from storm.
QBA	What is the horizontal visibility at .... ?	Horiz visibility at ... at ... hrs is ..... distance.
QBB	Amount, type, height, cloud over ... at ... ?	Amount, type, height cloud over ... at ... is ...
QBC	Report Met as observed at .... at ... hrs ?	Met as observed at ... at ... hrs are .....
QBD	How much fuel have you left ?	Fuel remaining is .... hrs ... minutes.
QBD ¶		IFF switched on in distress position.
QBE		I am about to wind in my aerial.
QBF	Are you flying in cloud ?	In cloud at ... above ... descending to ...
QBG	Are you flying above cloud ?	Above cloud at .... height above .....
QBH	Are you flying below cloud ?	Below cloud at .... height above .....
QBI ¶		The controlled zone regs are in force.
QBI	Is IFR compulsory at .... from .... to .... ?	IFR compulsory at .... from ... to .....
QBJ	Amt, type, height, above ... of top of cloud ?	At ... hrs at ... top of cloud is .... etc.
QBK	Have you no cloud in your vicinity ?	No cloud in my vicinity at ... above ...
QBL	May I make procedure let down on ..c/s.. Range Station ?	You are cleared to make procedure let down on ..c/s.. Range Station.
QBL	Can I leave local area on ... of .... ?	I may leave local area on ... of ...
QBL ¶	May I make procedure let down on c/s Range Stn ?	You may make procedure let down on c/s Range Stn .
QBM	Has ... sent any message for me ?	Here is message sent by ... at ... hrs.
QBN	Are you flying between 2 layers of cloud ?	Between two layers of cloud at ... hgt above ...

Radiotelegraph and Radiotelephone Codes, Prowords and Abbreviations

List of Radiotelegraph 'Q' and 'Z' Codes

Key to date of changes noted and references, NOT part of the Code Indicator.
*1912 $1924 #1933 %1938 ¶1943 ?1960 +1972 @1985 &1987 1990   ~ ARRL Codes » C&W

Q Codes etc. become a QUESTION when followed by the Question Mark (?).

CODE	QUESTION	ANSWER or NOTICE
QBO	What is the nearest suitable VFR drome ?	Suitable VFR drome at ....
QBP	Are you flying in and out of cloud ?	In and out of cloud at ... height above ....
QBQ	- unassigned -	
QBS	Ascend/descend to ... height above ... before instrument. met or visibility falls below ... & advise.	
QBT	What distance to see runway lights from approach?	Runway lights seen ... distance from approach?
QBT ¶		You are missing your dots.
QBU ¶	Are you certain of the accuracy of telegram ?	Telegram ... is not clear.
QBV	Have you reached ... height above ..... ?	Reached ... height above ... (datum/Place)
QBW	Did you receive msg ... sent at ... ?	Received message ... sent at ... hrs.
QBW ¶	Have you recd telegram sent at ... ?	Telegram sent at ... has not been received.
QBX	Have you left ... height above ... ?	Left ...... height above .... (datum/Place).
QBX ¶	May I approach using Beam Approach BABS installation ?`	You may approach using BABS Installation. The QDM of runway is ..... length .....
QBY	What's the height of important cloud ?	Height of important cloud layers is ....
QBZ	Report flying conditions relative to cloud ?	Use QBF, QBG, QBH, QBK, QBN, QBP as reqd
QCA	Can I change from ... height to ... above ... ?	May/am change from... height to ... above ...
QCA ¶		You are causing delay by slowness in answering.
QCB ¶		You are causing delay by answering out of turn ?
QCB	Delay caused by 1-tx out of turn. 2-slow reply. 3-your no reply to my	
QCC	- unassigned -	
QCD ¶		You are to - 1. maintain height of ... ft and report over the ..c/s.. Range Stn. 2. hold on to the ... leg of the beam ..c/s.. Range Stn. at height ... ft.
QCE	When can I expect approach clearance ?	Expect approach clearance at .../ No delay exptd
QCF	Delay indefinite.	Expect approach clearance not later than ... hrs.
QCG ¶	Shall I take guard from you (on ...Kc/s) ?	Take guard for me (on ...Kc/s).
QCH	May I taxi to .... ? (Place)	Cleared to taxi to.... (Place)
QCI		Make/making 360 deg turn to left / right immediately.
QCJ	- unassigned -	
QCK	- unassigned -	
QCL	- unassigned -	
QCM	Is my transmission defective ?	Your transmission in defective.
QCN	- unassigned -	
QCO ¶	How is my note ?	Your note is - 1. Good. 2. Bad. 3. Varies.
QCP		Your note is bad.
QCQ	- unassigned -	
QCR		My transmitter is faulty.
QCS		Receive on frequency ... broken down.
QCS ¶		My reception on low/med. freq has broken down.
QCT ¶		My reception on high frequency has broken down.
QCU	- unassigned -	
QCV	- unassigned -	
QCW	- unassigned -	
QCX	What is your full callsign ?	Full c/s is ... / use full c/s until .....
QCY ¶		Work/working on trailing aerial.
QCZ	Can I use abbreviated callsign ?	You can use abbreviated c/s until advised.
QDA		Act as relay between .... and ....
QDB	Have you sent message ...to..... ?	I have sent message ... to ....
QDC		Message ... is sent by landline.
QDD		Message ... refused by ... inform originator.
QDE	- unassigned -	
QDF	What is your D value at ... ? Position ?	D value at (Pos) at (height) is ... mb +/-
QDG ¶		Take guard for me on ... Kc/s.
QDH	What causes the interference ?	Interference is caused by ...

Radiotelegraph and Radiotelephone Codes, Prowords and Abbreviations

List of Radiotelegraph 'Q' and 'Z' Codes

Key to date of changes noted and references, NOT part of the Code Indicator.
*1912 $1924 #1933 %1938 ¶1943 ?1960 +1972 @1985 &1987 1990   ~ ARRL Codes » C&W

Q Codes etc. become a QUESTION when followed by the Question Mark (?).

CODE	QUESTION	ANSWER or NOTICE
QDI	- unassigned -	
QDJ	- unassigned -	
QDK		Answer in alphabetical order of callsigns.
QDL	Will you ask for a series of bearings ?	I will ask you for a series of bearings.
QDM	Give MAG brg to you /or with no wind	MB to me / no wind ... deg at ... hrs.
QDN ¶		Can't determine yr posn you are nearly in line with D/F Stn Base Line.
QDO	Station ... give sig on watch freq for ...?	Station ... will tx on freq ... for 1 / ... minute/s to DF.
QDP	Will you accept control of ... now / at ... hrs..?	I'll accept control of ... now / at ... hrs.
QDQ	- unassigned -	
QDR	What is my MAG bearing from U/or from ... ?	Your MAG brg from me/or from ... was ... at ... hrs.
QDS ¶		I cannot accept W/T control of.
QDT	Are you flying in visual met conditions ?	Fly / flying in visual met /at all times.
QDU		Cancel my IFR flight plan.
QDV	Are you in horizontal vision less than ..... ?	Horizontal visn less than (dist) at (ht) above ...
QDW	- unassigned -	
QDX		I accepted control and responsibility.
QDY ¶		Mag course with no wind to me/... is ....° at ...
		There is a balloon barrage within 60 miles of me on that track.
QEA	May I cross the runway ahead of me?	You may cross the runway ahead of you.
QEB	May I turn at the intersection?	Taxi LEFT/RIGHT/STRT AHEAD at ... into ....
QEC	Can I turn 180 deg & return down the runway?	You may turn 180 deg & return down runway.
QED	Shall I follow the pilot vehicle ?	Follow the pilot vehicle.
QEF	Have I/you reached the parking area?	I/you have reached the parking area.
QEG	Can I leave/ have you left the parking area?	You may leave/ I have left parking area.
QEH	Can I move / have you moved to holding position?	Cleared to/ I have moved to holding posn. no.
QEI	- unassigned -	
QEJ	Can I/ have you assume/d take off posn ?	Cleared to/ I have assumed take off position.
QEK	Are you ready for immediate take off?	I am ready for immediate take off.
QEL	Can I take off & then turn left/right ?	You can take off, turn as follows ....
QEM	What is the condition of the landing surface at ...	L S Condition at ... is ... (use NOTAM code)
QEN	Shall I hold my position ?	Hold your position.
QEO	Shall I/have you cleared runway?	Clear/ I have cleared / the runway.
QEP	- unassigned -	
QEQ	- unassigned -	
QER	- unassigned -	
QES	Is the right hand circuit in force at .... ?	A right hand circuit is in force at ....
QET to QEZ	- unassigned -	
QFA	What is met for (flt) for (hrs) to (hrs) ?	Met forcast for ... from ... to ... is ....
QFB ¶	Are fresh met observations req'd ?	Fresh met observations are required.
QFB		1) approach. 2) runway. 3) both lights are out of order.
QFC	Amount, type, height cloud base above ... at..?	At ... cloud base is ... at ...above ...
QFC ¶	Can you give me upper wind from ... to ...?	Here is upper wind from ... to ...
QFD	1) is visual beacon on at ...?	1) The... visual beacon at ... is operating.
	2) Put VB on. 3) Put VB off.	2) VB at ... will be off until you land.
QFD ¶	Altimeter adjusted at... at ... Give correction	At ... you must add .... metres.
	for ... or other drome.	At ... you must subtract ... metres.
QFE	Give barometric pressure at ground level.	The barometric pressure at ground level is .....
QFF	What is barometric pressure at sea level?	At ... barometric pressure is ... millibars.
QFF		Meteorological Office, Station.
QFG	Am I overhead ?	You are overhead.
QFH	May I descend below the clouds?	You may descend below the clouds.
QFI	Are the aerodrome lights lit ?	The aerodrome lights are lit.
QFI ¶		Please light aerodrome lights.
QFJ ¶		The aerodrome lights are in operation.

9

Radiotelegraph and Radiotelephone Codes, Prowords and Abbreviations

List of Radiotelegraph 'Q' and 'Z' Codes

Key to date of changes noted and references, NOT part of the Code Indicator.
*1912 $ 1924 # 1933 % 1938 ¶ 1943 ? 1960 + 1972 @ 1985 & 1987 1990 ~ ARRL Codes » C&W

Q Codes etc. become a QUESTION when followed by the Question Mark (?).

CODE		QUESTION	ANSWER or NOTICE
QFK	¶	Please send up maroons ?	I am about to send up maroons.
QFL	¶	Please send up pyrotechnical lights ?	I am about to send up pyrotechnical lights.
QFM		What height above .... (1) should I fly ? (2) are you flying ? (3) intend flying at ?	I am / you are flying at 1 / 2 / 3.
QFN	¶		Please do not wind in aerial until I transmit the "end of work" sign.
QFO		May I land immediately ?	You may land immediately.
QFP	¶		My navigation lights are not working.
			(From the ground) - Your navigation lights are not working.
QFP		Will you give info about .... at .....(place) ?	Info given as NOTAM Code Groups.
QFQ	¶		The landing lights / at ... are out of order.
QFQ		Are / please put approach / runway lights on ?	Approach / runway lights are on.
QFR		Does my landing gear appear damaged ?	Your landing gear appears damaged.
QFS		Is radio beacon at ..... in operation ?	Please have / radio at ... is in operation
QFS		Please place radio beacon at ... in operation.	Radio beacon at ... will be in oprn in ... mins.
QFT		Between what heights is ice formation seen at..?	Ice formation seen between hts... &... at ...
QFU		What is Mag dir/no of runway to use ?	Mag dir/ no of runway to use is ...
QFV		Are the floodlights switched on?	Switch on/ floodlights/ are switched on
QFV	¶	Give me direction of row of landing lights ? (Green, White, Red)	Direction of row of LL)Green, White, Red) is....
QFW		What is length of runway in (unit) ?	Length of runway ... in use is ...
QFW	¶	Is row of LLs (G,W,R) in operation ?	Row of LLs (G,W,R) is in operation.
QFX			Work / am working on fixed aerial.
QFY		Give met landing conditions at ... ?	Met landing conditions at ... are ...
QFZ		Give drome met for ... period ... to ...	Drome met for ... from ... to ... is ....
QGA	¶	Can I land immediately using beacon sigs ?	You may lan immediately using beacon sigs.
QGB	¶		You may not land at .... using radio beacon procedure.
QGC		Are there obstructions to the ... of runway ?	Obstructions to the ... of runway.
QGC	¶	Can you direct my landing ?	Cannot direct your landing. Stay outside controlled zone.
QGD		Any obstructions on track above my altitude?	Obstructions on track ... height above ...
QGE		What is my distance to your station?	Your dist to my station is ....
QGF	¶	Give my mag brg and dist to you, zero wind ?	Your mag brg is ..., dist... to me zero wind.
QGG			Send the pony by the next train. (satirical comment)
QGH		May I land using ..... procedure etc?	You may land using ... facility etc.
QGJ			Transmit to a minimum, I must work other aircraft.
QGK		What track should I / are you making good ?	Make / am making good track from ... to ....
QGL		May I enter control at .... ?	You may enter ... control at ...
QGM			You may not enter / leave .... control area / zone at ....
QGN		May I be cleared to land at ...... ?	You are cleared to land at ....
QGO			Landing is prohibited at ......
QGP		What is my number for landing ?	You are number ... to land.
QGQ		May I hold at ... (Place) ?	Hold at ... at (ht) above ... wait orders.
QGR		Can I land at ..... without left turn ?	You can land at ... without left turn.
QGS	¶		You may not land without left circuit.
QGS			Fly ... mins on heading to give reciprocal track.
QGT			Fly for ... mins on heading to maintain track reciprocal to your present one.
QGU			Fly .... mins on ... deg magnetic heading.
QGV		Do you see me / aerodrome / ... aircraft ?	I see you at ... / aerodrome / ... aircraft.
QGW		Is my landing gear down and OK ?	Your landing gear appears down and OK.
QGX	¶	May I land using ZZ procedure ?	You may land using ZZ procedure.
QGY	¶		You may not land using ZZ procedure.
QGZ			Hold on ... direction of ... facility.
QHA	¶		You are using authentication incorrectly. 1. Verify cipher set-up. 2. Place authenticator in proper part of transmission.
QHB	¶		Your attention is invited for 1. Action, 2. Info. to msg ... in your files.

Radiotelegraph and Radiotelephone Codes, Prowords and Abbreviations

List of Radiotelegraph 'Q' and 'Z' Codes

Key to date of changes noted and references, NOT part of the Code Indicator.
*1912 $ 1924 # 1933 % 1938 ¶ 1943 ? 1960 + 1972 @ 1985 & 1987 1990   ~ ARRL Codes » C&W

Q Codes etc. become a QUESTION when followed by the Question Mark (?).

CODE	QUESTION	ANSWER or NOTICE
QHC ¶		I am or have been (or ... is or has been) calling you (on ... Kc/s).
QHD ¶	What is cause of delay / bad transmission ?	Delay / bad transmission due to ...
QHE	Advise when you are on ... leg of approach ?	On 1) cross 2) down 3) base 4) final leg.
QHF ¶		Your freq is slightly (or ... Kc/s) high.
QHG	Can I enter traffic circuit ... high above ...?	Enter traffic circuit ... height above ...
QHG ¶	Is net free or directed ?	Net is free.
QHH	Are you making an emergency landing ?	Making / emergency landing / being made at ...
QHI	Are you 1) airborne, 2) on land ?	I am / ... is 1) airborne 2) on land at ... hrs.
QHI ¶		Now, until further orders (or until ...)
QHK ¶		Make preliminary call before transmission.
QHL ¶		From ... until ...
QHN ¶		Take over D/F guard as preordered (or ... Kc/s) from ... to ...
QHO ¶		I am (or ... is) unable to use ...
QHP ¶		At ...
QHQ	May I / are you making ... approach at ... ?	You may / I am making ... approach at ...
QHR ¶		Inform me when this msg(s) has been recd by addressees (or by ...)
QHS ¶		Switch of IFF sets for ten minutes in area denoted except for ship(s) whose c/s follow ...
QHU ¶		Waterborne.
QHW ¶		Set watch (on ... Kc/s).
QHX ¶		Pass to ... for info and BAMS transmitting action.
QHZ	Shall I circle drome (or go round) ?	Circle aerodrome (or go around).
QHZ ¶		Your lamp is out of focus.
QIA ¶		Check your authentication of last transmission (or message).
QIB ¶		The c/s of friendly shadowing aircraft is ....
QIC	Can I QSO with ... on (freq) now/ at ....?	Estab comms with ... on ... now/at ... hrs.
QID	Is your radio working well ?	My radio functions well.
QID ¶	Is your .... faulty ?	My .... is faulty.
QIE ¶	1. We have a glider in tow.	2. We are forced to release glider at .... (approx position).
QIF	What frequency is ... on ?	..... is on frequency .....
QIH ¶		Shift (or direct ...) to receive on ... Kc/s.
QIK ¶		C/s of strike (friendly striking force) aircraft is ...
QIN ¶		Shift to D/F freq ... and keep lookout for aircraft c/s.
QIO ¶		You are (or ...is) causing interference by inattention to order to wait.
QIZ ¶		Use flashing.
QJA ¶		Authentication of my last transmission (or message ...) is ... 1. Correct; 2. Incorrect, correct authenticator is ...
QJA	Is my 1) tape 2) mark/space reversed ?	Your 1) tape, 2) mark/space is reversed.
QJB	Will you use 1....... 8 ? (Code below) (1 Radio, 2 Cable, 3 Telegraph, 4 TTY, 5 Phone, 6 Receiver, 7 Transmitter, 8 Reperferator)	I will use 1 ..... 8. (Code below.)
QJC ¶	When will you call agn on present freq (or on ... Kc/s) ?	I will call you again on present freq (or on ... Kc/s)
QJC	Check your 1 ...... 8 ? (1 Tx-distr, 2 Auto head, 3 Perf, 4 Reperf, 5 Printer, 6 Printer motor. 7 Keyboard, 8 Antenna)	I will check my 1 ..... 8.
QJD	Am I transmitting in 1) letters 2) figures ?	I am transmitting in 1) or 2).
QJD ¶	Does my ... appear to be faulty ?	Your ... appears to be faulty.
QJE	Is my freq shift 1) wide 2) narrow 3) OK ?	Your freq shift is 1), 2) by ... Hz, 3) OK.
QJE ¶		... 1. Relay, 2. Remote control, 3. Tube (valve)
QJF ¶		Tune your stn to the proper freq (or to ... Kc/s).
QJF		My signal is satisfactory 1) locally, 2) as radiated.
QJG	Shall I revert to auto relay ?	Revert to automatic relay.
QJG ¶	Who is controlling stn (NCS) on this freq (or ...Kc/s) ?	
QJH	Shall I run 1) test tape, 2) text sentence ?	Run 1) test tape, 2) a test sentence.
QJH ¶		Shift (or direct ...) to transmit on ... Kc/s.
QJI	Will you transmit continuous 1) mark, 2) space?	I am transmitting continuous 1) mark, 2) space.

Radiotelegraph and Radiotelephone Codes, Prowords and Abbreviations

List of Radiotelegraph 'Q' and 'Z' Codes

Key to date of changes noted and references, NOT part of the Code Indicator.
*1912 $ 1924 # 1933 % 1938 ¶ 1943 ? 1960 + 1972 @ 1985 & 1987 1990   ~ ARRL Codes » C&W

Q Codes etc. become a QUESTION when followed by the Question Mark (?).

CODE	QUESTION	ANSWER or NOTICE
QJK	Are you receiving 1 .... 4 ?	I am receiving a 1 .... 4.
	1) cont. mark, 2) cont. space, 3) mark bias, 4) space bias.	
QJM ¶	Check encipherment (Cryptographing) of message ... (or portions indic.) and repeat.	
QJN ¶	Change to loop D/F on ...Kc/s (and home on transmissions made by ...)	
QJO ¶	Message (msg ...) is/has being passed out of proper sequence of stn serial numbers.	
QJP ¶		My ... apparatus temporarily out of action.
QJR ¶		Message was recd by addressees (or by ...) at ...
QJS ¶	What is readability of my (or ...) signals ? (1-5)	
QJT ¶		S/E (US radar) unserviceable.
QJV ¶		IFF switched off.
QJW ¶		Keep continuous watch until further notice (on...Kc/s).
QJY ¶		... is in W/T Company.
QJZ ¶		Stand by.
QK "	(WW2-SOE agents in Europe)	Initial letter or figure check follows immediately
QKA		Authentication of this message or transmission (or msg ...) is ...
QKA		I have effected rescue proceeding to with ... pers needing ambulance.
QKB ¶		The Beam Approach Installation is out of action.
QKC	Sea conditions at ...	1) permit landing, no take off, 2) landing hazardous.
QKC ¶	Shall I send by... 1. Direct (R) method ?	Send by ... (1, 2, 3, 4.)
	2. Broadcast (F) " ?	
	3. Intercept (I) " ?	
	4. Repeat back (G) " ?	
QKF	May I be relieved (at ... hrs)?	Relieved at ... hrs by a/c, vessel, c/s.
QKF ¶		Answer me (or ...) on ... Kc/s.
QKG ¶	Must I get permission from NCS before transmitting ?	You must obtain permission from NCS before transmitting.
QKG	Will relief be when .... makes 1) Visual, 2) Communications contact with survivors?	Relief will be when .... makes 1) or 2) contact with survivors.
QKH	Give details of parallel search ? Answers to 1, 2, 3.?	Parallel search details are -
		1. Sweep direction ... degs.
		2. With ... dist separation.
		3. At a height of ....
QKH ¶	Is the Beam Approach Installation in operation ?	The BAI is in operation.
QKI ¶		You may not land using the BAI.
QKJ ¶	May I approach using the BAI ?	You may approach using the BAI.
QKK ¶		Beacon of BAI is working but Inner Marker is out of action.
QKL ¶	May I land using the BAI ?	You may land using the BAI.
QKM ¶	Request BAI at ... be switched on.	The BAI at ... is switched on.
QKM	Has location of survival craft been marked ?	Loc of survival craft marked at ..... hrs by ...
	1) flame or smoke float 2) sea marker 3) sea marker dye 4) ...(specify other marker)	
QKN ¶		Aircraft plotted (believed to be you) in position ... course ... at ...
QKO ¶	May I use Radio Track Guide procedure ?	You may use RTG procedure.
QKO	What other Units are in the operation ?	In the operation ... other Units are ....
QKP ¶		You may not use RTG procedure.
QKP	What search pattern is being used ?	The search pattern is -
		1 parallel, 2 square, 3 creeping line,
		4 track crawl, 5 contour, 6 aircraft & ship,
		7 .... (specify).
QKQ ¶	Request RTG at ... be switched on.	The RTG at ... is switched on.
QKR ¶	Is the RTG at ... in operation ?	The RTG at ... is in operation.
QKS ¶		The RTG at ... is out of operation.
QKT ¶	Will you switch on the Range Stn. (at ...) ?	
QKU ¶	Is the Range Stn. (at ...) in operation ?	The Range Stn. (at ...) is in operation.
QKW ¶		The Range Stn. (at ...) is out of action.

Radiotelegraph and Radiotelephone Codes, Prowords and Abbreviations

List of Radiotelegraph 'Q' and 'Z' Codes

Key to date of changes noted and references, NOT part of the Code Indicator.
*1912 $ 1924 # 1933 % 1938 ¶ 1943 ? 1960 + 1972 @ 1985 & 1987 1990 ~ ARRL Codes » C&W

Q Codes etc. become a QUESTION when followed by the Question Mark (?).

CODE	QUESTION	ANSWER or NOTICE
QKW	What has rescue aircraft / vessel recovered ?	.... has recovered 1) ..... survivors. 2) wreckage 3) .... bodies.
QKY ¶		The main beacon of RTG at ... is working but the High marker is out of action.
QKY	Are you in the search area ..... or lat/long ?	I am in the .... search area.
QKZ	What is est drift of survival craft ?	Est drift of survival craft is .... (figs and units)
QLA ¶	Authenticate your last msg (or msg ...).	(When authentication system not in use reply will be coded.)
QLB ¶	Recommend aircraft c/s ... returns to base.	(warm front retarded low cloud approaches landing base).
QLB	Monitor station for range, quality ?	Monitor report is as follows ...
QLC ¶		Substitute code sign (c/s) of control stn of group (net) in place of this signal. (This signal for use with link sign procedure only.)
QLE ¶		... 1. Radio 2. Visual 3. Telegraph 4. Teletypewriter/Teleprinter 5. Telephone
QLF	Are you using left foot ?	Use left foot. (Insult to bad operators)
QLF ¶		Your freq is slightly (or ...Kc/s) low.
QLG ¶		Stn leaves net temporarily/ for... mins to comm with ... / will be on ... Kc/s.
QLH	Use simultaneous keying on ... freq and ... freq ?	Keying simultaneously on ... freq and ... freq.
QLI ¶		Am about to send call sign on my present freq (or on ... Kc/s).
QLJ ¶		Recommended aircraft c/s... returns to base. 1. Warm front retarded low cloud approaches landing base. 2. Continuous snow affecting visibility. 3. Severe icing following descent from cloud or through cloud on landing.
QLK ¶		Recommend aircraft c/s... return to base. (Continuing snow affecting visibility)
QLL ¶		Same as above, (Severe icing following descent from or through cloud on landing)
QLM	Can you tune down for replies ?	I am tuning down for replies.
QLM ¶		Hold my msg no... until correction confirmed.
QLN ¶		Bearing of unknown stn transmitting on ... Kc/s was ... (class ...) sense determined at ...
QLN		This is a repeat of a previous message ....
QLO ¶	Shall I use ...	Use ....
QLP ¶		Pass to ... for BAMS transmitting action only.
QLQ ¶		Bearing of you was ... (class ...). A balloon barrage within 60 miles of me on this bearing.
QLR ¶		Take no further action as regards sending msg no ... to ...
QLS ¶		Stn serial no(s) of last msg(s) recd from you (or...) is (are) ...
QLU		Tuning from top of band to lower end.
QLU ¶		Can't determine your posn. Your bearing from me (or ...) was ... (class...) sense determined at ...
QLV	Is the ... radio still required ?	... radio is still required.
QLW ¶		I am keeping watch on ... Kc/s for - 1. first 5 mins in each half hour. 2. from 10-15 and 40-45 mins past the hour
QLX ¶		Carry out short D/F procedure (as locally prescribed).
QLZ		Commence revolving beacon transmissions now (or at ...).
QMA ¶		Authenticate transmissions ... 1. on all circuits. 2. on this circuit. 3. on ...Kc/s.
QMC ¶		Am moving and will try to keep in comms while on move.
QMD ¶		My aerial (or of ...) has been damaged and carried away.
QME ¶		Ready to take your bearing (or brg of...) on my normal freq (or on ... Kc/s).
QMF ¶	How does my freq check ?	Your frequency is correct.
QMG ¶		Send reports in to me.
QMH	Will I tune up from mid-band for replies ?	I will tune up from mid-band.
QMH		Shift to freq ... if nothing heard in 5 mins, revert to present freq.
QMI	Report vertical distribution of cloud ?	Vertical distribution of cloud is ...
QMJ ¶	Msg ... indecipherable, check ... 1. Indicators. 2. Msg and machine settings.	and report.
QML	Tune down from mid-band for replies ?	I will tune down from mid-band.
QML ¶		Signal (transmit) bearing as determined approximately.
QMM ¶	Of what precedence and for whom are your msgs ?	I have ... msgs (number followed by O, OP, P, D precedence other than Routine) for you (or...).
QMN ¶		Bearing of you (or of ...) was ... (class...) sense determined from ... at ...
QMO ¶		Repeat msg ... (or portion of it).
QMQ ¶		Take bearing on rotating beacons.

Radiotelegraph and Radiotelephone Codes, Prowords and Abbreviations

List of Radiotelegraph 'Q' and 'Z' Codes

Key to date of changes noted and references, NOT part of the Code Indicator.
*1912 $ 1924 # 1933 % 1938 ¶ 1943 ? 1960 + 1972 @ 1985 & 1987 1990   ~ ARRL Codes » C&W

Q Codes etc. become a QUESTION when followed by the Question Mark (?).

CODE	QUESTION	ANSWER or NOTICE
QMR ¶	Retransmit msg ... to ... (for ...)	1. Action. 2. Information.
QMS ¶		Stn serial nos ... (from ...) has/have not been received.
QMU	Tune up for replies ?	I will tune up for replies.
QMU	Surface temp and dew point at .... ?	Surface temp and dew point at ... is ... etc.
QMU ¶	Cryptographic system indicated in your msg ... is -	1. Not held. 2. Inoperative.
QMV ¶		Pass in D/F brg (of ...) obtained on ...Kc/s (or between ... and ...Kc/s).
QMW ¶		Am keeping watch on ... Kc/s from 10 - 15 and 40 - 45 mins past the hour.
QMW	What is height of 0 deg C isotherm ?	At ... 0 deg C isotherm is at height ....
QMX	What is air temp at... height .... ?	At ... air temp is ... at height ....
QMZ	Have you amendments to flight forecast ?	Amendments to flight forecast are ....

QN...~ ARRL net codes indicated by ~ (NOT part of code sent) * Net Control Stations only.

CODE	QUESTION	ANSWER or NOTICE
QNA~*	Please answer in order ?	I will answer in order.
QNA ¶	Are you ready for high speed.	I am ready for high speed run at ... grps (... wds) per min.
QNB~*	Can you act as relay ?	I can relay.
QNB ¶		My position by rotating beacon bearings is ...
QNC	Is this net control traffic ?	This is net control traffic.
QNC~	All net stations copy .	I have a message for all net stations.
QNC ¶	When shall I call you agn on present freq (or on ... Kc/s)?	Call me again at ... on present freq. (or on ... Kc/s).
QND~*	Is this net control direction ?	This is net control direction.
QND ¶	Are you/or... radio W/T guard for ... (on...Kc/s)?	I am/...is radio W/T guard for ... (on ...Kc/s)
QNE~*	All stations please stand by ?	All stations standing by.
QNE		Standard Barometric Pressure at Sea Level (1013 millibars)
QNE	Altimeter will read ??? at ... if sub scale set to 1013.2 millibars?	At ... with sub-scale set to 1013.2 mbs, altimeter will read ..... millibars etc.
QNF~	Is this net free? (no NCS)	This is a free net.
QNF ¶	Shall I change to normal freq (or ... Kc/s) ?	Change to normal freq (or ...Kc/s).
QNG	Will you assume net control ?	I will assume net control.
QNG ¶		Resume normal W/T comms now (or at ...).
QNG~		Take over as Net Control Station.
QNH~	Is the net frequency high ?	The net frequency is high.
QNH	Give barometric Pressure at sea level ?	The barometric pressure at sea level is ......
QNH	What is alt setting for ground at your base ?	Set alt at .... (fig/unit) for ground here at ... hours.
QNI~	Please report to the net ?	I am reporting to the net.
QNI	Between what height is turbulence ?	Turbulence at ... of ... between ... and ....
QNI ¶		This is NOT a drill or exercise message.
QNJ~	Can you copy me ?	I can copy you.
QNK~*	Will you direct to relay ?	I will direct to relay.
QNL~	Is the net frequency low ?	Your net frequency is low.
QNM~*		You are interfering with the net, standby.
QNM ¶		Unable to locate msg(s) ... Give further ident data.
QNN~	Who is net control station ?	Net control station is .....
QNN ¶		Brg should be regarded as approx only, due to unfavourable circumstances.
QNO~		I am leaving the net.
QNO		Can't give info and facility required.
QNO ¶		Your/... message (...) not received.
QNP~		Unable to copy you (or ....)
QNQ~*		Move freq to .... and wait for ... to finish traffic. Then send him traffic for ....
QNQ ¶	What is my posn by D/F cross brgs by gridded map from nearest landmark (or frm ...)?	Your posn by D/F cross bearings by gridded map (or squared chart) method is ... (class...).
QNR	Can I use freq for message to .... ?	You can use freq for message to .....
QNR		I am approaching my point of no return.
QNR~		Answer ..... and receive traffic.
QNS~*	Request list of stations in net ?	Following stations are in the net ....
QNS ¶	Is my speech intelligible ?	Your speech is unintelligible.

Radiotelegraph and Radiotelephone Codes, Prowords and Abbreviations

List of Radiotelegraph 'Q' and 'Z' Codes

Key to date of changes noted and references, NOT part of the Code Indicator.
*1912 $1924 #1933 %1938 ¶1943 ?1960 +1972 @1985 &1987 1990 ~ARRL Codes »C&W

Q Codes etc. become a QUESTION when followed by the Question Mark (?).

CODE	QUESTION	ANSWER or NOTICE
QNT	What is gust speed at surface ?	Max gust speed of surf wind at ... is ....
QNT~	May I leave the net temporarily ?	Leaving net temporarily for ... mins.
QNU~*	Any net traffic for me ?	Net has traffic for you.
QNU ¶	What is my posn by D/F cross brgs from nearest landmark (or from ...) ?	Your posn by D/F cross brgs from nearest landmark (or from ...) is ... class....
QNV~*		Contact ... on this freq, move to ... freq and send traffic for ....
QNW~	How do I route messages for ..... ?	
QNW ¶	May I close down (until...) ?	Close down (reopen at ...).
QNX~	May I be excused from the net ?	You are excused from the net.
QNY	Give present weather and intensity at ..... ?	Present weather and intensity at ..... is ....
QNY~*		Shift to another freq (or ... Kc) for traffic with ...
QNZ~		Zero beat your signal with mine.
QNZ ¶		Your distance was approx ... miles from me (or ...) at ...

QOA - QQZ Allocated to the Maritime Services.

CODE	QUESTION	ANSWER or NOTICE
QOA	Can you communicate by telegraphy on 500 KHz ?	I can use radiotelegraphy on 500 KHz.
QOA ¶		Your tape is reversed.
QOB	Can you communicate by radiophone (2182 KHz) ?	I can use radiophone (2182 KHz).
QOC	Can you use 'phone (Ch 16, 156.8 MHz) ?	I can use 'phone (Ch 16, 156.8 MHz).
QOC ¶		Answer in alphabetical order.
QOD	Can you communicate with me in .. 1 — 9 ?	I can communicate with you in 1 - 9.
	0 = Dutch 1 = English 2 = French 3 = German 4 = Greek	
	5 = Italian 6 = Japanese 7 = Norwegian 8 = Russian 9 = Spanish	
QOD ¶		Your posn was ... (class...) by cross bearings (from ... and ...) at ...
QOE	Have you received safety signal from ... ?	I've received safety signal from ...
QOE...¶		... 1. Receiver 2. Transmitter 3. Power supply 4. Antenna system.
QOF	What is the commercial quality of my signal ?	The quality of your signal is --
	1 = Not commercial, 2 = Marginally commercial 3 = Commercial.	
QOF ¶		I am changing to normal freq (or ...Kc/s).
QOG	How many tapes have you to send ?	I have ... tapes to send.
QOG ¶		Assume W/T organisation forthwith (or at...)
QOH	Will I send phasing signal for ... seconds ?	Send phasing signal for ... seconds.
QOI	Shall I send my tape ?	Send your tape.
QOI ¶		Your brg appears to be between ... deg and ... deg, and sense indicates you are to the ... of this stn.
QOJ	Will you listen on ... freq for EPIRB ?	I am listening on ... freq for EPIRB.
QOK ¶		Your sigs are not sufficiently strong for determination of bearing in present unfavourable conditions.
QOK	Have you received EPIRB signal on ... KHz/MHz ?	I have received EPIRB sig on ... KHz/MHz.
QOL	Have you selcall ? / What is selcall ?	My selcall, selcallsign is ....
QOM	What is your selcall freqs ?	My selcall freqs are ... times ...
QOM ¶		Transmit only msgs of and above precedence ....
QON ¶		Can't determine your ... (or...) 1. Position. 2. Bearing.
QOO	Can you send on any working frequency ?	I can send on any working frequency.
QOQ		Beacon will be operating from ... to ...
QOR ¶		Transmit this msg/msg... to... now / by...
QOS ¶		Your speech is too weak to read, close distance.
QOT	Can you hear me, what is delay for traffic ?	I hear you, delay is ... minutes.
COU ¶		Beacon cannot be operated at present.
QOW ¶		Will call you again as soon as possible am closing down (due to)
	1. Air raid warning. 2. Electrical storm.	
	3. Possible attack by hostile aircraft. 4. To effect repair to equipment	
QOX ¶		Decrease freq slightly. Transmit c/s 5 times.
QOY ¶		Increase freq slightly. Transmit c/s 5 times.
QOZ ¶		Beacon ... no longer required.
QPA ¶		Authentication challenge is ... (based on time in the zone indicated by the suffix letter ...)

Radiotelegraph and Radiotelephone Codes, Prowords and Abbreviations

List of Radiotelegraph 'Q' and 'Z' Codes

Key to date of changes noted and references, NOT part of the Code Indicator.
*1912 $ 1924 # 1933 % 1938 ¶ 1943 ? 1960 + 1972 @ 1985 & 1987 1990   ~ ARRL Codes » C&W

Q Codes etc. become a QUESTION when followed by the Question Mark (?).

CODE	QUESTION	ANSWER or NOTICE
QPB ¶		Your freq has ... 1. Increased. 2. Decreased.
QPC ¶		Answer calls for me on present freq (or ...Kc/s).
QPD ¶		Beacon(s) now in operation is (are) ... (on ... Kc/s).
QPF		Broadcast transmission received.
QPF ¶		Am about to send c/s on present freq (or...Kc/s) Tune your transmitter to same freq.
QPG ¶	Shall I take control of net (for...) (until ....) ?	Take control of net (for...) (until ...).
QPH ¶		Decrease freq slightly to clear interference.
QPI ¶	Steer ... degs for 2 mins if possible	and send c/s and long dashes while doing so.
QPJ ¶		Increase freq slightly to clear interference.
QPK ¶		Accuracy of following msg (or grps ... in msg ...) is doubtful. Correction will be transmitted when received.
QPM ¶		The following msg has been read. (Received or transmitted)
QPN ¶		Increase height to enable more accurate brg to be completed.
QPO ¶		Following repetition (of ...) is made in accordance with your request. (Note: This signal is used in reply to QMO.)
QPO		Broadcast transmission unheard, please repeat.
QPR		Pay attention to correct procedure.
QPR ¶		Transmit following msg to ... on return to base.
QPS ¶		Change stn serial no of msg ... to read NR... or assign to msg ... stn serial no NR....
QPT ¶	Surface craft using c/s ... cooperating.	Change to ...Kc/s and follow D/F procedure when called.
QPV ¶		Send message for ... on ... Kc/s (by ... method)
QPW ¶		I am closing down (until ...)
QPX ¶		Check correctness of last QDM given.
QPY ¶	Have you recd (or sent) the executive signal ("Execute") for msg ... ?	Executive sig ("Execute") for last msg (or msg...) has been (or was) made at ...
QPZ ¶		Affirmative (Yes)
QQA ¶		Rerun number ... for message ...
QQB ¶		To be deciphered by an officer only.
QQC ¶		... will answer calls for me (or ...)
QQE ¶		Check sense of last QDM given.
QQF ¶	On what freq do you hear me best ?	I hear you best on ... Kc/s.
QQH ¶		Msg(s) ... have been passed to ... at ... (by ... or on ... Kc/s.)
QQJ ¶	When and on what freq was msg ... recd ?	Msg ... was received at ... on ... Kc/s.
QQK ¶		Report disposal of message.
QQL ¶		This msg (or msg...) is being (or has been) repeated for info to you (or to ...).
QQM ¶		This msg is an exact duplicate of a msg previously transmitted.
QQN ¶	Endeavour to obtain D/F bearing of stn now transmitting (or of ...) (on ...Kc/s).	
QQO ¶		Msg ... has been passed to ... for action.
QQP ¶		Check correctness of last QDR given.
QQQ also QQQQ (Early WW2, Discarded)	Have been ordered to stop by an unidentified merchantman. (Discarded, Merchant Radio Ops objected to Navy calling them 4Q. Response was 4Q2. –JWA)	
QQQ ¶		Air raid ... 1. Warning. 2. In progress. 3. All clear.
QQR ¶	Transmit traffic for me (or ...) by broadcast (F) method until further direction (or until ...)	
QQS ¶	What are sig strengths of grps (or ...) ?	Sig strength of grp(s) are ... (or of ... is ...)
QQT ¶	Is there any reply to msg for ... ?	There is no reply to message ...
QQU ¶	Can you accept msg for ... ?	Give me your message. I will dispose of it.
QQV ¶		Make call signs more distinctly.
QQW ¶	What stns are keeping watch on ...Kc/s (or in net)?	Following stns keeping watch on ...Kc/s (or in net).
QQX ¶		This msg may be sent as written by any means except radio (wireless).
QQY ¶		This msg must be sent in cypher if liable to interception or fall into enemy hands.
QQZ ¶		Negative (No, Not)

Radiotelegraph and Radiotelephone Codes, Prowords and Abbreviations

List of Radiotelegraph 'Q' and 'Z' Codes

Key to date of changes noted and references, NOT part of the Code Indicator.
*1912 $1924 #1933 %1938 ¶1943 ?1960 +1972 @1985 &1987 1990   ~ ARRL Codes » C&W

Q Codes etc. become a QUESTION when followed by the Question Mark (?).

CODE | QUESTION | ANSWER or NOTICE

QRA - QVZ is Allocated to the Radio Telecommunication Service (All Services).

CODE	QUESTION	ANSWER or NOTICE
QRA *	What is the name of your station ?	The name of my station is .....
QRB *	What distance are you from me ?	I am ... Kms/miles from you.
QRB	(WW2-SOE agents in occupied Europe)	Your message reference broadcast received OK.
QRC *	What is your true bearing ?	Your true bearing is ... degrees.
QRC #	Where will your account be sent ?	Send my account to ...
QRD *	Where are you going ?	I am going to ...
QRD %	Where are you bound and from ?	I am bound for ... from ...
QRE #	What nationality is your station ?	The nationality of my station is ......
QRE +	What is your estimated time of arrival ?	My estimated time of arrival is ....
QRF *	Where do you come from ?	I come from ....
QRF +	Are you returning to ... ?	I am returning / return to ....
QRG *	What line do you belong to ?	I belong to the ... Line.
QRG #	Will you tell me my frequency ?	Your frequency is ....
QRH *	What is your wavelength (freq) ?	My wavelength (freq) is .....
QRH %	Does my frequency vary ?	Your frequency varies.
QRHH $	What tune shall I adjust for ?	Adjust to receive on tune .....
QRI %	Is my note good ?	Your note varies.
QRI ''	(WW2-SOE agents in Europe) Is my note bad?	Your note is bad.
QRI ?	How is my tone ? (1-3)	Your tone is (1-3).
QRJ *	How many words have you to send ?	I have ... words to send.
QRJ #	Do you receive me badly ? Are my sigs weak ?	I cannot receive you.
QRJ ''	(WW2-SOE agents in Europe)	Nothing heard of you.
QRK *	Do you receive me well ?	I receive you well, good signal.
QRK $	How do you receive me ?	I receive you well.
QRK %	What is my legibility (1-5) ?	Your legibility is (1-5).
QRKIVI ''	(WW2-SOE agents in Europe)	How are you receiving me?
QRL *	Are you receiving badly ?	I am receiving badly.
QRLL $	Request permission to test ...... mins ?	Permission to test granted.
QRL #	Are you busy ?	I am busy, do not interfere.
QRM *	Are you being interfered with ?	I am being interfered with.
QRN *	Are you troubled by atmospherics ?	I am troubled by atmospherics.
QRO *	Must I increase power ?	Increase power.
QRO ''	(WW2 - SOE agents in occupied Europe)	Mistake encoding ... re-encode, repeat.
QRP *	Must I decrease power ?	Decrease power.
QRQ *	Must I send faster ?	Send faster (... wpm).
QRR %		Amateur (ARRL) distress "SOS" call, emergency use, U.S.A. only.
QRRR ?		Amateur (ARRL) distress "SOS" call, emergency use, U.S.A. only.
QRR +	Are you ready for auto transmission ?	I am ready for auto transmission.
QRS *	Must I send slower ?	Send slower (... wpm).
QRT *	Should I stop transmitting ?	I will stop transmitting.
QRT	How is the tone of my signals ?	Your tone is -1 good, 2 varies, 3 bad.
QRU *	Have you anything for me ?	I have nothing for you.
QRV *	Are you ready ?	I am ready. All right now.
QRV #	Should I send a series of V's ?	Send a series of V's.
QRV %	Are you ready ?	I am ready.
QRW +	Are you busy ?	I am busy. Do not interfere.
QRW #	Will I tell ..... you are calling ?	Please tell ... I am calling.
QRX *	Shall I stand by ?	Stand by.
QRX ¶	Will I wait ? Will you call me again ?	Wait, I will call you again on ....
QRY *	Which is my turn ?	Your turn is .....
QRZ *	Are my signals weak ?	Your signals are weak.
QRZ #	Who is calling me ?	You are being called by ...
QSA *	Are my signals strong ?	Your signals are strong.

Radiotelegraph and Radiotelephone Codes, Prowords and Abbreviations

List of Radiotelegraph 'Q' and 'Z' Codes

Key to date of changes noted and references, NOT part of the Code Indicator.
*1912 $ 1924   # 1933   % 1938   ¶ 1943   ? 1960   + 1972   @ 1985   & 1987   1990   ~ ARRL Codes   » C&W

Q Codes etc. become a QUESTION when followed by the Question Mark (?).

CODE	QUESTION	ANSWER or NOTICE
QSA #	What is my signal strength (1-5) ?	Your signal strength is (1-5).
QSB *	Is my tone / spark bad ?	Your tone / spark is bad.
QSB #	Does my signal strength var ?	Your signal strength varies.
QSC *	Is my spacing bad ?	Your spacing is bad.
QSC #	Does my signal disappear ?	Your signal disappears.
QSC +	Are you a cargo vessel ?	I am a cargo vessel.
QSC +	Are you a low traffic ship station ?	I am a low traffic ship station.
QSD *	What is your time ?	My time is ...
QSD #	Is my keying bad ?	Your keying is bad.
QSE	Are my signals distinct.	Your signals run together.
QSE +	What is the estimated drift of survival craft ?	Estimated drift of survival craft is ....
QSF *	Do I transmit alternately ?	Transmit in alternate order.
QSF #	Is my automatic transmission good ?	Your auto transmission fades out.
QSF +	Have you effected rescue ?	Effected rescue, ... injured to ....
QSG *	Will I send in series of 5 messages ?	Send in series of 5 messages.
QSG #	Will I send in lots of .... messages ?	Send in lots of 5 / 10 / .... messages.
QSH *	Will I send in lots of 10 messages ?	Send in lots of 10 messages.
QSH #	Will I send singly, repeating twice ?	Send singly, repeat twice.
QSH +	Can you DF ?	I can DF.
QSI #	Will I send alternately, no repeats ?	Send alternately, no repeating.
QSI +	Can you tell ... I can't break ?	Tell ... I can't break.
QSJ *	What rate / charge will I collect ?	Charge / collect ... for ...
QSK *	Is the last Radiogram cancelled ?	The last Radiogram is cancelled.
QSK #	Must I stop ? When will you call again ?	Suspend traffic. I will call at ......
QSK %	Will I continue, I can hear you ?	Continue, I will interrupt.
QSK &	Can I break in ?	Break in.
QSK+	Can you hear me between your signals?	I can hear you between my signals. Break in.
QSL *	Have you got the receipt ?	Please give a receipt.
QSL #	Can you acknowledge my receipt ?	I acknowledge your receipt.
QSLL		I will acknowledge when you do.
QSM *	What is your true course ?	My true course is ... degrees.
QSM #	Have you received my ack of receipt ?	I have not received your ack of receipt.
QSM %	Will I repeat the last Telegram ?	Repeat the last Telegram you sent.
QSM ''	(WW2-SOE agents in Europe)	Please repeat whole of last remarks.
QSN *	Are you in communication with land ?	I am not in communication with land.
QSN +	Did you hear me or ... on ... KHz ?	I heard you (or ...) on ......
QSO *	Can you communicate with ..... ?	I can communicate with ....
QSP *	Will I tell ..... you are calling ?	Inform ... that I am calling him.
QSP +	Will you relay to ... free of charge ?	I will relay to ... no charge.
QSQ *	Is ...... calling me ?	You are being called by .....
QSQ #	Must I send each word once only ?	Send each word once only.
QSQ +	Is there a Doctor on board ?	A Doctor is on board.
QSR *	Will you forward the Radiogram ?	I will forward the Radiogram.
QSR #	Has distress call from .. been attended to ?	Distress call from ... has been attended to by ....
QSR +	Will I repeat on calling frequency ?	Repeat call on calling frequency.
QSS $	Are my signals fading ?	Your signals are fading.
QSS	Will I use .... frequency ?	I will use ..... frequency.
QST *	Have you received the general call ?	General call to all stations.
QST%		General Call to all Amateurs. (ARRL). U.S.A. only.
QSU *	Please call me when finished or at ..... ?	I will call when I have finished.
QSU #	Will I transmit on .... freq, transmit mode .... ?	Send on ..... freq, mode ......
QSV *	Is Public traffic being handled ?	Public traffic is being handled.
QSV #	Need I change freq and send a series of V's ?	Shift to ..... and send a series of V's.
QSV %	Shall I send a series of V's ?	Send a series of V's.
QSV ''	(WW2-SOE agents in occupied Europe)	Send tuning call for 2 minutes.
QSW *	Will I increase my spark frequency ?	Increase your spark frequency.

Radiotelegraph and Radiotelephone Codes, Prowords and Abbreviations

List of Radiotelegraph 'Q' and 'Z' Codes

Key to date of changes noted and references, NOT part of the Code Indicator.
*1912 $ 1924 # 1933 % 1938 ¶ 1943 ? 1960 + 1972 @ 1985 & 1987 1990   ~ ARRL Codes » C&W

Q Codes etc. become a QUESTION when followed by the Question Mark (?).

CODE	QUESTION	ANSWER or NOTICE
QSW #	Will you send on .... freq, mode ..... ?	I will send on ...... freq, mode .....
QSW +	May I use this channel ?	I wish to use this channel.
QSX *	Will I decrease my spark frequency ?	Decrease your spark frequency.
QSX ♯	Does my wavelength (frequency) vary ?	Your wavelength (frequency) varies.
QSX %	Will you listen for ..... on frequency ..... ?	I am listening for ..... on frequency ....
QSY +	Will I change wavelength (frequency) ?	Change to a wavelength (frequency) ....
QSZ *	Will I send each word or group twice ?	Send each word or group twice.
QTA *	Will I repeat last Radiogram ?	Repeat last Radiogram.
QTA %	Will I cancel telegrams / messages no ..... ?	Cancel telegrams / messages no ......
QTA ''	(WW2-SOE agents in Europe)	Cancel No. ...... as if it has not been sent.
QTB *	Do you agree with my word count ?	I don't agree, repeat first letters.
QTC *	Have you anything to transmit ?	I have something to transmit.
QTC %	How many telegrams have you to send ?	I have ..... telegrams for you or .....
QTC +	Do you have traffic for ..... ?	I have traffic for ......
QTD +	What has the rescue vessel recovered ?	.... has recovered 1)... survivors, 2) ... wreckage 3)... bodies
QTE *	What is my true bearing relative to you ?	Your true bearing relative to me is ....
QTE ¶	What is the true bearing of ... (c/s) in relation to ... (c/s) ?	The true brg of .... in relation to ... is ...° at ...
QTF *	What is my position ?	Your position is ..... lat ..... long.
QTF	What is my DF'd location ?	Your DF'd location is ....
QTG *	Will I transmit c/s for 1 minute for bearing?	Transmit c/s for 1 minute to obtain bearing.
QTG %	Can I send callsign for 50secs plus 10sec dash ?	I will send callsign for 50sec plus 10sec dash.
QTG +	Can you send 2 long dashes before callsign ?	I will send 2 long dashes before callsign.
QTH	What is the location of your station ?	My location is ....
QTI	What is your true track ?	My true track is ....
QTISOL	What is your effective true bearing?	My effective true bearing is .... degrees.
QTJ	What is your speed ?	My speed is .....
QTK	What is your airspeed ?	My airspeed is ....
QTK ¶	What is date of Syko card you are using ?	Using Syko card for day .... of month.
QTL	What is your TRUE heading ?	My TRUE heading is ......
QTM +	What is your MAGNETIC heading ?	My MAGNETIC heading is ....
QTM	Send submarine signals to fix position.	I will send submarine signals to fix your positn.
QTN ¶		Send 20 sec dash followed by your c/s repeated ... times.
QTN	What is the departure time ?	The departure time is ......
QTO	Are you at sea (or airborne) ?	I am at sea (or airborne).
QTO ''	(WW2-SOE agents in occupied Europe)	I have .... messages for you.
QTP	Are you docking (or landing) ?	I am docking (or landing).
QTP ''	(WW2-SOE agents in occupied Europe)	Accept my priority message at once.
QTQ **	Can you use the International Code of Signals ?	I will use International Code of Signals.
QTR	What is the exact time?	The exact time is ....
QTR ''	(WW2-SOE agents in occupied Europe)	Can't decode prefix ...... Can't relay message.
QTS	What is your callsign ?	My callsign is ....
QTS	Send c/s for tuning or freq measurement now or at .... hrs on freq ... kHz / MHz.	
QTT	The following ID sign is superimposed on another transmission.	
QTU	What are your operating hours ?	My operating hours are ....
QTV	What is your guard frequency ?	My guard frequency is ....
QTW	What is the condition of survivors ?	Survivors in ..... condition, need ..... urgently.
QTX	Will you keep your station open ?	I will keep my station open.
QTY	Are you proceeding to destination ?	I am proceeding to destibation.
QTY	Are you proceeding to incident ? ETA?	Proceeding to incident, ETA ....
QTZ	Are you continuing the search ?	I am continuing the search.
QUA	Have you news of	I have news of .....
QUB	Info req'd on visibility, cloud, wind ?	Here is info requested ....
QUC	What is last message from .... ?	Last message from ...... is ....

Radiotelegraph and Radiotelephone Codes, Prowords and Abbreviations

List of Radiotelegraph 'Q' and 'Z' Codes

Key to date of changes noted and references, NOT part of the Code Indicator.
*1912 $1924 #1933 %1938 ¶1943 ?1960 +1972 @1985 &1987 1990   ~ ARRL Codes » C&W

Q Codes etc. become a QUESTION when followed by the Question Mark (?).

CODE	QUESTION	ANSWER or NOTICE
QUD	Have you received emergency signal from ...?	Emergency/urgency signal received from ....
QUE	Can you use phone in ...... (language) ?	I can use phone in ...... on ...... frequency.
QUF	Have you received a distress signal from ...... ?	Distress signal received from ....
QUG	Are you forced to abandon ship (land) ?	I am forced to abandon ship (land).
QUH	What is the barometric pressure at sea level ?	The barometric pressure at sea level is ......
QUI	Are there any navigation lights ?	There are no navigation lights.
QUI +	Are your navigation lights working ?	My navigation lights are not working.
QUJ	Will you give a true course instruction ?	The true course instruction is ....
QUK	What are the sea conditions ?	The sea conditions are .... (1 - 9)
QUL	What is the sea swell report ?	The sea swell report is .... (1 - 9)
QUM	Has emergency traffic ended ?	Emergency traffic has ended.
QUM +	May I resume normal working ?	Normal working may be resumed.
QUN	Please give a true course report ?	True course report is ....
QUO +	Can you search for .... ?	I will search for .... 1.A/c, 2.Ship, 3.Survival Craft.
QUO "	(WW2-SOE agents in occupied Europe)	Must stop transmitting, imminent danger, CU next sked.
QUP	Can you give a visual position indication ?	My visual position indication is ....
QUQ	Will you provide a landing beacon ?	I will provide a landing beacon.
QUQ	Will I train my searchlight vertical on a cloud?	Train searchlight vertical on cloud to assist location.
QUR	Did you pick up survivors ?	Survivors were picked up by ....
QUS	Have you sighted survivors / wreckage ?	I have sighted survivors. 1.In water, 2.On rafts, 3.Wreckage
QUT	Is the incident / your position marked ?	The incident / my position is marked by ....
QUU	Can you home to my position ?	I will home to your position.
QUV	Can you give my magnetic bearing ?	Your magnetic bearing is ....
QUW	Are you in the search area ...... ?	I am in .... search area.
QUX	Can you give a magnetic bearing instruction ?	The magnetic bearing instruction is ....
QUX	Do you have navig./gale warnings ?	I have following navig. /gale warnings in force........
QUY	Is the position of the survival craft marked ?	Survival craft position is marked by ....
QUZ ¶		Airborne.
QUZ +	May I resume restricted working ?	Distress phase still in force, resume restricted working.
QVA ¶		I am unable to read, use hand key.
QVB ¶		Check sense of last QDR given.
QVC ¶		Report when you are in radio comms with ....
QVF ¶	Shall I send a series of Vs on this freq (...Kc/s)?	Send a series of Vs on this freq (...Kc/s).
QVH ¶		Wait ... miles distance on a true brg of ... deg. from my stn.
QVJ ¶	Is the S/I Beacon (Mk...) in operation ?	The S/I Beacon is ... 1. in operation. 2 Out of order.
QVM ¶		Msg was incompletely recd. Parts missed indicated by QVM in the msg.
QVN ¶	Send c/s and 5 sec dashes at intervals so I (or ...) may home on you.	I will send c/s and 5 sec dashes at intervals so you (or ...) may home on me.
QVO ¶	Will you/... repeat what you sent at ... ?	Following is what I/... sent at ....
QVS ¶	What is/are stn serial no(s) of last msg(s) you transmitted to me (or to ...) ?	
QVU ¶		Exercise (drill) message.
QVV ¶	What is your dist from my stn in nautical miles?	My distance from your station in nautical miles is ...
QVY ¶		Repeat back each grp of text of message as it is transmitted. (For visual use only)
QVZ ¶		Unable to comply.
QWA ¶		Your perforation appears to be defective.
QWB ¶	What is your true brg and dist from me in nautical miles ?	True brg and dist from your stn is ... deg and ... nautical miles.
QWC ¶	Did you (or ...) hear ... at ... ?	I have (or ... has) been unable to comm with ... since ...
QWE ¶	Attention is drawn to - 1. RAF Signal Manual Part ... Art. ... Para ... 2. RAF CCO No ... 19.... para ... 3. RAF Command Signals Standing Orders para .... 4. AP 1927/BR777 page ... para ...	

Radiotelegraph and Radiotelephone Codes, Prowords and Abbreviations

List of Radiotelegraph 'Q' and 'Z' Codes

Key to date of changes noted and references, NOT part of the Code Indicator.
*1912 $ 1924 # 1933 % 1938 ¶ 1943 ? 1960 + 1972 @ 1985 & 1987 1990   ~ ARRL Codes » C&W

Q Codes etc. become a QUESTION when followed by the Question Mark (?).

CODE	QUESTION	ANSWER or NOTICE
QWF ¶	Send tuning sig on freq/...Kc/s for one minute or until AS is given ?	Will send tuning signal on freq/...Kc/s.
QWH ¶	May I home on S/I Beacon (Mk ...) ?	You may home on S/I Beacon (Mk ...).
QWM ¶		Do not forward this message by radio.
QWN ¶	Is bearing reliable ?	Bearing is reliable.
QWO ¶		Listen (out) for voice. (R/T)
QWR ¶		The first W/T link to handle this message was ...
QWT ¶	What is the time ?	The time is ....
QWV ¶		Request local weather report now/at ... / every ... hours.
QWX ¶		This 'drome/at... is unfit for landing owing to weather.
QWX		Last message sent to you is number ....
QWY ¶		Switch on IFF.
QWZ ¶	What is ...	I am using ....
	1. The date of the Syko card you are using ?	1. Syko card for ... day of the month.
	Syko replaced by Rekoh ? card later. These were encrypting methods. - Ed.	
	2. The date of the Bomber Card you are using?	2. Bomber Code Card for ... day of month.
	3. The date of the A/c Report Card you are using?	3. A/c Reporting Card for ... day of month.
	4. The indicator number of your Alametco card ?	4. Almetco (request) Card numbered ...
	5. The date of the ... net card you are using ?	5. ... net card for the ... day of the month.
QXA ¶	Please connect reperforator to this circuit.	Reperforator connected to your circuit.
QXB	What is .... (c/s) current (SPECIAL) weather?	SPL (foll by spcl wx report). (Prec by 10 bell signal).
QXB ¶		I am unable to furnish you (or...) brg now. Call agn in ... mins.
QXC ¶	When was I (or ...) last heard ?	Nothing heard from you (or...) since ...
QXC ¶	Latest wx rep fm stn incorrect? Verify?	Verify weather from ... origin from .... station.
QXD ¶		The S/I Approach beacon is out of order.
QXD ¶	Will you relay weather report from ..... ?	Please discontinue relaying ....
QXE ¶	What range printer opr do you get from .... ?	Printer range of ..... (pts) to ...... from ...... stn.
QXF ¶		Switch S/I Beacon ... 1. On; 2. Off.
QXF ¶	What was the last msg sent by you to ...... ?	Last msg sent by me to ...... was ....
QXG ¶	Will I check msg no ... ? How many words?	Recheck msg no .... I have ..... Words.
QXH ¶	Will I change yr msg no ... check to read ...?	Correct my msg no ... check ... to read ...
QXI ¶	What is your local range of printer operation?	My local range is ..... (points) to .... pts.
QXJ ¶	What is tx addr / time of your msg .... ?	My msg no ..... address ..... transmitted at ....
QXJ ¶		Carry on normal D/F work.
QXK ¶	Repeat ...... (or in ..... from ... to ...)	I repeat .... (or in ...... from ... to ...)
QXK ¶		Change over to loop D/F on 385 Kc/s (or on ... Kc/s) now or at ... and listen (out) for msg from (c/s of ship or Senior Officer).
QXL ¶	Will I get .... 'phone test to clear the trouble?	Get .... 'phone test room to clear the trouble.
QXM ¶	Is garble here? Will I change ptr, tx, reperf etc?	Garble at you. Change prtr, tx, perf, reperf etc.
	A. Garble occasionally. B. Garble frequently, read difficult. C. Garble badly, read nothing.	
	D. Line open / from ... to .... E. Carr Ret pulses missing. F. Line feed pulses missing.	
QXN ¶	What are my D/F bearings from ... ?	Bearing to you/of... was... (class...) from me/or ...
QXN ¶	Repeat ... c/s to me. Garbled unreadable.	Here is last ... c/s sent to you.
QXO ¶	Has reception yr stn interrupted? (QYG? ....)	Reception this stn interrupted. (add QYG ....)
QXP ¶	Your dots are :- 1. Too heavy. 2. Too light	3. Varying in bias.
QXP ¶	Was tx garbled on transferred circuit?	Transmit garbled on circuit from which it was transferred.
	Will you correct as soon as possible?	Corrections to be forwarded as soon as possible.
QXQ ¶		Modulation.
QXQ ¶	Advise whereabouts of .... / c/s, name, title?	.... is at / expected at ..... place .... time.
QXR ¶		Originating ciphering officer of this message is .....
QXR ¶	When .... was msg .... delivered to addressee?	Msg .... deld/not deld to addressee at .... because ....
QXS ¶	Is my procedure incorrect? What instructions?	Your procedure incorrect. Refer to instruction ....
QXT ¶	Monitor ... stn ... report keying, quality etc.	Monitored ... stn ... report ..... (briefly).
QXU ¶	Can ... CAA plane radiophone on .... freq?	... CAA plane can radiophone on ..... freq.
QXV ¶		Send 20 sec dash followed by your c/s on 385 (or...) Kc/s to give bearing to be obtained now/or at.... Listen for msgs from ...

Radiotelegraph and Radiotelephone Codes, Prowords and Abbreviations

List of Radiotelegraph 'Q' and 'Z' Codes

Key to date of changes noted and references, NOT part of the Code Indicator.
*1912 $ 1924 # 1933 % 1938 ¶ 1943 ? 1960 + 1972 @ 1985 & 1987 1990   ~ ARRL Codes » C&W

Q Codes etc. become a QUESTION when followed by the Question Mark (?).

CODE	QUESTION	ANSWER or NOTICE
QXV ¶	Has ... chain, stn, a/c, changed to day freq?	... chain, stn, a/c etc has/will change to day freq at ......
QXW ¶	Has ... chain, stn, a/c, changed to night freq?	... chain, stn, a/c etc has/will change to night freq at ......
QXY ¶		Listen on D/F on ... (or between ... and ...) Kc/s.
QXY ¶		Yes or affirmative when no other "Q" signal reply is available.
QXZ ¶		No or negative when no other "Q" signal reply is available.
QYA ¶	Use simultaneous keying on ...... and .... freq?	I will key simultaneously on ..... and .... freq.
QYB ¶	Shall I send RY for .... seconds?	Send RY for ..... seconds.
QYC ¶	What is present field condition at ..... C/s?	Field conditions at ...... c/s are ....
QYC ¶	Are you/is ... in comms with .... (by ....) ?	I am/ ... is in comms with .... (by ...)
QYDA		Teletype reception will be interrupted at ..... until further notice.
QYDB		Teletype reception resumed at ...... c/s at .... time.
QYE ¶	How many gallons avgas avail at .....?	.... gallons avgas available at ......
QYF ¶	How many gallons a/c oil avail at .....?	.... gallons a/c oil available at......
QYF ¶		I am about to shift receiver to ... Kc/s.
QYG ¶	What is last msg received by you from ......?	Last msg received by me from ...... is ......
QYM ¶		This msg may be sent as written by any means including radio (wireless).
QYN ¶		Bearing of you/... was ... or its reciprocal from me at ...
QYO ¶		The last group/word recd from you was .....
QYQ ¶		Repeat all enemy reports on 385/or... Kc/s followed by homing transmission.
QYR ¶		Relay this message via ....
QYT ¶	Request a timing signal now (or at ...)	Timing signal will be transmitted now (or at ...)
	(Numerals indicating time will be followed by as 5 sec dash, terminating exactly at the time indicated.)	
QYZ ¶	Your light is unreadable (...) 1. Not trained correctly. 2. Not bright enough. 3. Too bright.	
QZA ¶		Am working with aircraft in flight.
QZB ¶	Am I recleared/may I reclear from my present position to .... ?	You are recleared from your present position to ...
QZC ¶	Are you in radio comms with ... (on...Kc/s) ?	I am in radio comms with ... (on...Kc/s).
QZE	(German Police)	Your freq. is high, lower your freq.
QZF	(German Police)	Your freq. is low, raise your freq.
QZF ¶	Shall I zero beat (tune) my transmitter to your freq (or ...Kc/s) ?	Zero beat (tune) your transmitter to my freq (or ...Kc/s).
QZH ¶		Use CCBP ... (Attention is called to Article .....)
QZM ¶	Request you acknowledge message	Message / msg ... acknowledged.
QZN ¶	What is my true brg and dist from your stn ?	Your true bearing and dist from my stn is ... deg (and distance .... miles).
QZP	(German Police)	Transmitter trouble.
QZR ¶		Can't pass message .... in specified time or until ...
QZT	(German Police)	Receiver trouble.
QZY	(German Police)	You are unreadable.
QZZ ¶	Your operating sig (made at ....) (recd as ....) ... (1. Not understood: 2. Not held.)	

Z CODE.

Z Codes were initially developed by Cable & Wireless for management of their commercial traffic.
The military also developed Z Codes. The meanings are usually completely different.
   » indicates a C&W code. Listing may vary or be incomplete. Please advise of errors or omissions.
Suffix 1-5 may be added to any Z Code where applicable.
1. - Very slight. 2. - Slight. 3. - Moderate. 4. - Severe.   5. - Extreme.
Prefix INT converts Z codes to a question. Eg. INT ZAF
The ? is reserved for "(I) repeat" in military usage.

ZAA -- ZCZ is allocated to Air Traffic Control.

ZAA	You are not observing net discipline.
ZAB	Your speedkey is wrongly adjusted.

Radiotelegraph and Radiotelephone Codes, Prowords and Abbreviations

List of Radiotelegraph 'Q' and 'Z' Codes

Key to date of changes noted and references, NOT part of the Code Indicator.
*1912 $ 1924 # 1933 % 1938 ¶ 1943 ? 1960 + 1972 @ 1985 & 1987 1990 ~ ARRL Codes » C&W

Z Codes etc. become a QUESTION when preceded by the INT.

CODE	QUESTION	ANSWER or NOTICE
ZAC		Cease using speedkey (bug).
ZAC »		Advise ... c/s freq you read, ... running dual for you.
ZAD		Your Ops Signal at .... not understood.
ZAE		Unable to receive you, relay through ......
ZAF	Please patch me through ...... to .... ?	I will patch you through ...... to ....
ZAG		Break ...... 1) next tape 2) go back ..... feet 3) advance to ref no ...... and reprint last transmission.
ZAH		Can't relay, 1) wrong format 2) lines..... wrong 3) no on-line facility, 4) callsigns not encrypted 5) text not encrypted. We will file, you correct.
ZAI		Run ..... 1) Caller 2) Test tape 3) Sync tape 4) Traffic 5) Mark 6) Spaces 7) Reversals 8) Spacebars 9) Datel test at .... baud
ZAJ		I have been unable to break you.
ZAK		Transmit on ..... suspended ...., electrical hazard
ZAK »		Transmission interrupted at ..... hrs.
ZAL		I'm closing down due to ..... until ......
ZAL »		Alter wave length / change frequency.
ZAM		No QSL from TTY switch, you call please.
ZAN +»	Do you receive anything ?	I receive absolutely nothing.
ZAN @		Transmit messages of .... and above precedence ....
ZAO		Can't read speech, use telegraphy.
ZAP »	Acknowledge please.	
ZAP	Shall I work 1 ..... 8 ?	Work 1 ..... 8. 1 = Simplex, 2 = Duplex, 3 = Diplex, 4 = Multiplex, 5 = SSB. 6 = Auto correct, 7 = No auto correct, 8 = Time and frequency diversity.
ZAQ		Last word / group 1) received was ...... 2) transmitted was ......
ZAR »		Revert to automatic relay.
ZAR		This is my ..... request / reply (1=first etc.
ZAS	Rerun all tapes run on ..... since	1 = Present freq, 2 =... KHz/MHz, 3 = C/S..., 4 = This or ..... Channel
ZAT		I am perfing tape for transmission.
ZAU	What is TTY range on my signals ?	Your signal TTY range is from ..... to .....
ZAV		Transmit traffic for me by broadcast until advised.
ZAW	Will I transmit 12" blank tape at ..... WPM ?	Transmit 12" blank tape at intervals at ....WPM.
ZAX		You are 1) causing interf, listen before sending; 2) causing interf, wait order; 3) Sending over .... C/S; 4) Delay by slow answering; 5) Delay by slow reply to service / procedural messages; 6) Answering out of turn.
ZAY		Transmit traffic to me /... on ... freq without confirmation, I will confirm traffic later on... freq.
ZAZ		One or more transmissions on this b'cast are defective, b'cst will continue. Defective traffic will be repeated when full service is restored.
ZBA	What is cause of delay / bad transmission ?	Delay / bad transmission is due to .....
ZBB		..... copies of message are required.
ZBC		You are transmitting continuous ... 1) mark; 2) space
ZBD	Please repeat what you /..... sent at... ?	Following is what I / .... sent at .....
ZBE		Retransmit message .... to... for ... 1) Action 2) Info
ZBF		Use large message form.
ZBG		You are transmitting in upper case.
ZBH		Make prelim call before transmitting traffic.
ZBI		Listen to radio, formal message.
ZBI +		Listen for radiotelephony.
ZBK	Are you receiving my traffic clear ?	I receive your traffic 1= clear; 2= garbled
ZBL		Can't receive you while I'm transmitting, don't use break-in.
ZBM 1 or 2		Place .... on watch on this frequency. 1 = qualified speedkey op; 2 = competent op.
ZBN		Go ahead with your new slip.
ZBN 1 or 2		Your 1) tape; 2) mark / space is reversed.
ZBO	Of what precedence is message ?	Message follows, precedence .....
ZBP		Your .... 1) characters are indistinct; 2) spacing is bad.

Radiotelegraph and Radiotelephone Codes, Prowords and Abbreviations

List of Radiotelegraph 'Q' and 'Z' Codes

Key to date of changes noted and references, NOT part of the Code Indicator.
*1912 $1924 #1933 %1938 ¶1943 ?1960 +1972 @1985 &1987 1990   ~ ARRL Codes » C&W

Z Codes etc. become a QUESTION when preceded by the INT.

CODE	QUESTION	ANSWER or NOTICE
ZBQ	When and what freq was message ... rec'd?	Message ... was rec'd at ... on freq ...
ZBR +		Break Circuit, Retuning.
ZBR	Shall I send by ..... ? (1 to 4)	Send by ..... (1 to 4)
	1 = Direct (R) method. 2 = Broadcast (F) method.	
	3 = Intercept (I) method. 4 = Repeat back (G) method.	
ZBS		Your signals are blurring.
ZBS 1 to 6	Your... (1. dots too heavy; (2. dots too light; (3. dot bias varies;	
	(4. dots spacing bad; (5. dots missing; (6. dots burring.	
ZBT	How do you count the following text groups ... ?	Text groups ... count as ... groups.
ZBU		Report when you are in comms with ....
ZBV		Answer me / ... on ... KHz/MHz.
ZBW	Will you / ... change to ... frequency ?	I am /... is shifting to transmit on ..... freq.
ZBX	Will you (ask ....) shift to receive on ..... ?	I am (... is) shifting to receive on ..... freq.
ZBY		Pull your tape back one yard / metre.
ZBY 1 to 4	Pass ..... (1. on broadcast .....; (2. Broadcast ... single operator;	
	(3. broadcast ... 2. operators; (4. broadcast ... gen periods only.	
ZBZ	Is my /... print acceptable ?	Your / ... print acceptability is ... 1-5.
	1 = Unacceptable - totally corrupt. 2 = Unacceptable - very corrupt.	
	3 = Unacceptable - partly corrupt. 4 = Acceptable - now and then corrupt	
	5 = Acceptable - no corruption.	
ZCA »		Our circuit is affected - we need more readable signals.
ZCA		Satellite pre-empted from ... Z to ... Z
ZCB »		Our circuit is broken - we cannot hear your signals.
ZCB		Change to double-hop working using satellites ... West and ... East at ... hrs.
ZCC »		Collate your code.
ZCC		Establish ... on access ... channel (A/B).
	1 = 300 db Emergency patch. 2 = Phase-reversing-keying.	
ZCD »		Your collation is different than ours.
ZCD		Weight your access to ... c/s by ... db.
ZCE	Access satellite ... now (or at...) with ... 1-5	
	1 = Spread Spectrum Mod.(normal) 2 = Spread Spectrum Mod. to access ...	
	3 = Spread Spec Demod. chn 9 to access ... 4 = Frequency Modulation.	
	5 = Phase Shift Keying Modulation.	
ZCF »		Please check your centre frequency.
ZCF	Remove access now (or at...).	
	1 = Spread Spec Mod. 2 = FM. 3 = Ph-Rev-Keying. 4 = Ph-shift-Keying.	
ZCG	What is your FM deviation ?	My FM deviation is ...
ZCH	What is your tracking mode ?	My tracking mode is ....
		1= Autotrack. 2 = Manual tracking. 3 = Hand bearing.
ZCI »		Circuit is interrupted.
ZCI	What is your ... ? (1 - 4)	My 1 is .... watts.
	1 = total output power	2 ....%
	2 = quality meter reading	3 .... accesses
	3 = number of accesses	4 .... watts.
	4 = FM access power	
ZCJ	Have you equipment trouble ?	I have trouble with ....
	1= Spread Spect Modulator 2 = Freq Div Multiplexer. 3 = Line Modem.	
	4 = Time Div Multiplexer. 5 = Switching or Patching. 6 = Servo System.	
	7 = Transmitter. 8 = Receiver. 9 = Parametric Amp. 10 = Ph Shift Keyer	
ZCK »	How is my keying ?	Check your keying.
ZCK	Shall I loop my .... ?	Loop your ....
	1 = Spread Spec Mod. 2 = Line modem. 3 = Time Div Multiplexer.	
	4 = FM Division Multiplex Eqpt.	
ZCL »		Send your call letters intelligibly.
ZCL	Check speed of eqpt on ... ch / circuit ?	I have checked speed of equipment on ....

Radiotelegraph and Radiotelephone Codes, Prowords and Abbreviations

List of Radiotelegraph 'Q' and 'Z' Codes

Key to date of changes noted and references, NOT part of the Code Indicator.
*1912 $ 1924 # 1933 % 1938 ¶ 1943 ? 1960 + 1972 @ 1985 & 1987 1990 ~ ARRL Codes » C&W

Z Codes etc. become a QUESTION when preceded by the INT.

CODE	QUESTION	ANSWER or NOTICE
ZCM	May I do ... on satellite ....?	Carry out ... on satellite ...
	1= Spread Spectrum Mod. back-to-back check.	
	2 = Range measurement. 3 = Power Balance.	
ZCN	Can you sync Spread Spectrum Access ?	Ready to sync Spread Spectrum Access.
ZCO »		Your collation was omitted.
ZCO	On your FM/FDM access ... 1. Suppress telegraph ch 1-9; 2. Open telegraph ch 1-9.	
ZCP »		Local receiving conditions poor, please increase to maximum.
ZCP	Change total radiated power	
	1= on narrow band to ... watts 2 = on spread spectrum to ... watts.	
	3= of access ... (1-40, NI-N5, D or E) to ... watts.	
	4 = of access ... (1-40, RAE) to ... (0,3,6,9 db) below full access.	
ZCQ		Change FM/FDM to mode ... (AID) with deviation ....
ZCR		Am about to initiate ... 1. Serial; 2. Parallel sync of Accesses ..... and .....
ZCR »		Using concentrator, give preliminary call.
ZCS »		Cease transmitting.
ZCS		Switch spread spectrum access .... mode to .....
		1= Code off. 2 = Search. 3 = Sync 1. 4 = Sync 2. 5 = Traffic.
		6 = Ch A normal on. 7 = Ch B normal on.
ZCT »		Send all words/codes twice.
ZCT		My SSA demod is ......
		1= CW Tuned. 2 = In short-code lock. 3 = In long-code lock.
		4 = In long-code and date-lock on Channel A only.
		5 = In long-code and date-lock on both channels.
ZCU		Set SSA ..... to .... 1. Ch A only.
		2. Ch A and B retaining orig radiated power for this access
ZCV		Set speed of SSA ... Ch ... (A/B) to ....
		1 = 1300 baud 2 = 2600 bd. 3 = 600 bd.
		4 = 1200 bd 5 = 2400 bd. 6 = 4800 bd.
ZCW »	Are you in direct contact with ?	I am in direct contact with ....
ZCW	(To be used with ZCX). 1. Check your ... and advise. 2. I have lost	
	3. Perform back-to-back through .... 4. Bypass 5. I have bypassed ...	
	6. Retune demod.	
ZCX	1. Test loop 1. 2. Test loop 2. 3. Test loop 3. 4. Test loop 4.	
	5. Par amp. 6. Hi power amp. 7. Demodulator. 8. Mux Ch A.	
	9. Mux Ch B. 10. Demux Ch A. 11. Demux Ch B. 12. Coder.	
	13. Decoder. 14. Tracking (incl side lobe) 15. 5MHz standard.	
	16. Synthesiser. 17. Power supply. 18. Modulator. 19. Satellite.	
	20. Crypto eqpt. 21. Patching DC. 22. Patching RF. 23. Patch clock.	
ZCY	Operate at ... bauds P/S	
	1 = 75. 2 = 84. 3 = 150. 4 = 168. 5 = 300. 6 = 326. 7 = 600	
	8 = 672. 9 = 1200. 10 = 2400. 11 = 4800. 12 = 9600.	
ZCZ	1 = Coded. 2 = Uncoded. 3 = Satellite Access Ch at ... DBW.	
	4 = Relinquish Satellite Access due to sole access	
	5 = Relinquish Satellite Access due to violation of Power restrictions.	
	6 = Increase Power to .... DBW. 7 = Decrease Power to .... DBW.	
	8 = NB ALPHA. 9 = NB BRAVO. 10 = Change Satellite Access Control to .... at DBW.

ZDA — ZFZ is allocated to Message Procedures.

ZDA		Here is a message - the priority is ....
ZDA		I have a formal message for you.
ZDB	Expedite reply(ies) to my	
	1 = Previous signal. 2 = Repeat / correct request. 3 = Service message.	
ZDC »		I am diagnosing circuit faults and will advise.
ZDC	Does last message require signal of execution ?	Last message requires signal of execution.
ZDD		Bring message .... to the circuit.

Radiotelegraph and Radiotelephone Codes, Prowords and Abbreviations

List of Radiotelegraph 'Q' and 'Z' Codes

Key to date of changes noted and references, NOT part of the Code Indicator.
*1912 $1924 #1933 %1938 ¶1943 ?1960 +1972 @1985 &1987 1990 ~ ARRL Codes » C&W

Z Codes etc. become a QUESTION when preceded by the INT.

CODE	QUESTION	ANSWER or NOTICE
ZDE		Message ... undelivered, station closed. 1-6.
ZDF »	Does my frequency drift ?	Your frequency is drifting.
ZDF		Message received by addressees 1-5.
ZDF 1-5 +		Your freq is drifting 1-5.
ZDG		Message doubtful. Confirmation coming.
ZDH »		Your dots are too heavy (long); adjust lighter.
ZDH		Corrected copy of message ...... forward to ......
ZDI		Put message ..... on 1) Mercast. 2) Mercast one operator pai―
ZDJ	How many groups in your message ?	Message ..... groups to transmit to you.
ZDK	Will you repeat message or portion .... ?	Following repetition is made ....
ZDL »		Your dots are too light (short); adjust heavier.
ZDL		Confirmation 1) omitted. 2) differs to text
ZDM »		Your dots are missing.
ZDM		I am holding your message. Multiple address.
ZDN		Report disposal of message .... your station, why delay?
ZDO		I could not send message ..... to ....
ZDP		Hold message ..... until confirmed correct.
ZDQ		Message .... relayed to .... before .... at ... on ... freq
ZDR		Here is multi-adr or book message tape with ... normal routing indicators
ZDS		Message just transmitted is wrong, correction is .....
ZDT »		The following transmitters are running dual.
ZDT		Exercise msgs not to be sent until further orders (or until ....)
ZDU		Pass following 1) private msg. 2) service msg. Number words charged for is ....
ZDV »		Your dots varying in length; please remedy.
ZDV		Private message recd for ...... Request instructions.
ZDW		In addit to regular skeds, hydrographic msg will be sent out on .... skeds.
ZDX		Msgs up to/incl no. have been previously sent.
ZDY		Private msgs are not to be sent until further orders or until .....
ZDZ		On .... msgs were mailed to ...... bearing serial nos. ....
ZEA		Pass plain language copy to ..... by secure means.
ZEB		This is a reprocessed ICAO message.
ZEC	Have you received message ?	Message ... 1) not rec'd 2) unidentified. Give better ID.
ZED »		We are experiencing dropouts 1-5.
ZED		Confirmation info received varies with the text.
ZEE		Your signal is dropping out.
ZEE		Request message .... be transmitted.
ZEF		Your signal is being filled in 1-5.
ZEF		This msg has been rec'd/intercepted from a ship at sea.
ZEG »		Your signal is garbled 1-5.
ZEG		Msg not to be decrypted/reported outside COMCEN in 1) aggressor 2) friendly force
ZEH		The accuracy of the following is doubtful - confirm (1) Heading (2) Text (3) Group Count.
ZEI		Accuracy of msg doubtful. Check with originator and repeat.
ZEJ		Replies to this msg (or ...) to be sent now (or at ...)
ZEK		No answer is required.
ZEL	Is msg .... a correction to doubtful msg ...?	Msg is correction to msg .... to .... (Use only with ZDG)
ZEN		Msg del'd by separate tx or other means immediately following this op signal.
ZEO		Transmit msg by rapid means if no charge, to all others by mail.
ZEP		Msg incomplete. Missed grps indic by ZEP to be sent as soon as recd.
ZEQ		Msg missent to this stn. Retx to correct addr. / I will retransmit to correct address.
ZER		Book msg incl ... routing indics. Pilot station responsible.
ZES		Your msg 1) Incomplete 2) Garbled. Retransmit.
ZET		Msg is protected no further action by ..... is reqd.

Radiotelegraph and Radiotelephone Codes, Prowords and Abbreviations

List of Radiotelegraph 'Q' and 'Z' Codes

Key to date of changes noted and references, NOT part of the Code Indicator.
*1912 $ 1924 # 1933 % 1938 ¶ 1943 ? 1960 + 1972 @ 1985 & 1987 1990   ~ ARRL Codes » C&W

Z Codes etc. become a QUESTION when preceded by the INT.

CODE	QUESTION	ANSWER or NOTICE
ZEU		Exercise (drill) message.
ZEV	Acknowledge message.	Message .... is acknowledged.
ZEV	Can you authenticate ?	I authenticate ...
ZEW		Attention for 1) Action 2) Info to msg ... in your files.
ZEX		Book message - to List of addressees, not listed in msg.
ZEY		Msg .... has/will be put on broadcast schedule .....
ZEZ		Msg sent commercially / by phone to be sent as single address. (Use only with ZEX)
ZFA »		Your auto is failing.
ZFA		Following message read/received/intercepted.
ZFB »		Your signals are fading badly.
ZFB		Pass msg to ... 1) on arrival 2) on return to base (BASEGRAM)
ZFC »		Check your TTY shift.
ZFC	Have U sent/recd "Execute" for msg ...?	"Execute" for message ..... sent at ......
ZFD »		Your signal is fading.
ZFD		Your depth of fading is ..... (1 to 5 grading).
ZFD %		Send V's.
ZFD '49		This message is a suspected duplicate.
ZFE		Pass yr file msg ... using supplementary heading you have.
ZFF »		Please observe and furnish frame code reports on .... (C/s, freq) kilocycles.
ZFF		Inform me when msg ... recd by ... 1)Action 2)Info 3)All addressees 4-6) 1-3 Msg Centres.
ZFG		Msg is a duplicate of previous msg, deliver to all addressees.
ZFH		Extra addressees if message is readdressed.
ZFH		Message to you for action/info/comment for .....
ZFI	Is there any reply to msg ....?	There is no reply to message ....
ZFJ		Msgs ... not transmitted on this sked are no longer required.
ZFK »		Revert to FSK.
ZFK	Does msg .... concern me ?	Msg ... does not / no longer concerns you or ....
ZFL	Any tfc fr me on sked ... between ... and ...?	Traffic for U on bcast sked ... between ... and ...
ZFM		Msgs ... to ... sent on unserviceable txr, simultaneously keyed, will be sent again
ZFO »		Your signal is fading out.
ZFO	Are my signals fading ?	Your signals have faded out.
ZFO		Msg ... being delivered as basegram message.
ZFP		Basegram - Hold message at base or port for arrival of ......
ZFQ »		The frequency shift of your signal is now ...... Hz.
ZFQ		Two msgs ... and ... recd under ch no .... Both released.
ZFR		Cancel message ..... under TI number ...
ZFR »		You have rapid fading (1 to 5 grading).
ZFS »		There is a slight fade to your signal.
ZFS		Make msg ... same ser no. as this procedure message.
ZFT		Msg ... recd without ser no. following msg no. ... Both released.
ZFU		Ch nos. ... and ... before msg ... Lower no. recorded, higher no. blanked.
ZFV		Msg ... with ch no .... separated by parts of msg released subject to correction. Provide corrected copy.
ZFW		BLANK Ch no ..... Forward message ... as ch no ...
ZFX		Channel no / Stn serial no ..... is open.

ZGA — ZGM is allocated to Calling Procedure.

CODE	QUESTION	ANSWER or NOTICE
ZGA	What is my callsign on this circuit ?	Your callsign on this circuit is ....
ZGB		Answer in 1) Alphabetical order 2) Following order of callsigns.
ZGC		ZGB transmit your c/s .... times.
ZGD		Two stns using same c/s on ...kHz/MHz. Both to select different c/s
ZGE		Send callsign ... times on ... frequency.
ZGF »		Your signal is good for ... wpm.

Radiotelegraph and Radiotelephone Codes, Prowords and Abbreviations

List of Radiotelegraph 'Q' and 'Z' Codes

Key to date of changes noted and references, NOT part of the Code Indicator.
*1912 $ 1924 # 1933 % 1938 ¶ 1943 ? 1960 + 1972 @ 1985 & 1987 1990   ~ ARRL Codes » C&W

Z Codes etc. become a QUESTION when preceded by the INT.

CODE	QUESTION	ANSWER or NOTICE
ZGF		Make callsigns more distinctly.
ZGG	What is callsign of ?	Callsign of .... is .....
	1) Friendly strike a/c. 2) Friendly shadowing a/c. 3) Incoming vessel. 4) Senior Officer IC 5) Flagship.	
ZGH		Using txmtr on two or more freqs. Answers may be delayed.
ZGI		..... has been calling you on .... freq.
ZGJ	When will you call me on this / ....freq ?	I will call you on this / ... freq ASAP or at ... hrs.
ZGK	When will I call you on this / ... freq ?	Call me agn on present / ... freq .
ZGL		... will answer calls for me / or for ...
ZGM	Did you (or ...) hear ... at ... ?	... been unable to communicate with ... (since) ...
ZGN	When was I (or.....) last heard ?	Nothing heard from you (or ....) since.....
ZGO	What is my callsign and sequence ?	Your callsign is ..... Answer after ......
ZGP »		Please give priority.
ZGP		Answer calls for me on present / ... freq.
ZGS »		Your signals are getting stronger.
ZGW »		Your signals are getting weaker.

ZHA - ZHM is allocated to Interference and Delay.

CODE	QUESTION	ANSWER or NOTICE
ZHA »	Do conditions permit auto transmission ?	Conditions permit automatic reception.
ZHA	Will I decrease freq to clear interference ?	Decrease freq slightly to clear interference.
ZHB	Will I increase freq to clear interference ?	Increase freq slightly to clear interference.
ZHC		My receiving conditions are .....
ZHM »	What is extent of reception of harmonic radiation ?	

ZHN - ZHZ is allocated to Automatic Transmissions.

CODE	QUESTION	ANSWER or NOTICE
ZHN	How do you recv my auto transmission ?	Your auto transmissions are - (1- good 2 - fair 3 - unreadable)
ZHO	What is your speed of auto transmission ?	My auto transmission speed in (1- rpm, 2- wpm, 3- bauds) is ...
ZHP	What is preventing auto reception ?	Auto reception is prevented by ......
ZHQ		Listen for me on .... freq., transmit to me on .... freq.
ZHR	Is my auto transmit speed correct ?	Auto trans speed is 1 - fast, 2 - slow, 3 - erratic, 4 - correct.
ZHS »		Send high speed auto ..... wpm.
ZHY »		We are holding your ......

ZIA - ZIZ is allocated to Serial Numbers.

CODE	QUESTION	ANSWER or NOTICE
ZIA		Msg is out of proper sequence of serial numbers.
ZIB	Msgs ... and ... have same serial no. ? What are correct numbers ?	Change / give msg ... serial number ....
ZIC	How many messages have I sent you?	
ZIC	What is ser. no. of last msg sent to me ?	Ser. no. of last msg transmitted to you is ......
ZID	How many messages have you sent me?	
ZID	What is ser. no. of last msg recd from me ?	Ser. no. of last msg recd from you is ....
ZIE		Serial numbers not recd, Repeat msg or cancel ser. nos.
ZIF		I / .... did not use serial numbers.
ZIG	Is / are number/s ... to ... blank ?	Numbers ... to ... are blank.
ZIH		Repeat msg headings ... to .... to check serial nos.
ZII	What was 1- DTG. 2- filing time of your ... ?	My ... had 1- DTG or 2- filing time of ....
ZIJ		Changing Ch no. /letter. This msg is last in this series.
ZIK	This is a weather controlled msg. not to be transmitted in clear over radio circuits.	
ZIM »		Interruption by ISM interference 1-5.
ZIP »		Increase power.
ZIP	Have set continuous watch or 1- single opr, 2- Two opr, 3- general, 4- reduced single opr on bcast indicated.	
		First serial number recd is .... / No number yet recd.
ZIR		Your transmitter has strong idle radiation.
ZIS 1-5 +		Atmospheric interference on .... freq is 1-5.

Radiotelegraph and Radiotelephone Codes, Prowords and Abbreviations

List of Radiotelegraph 'Q' and 'Z' Codes

Key to date of changes noted and references, NOT part of the Code Indicator.
*1912 $ 1924 # 1933 % 1938 ¶ 1943 ? 1960 + 1972 @ 1985 & 1987 1990   ~ ARRL Codes » C&W

Z Codes etc. become a QUESTION when preceded by the INT.

CODE	QUESTION	ANSWER or NOTICE

ZJA - ZJZ is allocated to Optical.

CODE	QUESTION	ANSWER or NOTICE
ZJA		Read signalling light of ....
ZJB	May I close down visual watch now /at ... ?	Close down visual watch now / or at ....
ZJC		Repeat all flag signals made by the senior officer (senior officer afloat).
ZJD		Use .. 1 - better light. 2 - better background.
ZJE		Set visual watch now / or at ......
ZJF		Visual relay stn btwn snr offr (or ...) and ... is to be ...
ZJF 1-5 +		Your freq is jumping 1-5.
ZJG		Repeat all flashing/semaphore msgs made by snr officer.
ZJH		Your light is unreadable - 1 - not trained correctly, 2 - not bright enough, 3 - too bright.
ZJI	What are c/s of ships accompanying you ?	C/s of ships accompanying me are ... (Visual use only)
ZJJ		Use double flash procedure.
ZJK	Are you / is ... visual guard for .... ?	I am / .... is visual guard for ......
ZJL		Hoist the following signal.
ZJM		..... 1 - Flaghoist; 2 - Semaphore; 3 - 20-inch sig projector; 4 - 10-inch sig projector; 5 - ALDIS; 6 - Intermediate; 7 - Heather; 8 - Daylight sig lantern; 9 - Masthead flashing light; 10 - Infrared; 11 - Sig. searchlight; 12 - Omnidirectional flashing light; 13 - Directional flashing light.
ZJN		Message .... passed to ... at ... but "L" not yet recd.
ZJO		Read back each group of text of message as it is sent.
ZJP		Encrypt msg and pass to all addressees. (Only used with visual, not liable to interception)
ZJQ		Pepeat msg snr offr /ship now / is about to transmit.
ZJR		Only semaphore to be used for visual sigs between ... and ... / from ...
ZJS		Directional lights of min brilliance to be used for all visual traffic between ... and ... except msgs of priority and above requiring transmission to two or more ships.
ZJT		Bcast tx ... to be taken off for .... mins (or until ....)

ZKA - ZKZ is allocated to Radio Guard.

CODE	QUESTION	ANSWER or NOTICE
ZKA	Who is NCS on this or ..... freq ?	...... is Net Control Station on ..... frequency
ZKB	Is permission required before transmitting ?	Permission is required from NCS.
ZKC		Net control station.
ZKD	Will I take net control from ..... to ...... ?	Take net control for ...... until ....
ZKE		I or ..... report into net / circuit.
ZKF		...... station leaving net temporarily to ......
ZKG		Observe (... to obs) sked with ... on ... at .... time.
ZKH	Did you (or ...) obs sked with ... at ...?	I (or ...) observed sked with ... at ...
ZKI		Listen on .... Freq 1. Continuously. 2. Until new order.
ZKJ	May I close down (until .....) ?	1 - Close down (until ......) 2 - I am closing down (until)
ZKK		Assume radiotelegraph (wireless) organisation forthwith (or at ....)
ZKL		Resume normal radio comms now (or at ...)
ZKM		Take guard (for ...) (on ... kHz / MHz)
ZKN		I have taken over guard on ... kHz / MHz.
ZKO »		Revert to on/off keying.
ZKO		I have handed over guard to ... on ... kHz / MHz. Ser no. of last msg was ....
ZKP	Are you (is ...) radio guard for ... on ... kHz/MHz ?	I am (is ...) radio guard for ... on ... kHz / MHz.
ZKQ »		Say when you are ready to resume.
ZKQ		Indicate ships / stns you are / or ... is guard. (1. Radio on .... kHz / MHz.; 2. Visual.)
ZKR	On what freqs are you /or ... maintaining watch ?	I am / or ... is maintaining watch on ... kHz / MHz.
ZKS	What stns keeping watch on .... / or in net ?	Following stns keeping watch on .... kHz/MHz / or in net.
ZKT		Am keeping watch on ... kHz / MHz for ..... 1. First 5 mins in ea half hr.; 2. From 10 to 15, 40 to 45 min past hr.; 3. Betwn ... and ... mins past the hr.
ZKU		I am / ... is maintaining continuous watch, or

Radiotelegraph and Radiotelephone Codes, Prowords and Abbreviations

List of Radiotelegraph 'Q' and 'Z' Codes

Key to date of changes noted and references, NOT part of the Code Indicator.
*1912 $ 1924 # 1933 % 1938 ¶ 1943 ? 1960 + 1972 @ 1985 & 1987 1990   ~ ARRL Codes   » C&W

Z Codes etc. become a QUESTION when preceded by the INT.

CODE	QUESTION	ANSWER or NOTICE
		1. Single opr; 2. Two opr; 3. General; 4. Reduced single opr; period on ... c/s ... bcast.
ZKV		I am / ... is standing splitphone watch on .... and .... kHz/MHz.
ZKW »		The key weight of your sigs is .... percent.

ZLA - ZLM is allocated to Facsimile.

ZLA		I have pics of following types to transmit ...
		1. Photographs; 2. Wx maps; 3. Blueprints; 4. Printed matter; 5. Test
ZLB »		Give me longer breaks.
ZLB	What drum rotation speed shall I use ?	Transmit at ... rpm. (1. 30; 2. 45; 3. 50; 4. 60; 5. 90; 6. 100)
ZLC		Your transmission .... (1. Shows objectional modulation: 2. Suitable for comms but not for picture; 3. Shows caption too close to edge of picture; 4. Shows buckled print; 5. Shows fork drift; 6. Picture shows too much contrast; 7. Picture shows insufficient contrast; 8. Picture shows cross-over.
ZLD »		We are getting a long dash (mark/space) from you.
ZLD		I am unable to ... 1. Sync with you; 2. Transmit pictures; 3. Copy pictures.
ZLE		Send .... (1. Fence; 2. White; 3. Black; 4. Picture; 5. Synchronise; 6. Fence swinging black; 7. Fence swinging white until I stop you.)
ZLF		... (1. Inverter; 2. Converter; 3. 96-line 12x18 tcvr; 4. 100-line tcvr; 5. 300-line tcvr).
ZLG	Shall I transmit (1. Negative; 2. Positive) ?	Transmit (1. Negative; 2. Positive)
ZLH	Will you transmit map(s) ... area ... time ... type ?	I will transmit map(s) ... area ... time ... type.
ZLI		Reverse material on drum, run until I break you.
ZLJ	What size lettering will I use ?	Use .... (1. Standard telegraphic typewriter; 2. Jumbo twriter (if avail); 3. Hand lettering at least 3/16 inch high)
ZLL +		Distorted landline control sigs apparently caused by control wire pickup.

ZLN - ZLZ is allocated to Radionavigation and Landing Facilities.

ZLN		Facility indicated can't be operated at present.
ZLO	Is/are facilities operative at your station ?	Following facilities operative at this station /or at ..... (1. Homing beacon; 2. Radar beacon; 3. Revolving/flashing beacon; 4. Radio beacon; 5. Instr landing sys; 6. Grnd control approach; 7. Approach control; 8. Tower txmtr, (LF, MF, VHF, UHF); 9. MF DF; 10. VHF DF; 11. UHF DF; 12. Runway lights; 13. Sandra lights; 14. Radio track; 15. Radio range.)
ZLP »		Reduce power.
ZLP	What is/are mag lines of shoot of ... facil ?	Mag lines of shoot of .... facility/ies are .... degrees.
ZLS »		We are suffering from a lightning storm.

ZMA - ZMZ is allocated to Direction Finding.

ZMA %		I have a message.
ZMA (1949)	What was bearing of stn .... at ...... on ..... freq?	Brg of stn ... at ... on .... freq is ...degrees.
ZMB		Brg of you/.... was .... (class ...) from me/.... at .... hrs.
ZMC		Brg of stn answd msg frm ... was ... at ... time class .... kHZ/MHz.
ZMD		1. Yr brg is btwn ... deg and ... deg, sense indics you are ... of this stn. 2. Your bearing is changing rapidly.
ZME		Pass in DF brg ... on/between kHz/MHz etc.
ZMF	Will you get DF brg of stn now on ... kHz/MHz ?	Brg of stn on ... kHz/MHz was ... at ... time.
ZMG		Bearing unreliable, Error may be .... deg/miles.
ZMH »		Magnetic activity.
ZMH		Surface craft c/s ... cooperating. Change to ... kHz/MHz. Follow DF procedure when called.
ZMI	Will you send c/s, 5sec dash to home on you ?	I'll send c/s, 5sec dash. You home on me.
ZMJ		Check ... (1. Correctness of last QUV; 2. Sense of last QDR;

Radiotelegraph and Radiotelephone Codes, Prowords and Abbreviations

List of Radiotelegraph 'Q' and 'Z' Codes

Key to date of changes noted and references, NOT part of the Code Indicator.
*1912 $1924 #1933 %1938 ¶1943 ?1960 +1972 @1985 &1987 1990   ~ARRL Codes »C&W

Z Codes etc. become a QUESTION when preceded by the INT.

CODE	QUESTION	ANSWER or NOTICE
		3. Correctness of last QDM; 4. Sense of last QDM).
ZMK		Can't determine your /...'s (1. Position; 2. Bearing).
ZML		Steer ... deg 2 mins, send c/s, long dash while doing.
ZMM		Increase height for more accurate bearing.
ZMN		Change to loop DF on ... freq (home on tranmit by ...)
ZMO »		Stand by for a moment.
ZMO	What is my DF bearing from landmark /.... ?	Your bearing from landmark is ... at ... time.
ZMP »		Mispunch or perforator failure.
ZMP		Plot position from bearings of stns on ... freq
ZMQ »		Stand by for ......
ZMQ		Can't determine your posn, ur in line with DF baseline.
ZMR		Take over DF guard on ... freq.
ZMS		Carry out short DF procedure, locally prescribed.
ZMT		Sense determination unreliable, brg may be reciprocal.
ZMU »		Multipath effect causing distortion.
ZMU	... (1. Listen (for	...0 on DF on ... freq). 2. Shift to DF ... listen for c/s ...).
ZMV	What is Grid Course from me to you ?	Grid Course from you to me is ... at ... time.

ZNA - ZNZ is allocated to Communication Security.

CODE	QUESTION	ANSWER or NOTICE
ZNA		You are encrypting ... incorrectly (1. operating signals; 2. Radio callsigns; 3. Address groups).
ZNB »		We do not get your breaks, we send twice.
ZNB		Give me longer breaks.
ZNB	What is authentication of .... ?	Authentication of .... is
ZNC »		There is no communication with .....
ZNC		All transm will be authenticated ... (1. On all ccts; 2. On this cct; 3. On ... freq).
ZND		You are authenticating incorrectly. (1. Verify authenticator key; 2. Check authen of yr last transm).
ZNE		I am prepared to authenticate.
ZNF		Addressees not holding the crypto system, need not decrypt, read decrypt and obtain copy if needed.
ZNG »		Receiving condition no good for code.
ZNG		Addressees not holding the crypto are exempted.
ZNH		Prepare plaintext tape during decipherment.
ZNI »		No call letters / ident heard.
ZNI		Shift to ... (1. On-line; 2. Plain) operation now. Msg
ZNJ		may be forwarded by radio or unsafe liaisons.
ZNK		Addressees not holding crypto facilities are exempted.
ZNL		Crypto receiver direct queries to ..... (address designators except plain language).
		Note: Use in codress msgs, limit to msgs Immediate and above.
ZNM		May be transferred into addressee nets, secure or of same classification as msg.
ZNN »		Clear of traffic.
ZNO »		Not on the air.
ZNO		Unable to decrypt msg. Use only as laid down in cryptog. instructions.
ZNP		Transfer ch to .... (1. Normal; 2. Top Secret; 3. Conference; 4. Engineering;) on-line cipher operation.
		Note: This signal is for use only when already in on-line operation.
ZNQ		Msg ... recd (1. Without authentication: 2. Incorrectly authenticated.)
ZNR »		Not received.
ZNR		Msg may be fwd without change by radio or non-approved circuit.
ZNS »		Here's new slip.

ZOA - ZOM is allocated to Relay.

CODE	QUESTION	ANSWER or NOTICE
ZOA		On the air.
ZOA »¶		Have checked tx c/s ..... Sigs radiating on air OK.
ZOA		Relay msg ... to ... by visual.
ZOB		(I will) take no further action to fwd msg ....
ZOC		Stations called relay msg .... to your addressees.

Radiotelegraph and Radiotelephone Codes, Prowords and Abbreviations

List of Radiotelegraph 'Q' and 'Z' Codes

Key to date of changes noted and references, NOT part of the Code Indicator.
*1912 $ 1924 # 1933 % 1938 ¶ 1943 ? 1960 + 1972 @ 1985 & 1987 1990   ~ ARRL Codes » C&W

Z Codes etc. become a QUESTION when preceded by the INT.

CODE	QUESTION	ANSWER or NOTICE
ZOD »		Observing .... conditions - will relay when better
ZOD		Act as radio link (relaying stn) between me / ... and ...
ZOE	Can you accept message for .... ?	Send message, I will pass to ....
ZOF		Pass this message to ...... now / at ....
ZOG		Transmit your message. (give info).
ZOH ¶	What traffic have you on hand?	
ZOH		Send on ... freq by ...(1. Receipt; 2. Bcast; 3. Intercept) method.
ZOI		Pass message to nearest / ... weather control.
ZOJ		Unable to relay ... (1. C/s 2. Text) not encrypted.
ZOK »+	Are you receiving OK ?	We are receiving OK.
ZOK @		Relay this message via ....
ZOL »		OK, I am on line.
ZOL		I will relay your c/s to senior offr afloat, c/s ...
ZOM »		Deliver msg by mail to ... instead of broadcast.

ZON - ZOZ is allocated to Routing.

CODE	QUESTION	ANSWER or NOTICE
ZON		Put this/... msg on (1. CW; 2. RTTY;) bcast by designator ....
ZOO		Put msg on MERCAST indicated by designator ....
ZOP		Msg has been delivered to all / .... bcast areas.
ZOQ		Deliver message to all / .... broadcast areas.
ZOR »		Transmit only reversals.
ZOR		1. Route traffic for ... via ... area broadcast. 2. From ... traffic for you /... will be routed via ... area bcast.
ZOS	Request area routeing for msgs for	Area routeing for messages for ..... is .....
ZOT %		Go ahead.
ZOT +		Transmit at lower Precedence to ....
ZOU	How should traffic for ... be routed ?	Route traffic for ... through .... on .... freq.
ZOV		Stn desig preceding this op sig is correct routing for msg, rerouted by ....
ZOW		Bcast msg at watch periods for ships with (1. One; 2. Two;) radio ops.
ZOX		Put msg / ... on submarine bcast indic by designator .....
ZOY		Relay only to stns whose designations precede this op sig.
ZOZ		Relay this msg /..... as is without decryption.

ZPA - ZPM is allocated to Signal Strength and Readability.

CODE	QUESTION	ANSWER or NOTICE
ZPA	Am I distorted ?	You are distorted.
ZPA »		Printer (TTY) line feed signal not received.
ZPB		Your transmitter has strong radiation while idling.
ZPC »		Printer carriage return signal not received.
ZPC		Your sigs are ... (1. Fading badly; 2. Fading slightly; 3. Good for ...wpm; 4. Getting stronger; 5. Getting weaker).
ZPD	Is your monitored signal ... satisfactory - (1. Locally; 2. As radiated)	My monitored signal ..... is satisfactory - (1. Locally; 2. As radiated)
ZPE »		Punch everything you have.
ZPE		Maximum power is now being radiated.
ZPF »		Motor running fast.
ZPF	What is readability of net signals ?	Readability of net signals is 1-5.
ZPG	What is / are signal strengths of net or .... ?	Signal strengths of ...... is / are .... (1-5).

ZPN - ZPZ is allocated to Search and Rescue.

CODE	QUESTION	ANSWER or NOTICE
ZPN		IFF switched ON in distress position.
ZPO		Relay exactly as is, no changes to text, functions or groups etc.
ZPO »		Send plain text once.
ZPP »		Punch plain only.

Radiotelegraph and Radiotelephone Codes, Prowords and Abbreviations

List of Radiotelegraph 'Q' and 'Z' Codes

Key to date of changes noted and references, NOT part of the Code Indicator.
*1912 $ 1924 # 1933 % 1938 ¶ 1943 ? 1960 + 1972 @ 1985 & 1987 1990   ~ ARRL Codes » C&W

Z Codes etc. become a QUESTION when preceded by the INT.

CODE	QUESTION	ANSWER or NOTICE
ZPP		Msg is submarine surfacing msg, clear on calling freq.
ZPR »		Return slip at present running.
ZPR		I have ... msgs in tape relay format for you. (receive directly to reperf. m/c)
ZPS »		Printer motor is running low.
ZPT »		Send plain text twice.
ZPT		This is a transmitter pre-acceptance trial. Send strength and readability reports ASAP.
ZPU		Send highest serial number first of waiting Tropical Wind Warning msgs.
ZPV		File earlier wind warnings (by DTG's) without further transmission.
ZPW		Msg cancelled at ... time. File without transmission.
ZPX		Msg for screening for broadcast. Advise bcast control of determination.

ZQA - ZQZ is allocated to Take-off and Landing Instructions.

ZQA		Landing lights at .... are out of order.
ZQB	What is magnetic direction for landing ?	Magnetic direction for landing is .... deg.
ZQC	Are you /... (1. Airborne; 2. Waterborne; 3. On land) ?	I am /... is (1.; 2.; 3.)
ZQD	Will I use procedure for .... facility ?	Use procedure for ..... facility.
ZQE	What rate of descent (ft/min) do you want ?	I want ... hundreds ft/min rate of descent.
ZQF	How long is runway in use in yards ?	Runway in use is ..... yards long.

ZRA - ZRZ is allocated to Frequencies.

ZRA 1-7	How does my frequency check ?	Your frequency is 1 - 7
	1 - correct. 2 - high. 3 - low. 4 - Stable mark.	5 - Stable space. 6 - Unstable. 7 - Erratic.
ZRA »		Reversed auto tape.
ZRB »		Your relay is poor, retune your receiver.
ZRB		Check your frequency on this circuit.
ZRC »	Can you receive CW?	
ZRC	Shall I tune my transmitter to ...... ?	Tune your transmitter to ....
ZRD	What is freq of radio in operation ?	.... radio in operation is on freq ......
ZRE	On what frequency do you hear me best?	I hear you best on ..... Kcs.
ZRF »		Run foxes (Send a QBF test tape).
ZRF	Send tune signal on frequency 1 min or .... ?	Will send tuning signal on frequency ....
ZRG	When will change freq ... be needed ?	Change freq to ... needed at .... time.
ZRH	Is my frequency shift correct ?	Your freq shift is .... (1. Too wide; 2. Too narrow; 3. Not linear; 5. Correct.) (by Hz).
ZRJ	Will you check your ..... ?	I will check my ......
ZRK »		Your keying tape is reversed.
ZRK	Shall I revert to single ch working ?	Revert to single ch working.
ZRL »		Rerun slip before one now running.
ZRL	Are you working on the correct code ?	I am working on the correct code.
	Note: This meaning applies only to frequency shift diplex.	
ZRM »		Remove the modulation from ....
ZRM	Can you rec both sidebands of my independent sideband transmissions ?	I can receive ... (1. The upper sideband; 2. The lower sideband; 3. Both sidebands).
ZRN »	Is my note rough ?	You have a rough note.
ZRN	Do you intend to transmit on ..... ? (1. The upper sideband; 2. The lower sideband; 3. Both sidebands independently).	I intend to transmit on ......
ZRO »		I am receiving you OK.
ZRO	Can you read me on ... ? (1. Ch A; 2. Ch B; 3. Ch(s) ....; 4. All Chs).	I can read you on ..... (1. - 4.)
ZRP		Transfer sig on Ch .... to Ch .....
ZRQ		Change to other sideband.
ZRR »		Run reversals.
ZRR		Msgs .... no longer bcast but effective and of interest to ....
ZRS »		Rerun slip number ......

Radiotelegraph and Radiotelephone Codes, Prowords and Abbreviations

List of Radiotelegraph 'Q' and 'Z' Codes

Key to date of changes noted and references, NOT part of the Code Indicator.
*1912 $ 1924   #1933   %1938   ¶1943   ?1960   +1972   @1985   &1987 1990   ~ ARRL Codes   » C&W

Z Codes etc. become a QUESTION when preceded by the INT.

CODE	QUESTION	ANSWER or NOTICE
ZRS		Your carrier is (1. Over-suppressed; 2. Under-suppressed).
ZRT »		Return to traffic handling.
ZRT		Radiate full unmodulated power for ... mins.
ZRU	Are my tone freqs correct ?	Your tone for ...(1. Marking and spacing are high; 2. Marking and spacing are low; 3. Marking and spacing are correct).
ZRY »		Run a test tape.

ZSA - ZSZ is allocated to Air & Sea Traffic Control.

CODE	QUESTION	ANSWER or NOTICE
ZSA	May I ascend to .... height ?	You may ascend to .... height.
ZSB	May I descend to .... height ?	You may descend to .... height.
ZSC		Switch on IFF.
ZSD		IFF switched OFF.
ZSE	Do you have glider in tow ?	..... (1. have glider in tow; 2. released glider at ... height).
ZSF »		Send faster.
ZSF		Switch off .. (1. IFF; 2. IFF for 10 mins in area denoted except ships c/s).
ZSH »		There is heavy static here.
ZSI »	What is my signal intensity?	Your signal intensity is ....
ZSI		.... (1. Maintain height ... ft report over ... c/s stn; 2. Hold ... leg of beam ... c/s stn at .... ft.).
ZSJ		Stop, Auto jam.
ZSM »		Microvolt input to receiver is ......
ZSN »		Give me a SINPO report on my signal.
ZSO »		Transmit your slips once.
ZSO		Send your tapes/messages 1. Once. 2. Twice.
ZSR »		Your signals are strong and readable.
ZSS »		Send slower.
ZST »		Transmit your slips twice. (Wheatstone tx)
ZST		Transmit revs continuously.
ZSU »		Your signals are unreadable.
ZSV »		Your speed is varying.
ZSW		Stop auto, signals too weak.
ZSX		Stop auto, signals too weak.

ZTA - ZTZ is allocated to Equipment.

CODE	QUESTION	ANSWER or NOTICE
ZTA »		Transmit by auto.
ZTA		.... (1. Radio; 2. Visual; 3. Landline; 4. Teletypewriter; 5. Telephone; 6. Automatic; 7. Facsimile; 8. Shore telephone; 9. Shore TTY; 10. RTTY).
ZTB		.... (1. Transmitter-distributor; 2. Auto-head; 3. Perforator; 4. Reperforator; 5. Printer; 6. Undulator; 7. Keyboard; 8. Freq shift keyer; 9. Multiplexing carrier base; 10. On-line crypto device).
ZTC	... (1. Does my ...; 2. Is your ....) faulty ?	.... (1. Your ....; My .....) appears to be faulty.
ZTD	Shall I use .... ?	Use ....
ZTE	Are you (is ....) able to use .... ?	I am (.... is) able to use.
ZTF		Send fast and twice.
ZTF	Are repairs completed ?	Repairs completed.
ZTG		... (class of emission / type of transmission).
ZTH »		Transmit to me by hand.
ZTH		1. FM 2. AM 3. PM 4. FSK 5. AJ ... transmission.
ZTI »		My transmission will be temporarily interrupted
ZTI		.... (1. Rcvr; 2. Transmitter; 3. Power supply; 4. Antenna system; 5. Radio direction finder).
ZTJ		Cease using ......
ZTK	Are you / is ..... connected to .... ?	I am / ... is connected to ....

Radiotelegraph and Radiotelephone Codes, Prowords and Abbreviations

List of Radiotelegraph 'Q' and 'Z' Codes

Key to date of changes noted and references, NOT part of the Code Indicator.
*1912 $1924 #1933 %1938 ¶1943 ?1960 +1972 @1985 &1987 1990   ~ ARRL Codes » C&W

Z Codes etc. become a QUESTION when preceded by the INT.

CODE	QUESTION	ANSWER or NOTICE
ZTL	Are you / is .... about to disconnect ?	I am / ... is about to disconnect.
ZTM		I (or ...) is unable to use .....
ZTN	What is my bias distortion ?	Your bias distortion is ... (1. Excessive; 2. .... % marking; 3. ... % spacing; 4. ... % total distortion).
ZTO	Is my character formation correct ?	Your character formation is .... (1. Correct; 2. Defective in start element; 3. Def. 1st el.; 4. Def. 2nd element; 5. Def. 3rd el.; 6. Def. 4th el.; 7. Def. in 5th element; 8. Def. in stop element).
ZTP	What is the duration of your modulation cycle ?	The duration of my modulation cycle is ..... **50 Baud Equipment.** 1. 148 milliseconds (7.42 units) fast. 2. 150 milliseconds (7.5 units) correct. 3. 152 milliseconds (7.6 units) slow. 4. .... erratic per character. **45.5 Baud Equipment.** 1. 161 milliseconds (7.35 units) fast. 2. 163 milliseconds (7.42 units) correct. 3. 165 milliseconds (7.5 units) slow. 4. .... erratic per character.
ZTQ	Will you .... (1. Get Chief Tech. on this/... cct; 2. Hand line over to Cct Engineer) for check?	I will ... (1. Get Chief Technician on this/... circuit; 2. Hand line over to Circuit Engineer) call when complete.
ZTR	Will you ... (1. Disconnect, carry out local test, reconnect in ... mins; 2. Connect transmit to receive for me to do loop test for ... mins) ?	I will ... (1. Disconnect, carry out local test, reconnect in ... mins; 2. Connect my transmit to recv for you to do loop test for ...
ZTS	Is the line satisfactory ?	The line is ... (1. Satisfactory; 2. Unsatisfactory).
ZTV		Send with Vibroplex.

ZUA - ZUM is allocated to Miscellaneous.

CODE	QUESTION	ANSWER or NOTICE
ZUA	Request time signal now (or at ....) ?	Time signal will be transmitted now (or at ....).
ZUA »¶		Our conditions unsuitable for undulator or automatic recording.
ZUB »		We have been unable to break in on you.
ZUB		At ...... hrs.
ZUC »		Unable to comply - will do so at ......
ZUC		From ..... to ....
ZUE		Affirmative (yes)
ZUF		Air raid .... (1. Warning; 2. In progress; 3. All clear).
ZUG		Negative (no).
ZUG		Lift emergency silence.
ZUH		Unable to comply.
ZUI		Your attention is invited to ....
ZUJ		Stand by.
ZUK	.... wants key conversation with	.... ready for key conversation with ....

ZUN - ZUZ is allocated to Meteorology.

ZUT   Unofficial sign-off signal used at first by US service operators.   Colloq. "CW forever"

ZVA - ZVZ is allocated to Relay.

CODE	QUESTION	ANSWER or NOTICE
ZVA		Stn called is responsible for relay to all stns line 2, or as indicated.
ZVB »		You have varying bias.
ZVB	What was time over RV, ETA next RV ?	My time over RV was ... , ETA next compulsory RV is .....

Radiotelegraph and Radiotelephone Codes, Prowords and Abbreviations

List of Radiotelegraph 'Q' and 'Z' Codes

Key to date of changes noted and references, NOT part of the Code Indicator.
*1912 $1924 #1933 %1938 ¶1943 ?1960 +1972 @1985 &1987 1990 ~ ARRL Codes » C&W

Z Codes etc. become a QUESTION when preceded by the INT.

CODE	QUESTION	ANSWER or NOTICE
ZVE	What is security at your / ... stn / ch. ?	My security level is ... (1. Restricted; 2. Confidential; 3. Secret; 4. Top Secret).
ZVF »		Your signal is varying in frequency.
ZVF		This stn/ch is unserviceable for classified traffic.
ZVP »		Send V's.
ZVQ		Msgs ref warning, distress, emergency to be relayed without prior arrangement.
ZVR		Retransmit msg /.... at once to all substations.
ZVS »		Your signals are varying in intensity.

ZWA - ZWZ is allocated to Communication Exercises.

ZWB		Name operator on watch.
ZWC »		Wipers or clicks here.
ZWF	Am I / is ...... wrong ?	Wrong.
ZWG		You are correct.
ZWH		Try again.
ZWI		Answer last question.
ZWL		Except ....
ZWL		Don't fwd to designation immed following reqd.
ZWM		Correct answer to last / .... question is .... / in ....
ZWN		Correct version of wrong msg is .... / found in .....
ZWO »	Will I send words once ?	Send words once.
ZWO		Following msg for exercise of ... (1. Jnr ops; 2. Snr Ops; 3. Ratings on watch).
ZWP		A Jnr Op is to carry out - (1. Std flashing ex.; 2. Std semaphore ex.; 3. Std radio teleg tx ex.; 4. Std radio teleg recv ex.).
ZWR »		Your signals are weak but readable.
ZWS »		Frequency varies.
ZWT »	Will I send words twice ?	Send words twice.

» ZXA - ZXZ Radiophoto and Facsimile.

ZXA »		Adjusting / please adjust to receive speeds ......
ZXA		Following is a callsign or address delivery group.
ZXB		Addressee get complete copy of interrupted msg from orig stn.
ZXC »		Pictures ... conditionally accepted. Will advise.
ZXD »		Send dashes. (RADIOFAX for most ZX-'s)
ZXD		Deliver msg to addressee in tape form.
ZXF »		You are floating badly.
ZXH »		Your limits are too high. Reduce to ... Hz.
ZXJ »		You are jumping out of phase.
ZXK »		Your sync is correct.
ZXK		Relay message /.... to .... in addition to normal duties.
ZXL »		Your limits ae too low. Reduce to .... Hz.
ZXO »		Last run defaced (due to ...)
ZXO		Obtain retrans of messages ..... from stn ......
ZXP »		Go ahead with pictures.
ZXP		Have for you - (1. Req for dir air spt.; 2. Reply to spt req. Precedence is ....).
ZXQ		Have for you - (1. Req for tactical recce; 2. Req for photo recce; 3. req for artillery recce. Preced. is ....)
ZXR		Extensive flag signalling will occur shortly / in ... mins.
ZXS »		You are floating slowly.
ZXS		Msg to be handled by - (1. Offr Emerg Crypto Team; 2. Ratings ECT; 3. Snr Comms Rating; 4. Jnr Comms Rating; 5. Coder (Educational)).
ZXT		Msg not to be sent by radio teleg/telephone in any form over part of its route.
ZXV »		Your modulation varies.
ZXW		Msg has been deld to all addressees following this op sig.
ZXX		Msg been deld to all info addressees following this op sig.
ZXY		Transmit this message to addressees ....

Radiotelegraph and Radiotelephone Codes, Prowords and Abbreviations

List of Radiotelegraph 'Q' and 'Z' Codes

Key to date of changes noted and references, NOT part of the Code Indicator.
*1912 $ 1924 # 1933 % 1938 ¶ 1943 ? 1960 + 1972 @ 1985 & 1987 1990   ~ ARRL Codes » C&W

Z Codes etc. become a QUESTION when preceded by the INT.

CODE	QUESTION	ANSWER or NOTICE

ZYA - ZZZ reserved for assignment as required by national authorities (ACP-131, c1955) » Multiplex

Code	Question	Answer or Notice
ZYA »		Cease traffic on all channels. Send A's on "A" channel for sync.
ZYC »		Cycling on ARC with errors stored your end.
ZYK »		Your keying on channel .... affected; please check.
ZYM		Change from single printer to multiplex.
ZYN »		Reduce bias.
ZYO		Message originated with mobile units.
ZYP »		Change from multiplex to single channel.
ZYR »		Put .... on multiplex reversals.
ZYS »	What is your speed of transmission?	Transmission speed is ....
ZYT +		Check your thyratrons.
ZYX »		Revert to multiplex reversals ..... channels.

ZZA - ZZZ is allocated to Communication Exercises.

Code	Question	Answer or Notice
ZZA	Standby.	I will standby.
ZZA		Tell name of opr who sent last msg (or msg …)
ZZC		Operator to Operator message.
ZZD	(Russian military)	Readability is … ("ich hoere Sie gut"); QRK.
ZZF		Incorrect.
ZZG		You are correct.
ZZH		Try again.
ZZN		Msg is drill msg for 1. Beginning oprs. 2. Advanced oprs. 3. Oprs on watch.
ZZO		I am a Junior Operator. (Sometimes used to chastise a LID (poor operator))
ZZS	(Russian military)	Change freq to … ("gehen Sie auf …"); QSY/QDW

** The 1931 International Code of Signals (Suppl 1950) Marine flag signals.
"" WW2-SOE Special Operations Executive. British secret agents in Europe.
»   C&W - Cable and Wireless Service. US commercial telegraph company.

Some codes do not comply with the international allocations as commercial systems devised their own arrangements and often pre-dated the international agreements.

Definitions have been abbreviated to conserve space. This is only a Partial List and may contain errors.
Please send corrections or additions to the author to enable updating.
Photocopies / emails of additional lists would be appreciated to   jalcorn@nor.com.au

> 73,
> John, VK2JWA, QTHR.
> Compiler.

Radiotelegraph and Radiotelephone Codes, Prowords and Abbreviations

List of Radiotelegraph 'Q' and 'Z' Codes

Key to date of changes noted and references, NOT part of the Code Indicator.
*1912 $ 1924 # 1933 % 1938 ¶ 1943 ? 1960 + 1972 @ 1985 & 1987 1990   ~ ARRL Codes » C&W

Z Codes etc. become a QUESTION when preceded by the INT.

CODE	QUESTION	ANSWER or NOTICE

Radiotelegraph and Radiotelephone Codes, Prowords and Abbreviations

Telegraphic Code to Insure Secrecy in the Transmission of Telegrams - 1885
US War Dept., Secretary of War. - US Govt Printing Office.

This numerical system was adopted from the French Atlantic Telegraph Co's commercial code. Reconstructed for military usages it contained 25,000 words. (Not reproduced here)
Groups of five figures are produced. This was/is the standard telegram definition of a 'word' for which the minimum charge was made. Economy was the aim, as much as secrecy.

The message was composed from the dictionary and the number listed.
A prearranged/derived "key" was added/subtracted to this number as arranged.
The new number was referred to the dictionary to give its word equivalent.
This word sequence was sent and decoded by reverse process by the receiver.

Example from the manual - (Explanation simplified)
Add any number below 25000 (say 3333) to the vocab number to give the new word.
If the new number exceeds 25000 then deduct 25000 and use that number.

Word to be transmitted	Number in Vocabulary	Plus 3333	Representing in Vocabulary
War	23724	27057	Barker
is	12373	15706	ovation
a	00001	03334	cairn
punishment	17893	21226	sousing
whereof	23887	27220	begetting
death	06202	09535	frequent
is the	12373	15706	ovation
maximum	22327	25660	agape
	14032	17365	priggish

Subtract any number below 25000 (say 3333) from the vocab number to give the new word.
Where this exceeds the vocab number, add 25000 and use the resulting number.

Word to be transmitted	Number in Vocabulary	Minus 3333	Representing in Vocabulary
War	23724	20391	Servant
is	12373	09040	filbert
a	00001	21668	straw
punishment	17893	14560	mobility
whereof	23887	20554	shingle
death	06202	02869	bounden
is the	12373	09040	filbert
maximum	22327	18994	remunerating
	14032	10699	helmet

Various other methods of message transposition and key number derivation were applied to increase the security and avoid decryption by others.

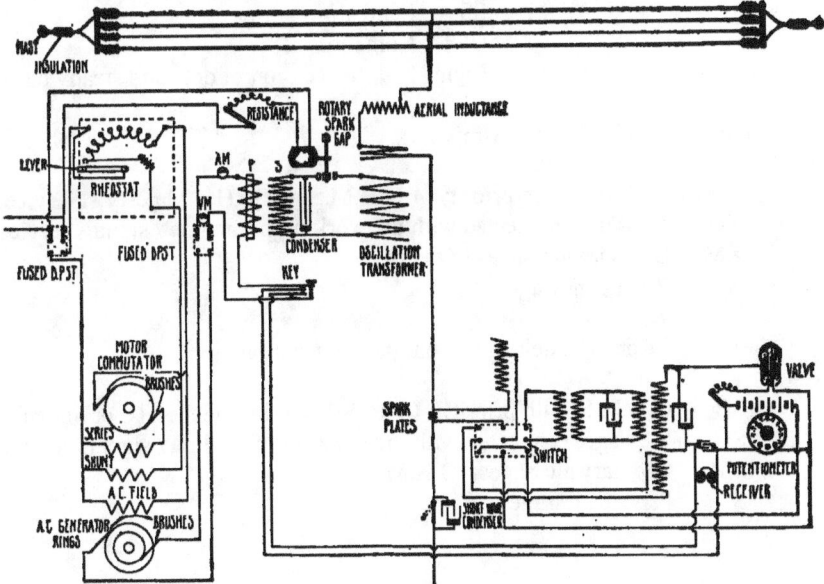

Diagram of a complete Marconi sending and receiving system using an Alternator primary, Rotary Spark Gap and Valve detector.
Hawkins Electrical Guide, 1917.

Radiotelegraph and Radiotelephone Codes, Prowords and Abbreviations

List of Procedures and Priorities Indicators 1896

From 'Signalling Instructions' 1896 by the British Army.
Designed for visual and electric Morse signalling, these carried into wireless.

Abbreviations and Prosigns.   (Sequence as in the manual)

Morse	Code	Meaning
—	T	Answer or Acknowledgment of Call or Correct copy.
......	III	Full stop.
—————		Stop - As required to break a transmission. Send until answered.
...— .	VE	End of message.
.—— —..	WB	Word before.
.—— .—	WA	Word after.
—.— —..	RD	When all corrections, if required, have been obtained.
——.	G	Go on. Invite to continue, message received so far.
....		Preparative. Succession of dots to attract unknown station.
.. —— ..	IMI	Repeat. Usually followed by WB ..., WA ..., etc.
—.—. —.—.	CC	Cipher. Preceding and following cipher groups.
.. ..	II	Break. Preceding and following the text.
.—.—.—.—	AAAA	Erase. To erase incorrectly sent word etc.
... ...	SSS	Oblique Stroke. As in fractions, punctuation etc.
—.—.— —.—.—	KK, KK	Each word will be repeated, no acknowledgment expected from receiving station. Dangerous or difficult situations.
.—— .——	WW	Obliterator or Annul. Delete concerned or preceding message.
——— ——— ———	OOO	Stop traffic, clear the line. Prior to sending very urgent message.
——..	Z	Blocks. Before and after letters to be in capitals.
..—. ..	FI	Figures intended. Before figures.
..—. ..—.	FF	Figures finished. After figures, letters follow.
—..— —..—	XX	Naval. By Army or land party wanting to work navy ship.

Visual Signalling

Morse	Code	Meaning
.—.	R	Move to your right.
.—..	L	Move to your left.
....	H	Move higher or further off.
———	O	Move lower down or closer.
... ..—.	SF	Separate your flags.
—... ..—.	BF	Use large blue flag. If prefixed by 'S', use small flag.
.—— ..—.	WF	Use large white flag. If prefixed by 'S', use small flag.
—.. ...	DS	Drop shutter or turn off light from your heliograph. It does not obscure.
—— ——.—	MQ	Wait.
—.— ——.—	KQ	Are you ready?
.—. ..—	RU	Who are you?
—. .—	NA	Send KK, KK message. Enemy near unsafe to answer or light wrong.
—. —.	NN	No more messages coming.
... ——.—	SQ	Send quicker.
... ...	SS	Send slower.
—.—. ..	CI	Come in.
........———		Light bad. Succession of dots and steady dash until adjusted.

Message Priority for Transmission.

- **XB** O.H.M.S. with priority. (O.H.M.S. = On Her Majesty's Service. ie Army etc.)
- **XG** Messages connected with the working of the line / signals service.
- **XM** Ordinary messages, O.H.M.S.
- **X**   Private messages.

Messages for or to be delivered from the next station.

- **SB** O.H.M.S. with priority. (XB, SB sent by a General's or higher authority only.)
- **SG** Messages connected with the working of the line / signals service.
- **SM** Ordinary messages, O.H.M.S.
- **S**   Private messages.

Radiotelegraph and Radiotelephone Codes, Prowords and Abbreviations

Method of Coding Time for Message Handling 1896

From 'Signalling Instructions' 1896 by the British Army.
Times in the text of a message are sent as is, not encoded as below.

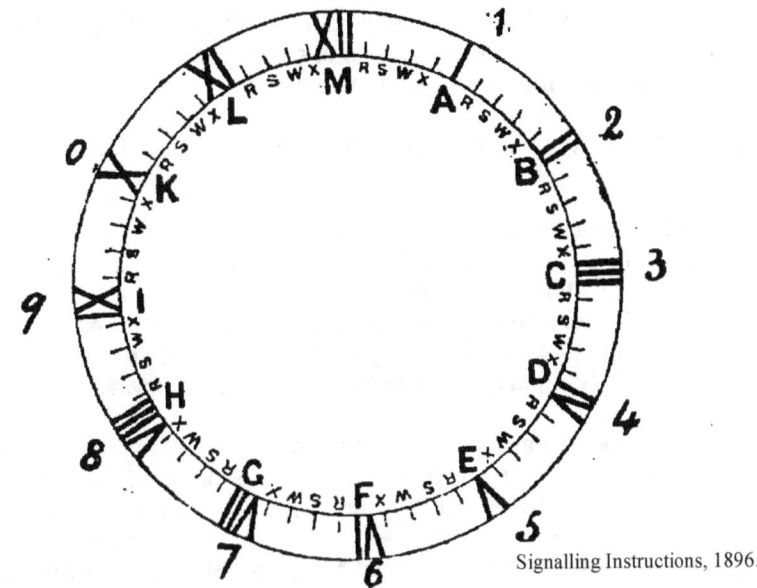

Signalling Instructions, 1896.

This encoding is for message handling, e.g. TOR, TOD etc. NOT for times in the Text.
The method is simple -
Morning, a.m. is sent AM, and afternoon, p.m. is sent PM after time groups.
The figure denoting the hour is put first   (E=5) so 5.00 am   = EAM
If the minute is an exact five minute point (40=H) so 5.40 am   = EHAM
If the minute is between on R,S,W or X is next, so   5.43 am   = EHWAM
            12 noon is coded as   MRPM,   12 midnight as   MRAM.

Examples -

MRAM is	12 am	BPM is	2 pm	
FPM is	6 pm	IAM is	9 am	
MFAM is	12.30 am	BIPM is	2.45 pm	
MFSAM is	12.32 am	BIXAM is	2.49 am	

The 24 hour time format was adopted during WW1. and is in the 1918 instructions.

Ciphers and Cryptograms.

Two methods of encoding or ciphers were used. They were 'Playfair' and the 'Cipher Wheel'.
Both were (and still are) perfectly satisfactory short term field ciphers.
Both are well known and described in many books on cryptology and will not be done here.
However the 'Cryptogram' was written on the message form with the encoded words in their real
position and length and mixed with plaintext. This is a security risk. They are now written in five
figure groups regardless of word length.   They were however transmitted as five figure groups.

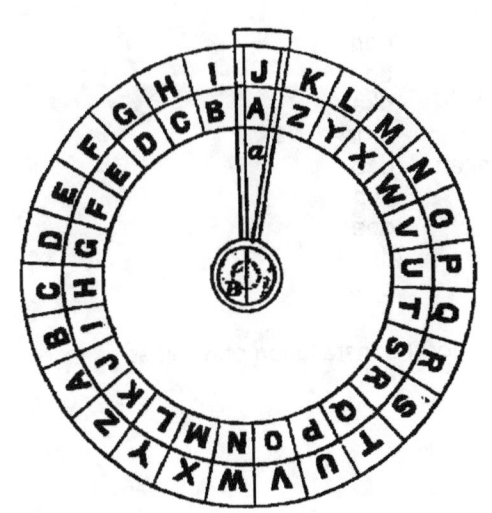

41

Radiotelegraph and Radiotelephone Codes, Prowords and Abbreviations

German Regulations for the Control of Wireless Telegraphy - 1905
Regelung der Funkentelegraphie im Deutschen Reich - 1 April 1905
Brief extracts only. From Internet - http://www.ipass.net/~whitetho/1905germ.htm
Full German text is also available on the Internet.

The International Service Regulations, as revised in London in 1903, and the German Government Telegraph Regulations with regard to submarine telegrams are to apply to wireless telegraphy across the sea unless modified by any of the present special regulations. ......

....

Regulation 4 prescribes that ordinary Morse signals are to be used, together with the following additional signals :-

— — — — — —   "Cease sending" signal (Ruhezeichen). This may only be given by public coast stations.

··· — — — ···   [SOS] Distress signal (Notzeichen). This is to be repeated by a ship in distress until all other stations have stopped working.

··· — — —·   [SOE] Quest signal (Suchzeichen). This may be repeated by ships on the high sea, the signal to be followed by the name of the ship. [Equiv to 'CQ' - JWA.]
It is to be replied by the word "hier" (here), followed by the name of the replier.

....

Ship calling coast station - [Paraphrased to save space, much procedural text omitted. - JWA.]
To Call -   ··— — — · c/s c/s c/s of stn called ···— — c/s or name of ship calling.
Reply -   ··— — — · c/s of ship ···— — c/s of stn called — ·— if ready to go on.   or
·— — — — # (mins to wait).
If more than 10 mins, the reason must be given. Ship must await a call from the shore station.

Telegram Prefixes / Preamble -   Instructions indicating -
   s Government telegram.   ss Free Government telegram.
   a Service telegram.   d Urgent private telegram.   followed by -
destination, v or de,   name of ship,   no. of telegram (if destined abroad),   no. of words,   and time of handing in (three figs - day of month, hour and minutes)   followed by -
Telegram address, text and signature.

Regulation 5 gives a list of the code names of the (then) German coast stations and merchant vessels -

   a. Public Coast Stations.

1.	Rixhöft	krx	5. Heligoland	khg
2.	Arcona	kar	6. Cuxhaven	kcx
3.	Marienleuchte	kmr	7. Borkum lighthouse.	kbm
4.	Bülk	kbk	8. Borkumriff lightship.	fbr

   b. Coast Stations for Limited Public Traffic.

1.	Bremerhaven Lloydhalle.	kbh
2.	Weser Lightship.	fwf
3.	Elbe 1. Lightship.	fef

   c. Merchant Steamers.

1.	"Kaiser Wilhelm der Grosse"	North German Lloyd	dkw
2.	"Kronprinz Wilhelm"	ditto	dkp
3.	"Kaiser Wilhelm II"	ditto	dkm
4.	"Deutschland"	Hamburg American	ddl
5.	"Moltke"	ditto	ddm
6.	"Blücher"	ditto	ddb
7.	"König Albert"	ditto	dka
8.	"Meteor"	ditto	dmr
9.	"Cap Oregal"	Hamburg S. American.	dco
10.	"Cap Blanco"	ditto	dcb
11.	"Prinz Adalbert"	Keil-Korsör	dpa
12.	"Prinz Sigismund"	ditto	dps
13.	"Prinz Waldemar"	ditto	dpw

Code names are fixed by the department which gives permission for the installation of wireless telegraph stations. [1905]

Radiotelegraph and Radiotelephone Codes, Prowords and Abbreviations

List of Original Z-Codes and Procedures

From 'The British Signal Manual' 1907 by the Admiralty for marine and coastal use.
Used between British Navy and Merchant Ships and Coastal Stations.
Z-Codes even into modern times seem to be mostly used by the Armed Services.

Procedure Signals

Morse	Code	Meaning
—..—..——	etc	Use the British Signal Manual
.———.——.—	etc	Answering sign
..—...	FI	Figures follow.
..—...—.	FF	Figures finished, Spelling Sign
..———..	IMI	Repeat Sign
.———.—	WA	Word after. Used with repeat.
.—.—	AA	All after. Used with repeat.
.—.———..—	ALL	All message. Used with repeat.
.—.—.—.—.—	AAAAA	Erase Signal Sent after a wrong word.
.———.——	WW	Annul, Delete entire message.
.—.—.—	A A A	Full Stop
—————— etc		Stop sign. End of message.
————		'Code Flag' indicates the following are signals which use the 'Code Flag' in the International Code Signal Book, eg. Urgent, Important, Numeral, Latitude and Longitude Tables.

Z-Codes -

ZOA - ZOY   Ammunition and Gunnery

ZOA   Have you spare guns for the fleet?
ZOB   Have you spare gun mountings for the fleet?
ZOC   Have you ammunition for the fleet?
ZOD   What ammunition have you on board?
ZOE   I have ammunition on board.
ZOF   I have (no. of rounds) of ammunition on board, 13.5 inch.
ZOG   I have (no. of rounds) of ammunition on board, 12 inch.
ZOH   I have (no. of rounds) of ammunition on board, 10 inch.
ZOI   I have (no. of rounds) of ammunition on board, 9.2 inch.
ZOJ   I have (no. of rounds) of ammunition on board, 7.5 inch.
ZOK   I have (no. of rounds) of ammunition on board, 6 inch.
ZOL   I have (no. of rounds) of ammunition on board, 4.7 inch.
ZOM   I have (no. of rounds) of ammunition on board, 4 inch.
ZON   I have (no. of rounds) of ammunition on board, 12 pounder.
ZOP   I have (no. of rounds) of ammunition on board, 6 pounder.
ZOQ   I have (no. of rounds) of ammunition on board, 3 pounder.
ZOR   I have (no. of rounds) of ammunition on board, aiming rifle.
ZOS   I have (no. of rounds) of ammunition on board, machine gun.
ZOT   I have (no. of rounds) of ammunition on board, rifle.
ZOU   I have (no. of rounds) of ammunition on board, Morris tube.
ZOV - ZOY   Spare.

ZPA - ZQK   Coal and Oil etc.

ZPA   What quantity of coal have you on board?
ZPB   How many hatches have you?
ZPC   What is the length of your ship in feet?
ZPD   What is the distance in feet from your stem to centre of each hatch.
ZPE   Are you fitted with Temperley transporters?
ZPF   How many Temperley transporters have you?
ZPG   Rig Temperley transporters (or coaling gear) for coaling from your starboard side.
ZPH   Rig Temperley transporters (or coaling gear) for coaling from your port side.

Radiotelegraph and Radiotelephone Codes, Prowords and Abbreviations

List of Original Z-Codes and Procedures
From 'The British Signal Manual' 1907

ZPI	Rig Temperley transporters (or coaling gear) for coaling me (or ship indicated) alongside my (or her) starboard side.
ZPJ	Rig Temperley transporters (or coaling gear) for coaling me (or ship indicated) alongside my (or her) port side.
ZPK	Be prepared to come alongside starboard side (or go alongside the starboard side of ship indicated) to commence coaling directly we anchor.
ZPL	Be prepared to come alongside port side (or go alongside the port side of ship indicated) to commence coaling directly we anchor.
ZPM	Have everything ready to commence coaling the fleet as soon as we anchor.
ZPN	Have everything ready to commence coaling me (or ship indic.) when opportunity offers.
ZPO	Have everything ready to commence coaling me (or ship indicated) when the weather moderates.
ZPQ	Are you fitted with Metcalf's coaling gear?
ZPR	I am fitted with Metcalf's coaling gear.
ZPS	Prepare to be taken in tow by me (or ship indicated) and commence coaling as soon as possible (or at the time indicated).
ZPT	Proceed to (place indicated) and have everything ready to commence coaling the fleet on its arrival.
ZPU	Have you any coal bags? (indicate number)
ZPV	Have you any coal bags ready filled? (indicate quantity)
ZPW	I have (number indicated) tons of coal in bags ready filled.
ZPX	Have you liquid fuel for the fleet?
ZPY	What quantity of liquid fuel have you on board?
ZQA	I have (number indicated) tons of liquid fuel on board.
ZQB	I shall want (number indicated) tons of liquid fuel.
ZQC	I have (number indicated) tons of patent fuel.
ZQD	Have you engine oil for the fleet?
ZQE	What quantity of engine oil have you on board?
ZQF	I shall require (quantity indicated) of engine oil.
ZQG - ZQK	Spare.

ZQL -	ZRJ	Convoy

ZQL	Convoy is to anchor in the position indicated.
ZQM	Convoy will anchor for the night at the place indic'd, and rejoin at daylight or time denoted.
ZQN	Convoy will weigh and proceed independently now or at time indicated.
ZQO	Convoy to weigh and proceed independently now or at time indicated.
ZQP	Convoy to disperse and proceed independently.
ZQR	Convoy to follow the route indicated.
ZQS	Convoy to proceed through the following rendezvous.
ZQT	Convoy to keep station on the fleet or escort.
ZQU	Convoy to take station ahead at the distance indicated.
ZQV	Convoy to take station astern at the distance indicated.
ZQW	Convoy to take station on starboard beam at the distance indicated.
ZQX	Convoy to take station on port beam at the distance indicated.
ZQY	Convoy must keep nearer to escort.
ZRA	Convoy must keep further from escort.
ZRB	Convoy to disperse and reassemble in latitude and longitude or at place or rendezvous indicated.
ZRC	Convoy to rendezvous in latitude and longitude or at place or rendezvous indicated.
ZRD	All ships of convoy are to rejoin company.
ZRE	You should join the convoy in latitude and longitude or at the place indicated.
ZRF - ZRJ	Spare.

Radiotelegraph and Radiotelephone Codes, Prowords and Abbreviations

List of Original Z-Codes and Procedures
From 'The British Signal Manual' 1907

ZRK - ZSR   Enemy - General Reports.

ZRK	Saw the smoke of a large fleet (in position and at time indicated).
ZRL	Saw the smoke of a small fleet (in position and at time indicated).
ZRM	Have you been stopped by any men-of-war?
ZRN	We were stopped by a man-of-war (nationality, time, and position indicated).
ZRO	Enemy is at anchor.
ZRP	Enemy's ships are getting under weigh.
ZRQ	Enemy's ships are coming out of port.
ZRS	The enemy has put to sea.
ZRT	The enemy has altered course to the northward.
ZRU	The enemy has altered course to the southward.
ZRV	The enemy has altered course to the eastward.
ZRW	The enemy has altered course to the westward.
ZRX	The enemy's torpedo-boat destroyers (or torpedo boats) are approaching from the northward.
ZRY	The enemy's torpedo-boat destroyers (or torpedo boats) are approaching from the southward.
ZSA	The enemy's torpedo-boat destroyers (or torpedo boats) are approaching from the eastward.
ZSB	The enemy's torpedo-boat destroyers (or torpedo boats) are approaching from the westward.
ZSC	Passed the enemy's fleet in latitude ..., longitude ... at the time indicated steering to the .....
ZSD	Passed the British fleet in latitude ..., longitude ... at the time indicated steering to the ..... (The number of ships should be stated if possible)
ZSE	Passed British battleships in latitude ..., longitude ... at the time indicated steering to the ..... (The number of ships should be stated if possible)
ZSF	Passed British cruisers in latitude ..., longitude ... at the time indicated steering to the ..... (The number of ships should be stated if possible)
ZSG	Passed British destroyers in latitude ..., longitude ... at the time indicated steering to the ..... (The number of ships should be stated if possible)
ZSH	Passed enemy's battleships in latitude .., longitude .. at the time indicated steering to the ..... (The number of ships should be stated if possible)
ZSI	Passed enemy's cruisers in latitude ..., longitude ... at the time indicated steering to the ..... (The number of ships should be stated if possible)
ZSJ	Passed enemy's destroyers in latitude ..., longitude ... at the time indic. steering to the ..... (The number of ships should be stated if possible)
ZSK -ZSR	Spare.

ZST -ZTH   Hospital Ships.

ZST	How many surgeons have you on board?
ZSU	Can you spare a surgeon?
ZSV	Surgeon to bring instruments with him.
ZSW	How many cots have you?
ZSX	Can you spare any cots (indicate number)?
ZSY	How many cases can you take?
ZTA	How many cot cases can you take?
ZTB	Land your cases at .... hospital and return to the fleet, or place indicated.
ZTC	Have an (or number) infectious case for you.
ZTD -ZTH	Spare.

Radiotelegraph and Radiotelephone Codes, Prowords and Abbreviations

List of Original Z-Codes and Procedures
From 'The British Signal Manual' 1907

ZTI -ZTY   Torpedo.

ZTI	Have you torpedoes for the fleet?
ZTJ	What torpedoes have you (indicate number and size) ?
ZTK	18-inch torpedo.
ZTL	14-inch torpedo.
ZTM	I have torpedoes for the fleet.
ZTN	I have (number) 18-inch torpedoes for the fleet.
ZTO	I have (number) 14-inch torpedoes for the fleet.
ZTP -ZTY	Spare.

ZUA - ZUH   Water Distilling, etc.

ZUA	How many tons of water have you?
ZUB	I have (number indicated) tons of water.
ZUC	What quantity of water can you distil per day?
ZUD	I can distil (number indicated) tons of water per day.
ZUE	Require (number indicated) tons of boiler water.
ZUF -ZUH	Spare.

ZUI - ZUS   Signalling.

ZUI	Have you got the British Signal Manual ?
ZUJ	Can you communicate at night by flashing ?
ZUK	Please signal a little faster.
ZUL	Please signal at a slower rate.
ZUM	Please make a longer pause between the letters.
ZUN	Please make a longer pause between the words or groups.
ZUO	I cannot read your flashing as your light is too indistinct.
ZUP	Keep within signalling distance on the bearing indicated from me.
ZUQ - ZUS	Spare.

ZUT - ZVY   Miscellaneous.

ZUT	Prepare to come alongside my (or go alongside ship indicated her) starboard side, at time indicated.
ZUV	Prepare to come alongside my (or go alongside ship indicated her) port side, at time indicated.
ZUW	Come alongside (or go alongside ship indicated) starboard side,
ZUX	Come alongside (or go alongside ship indicated) port side,
ZUY	Prepare to go alongside place indicated, at time indicated.
ZVA	What is the size of your largest wire hawser?
ZVB	Prepare to be taken in tow.
ZVC	Are you ready to be taken in tow?
ZVD	I am ready to be taken in tow.
ZVE	I am ready to take you in tow.
ZVF	Come under my stern (or go under the stern of ship indicated) to be taken in tow.
ZVG - ZVY	Spare.

ZWA - ZYX   Spare Signals

ZWA

ZYX

Radiotelegraph and Radiotelephone Codes, Prowords and Abbreviations

List of Procedure Signs and RA - SF Abbreviations - 1908
From 'Handbook for Wireless Telegraph Operators' 1908
By the British Postmaster-General for use by British ships and coastal stations.

Procedures and Prosigns

Note: Bracketted letters (..) not in the manual.

Code	Prosign	Meaning
—·—·—	(CT)	Commencing Call - Followed by the Called Station's callsign three times.
—·· ·	(de) (K)	From (French) followed by Calling Station's callsign three times.
—·—	(AR)	Close of Call. Go on, Inviting reply.
·—·—·	(TT)	Close. Sent at end of message.
—·—		Fraction bar.
— — — — —	(MMM)	Separates no. of words sent and no of words charged if different.

Punctuation and Other Signs

Code	Prosign	Meaning
·· ·· ··		Full Stop.
—·—·—·		Semicolon.
·—·—·—		Comma.
— — — ···		Colon.
··— —··		Question Mark or Request for Repetition.
— —··——		Exclamation Mark.
·————·		Apostrophe.
—····—		Hyphen or Dash.
—··—·		Bar indicating fraction (added in 1916 Edition)
—·——·—		Parenthesis (before and after the words)
·—··—·		Inverted commas. (before and after each word or group in quotes).
··— — —·—		Underline. (before and after each word or group underlined).
—·—·—		Call. (preliminary of every transmission).
—···—	(=)	Equals or Double Dash. Seperates preamble, address, text, signature.
···—·		Understood.
········		Error.
·—·—·	(+)	Cross (end of transmission) (Now AR).
—·—	(K)	Invitation to transmit.
·—···	(AS)	Wait.
·—·	(R)	Received signal.
···—·—	(SK)	End of work.
— — —	(T T T)	Safety Signal. (added in 1916 Edition)

Abbreviations.

These formed the basis for the Q-Codes adopted in 1912.
French equivalents in italics.
These abbreviations must be repeated three times and followed by ·· — — ··

RA	What station is corresponding?	Quelle est la station en correspondance?
RB	At what distance are you from my station?	A quelle distance vous trouvez-vous de ma station?
RC	What is your wavelength in metres?	Quelle est votre longuer d'onde en mètres?
RD	How many words have you to transmit to me?	Combien de mots avez-vous à me transmettre?
RE	How are you receiving?	Comment recevez-vous?
RF	I am receiving badly.	Je reçois mal.
RG	Send me ·——·- twenty times to regulate my apparatus.	Transmettez-moi vingt fois ·——·- pour régler mes appareils.
RH	Are you being interfered with?	Etes-vous troublé?
RJ	I am being interfered with.	Je suis troublé.
RK	Atmospherics are very strong.	Les atmosphériques sont très fortes.

Radiotelegraph and Radiotelephone Codes, Prowords and Abbreviations

List of Procedure Signs and RA - SF Abbreviations - 1908
From 'Handbook for Wireless Telegraph Operators' 1908
By the British Postmaster-General for use by British ships and coastal stations.

RL	.... Tell me the wire charge to	Indiquez-mois la taxe à percevoir pour transmission par fil à ....
RM	Engaged with public correspondence. The ship is requested not to interfere.	Correspondence publique est engagée. Prière au navire de ne pas troubler.
RN	Stop transmitting.	Cessez votre transmission,
RQ	Transmit more slowly.	Transmettez plus lentement.
RS	Increase your power.	Augmentez votre énergie.
RT	Diminish your power.	Diminuez votre énergie.
RU	Repeat everything.	Répétez tout.
RV	From ... to ... Repeat from such to such a word.	Répétez de .... à ....
RW	... from ...., Repeat ..... words from	Répétez .... mots à partir de ....
RX	Your turn is number	Votre tour est numéro ....
RY	General call to all stations.	
RZ	Nothing more.	Rien de plus.
SA	I have nothing for you.	Je n'ai rien pour vous.
SB	Everything in order.	Tout est en ordre.
SC	Wait. I will call you as soon as I've finished.	Attention. Je vous appellerai dès que j'aurai fini.
SD	Can you transmit faster?	Vous pouvez transmettre plus vite.
SF	I am occupied with another station.	Je suis occupé avec une autre station.

Operator's Qualifications, 1896 and 1908.
The 1896 British Army School of Signalling, Aldershot, Qualification for -
"Certificate of Signalling" - (Officers) was -

Reading from small flag.	12 WPM	Passes required on each apparatus -		
Read and send Lamp or Limelight.	12 "			
Read and send Heliograph.	12 "	'Special' Cert.	97.43%	Theory 80%
Read and send Semaphore.	15 "	'Instructor's Cert.	94.87%	Theory 66%
Read and send Sounder.	12 "			

Officers must show a satisfactory ability to send accurately on the large and small flags.

"Assistant Instructor's Certificate of Signalling" - (NCO's).

Read & Send -	Large Flag.	10 WPM	Passes required on each apparatus -
"	Small Flag.	12 "	
"	Lamp or Limelight	12 "	97.43% Send and Receive.
"	Heliograph.	12 "	
"	Semaphore.	15 "	Theory Exams - 66% for each paper.
"	Sounder.	12 "	

Three Courses per year. Officers or NCO's who failed the Course could not try again.

The 1908 qualifying speed for a Ship's Wireless Telegraphy Operator was 20 WPM send and receive.
There were also Theory and Practical tests.

Radiotelegraph and Radiotelephone Codes, Prowords and Abbreviations

List of Procedure Signs and QRA - QSJ Abbreviations - 1909

From 'Handbook for Wireless Telegraph Operators' 1909
By the British Postmaster-General for use by British ships and coastal stations.
Q Codes etc. become a QUESTION when followed by the Question Mark (?).

CODE	ANSWER or NOTICE	QUESTION
QRA	Here the	What ship or coast station is that?
QRB	My distance is	What is your distance?
QRC	My bearing is	What is your bearing?
QRD	I am bound for	Where are you bound for?
QRF	I am bound from	Where are you bound from?
QRG	I belong to the ..... line.	What line do you belong to?
QRH	My wave-length is .... metres	What is your wave-length in metres?
QRJ	I have .... words to transmit	How many words have you to transmit?
QRK	Signals are satisfactory	How are signals?
QRL	I am receiving badly. please send 20 - - - — for adjustment.	Are you receiving badly? Shall I send 20 - - - — (V) for adjustment?
QRM	I am being interfered with	Are you being interfered with?
QRN	Atmospherics are very strong	Are atmospherics strong?
QRO	Increase your power	Shall I increase power?
QRP	Decrease your power	Shall I decrease power?
QRQ	Transmit faster	Shall I transmit faster?
QRS	Transmit slower	Shall I transmit slower?
QRT	Stop transmitting	Shall I stop transmitting?
QRU	I have nothing for you	Have you anything for me?
QRV	All right now, everything is in order	Is everything in order?
QRW	Engaged, Please do not interfere	Are you busy?
QRX	Stand by. I will call you when required	Shall I stand by?
QRY	Your turn will be number	When will be my turn?
QRZ	Your signals are weak	Are my signals weak?
QSA	Your signals are strong	Are my signals strong?
QSB	Your spark is bad	Is my spark bad?
QSC	Your spacing is bad	Is my spacing bad?
QSD	My time is	What is your time?
QSF	Transmission will be in alternate order	
QSG	Transmission will be in series of 5 messages	
QSH	Transmission will be in series of 10 messages	
QSJ	Please give me your rate to	Do you want my rate to ....

In addition to these signals, which, it will be observed, are uniform in construction, the following signals of the international telegraph code may be used in these communications:-

- — — --   Repeat sign (as well as mark of interrogation)
- - - — -   Understood
- - — - - -   Wait

Local Sounder
C1866 – USA

LOCAL SOUNDER.

Radiotelegraph and Radiotelephone Codes, Prowords and Abbreviations

Machine-gun Fire Observation Signals - WW1
From British Army - 'Infantry Training.' 1911

Sent by semaphore from forward observers of indirect fire not visible from the gun position.

- P = Plus: meaning fire observed at least 50 yards beyond target.
- M = Minus: meaning fire observed at least 50 yards short of target.
- T = Right: meaning fire observed to right of target.
- L = Left: meaning fire observed to left of target.
- C = Centre: meaning direction of fire correct.
- U = Unobserved: meaning no observation obtained.
- Q = Query: meaning fire observed but its position uncertain.
- R = Range: meaning range correct.

Observers give the 'call up' signal to indicate they are ready.
'P' and 'M' may be repeated to indicate multiples of 50 yards. i.e. 'PP' = 100 yards beyond target.
Signals should be repeated back from the gun if this does not disclose the position to the enemy.

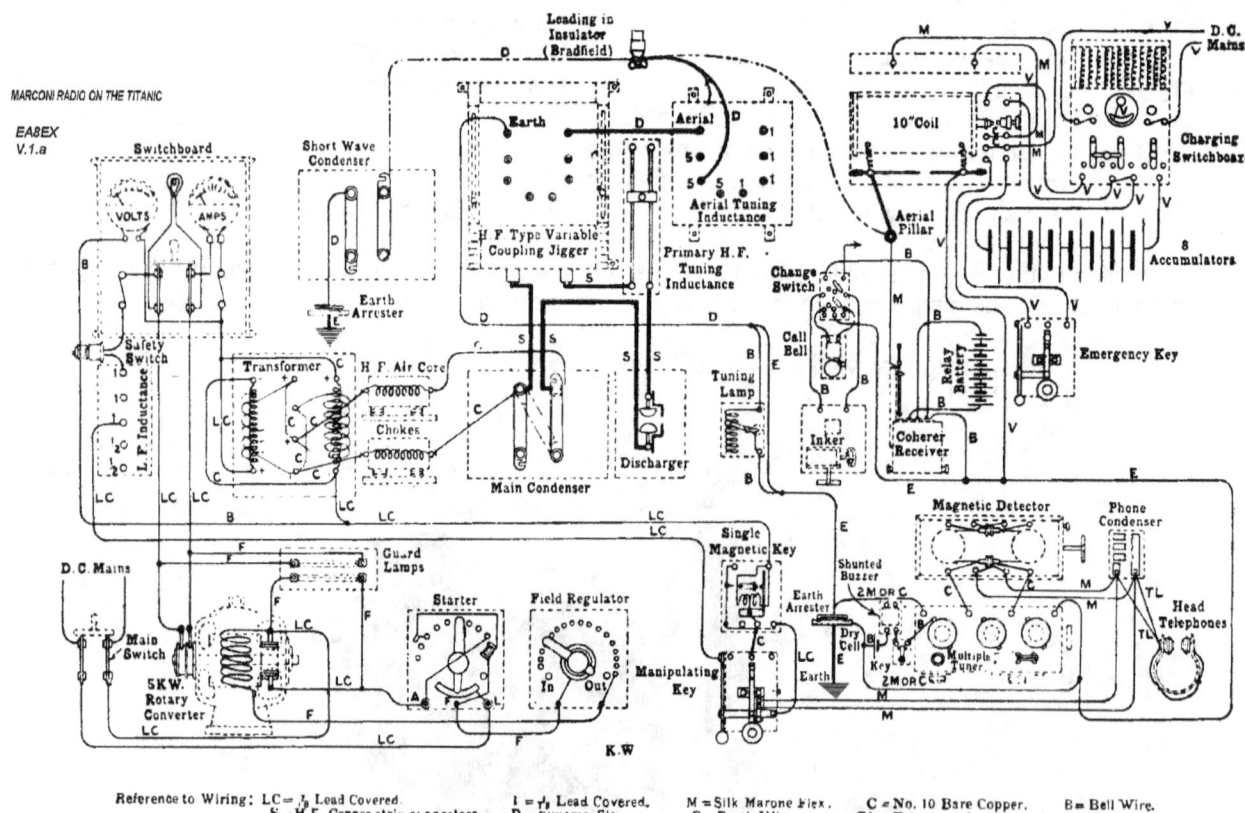

Fig. Connections of 1½/5-kw. Marconi Converter Set.

Radio Installation as on the 'Titanic' 1912

50

Radiotelegraph and Radiotelephone Codes, Prowords and Abbreviations

Miscellaneous Procedures - WW1
From British Army - 'Signal Training. Part VI. Procedure' 1918

	Morse	Semaphore	Use
Hyphen	—·····—	NV	In the body of message.
Separate Whole nos from Fractions.	—···—	MM	Between 1 and ½ of 1½.
Oblique Stroke	—··—·	LT	As written by originator.
Horizontal Bar.	—··—·	NR	Fraction Separator.
Brackets	—·—·—·	KK	Before and after enclosed wds.
Inverted Commas	·—··—·	RR	Same as for brackets.
Block Letters	··——·—	UK	Same as for brackets.
Decimal Point	······	iii	Sent as three i's.
Full Stop.	·—·—·—	aaa	Sent as one sign.

The following are met with in international working and will be written down as below:

Morse sign.	When receiving a message in a foreign language in clear.	In French and Belgian.	In Portuguese.	In German.	When intercepting a foreign cipher message
·—·—	ä		ã or á	ä	A'
—···					B'
—·—·					C'
—··—··			ç		L'
————	ch	ch	ch	ch	ch
··—··	è	è or é	è	ë	E'
——·—·					G'
——·——	ñ				N'
———·	ö		õ or ó	ö	O'
·——·——	à or á				P'
————					T'
·—·—·					R'
··——	ü			ü	U'
—··—·					X'
——··—					Z'

The Germans use the following miscellaneous signs &c. :-   (1918 - JWA.)

Full Stop	······	Column	—·—·—	Msg. Understood	···—·
Semicolon	—·—·—	Call Signal	—·—·—	Wait	·—···
Comma	·—·—·—	Begin Msg.	—·—·—·	Acknowledged	·—·—·—·
Colon	———— ——— ···	Answer	—·—	Roman Numerals	·— ——— —

The following signals are used to designate special messages :-

War messages (KR) —·— ·—·   Telegraphic Service (A) ·—

Urgent Military Msgs (SSD) ··· ··· —··   Urgent Private (D) —··

State or Military (SS) ··· ···

KR messages can only be used by Imperial Headquarters, Imperial Chancellor, Army Headquarters, War Ministry, Admiralty, Foreign Office, &c.

Radiotelegraph and Radiotelephone Codes, Prowords and Abbreviations

The 'X' Codes

These were operating signals used by British Empire Forces and others from about 1918 to 1943.
They were similar in purpose to the Q Codes and were replaced by Q Codes in 1943 for uniformity after the USA entered the war. They were the letter X followed by numerals. Some were in unofficial use until about 1946.

From the British 'Signal Training. Part VI. Procedure' 1918
'British W/T Operating Signals' O.U. 5371 1926, 1931.
and 'Army Wireless Operating Signals.' B.R.266/1941.
The Signals marked "A" are in possession of Aircraft

* Not used by Navy or Royal Air Force.   # Other Source, NOT in the B.R.266/1941.
Indicators – (NOT part of signal) ^ 1918, @ 1926, % 1931, ¶ 1941.

X Codes become a QUESTION when preceded by the "Interrogative" X112.
X Codes become NEGATIVE when preceded by "Negative" X114

CODE		QUESTION	ANSWER or NOTICE

ADDRESSEES. (1931) %

X00		Pass to Addressee / All Addressees
X0		Initial distinction for forwarding group. Numerals follow to indicate addressees.
X01		Pass to 1st addressee.
X023		Pass to 2nd and 3rd addressees.
X03469		Pass to 3rd, 4th, 6th and 9th addressees.
		Addressees above the 9th are denoted by separate numeral groups:-
X0578-12		Pass to 5th, 7th, 8th and 12th addressees.
X0-10		Pass to 10th addressee.

GENERAL.(1918) ^ In Numerical Order, not Meaning – X01 to X152.
For use with W/T (Wireless Telegraphy) Operating Signals Only.
  THI = Time Handed In

X01	^	Your spacing is bad.
X02	^	I am using full power for transmission.
X03	^	Increase strength of signals.
X04	^	Decrease strength of signals.
X05	^	Tighten coupling.
X06	^	Loosen coupling.
X07	^	Raise your note.
X08	^	Lower your note.
X09	^	Send faster.
X10	^	Send slower.
X11	^	I have been calling you since the time specified or for the number of hours specified.
X12	^	Can you hear the station denoted? What is his strength to you?
X13	^	There appears to be something wrong with your receiving instruments.
X14	^	There appears to be something wrong with your transmitting instruments.
X15	^	W/T apparatus now correct.
X16	^	Your aerial appears to be earthing.
X17	^	Fragments only received.
X18	^	Your signals are broken.
X19	^	You are causing interference.
X20	^	You are delaying message by answering out of turn.
X21	^	Stations addressed are causing delay by slowness in answering.
X22	^	Have you anything to communicate?
X23	^	Have nothing to communicate.
X25	^	Answer every word or group by K.
X26	^	Your last msg, or msg with THI specified, appears to have been wrongly ciphered.
X27	^	Has the message with THI specified been received by the station denoted?
X28	^	The message with THI specified has been received by the station addressed or that denoted.
X29	^	Have been unable to pass the message timed as specified.
X30	^	Have to dismantle in number of hours specified.
X31	^	How many signals have you for transmission ?
X32	^	I have a number of signals indicated awaiting transmission.
X33	^	Messages, numbers as indicated, have not been transmitted.
X34	^	I am handing over.
X34	#¶	Your Morse is bad. (Probably unofficial - Ed.)

Radiotelegraph and Radiotelephone Codes, Prowords and Abbreviations

List of Radiotelegraph 'X' Codes

The Signals marked "A" are in possession of Aircraft
* Not used by Navy or Royal Air Force.   # Other Source, NOT in the B.R.266/1941.
Indicators – (NOT part of signal) ^ 1918, @ 1926, % 1931, ¶ 1941.

X Codes become a QUESTION when preceded by the "Interrogative" X112.
X Codes become NEGATIVE when preceded by "Negative" X114

SIGNAL		MEANING
X35	^	I am not ready to take (or hand) over.
X36	^	My station is erected and ready for work.
X37	^	I am ready to take (or hand) over.
X38	^	Take (or hand) over at once.
X39	^	Have you deciphered msg no ....? Have you deciphered (THI of message) ?
X40	^	Acknowledge call and then change to wave index No. ....
X41	^	Shall send to you on wave index No. ....
X42	^	Shall receive from you on wave index No. ....
X43	^	Cancel message being sent or message with THI ....
X44	^	Denote ships for which you are W/T guard.
X45	^	I am W/T guard for the ships denoted.
X46	^	Man W/T office at every odd hour, and call directing station or station denoted.
X47	^	Man W/T office at every hour, and call directing station or station denoted.
X48	^	Please reply in the following order (to be followed by station numeral calls).
X49	^	With what stations are you, or station denoted, in W/T or visual communication.
X50	^	Station(s) denoted is (or are) keeping W/T watch.
X50	#¶	Your Morse is perfect. (Probably unofficial - Ed)
X51	^	Are you in W/T communication with the station denoted ?
X52	^	Am in W/T communication with the station denoted. Proceed with your message.
X53	^	Am not in communication with the station denoted.
X54	^	Transmit message which follows to station denoted.
X55	^	The message which follows is from the station denoted.
X56	^	All the stations of this group to reply in alphabetical order, giving strength of signals received from me.
X57	^	Are you in visual or cable communication with the station denoted ?
X58	^	Station making this signal is in visual or cable communication with the station denoted.
X59	^	Station making this signal is not in visual or cable communication with the station denoted.
X60	^	What wave-length is the station denoted using ?
X61	^	Station denoted is using the wave-length denoted.
X62	^	What wave-length are you signalling on ?
X63	^	Station making this signal is using the wave-length denoted.
X64	^	The signal which follows is a timing signal for correcting W/T office clocks. (When sent without the timing signal — "What is the time ?")
X65	^	How are your accumulators ?
X66	^	My accumulators are O.K.
X67	^	My accumulators are run down.
X68	^	Send more accumulators.
X69	^	Reply yes. (For use with operating signals only).
X70	^	Reply no. (For use with operating signals only).
X71	^	What percentage of coupling are you using ?
X75	^	Do my instruments appear to be in tune ?
X76	^	Your tuning appears to be correct.
X77	^	You do not appear to be in tune.
X78	^	Send "Vs" on your present wave-length, or wave-length denoted for ...... seconds. (Only to be used when a station is newly erected and getting into communication for the first time.)
X80	^	Keep continuous watch.
X82	^	Unable to receive signals, but will continue transmitting.
X83	^	Am now able to receive signals.
X84	^	Unable to transmit without jamming R.A.F. but will continue receiving.
X85	^	Now able to transmit.
X88	^	Can get no reply from station denoted.
X89	^	Reply quicker.
X90	^	You are replying too quickly.
X95	^	I desire to correct message signalled to you. (Quotes THI of message).
X99	^	Readjust speed of your spark gap to improve the note.

Radiotelegraph and Radiotelephone Codes, Prowords and Abbreviations

List of Radiotelegraph 'X' Codes
The Signals marked "A" are in possession of Aircraft
* Not used by Navy or Royal Air Force.   # Other Source, NOT in the B.R.266/1941.
Indicators – (NOT part of signal) ^ 1918,   @ 1926,   % 1931,   ¶ 1941.

X Codes become a QUESTION when preceded by the "Interrogative" X112.
X Codes become NEGATIVE when preceded by "Negative" X114

SIGNAL   MEANING

GENERAL (1926) @ (1931) %
NOTE: From 1931 – wave ….. metres is replaced by frequency …… Kc/s

	X100 ^	How is my note ?
A	X100 @	Negative, no, not.
A	X100*%	Affirmative, Yes.
	X101 ^	Your note is very bad.
	X102 ^	Your note is bad.
A	X102 @	Interrogative.
A	X102*%	Am (or ……. is) able to (comply)
	X103 ^	Your note is non-musical.
	X103*%	Am (or ……. Is) using ……. (or …… Kc/s)
	X104 ^	Your note is musical.
A	X104 @	Affirmative, Yes.
A	X105 @	Am (or …… is) unable to
	X105 ^	Your note is low.
	X106 ^	Your note is about 350 cycles.
A	X106 @	At …….. (time).
	X106*%	Decrease.
	X107 ^	Your note is high.
A	X107 @	(on) Wave ……. (metres) Kc/s.
	X108 ^	Your note is very high.
	X108*%	From ……… (until …….)
	X109 ^	Your note is confused.

CALLS (1926) @

	X110 ^	Your note is clear.
A	X110 @	Call me again at …….. On present wave (or on ….. Metres) Kc/s.
	X110 %	Increase.
	X111 ^	Your note is very clear.
A	X111 @	I will call you again as soon as I can (or at ……).
	X112 ^	Your note is very unsteady.
A	X112 @	Have been (…….. Is, or has been) calling you (or ……) (on …… Kc/s) since ……..)
A	X112*%	Interrogative.
	X113 ^	Your spark is broken.
A	X113 @	Inform …. That I am calling him (on …….. Metres / Kc/s)
	X114 ^	Your spark is very broken.
A	X114 @	Call me every ……… minutes until ……..
A	X114*%	Negative, No, Not
	X115 ^	Your spark is good.
	X115 @	Following call has been received. No station has been heard to answer.
	X116 ^	Your spark is very good.
	X115*%	Now (or at …….)
	X117 ¶	Where is your station ?
	X118*%	(On) ……… Kc/s
	X118 ¶	This station is at ………….. (cipher)
	X119 ¶	Am closing now and expect to come in at ………. (Time.)

(When sent without the time, "I am closing now.")

ANSWERING CALLS (1926) @

	X120 ¶	Dismantle at once and report at …………. (followed by place, &c., in cipher).
	X120 @	Answer ……. and take any message for me (or for ……)
	X120*%	Since.
	X121 ¶	Close now. Re-open at ……….. (followed by time).
A	X121 @	Answer calls for me (or for …) on present wave (or on …… metres / Kc/s).
	X122 ¶	……….. operator casualties. Send reinforcements.

Radiotelegraph and Radiotelephone Codes, Prowords and Abbreviations

List of Radiotelegraph 'X' Codes

The Signals marked "A" are in possession of Aircraft
* Not used by Navy or Royal Air Force.   # Other Source, NOT in the B.R.266/1941.
¶ - 1941, not listed in 1918 although they may have existed. Not a full list.
Indicators – (NOT part of signal) ^ 1918, @ 1926, % 1931, ¶ 1941.

X Codes become a QUESTION when preceded by the "Interrogative" X112.
X Codes become NEGATIVE when preceded by "Negative" X114

SIGNAL	MEANING
A X122 @	Answer me (or …..) on …… metres / Kc/s.
X122*%	Use (……..) or (…….. Kc/s)
X123 ¶	Cipher list of words has been captured (or otherwise lost).
A X123 @	Senior Officer (Controlling Station) (or …..) will answer calls (on …… metres / Kcs.
X124*%	Via …….(call sign)
X124 ¶	Change to emergency cipher word until new list is sent out.
X125 ¶	I am going to call the station denoted. (to be followed by wave-length which will be employed if different from that of station making the signal).
X126 ^	Station(s) denoted has/have closed down.
X126*%	What …….. Are you (or is …..) using?
X127 ^	I have taken over from the station denoted.

COMMUNICATION (1926) @

X128 ^	Please call the station denoted. (On wave-length denoted.)
A X128 @	Have something to communicate (or have message for ……) (at ……).

AIRCRAFT (1931) %

X128 %	Aircraft call signs ….. are up and working (on …… Kc/s).
X129 ^	Shall I call the station denoted ? (On wave-length denoted.)
A X129 @	Have nothing to communicate. (Series number of last message was ……)
X130 ^	The station denoted is calling you. (On wave-length denoted.)
A X130 @	Am in W/T (or ….) communication with …...
X130 %	Aircraft fitted with ………, call signs …….., leaving for you (or …..) now (or at …..).
X131 ^	Other stations of the group are now working.
A X131 @	Report when you are in W/T (or ….) communication with …...
X132 ^	Transmit your message through control station.
X132 @	Report with what stations you are in W/T (or ….) communication with …...
A X132 %	Aircraft (call sign ……) has (have) landed.
X133 ^	You are using excessive procedure.
A X133 @	I can hear ………. Strength of Signals is ………..
X134 ^	I am going to send a message without prefix or waiting for "K", keep careful watch.
A X134 @	Wait. I must shift to read another station (or ……..) but will call (answer) you as soon as I can.
A X134*%	Am about to work camera obscura by W/T.
X135 ^	Answer every ……. groups by "K".
X135 @	Have …… messages awaiting transmission.
X136 ^	My apparatus is going faulty and I will have to shut down to examine it.
X136 @	Only messages of an immediate nature are to be passed until further orders.
A X136*%	Am reeling in aerial (preparatory to landing at ……. (or on ……..))
X137 ^	Is my wave-length correct ?
A X137 @	Resume normal W/T communication now (or at …….).
X138 ^	Your wave-length is correct.
A X138 @	Report time …….. Was last heard.
A X138*%	Am reeling in to pick up a message.
X139 ^	Your wave-length is ...... metres too short.
X139 @	Only Service messages are to be transmitted until further orders (or from …. until ….).
X140 ^	Your wave-length is …... metres too long.
A X140*%	Am working with aircraft in flight (on ……)
X141 /	Give me my proper wave-length.
X142 /	Followed by calls to tune in by. This is your wave-length.
A X142*%	Forced landing (at ……..)

MESSAGES (1926) @

Radiotelegraph and Radiotelephone Codes, Prowords and Abbreviations

List of Radiotelegraph 'X' Codes

The Signals marked "A" are in possession of Aircraft
* Not used by Navy or Royal Air Force. # Other Source, NOT in the B.R.266/1941.
¶ or blank - 1941, not listed in 1918 although they may have existed. Not a full list.
Indicators – (NOT part of signal) ^ 1918, @ 1926,   % 1931,   ¶ 1941.

X Codes become a QUESTION when preceded by the "Interrogative" X112.
X Codes become NEGATIVE when preceded by "Negative" X114

SIGNAL	MEANING
X143 ^	Your wave-length is varying.
A X143 @	Send message for …. (via ….) (on ….. KC/s) (by …….. method).
X144 ^	Are your "H.T." Batteries O.K. ?
X144 @	Have a Service message to transmit.
A X144 %	Restrict volume of traffic while aircraft are up.
X145 ^	Change your transmission valve.
X145 @	This message (or message ….) is being (or has been) repeated for information to ….
X146 ^	Change to "H.T." unit.
X146 @	Message …. Does not concern you (or …..).

RADIOTELEPHONE (1931) %

A X146*%	I can hear your speech, strength ………
X147 ^	I am changing to "H.T." unit.
A X147 @	Hasten reply to last message (or message …..).
X148 ^	Change to "H.T." battery.
X148 @	Replies to message ….. are to be transmitted now, or at ……..
A X148 %	I cannot hear your speech, use W/T (on ……. Kc/s)
X149 ^	I am changing to "H.T." battery.
X149 @	Ships or stations intercepting this message need not decipher it.
X150 ^	Message No. ….. has been deciphered. Message with THI specified has been deciphered.
X150 @	Message transmitted at …. by ….. received.
A X150*%	Listen out for R/T (on ……. Kc/s)
X151 ^	Message from station denoted and with THI as specified has been forwarded by landline.
X151 @	Request reply may be made to my ………
X152 ^	I can receive but my transmitting apparatus is failing.

NOTE: End of available 1918 list.

X152 @	Clear traffic on guard wave or wave denoted.
A X152* %	Use R/T (on …….. Kc/s)
A X154* %	Your speech is distinct.
A X156*%	Your speech is too weak to read: close distance.

APPARATUS AND SYSTEMS (1931) %

X158*%	Aerial.
X159*%	Aerial (Diving).

ACCURACY OF MESSAGES (1926) @

For use with R/T (Radio Telephony) 1941

X160 @	Accuracy of reception of message …. (or of groups ……. in message …. is / are doubtful.
X160* %	Aerial (Jury)
A X161* @	Fragments only received (or received from …..)
X161* %	Aerial (Kite)
X162 @	Number of groups in text and time of origin in message following (or in message ….) is ….
X162* %	Aerial (Mast)
X163 @	Message following was incompletely received. Portions missed are indicated by the position of this operating signal in the message.
X163*%	Aerial (Roof)
X164 @	Group(s) …… in message …… should apparently read as follows.

Radiotelegraph and Radiotelephone Codes, Prowords and Abbreviations

List of Radiotelegraph 'X' Codes

The Signals marked "A" are in possession of Aircraft
* Not used by Navy or Royal Air Force.   # Other Source, NOT in the B.R.266/1941.
Indicators – (NOT part of signal) ^ 1918,   @ 1926,   % 1931,   ¶ 1941..

X Codes become a QUESTION when preceded by the "Interrogative" X112.
X Codes become NEGATIVE when preceded by "Negative" X114

SIGNAL	MEANING

X164*%	Aerial amperes.
X165 @	Message which you have just forwarded (or message .....) was incorrectly transmitted, correct version is.
X165*%	Anode Volts.
X166* %	Arc. Array.
X167* %	Automatic.
X168* %	Auxiliary Office.
X169* %	Auxiliary Set.
X170*%	

RETRANSMISSION OF MESSAGES (1926) @

A	X170 @	Pass this message (or message ......) by .... to ....
	X171 @	Transmit this message (or message ....) now or at ....
	X172 @	Message(s) .... has (have) been passed to .... (at ....)
A	X173 @	Inform me when this message (or message....) has been received by the addressee(s) or by ....
	X173*%	Coupling.
A	X174 @	Message ...... has been received by addressee(s) (or by ......)
A	X174* %	C.W.
A	X175 @	Give me your message (for ......) I will forward it.
	X175* %	D/F Set.
	X176 @	Pass this message (or message .....) to stations addressed (or whose call signs follow) for which you are responsible.
	X176*%	Emergency Set.
	X177 @	Transmit this message (or message ....) now (or at .....) without preliminary call.
	X177*%	G/C Set.
	X178 @	Take no further action with regard to forwarding message .... to ....
	X179 @	Repeat message(s) read from .... at ....
A	X180 @	Did ...... send any messages for me? If so please repeat.
	X181 @	Pass message (or message .....) direct (to ......)
	X181*%	H/F (High Frequency).
	X182 @	Following message has been read.
A	X182* %	I.C.W.
	X183 @	Repeat last message (or message ......) on .... Metres / Kc/s (to ....)
	X183* %	Key (Magnetic)
	X184* %	L/F (Low Frequency)
A	X186*%	Listening-through apparatus.

TRANSMITTED MESSAGES (1926) @

	X187 @	Transmit your message by "up and down" working.
	X187*%	Low Power.
	X188 @	Message up to and including No. .... Have been broadcast at previous transmissions.
A	X189 @	Nothing received from (or heard of) .... at ....
A	X190 @	Following is what .... made at ....
	X190*%	Main Office.
	X191 @	Have message(s) bearing series number(s) .... for ....
	X191* %	Master Oscillator.
	X192 @	Report series number(s) of last message(s) received from ....
	X192* %	Note Frequency (...... cycles per second).
	X193 @	Series number(s) of last message(s) received from .... (is) (are) ....
A	X193* %	Power.
	X194 @	Message bearing series number .... was a service message.

Radiotelegraph and Radiotelephone Codes, Prowords and Abbreviations

List of Radiotelegraph 'X' Codes
The Signals marked "A" are in possession of Aircraft
* Not used by Navy or Royal Air Force.   # Other Source, NOT in the B.R.266/1941.
Indicators – (NOT part of signal) ^ 1918, @ 1926,   % 1931, ¶ 1941..

X Codes become a QUESTION when preceded by the "Interrogative" X112.
X Codes become NEGATIVE when preceded by "Negative" X114

SIGNAL	MEANING
X194*%	Quartz Crystal.
X195 @	Repeat message made by ……. at …….. (or message series number …..) is a service message.
X195* %	Receiver (Receiving model …….) No. of valves in use ……..))
X196 @	Message made by ….. at …… was NOT a service message.
X196* %	Remote control.
X197 @	W/T Operating Signals only were made by ……. at ……..
A X197*%	R/T.
X198 @	Message transmitted by ……… at ……. NOT received.
X199 @	Pass all service messages received from group or single stations (or from ….) on your wave between …… and …… times.
X200 @	Transmit the following message (or message ….) on normal wave to one of the group stations (or to …….) at the next routine time, inserting the correct series number and carrying out the procedure for "I" method group stations.
X200*%	Second (Office).
X201 @	Executive signal for last message (or following message) has been made, or was made at …..
X201*%	Spark.
X202 @	Have you received the Executive Signal for the last message (or following message).
X202*%	S/T.
X203 @	Messages will be sent by the "F" method. Reply at the next routine time (or at time indicated).
X203*%	Telephone.
X204 @	This message (or message …..) is being (or has been) passed out of its proper sequence.
A X204*%	Transmitter.
A X204 ¶	I cannot hear your speech, use W/T.
X205 @	Originator's number of message timed …… to ……. from ……. is ……..
X205*%	Type number or set …….
A X206 @	Send messages by "F" method.
X206*%	Valve.
A X206 ¶	Listen out for R/T.
A X207 @	Message(s) will be sent by "F" method.
A X207*%	V/S (Visual Signalling)
A X208 ¶	Use R/T.
X208 @	Pass messages for me (or for ……) by "F" method until further orders (or until ……).
X209 @	Transmit your messages in batches of …… messages at a time.

TELEGRAMS (1926) @

X215 @	Private telegram(s) received for ………
X216 @	Open and Signal contents of private telegram for …………
X217 @	Have …….. service telegram(s) awaiting transmission.
X218 @	Have …….. private telegram(s) awaiting transmission.
X219 @	Pass service telegrams (on ……… metres / Kc/s)
X220 @	Pass private telegrams (on ……… metres / Kc/s)
X221 @	Charges on this private telegram have been prepaid.

AUTOMATIC SIGNALLING (1931) %

X212*%	Conditions favourable for automatic reception.
X214* %	Transmit by hand.
X216 %	Traffic tape received. Receipt will be given later (or at ……..)
X218* %	Transmit traffic by perforated tape at ….. words per minute.
X220*%	transmit your call sign for …. minutes at ….. words per minute.

Radiotelegraph and Radiotelephone Codes, Prowords and Abbreviations

List of Radiotelegraph 'X' Codes
The Signals marked "A" are in possession of Aircraft
* Not used by Navy or Royal Air Force.   # Other Source, NOT in the B.R.266/1941.
Indicators – (NOT part of signal) ^ 1918,   @ 1926,   % 1931,   ¶ 1941.

X Codes become a QUESTION when preceded by the "Interrogative" X112.
X Codes become NEGATIVE when preceded by "Negative" X114

SIGNAL	MEANING
X222*%	You are transmitting a continuous long.
X224*%	your cut off is bad.

S.O.S. TIME AND WEATHER (1926) @

A	X225 @	S.O.S. message made at .... (by ....) received.
A	X226 @	Request local weather report at .... (or every .... hours)
A	X227 @	Am about to transmit timing signal for correcting clocks.

COMMUNICATION. NOTE AND STRENGTH (1931) %

A	X227*%	Am in W/T (or ....) communication with .... (on .... Kc/s).
	X228 @	Request a timing signal for correcting clocks.
	X229 @	Request permission to shift receiving gear to read timing signal now (or at ....)
A	X229 %	Am moving and will call immediately on re-opening (or at ....)
A	X231 %	Am moving and will endeavour to keep in communication while on the move.

GUARDS AND DUTIES (1926) @

A	X233 @	Take over W/T guard (or duty) on your present wave (or on .... metres / Kc/s).
A	X233*%	Am shifting to read another station (or ....) but will call you as soon as I can (or at ......).
	X234 @	Take over stand-by guard on your present wave (or on .... metres / Kc/s)
	X235 @	Am prepared to take or hand over the W/T guard (or duty).
	X235 %	Docket No. ...... arrived at .... (hours).
	X236 @	W/T guard correct.
	X237 @	Denote the station(s) for which you are W/T guard.
	X237 %	Docket No. ...... left for your office at ..... (hours). Report arrival.
	X238 @	Senior Officer is keeping constant watch on .... metres / Kc/s.
		W/T guards are not to pass in messages received on this (these) wave(s) unless directed to do so.
	X239 @	Have heard nothing on my wave (or .... metres / Kc/s) since taking over W/T guard (or assuming watch).
	X239 %	Establish communication with me (or .....) on your guard wave (or on ...... Kc/s).
	X240 @	Act as W/T link between me and .... (or between .... and ....)
A	X241 @	Keep watch on .... Metres / Kc/s.
A	X241 %	Have nothing to communicate (Series and/or originator's number of last message was ....)

COMMUNICATION, NOTE and STRENGTH. (1941) ¶

A	X242 @	Listen out for messages from .... (on .... metres / Kc/s).
	X242 ¶	We are under air attack.
	X243 @	Set watch (direct .... to set watch) (on ....)
A	X243 %	Have something to communicate (or have message, or number of messages denoted for ... at...)
	X243 ¶	Air attack all clear.
	X244 @	I have set watch (have directed .... to set watch) (on ....).
A	X244 ¶	Am closing down during air raid warning.
	X245 @	Close down until ....
	X245 %	Maintain communication with me (or ......) on your guard wave (or on ..... Kc/s)
A	X245 ¶	Am moving and will maintain comms while moving.
A	X246 @	Am closing down owing to electrical storms, will call immediately reception is possible.
A	X247 @	My (or ....) station is now ready for work.
A	X247*%	Nothing heard from .... (at ......)
A	X247 ¶	Am shifting to read another stn, will call you ASAP (or at ....)
A	X248 @	Am about to reel in aerial.
A	X249 @	Am reeling in preparatory to landing.
A	X249 %	Report time .... was last heard (on ...... Kc/s)
	X250 @	Dismantle W/T station at once.

Radiotelegraph and Radiotelephone Codes, Prowords and Abbreviations

List of Radiotelegraph 'X' Codes

The Signals marked "A" are in possession of Aircraft
 * Not used by Navy or Royal Air Force.   # Other Source, NOT in the B.R.266/1941.
Indicators – (NOT part of signal) ^ 1918,   @ 1926,   % 1931,   ¶ 1941..

X Codes become a QUESTION when preceded by the "Interrogative" X112.
X Codes become NEGATIVE when preceded by "Negative" X114

SIGNAL	MEANING
X251 @	Am closing now.
A X251 %	Report when you are in W/T (or ……) communication with ……..
X252 @	Close now, reopen at ……….
X253 @	This station (or ….) listens out on normal wave (or on…. metres / Kc/s) between … and …
X253 %	Report with what stations you are in W/T (or ….) communication (on ….. Kc/s)
A X254 @	Forced landing (at ………)
X255 @	Man remote control on …… metres / Kc/s now (or at …….)
A X255 %	Resume normal W/T communication now (or at ……)
X256 @	Report blank.
A X257 ¶	Have nothing for you, last message number was ….
A X257*%	Decrease strength of signals.
A X259*%	Increase strength of signals.
A X259 ¶	Have something / ... msgs for you.
X259 #	What is my signal strength?
A X261*%	Lower your note.
A X261 ¶	Increase strength of signals.

NOTE AND STRENGTH (1926) @

A X263 @	How are my signals?
A X263*%	Raise your note.
A X264*@	Your signals are clear and readable strength ……….
X265 @	………. reports that strength of my signals is ……….
A X265*%	What strength are my signals (or those of ……..)
A X266*@	Decrease strength of signals.
A X267 @	How is my note?
A X267*%	What is quality of my note?
A X267 ¶	Nothing heard from you (at …..)
A X268*@	Increase strength of signals.
A X269*@	Your note is clear and musical.
A X269*%	Your note is bad – try to improve.
A X270*@	Your note is bad (or spark broken).
A X271*@	Your signals are unreadable owing to your bad note.
A X271*%	Your note is clear and musical.
A X271 ¶	Report time I (or ...) was last heard.
A X272*@	Your signals are unreadable. Clicks only being received.
A X273*@	Lower your note.
A X273*%	Your note is unsteady (rising and falling).
A X274*@	Raise your note.
A X275*@	Try to improve your note.
A X275*%	Your signals are fading strength …….. to ……..
A X276*@	Your note is jumping (unsteady) (rising and falling).
A X277 ¶	Resume normal W/T comms now (or at ...)
A X277*%	Your (or …..) signals are (or were at ……..) readable and clear strength.
A X279*%	Your signals are unreadable owing to your bad note.
A X279 ¶	What are the strength of my /....'s signals?
X279 #	Do you have any traffic?

WAVES AND TUNING (1926) @

A X280 @	Please send call sign on your present wave (or on ….. metres) for one minute, or until "Q" is received.
A X281 @	Am about to send call sign on my present wave (or on …….. metres).
A X281*%	Your signals are unreadable. Clicks only being received.
X282 @	Am about to send call sign on my present wave (or on …….. metres), obtain receiving adjustments and then tune in the same way.

Radiotelegraph and Radiotelephone Codes, Prowords and Abbreviations

List of Radiotelegraph 'X' Codes
The Signals marked "A" are in possession of Aircraft
* Not used by Navy or Royal Air Force.   # Other Source, NOT in the B.R.266/1941.
Indicators – (NOT part of signal) ^1918,   @ 1926,   % 1931,   ¶ 1941.

X Codes become a QUESTION when preceded by the "Interrogative" X112.
X Codes become NEGATIVE when preceded by "Negative" X114

SIGNAL   MEANING

CALLS AND ANSWERS (1931) %

	X282 %	Answer in alphabetical order of callsigns.
A	X283*@	Am (or ..... is) adjusting (shifting) to normal wave (on .... metres / Kc/s)
A	X283 ¶	Your note is bad - try to improve.
A	X284 @	Adjust (shift) to normal wave (or .... metres /Kc/s).
A	X284 %	answer calls for me (or for ......) on present frequency (or on ...... Kc/s).
	X285 @	What wave are you (or is ....) using?
	X286*@	Am (or is ....) using .... metres / Kc/s.?
A	X286 %	Answer me (or .....) (on ...... Kc/s).
A	X287*@	Am about to transmit on .... metres / Kc/s.
A	X287 ¶	Your note is unsteady (rising and falling)
A	X288*@	Am about to shift receiving gear to .... metres / Kc/s.
A	X288 %	Call me again at .... On present frequency (or on ...... Kc/s).
A	X289 @	Shift receiving gear to .... metres / Kc/s.
A	X289 ¶	Your signals are fading, Strength ... to ...
	X290 @	Direct ...... (by .... method) to shift receiving gear to .... metres / Kc/s.
A	X290 %	Call me (or ....) (on ...... Kc/s) every ..... minutes (until .....)
	X291*@	Have (or has ....) shifted receiving gear to .... metres / Kc/s.
A	X291 ¶	Your / .... sigs are/were at .... readable and clear, strength .....
A	X292 @	Please measure my wave.
A	X293 @	Transmit on .... metres and receive on .... metres / Kc/s.
A	X294*@	Your wave appears to be correct.
A	X294 %	Have been (...... is, or has been) calling or answering you (or .....) (on ......Kc/s) since .....
A	X295*@	Your wave appears to be long, decrease .... metres.
A	X295 ¶	Your sigs are unreadable, clicks only received.
A	X296*@	Your wave appears to be short, increase .... metres.
A	X296 %	Inform ..... that I am calling or answering him (on .... Kc/s).
A	X297*@	Your wave is .... metres / Kc/s.
	X298 @	Tune your station (or ......) to .... metres.
A	X298 %	...... will answer calls (on .... Kc/s)

CALLS and ANSWERS. (1941). ¶

A	X298 ¶	Answer calls for me on present frequency.
	X299 @	Do I appear to be in tune with .... ?
	X300* @	Your wave is steady.
A	X300 %	Will you call again as soon as possible (or at ....) on present frequency.
	X301* @	Your wave is decreasing (falling).
	X302*@	Your wave is increasing (rising).

TIME (1931) %

A	X302 %	Request a timing signal now (or at ....)
	X302*¶	Call me again at .... on present frequency.
	X303*@	Your wave length changed during last transmission.
A	X304*@	Your wave length has changed since last transmission (or since ....)
A	X304 %	Shift receiver to read timing signal now (or at ....)
	X305 @	My normal working wave is .... metres.
A	X306 %	Timing signal will be transmitted now (or at ....)
	X306 #	Increase your wave frequency very slightly.
	X307 #	Decrease your wave frequency very slightly.

DEFECTS AND DELAYS (1931) %

Radiotelegraph and Radiotelephone Codes, Prowords and Abbreviations

List of Radiotelegraph 'X' Codes
The Signals marked "A" are in possession of Aircraft
* Not used by Navy or Royal Air Force.   # Other Source, NOT in the B.R.266/1941.
Indicators – (NOT part of signal) ^ 1918,   @ 1926,   % 1931,   ¶ 1941.

X Codes become a QUESTION when preceded by the "Interrogative" X112.
X Codes become NEGATIVE when preceded by "Negative" X114

SIGNAL   MEANING

A	X308*%	Delay was due to a fault in my receiver.
	X308 #	Your signals are fading strength …… to ………
A	X308 ¶	Have been / …is / has been calling / answering you / or … since ….

WAVES and TUNING (Special) (1926) @

A	X310 @	Shift to Divisional wave.
A	X310*%	Delay was due to a fault in my transmitter.
A	X310 ¶	Inform … that I am calling / answering him.
A	X311 @	Shift to Sub-divisional wave.
	X312 @	Shift to Flotilla wave.
A	X312*%	Delay was due to failure of power supply.
A	X312 ¶	…… will answer calls.
A	X313 @	Tune in on Divisional wave (or on ……. metres).
A	X314 @	Tune in on Sub-divisional wave.
	X314*%	Delay was due to man aloft.
A	X314 ¶	Will call you again ASAP / or at … on present freq.
	X315 @	Adjust tuning of aerial circuit until maximum radiation is (or until …. amperes are obtained without altering primary tuning.
	X316 @	You appear to be ….. degrees long on fine tuner.
	X316*%	Delay was due to raising or lowering W/T mast.
	X317 @	You appear to be ….. degrees short on fine tuner.

MESSAGES (1941) ¶

	X317 ¶	Cannot pass your message (….) in specified time / or till …
	X318 @	Increase your wave, primary coil variometer to be moved …. degrees. When in new position station is to make its call sign three times.
	X318*%	Delay was due to working with another station.
	X319 @	Decrease your wave, primary coil variometer to be moved …. degrees. When in new position station is to make its call sign three times.
	X320 @	Send in alphabetical sequence of call signs. Each station to make its call sign once (or …. times)
A	X320*%	Have been closed down due to electric storms.

AIRCRAFT (1926) @

	X322*%	Have man aloft, am unable to transmit from ….. office (or from …….)
	X324* %	My aerial (or aerial of …….) has been damaged or carried away.
A	X325 @	Restrict volume of traffic while aircraft are up …..
A	X326 @	Aircraft fitted with W/T leaving now (or at …….)
A	X326*%	My accumulators are correct.
A	X326 ¶	Following message in SYKO.
A	X327 @	Am working with aircraft in flight on ……….
A	X328 @	Am about to work camera obscura by W/T ……
A	X328*%	My accumulators are run down.
A	X329 @	Aircraft has (have) landed. Resume watch on normal wave (or …… metres).
	X329 ¶	Following message has been read.
A	X330*%	My ……. apparatus is out of order.
	X331 ¶	Following msg /… incompletely received.

Radiotelegraph and Radiotelephone Codes, Prowords and Abbreviations

List of Radiotelegraph 'X' Codes

The Signals marked "A" are in possession of Aircraft
* Not used by Navy or Royal Air Force.   # Other Source, NOT in the B.R.266/1941.
Indicators – (NOT part of signal) ^1918, @ 1926, % 1931, ¶ 1941.

X Codes become a QUESTION when preceded by the "Interrogative" X112.
X Codes become NEGATIVE when preceded by "Negative" X114

| SIGNAL | MEANING |

(Portions missed are indicated by the position of this operating signal in the message)
A X332*%   My (or ......) .... appears to be correct.

RADIO TELEPHONY (1926) @

A X333 @   Your speech is too weak to read; proceed in direction of this office.
A X334 @   I cannot hear your speech, use W/T (on ...... metres).
A X334*%   My ..... (or .... of ....) is defective.
A X335 @   Use R/T on .... metres.
A X336 @   Listen out for R/T on .... metres.
A X336*%   My .... installation correct (repairs completed)
A X337*@   I can hear you speaking. Your speech is strength ......
A X338*@   Your speech is indistinct.
A X338 %   There appears to be a fault in your .... apparatus (on .... Kc/s).
A X338 ¶   Give me your message (or msg ...) I will dispose of it.
A X339*@   Your speech is good.
  X339 ¶   Report time this msg / msg ... has been rec'd by addressees for whom you are responsible.
  X340 @   Your microphone appears to be packing.
  X340 %   Transmission on high frequency suspended until further notice on account of
             high frequency hazards.
  X340 ¶   Is there any reply to message .... ?
A X342 %   What is the cause of delay in answering.

DIRECTION FINDING (1926) @

A X343 @   What is my bearing?
  X343 ¶   Msgs with priority / priority ... only are to be passed until further orders.
A X344 @   What is my position by D.F. cross bearings?
  X344 %   What was delay in re-transmitting message .... (to ....)
  X345 @   Pass in D.F. bearings (of ....)
  X346 @   Endeavour to obtain a bearing of ......
  X346*%   Your aerial appears to be earthing.
A X347 @   Am ready to take your bearing (or bearing of ....) on my normal wave or on ..... metres.
A X348 @   Bearing of you (or of ....) obtained at ..... was .... from me (or from ....) class ...
             or its reciprocal.
A X348*%   Your .... appears to be defective.
A X349 @   Am unable to determine bearing.
  X350 @   Send a dummy message in order that a bearing may be obtained .
             (Body of message to be preceded by "X")
A X350*%   You are missing shorts.
A X351 @   Send your call sign for two minutes on your present wave (or on .... Metres) in order that a
             bearing may be obtained.
A X352 @   Bearing of you (or of ....) obtained at ..... was .... from me (or from ....) class ... ,
             sense determined.
A X352 %   You are causing delay by answering out of turn.
A X353 @   Bearing of station which answered message from .... at .... was ..... class .... or its
             reciprocal.
A X354 @   Your distance was approximately ..... miles from me (or from ....) at ......
A X354 %   You are causing delay by slowness in answering me (or ....).
A X355 @   Bearing should be regarded as approximate only owing to unfavourable circumstances.
A X356 @   Your signals are not sufficiently strong for good determination of bearing under present
             unfavourable circumstances.

Radiotelegraph and Radiotelephone Codes, Prowords and Abbreviations

List of Radiotelegraph 'X' Codes
The Signals marked "A" are in possession of Aircraft
* Not used by Navy or Royal Air Force.   # Other Source, NOT in the B.R.266/1941.
Indicators – (NOT part of signal) ^ 1918,   @ 1926,   % 1931,   ¶ 1941.

X Codes become a QUESTION when preceded by the "Interrogative" X112.
X Codes become NEGATIVE when preceded by "Negative" X114

SIGNAL	MEANING

EXERCISES (1931) %

A	X356	%	W/T exercise (No ……..) will be carried out now (or at ………).
A	X357	@	Signal bearing as determined approximately ……..
A	X358	@	Am (or ….. is) listening out on ……. metres D.F.
A	X358	%	W/T exercise will now cease.

REFERENCE TO ORDERS (1931) %

A	X359	@	Listen out on D.F. on …… metres (or between ……. and ……. metres.
A	X360	@	Your position at …… was …… class ……. by cross bearings (from …. and ….)
	X360	%	Attention is called to R.A.F. Command Routine Order no. …….. paragraph ……...
	X361	@	Take a bearing of station now transmitting on …. metres.
	X361	%	Attention of W/T operator of the watch is called to "Confidential Communication Orders" No. ………. paragraph ……...
	X362	@	Bearing of unknown station transmitting on ….. metres at …. was …. or its reciprocal.
	X362	%	Attention of W/T operator of the watch is called to R.A.F. Signal Manual, Part …… , Article ………, paragraph …………
A	X363	@	Stand by to determine my position by means of the Radio Acoustic method. The executive Signal will follow.
	X363	%	Attention of W/T operator on duty is called to Army Signal Training, Part …… Article …….. para ……..
A	X364	@	When ready (or at ….) carry out the procedure to enable me to fix your position by means of the Radio Acoustic method.
	X364	%	Attention of W/T rating in charge of watch is called to Fleet (Station) Communication Orders, Article ………, paragraph ………..
A	X365	@	Commence revolving beacon transmissions now (or at ……)
	X365	%	Attention of W/T rating in charge of watch is called to P.M.G.'s Handbook, Article ………, paragraph ……..
	X366	%	Attention of W/T rating in charge of watch is called to Signal Manual (Naval), Article ………, paragraph ……..
	X366	¶	Report disposal of message ……..
	X367	%	Attention of W/T rating in charge of watch is called to Wireless Signalling Instructions, Article ………, paragraph ……..

MESSAGES (1931) %

X369*%		Accuracy of following message or of message ……. (or of groups …….. in a message ……..) is doubtful.
X370 %		Acknowledge in due course.
X371*%		Cannot pass your message (identity …….) in the specified time (or till ……..)

OPERATORS (1926) @

	X372	@	For the purpose of record denote the name of operator of the watch.
	X373	@	A competent operator is to take operator of the watch.
A	X373*	%	Can you accept message for ………
	X374	@	A junior operator is to take operator of the watch.
	X375	@	A senior operator is to be on watch (during Ex. No. ……..)
A	X375*	%	Distress message made at ……… (by ………) received.
A	X377*	%	Executive Signal for last message (or following message) has been made, or was made at …….

REFERENCE TO ORDERS (1926) @

Radiotelegraph and Radiotelephone Codes, Prowords and Abbreviations

List of Radiotelegraph 'X' Codes

The Signals marked "A" are in possession of Aircraft
* Not used by Navy or Royal Air Force.   # Other Source, NOT in the B.R.266/1941.
Indicators – (NOT part of signal) ^ 1918, @ 1926, % 1931, ¶ 1941.

X Codes become a QUESTION when preceded by the "Interrogative" X112.
X Codes become NEGATIVE when preceded by "Negative" X114

SIGNAL	MEANING
X379 @	Attention of W/T operator of the watch is called to Fleet (Station) Communication Orders …… Orders Article …….. para ……..
X379*%	Following is a service message.
X380 @	Attention of W/T operator of the watch is called to "Wireless Signalling Instructions" (Naval) Article …….. para ……..
X381 @	Attention of W/T operator of the watch is called to "Signal Manual" (Naval) Article …….. para ……..
X381*%	Following is what ……… made (or was made) at ……….
X382 @	Attention of W/T operator of the watch is called to "Confidential Communication Orders" No. …… para …….
X383 @	Attention of W/T operator of the watch is called to "R.A.F. Signal Manual," Part …….. Article …….. para ……..
X383*%	Following message has been read.
X384 @	Attention of W/T operator on duty is called to Army Signal Training, Part …… Article …….. para ……..
X385 @	Attention of W/T operator of the watch is called to message ….. from this station (or from …..)
X385*%	Following message (or message …….) was incompletely received. (Portions missed are indicated by the position of this operating signal in the message).
X386 @	Attention is called to Coding Instructions (Naval) Article …….. para ……..
X387 @	Attention is called to Admiralty Fleet Orders "S" Series No. ….. para …….
A X387 %	Give me your message (for ……..). I will dispose of it.
A X389*%	Have you received the Executive Signal for message ……. ?
A X389 ¶	Transmit messages in batches of ... messages at a time.

INSTRUCTIONS TO OPERATORS (1926) @

X390 @	………. is (are) in company for W/T purposes.
X391 @	………. Is (are) not keeping W/T watch.
X391 %	Have one (or ……) service messages for ……… Request route.
X392 @	W/T operator is to pay more attention.
A X393*@	You are missing shorts.
X393 %	Inform me when this message (or message ……) has been received by those of the addressees for whom you are responsible (or by …….)
X394 @	Separative signs must be made more distinctively
A X395 @	Calls must be made more distinctly.
X395 %	Messages will be sent by Broadcast method. Answer at next routine time (or at ……).
X396*@	Send faster.
A X397*@	Send more slowly.
X397 %	Messages bearing an indication of priority (or indication of priority ……..) only are to be passed until further orders.
A X398 @	Your morse is bad (difficult to read)
X399 @	Pay more attention to your spacing.
X399 %	Message …….. does not concern you (or ……..).

DEFECTS and DELAYS (1941) ¶

A X399 ¶	Delay was due to default in …..
X400 @	Answer in alphabetical order of call signs.
X401 @	You are causing delay by answering out of turn.
X401 %	Message(s) ……. has (have) been passed to …….. (at …….) (by ……….)
X402 @	You are causing delay by slowness in answering.
X403 @	"Q" was made by me (or by …..) during your last transmission.
X403 %	Message(s) ……. has (have) been received at …… by addressees for whom I am responsible (or by …….)
X405*%	Message ……. was received at ……. on ……… Kc/s.

Radiotelegraph and Radiotelephone Codes, Prowords and Abbreviations

List of Radiotelegraph 'X' Codes

The Signals marked "A" are in possession of Aircraft
* Not used by Navy or Royal Air Force.   # Other Source, NOT in the B.R.266/1941.
Indicators – (NOT part of signal) ^ 1918, @ 1926, % 1931, ¶ 1941.

X Codes become a QUESTION when preceded by the "Interrogative" X112.
X Codes become NEGATIVE when preceded by "Negative" X114

SIGNAL	MEANING
A X405 ¶	Delay was due to working another station.
X407*%	Messages up to and including No. ……. have been have been transmitted at previous transmissions.
A X407 ¶	Have been closed down due to electrical storm.

INTERFERENCE (1926) @

A X408 @	Listen out before transmitting. You are causing unnecessary interference.
A X409 @	Please do not interfere. I am receiving from …….
X409*%	Message which you (or …..) have (has) just forwarded (or message …..) was incorrectly transmitted; correct version is ……….
A X410 @	You are causing interference on ……. metres.
X411 @	You are causing interference with aircraft communications.
X411*%	Originator's or series number of message timed ……… to ………. from ……… is ……..
A X412 @	You are causing interference by inattention to order to wait.
X412 %	Pass this message (or message …..) to those addressees for whom you are responsible (or to …..)
X413 @	You are causing interference by careless handling of your receiving gear.
X413 ¶	My accumulators are correct.
X414 @	From what is interference being experienced (or who is interfering with you).
X414 %	Pass this message (or message …..) (via ……..) to …… (by ……..) (on …… Kc/s)
X515*@	Interference from …… is apparently deliberate.
X416 @	I am being deliberately interfered with by the enemy (call sign ………).
X416 %	Repeat any messages (for …….) made at …….. (by ……..)
A X417*@	Interference is being experienced from ……. (on …….. metres).
A X417 ¶	My …. apparatus is temporarily out of action.
A X418*@	Interference is being experienced (in ……..) from your valve.
X418 %	Replies to message …… are to be transmitted now (or at ……)
A X419*@	Interference is being experienced from local noises.
A X419 ¶	My /…..'s …. appears to be correct.
A X420*@	You were sending at the same time as ………
X420 %	Report disposal of message.
A X421 ¶	My …. (or …. of ….) is defective.
A X422 ¶	My remote control is out of action, using close control.
X422 %	Report series number(s) of last message(s) received from ………
A X423 ¶	My …. installation correct (repairs completed).
X424*%	Series number(s) of last message(s) received from …… is (are)

DELAYS (1926) @

A X425*@	Delay was due to a fault in my transmitting gear.
A X425 ¶	There appears to be a fault in your …. apparatus.
A X426*@	Delay was due to a fault in my receiving gear.
X426 %	Send by Broadcast method.
X427 @	Delay was due to man aloft.
X428 @	Have man aloft, am unable to transmit from main or second office (or on …… type or method).
X428 %	Service messages only are to be transmitted until further orders (or from …… till …….)
A X429 @	what is the cause of delay in answering?
X430 @	Am about to lower main aerials and connect up to jury aerials. Wait 5 minutes.
X430 %	Ships or stations intercepting this message need not decode (decipher) it.
X431 @	Am about to disconnect from jury aerials and connect up to main aerials.
X432 %	Send message for ……. (via …….) (on …… Kc/s) (by ……. method).
X433 %	Spell out the ordinal numbers in the message just transmitted or in message timed ……..
X434 %	Take no further action as to forwarding message ……. (to ……..)

DEFECTS (1926) @

Radiotelegraph and Radiotelephone Codes, Prowords and Abbreviations

List of Radiotelegraph 'X' Codes
The Signals marked "A" are in possession of Aircraft
* Not used by Navy or Royal Air Force.   # Other Source, NOT in the B.R.266/1941.
Indicators – (NOT part of signal)   ^ 1918,   @ 1926,   % 1931,   ¶ 1941.

X Codes become a QUESTION when preceded by the "Interrogative" X112.
X Codes become NEGATIVE when preceded by "Negative" X114

SIGNAL	MEANING
X436*@	My aerial (or aerial of ......) has been damaged or carried away.
X436 %	This message (or message ......) is being (or has been) passed out of its proper sequence.
X437*@	My .... transmitting gear is temporarily out of action.
A X438*@	My .... receiving gear is temporarily out of action.
X438 %	This message (or message ......) is being (or has been) repeated for information to ....
A X438 ¶	Your relay appears to be sticking.
A X439*@	My .... (or .... of ....) is defective.
A X439 ¶	You are causing delay by answering out of turn.
A X440 @	Your ...... appears to be defective.
X440 %	Transfer messages for .... to W/T guard on ...... Kc/s (or to ....)
A X441 @	There appears to be a fault in your (........) transmitting gear.
A X441 ¶	You are causing delay by slowness in answering me (or .....)
A X442 @	There appears to be a fault in your (........) receiving gear.
X442 %	transmit following message (or message ......) on normal wave to one of the group stations (or to .....) at the next routine time, inserting the correct series number and carrying out the procedure for "I" method group stations.
A X443 @	There appears to be a fault in your gear for listening through.
X443 #	Transmit the following message using a Naval Board Call Sign.

TIME (1941) ¶

A X443 ¶	Request a timing signal now (or at ...)
X444 @	Your aerial appears to be earthing.
X444 %	Transmit messages for me (or for .....) by Broadcast method until further notice (or until ......)
A X445 @	(......) installation correct (repairs completed)
A X445 ¶	Timing signal will be transmitted now (or at ...)
X446 @	Report when your installation is correct (repairs completed)
X446 %	Transmit messages in batches of .... messages at a time.
A X447 @	My accumulators are correct.
A X448 @	My accumulators are run down.
X448 %	Transmit messages by "up and down" working.
A X449 @	Send more accumulators.
X450 @	My (or ......) .... appears to be correct.
X450 %	transmit this message (or message ....) by H/F.
X452 %	When and on what frequency was message .... received.

W/T GUARDS AND DUTIES (1931) %

X453 %	Assume W/T organisation ...... (in order of call signs following) (or at ....)

MISCELLANEOUS (1926) @

X454 @	Increase
X455 @	Decrease
X455 %	Assume W/T responsibility forthwith for ships or stations whose call signs follow ....
A X456 @	Am about to use (or am shifting to ....)
A X457 @	Am (or .... is) using.
X457 %	Take over D/F guard as previously ordered (or on ...... Kc/s) (or from ..... to ...... Kc/s)
A X458 @	Am (or .... is) unable to use.
A X459 @	Use.
A X459 %	Take over W/T guard on your present frequency (or on .... Kc/s)
A X461 @	Am (or was) unable to send on ....
X461 %	Take over stand-by guard on your present frequency (or on .... Kc/s)
A X462 @	Am unable to receive ....

Radiotelegraph and Radiotelephone Codes, Prowords and Abbreviations

List of Radiotelegraph 'X' Codes

The Signals marked "A" are in possession of Aircraft
* Not used by Navy or Royal Air Force.   # Other Source, NOT in the B.R.266/1941.
Indicators – (NOT part of signal) ^ 1918, @ 1926, % 1931, ¶ 1941.

X Codes become a QUESTION when preceded by the "Interrogative" X112.
X Codes become NEGATIVE when preceded by "Negative" X114

SIGNAL		MEANING
X463	%	Am handing over W/T guard (on ….. Kc/s) (Messages have not been cleared to ……..)
X464	@	What …… are you (or is ……..) using.
X465	%	Am handing over W/T guard (on ….. Kc/s). Originators and/or series numbers of last messages read are ……..
X467	%	Am prepared to take over W/T guard (on …….. Kc/s)
X469	%	Am W/T guard for …….. (on ……. Kc/s)

TYPES AND OFFICES (1926) @

X470	@	Main (office)
X471	@	Second (office)
X471	%	Answers to message(s) …….. have not yet been received from ……..
X472	@	Third (office)
X473	@	Auxiliary (office)
X473	%	Have taken over stand-by guard on …….. Kc/s (at ……)
X474	@	Direction finding (office)
X475	@	Emergency set.
X475	%	Have (or …….. has) taken over W/T guard on …… Kc/s (at …….)
X476	@	Type No. or Set.
X477	@	Remote control.
X477	%	Clear traffic on guard wave (or on …… Kc/s) (for ………)

W/T GUARDS and DUTIES. (1941) ¶

X478	¶	Act as W/T link between me and .... (or .... and ....)
X479	%	Control …… to answer message which you have just retransmitted on your guard wave (or message ………)
X481	%	Denote the stations for which you are W/T guard (or are you W/T guard for ……..?)

APPARATUS (1926) @

X482	@	Aerial.
X483	@	Jury aerial.
X483	%	Retransmit this message (or message …..) (to …….) on your guard wave.
X484	@	Aerial amperes.
X485	@	Amplifier(s)
X485	%	Transfer messages for ……. to W/T guard on …….. Kc/s (or to ……..)
X486	@	Anode Volts.
X487	@	Generator.
X487	%	Act as W/T link between me and ……… (or between …….. and ……..)
X488	@	Plug position.
X488	¶	Answer(s) to message(s) has/have not yet been received from …..
X489	@	Receiving model ……. (if a multivalve model the number of valves in use to be stated).
X489	%	Close down (reopen at ……..)
X490	@	Coupling.
X490	¶	Assume W/T organisation .... forthwith (or at ...)
X491	@	Frequency.
X491	%	Closing down (now or at …….)
X492	@	Stream electrodes.
X493	@	Key (Magnetic key).
A X493	%	Closing down owing to electrical storms; will call immediately reception is possible (or at …….)
X494	@	Transmitting apparatus.
X494	¶	Close down (re-open at ....)
X495	@	Receiving apparatus.
X495	%	Have (or has …….) set watch (on …… Kc/s) (on …….. Set or office)

Radiotelegraph and Radiotelephone Codes, Prowords and Abbreviations

List of Radiotelegraph 'X' Codes

The Signals marked "A" are in possession of Aircraft
* Not used by Navy or Royal Air Force.   # Other Source, NOT in the B.R.266/1941.
Indicators – (NOT part of signal) ^ 1918,   @ 1926,   % 1931,   ¶ 1941.

X Codes become a QUESTION when preceded by the "Interrogative" X112.
X Codes become NEGATIVE when preceded by "Negative" X114

SIGNAL	MEANING
A X496 ¶	Closing down now (or at ....)
A X497 %	…….. is in W/T company.
A X498 ¶	Closing down due to electrical storms; will call immediately reception is possible (or at ...)
A X499 %	…….. is not keeping W/T watch.

SIGNALLING SYSTEMS (1926) @

X501 @	Low power (buzzer)
A X501 %	Keep continuous W/T watch until further notice.
A X502 @	Power.
A X503 @	C.W.
A X503 %	Listen out for messages from ……… (on …….. Kc/s)
X504 @	Valve.
X505 @	Arc.
X505 %	Remote control on ……. Kc/s is to be manned now (or at …….)
A X506 @	I.C.W.
X507 @	Spark.
X507 %	Resume normal W/T watch.
X508 @	Quenched spark.
A X509 @	R/T.
X509 %	Set watch (on …….. Kc/s) (on …… set or office)
X510 @	S/T (Sound Telegraphy)
A X511 @	V/S (Visual)
X511 %	This station (or ……) listens out on normal frequency (or on …… Kc/s) between ….. and ……
X512 @	Telephone.

INTERFERENCE AND OPERATING (1931) %

X512 %	Competent operator is to take operator of the watch.
X513 @	L/T.
A X513 ¶	Keep continuous W/T watch until further notice.
X514 @	Electrode signalling.
X514 %	Indicate the name of the operator of the watch (at ………)
X515 @	S/W (short wave).
X516 @	High frequency.
X516 %	Indicate the name of the W/T rating in charge of watch (or of ……. Office)
X517 @	Low frequency.
X518 @	Supersonic.
X418 %	Interference by the enemy (call sign ……) is deliberate.
X519 @	Automatic.
X520 %	Interference by ……… is apparently deliberate.
A X522*%	Interference is being experienced from local noises.
X523 ¶	Resume normal W/T watch.

EXERCISES (1926) @

A X524 @	W/T exercise (Number ….) will be carried out now (or at ……..)
X524 %	Interference is being caused (in ……) by your receiver.
X525 @	W/T exercise for regular operators will be carried out now (or at …….)
X526 @	W/T exercise for operators under training will be carried out now (or at ……..)
X526 %	Junior operator is taking over watch.
X527 @	Ready for fire control exercise.
A X528 @	Dummy run denoted by letter (or number) following will start now.
X528 %	Junior operator is to take operator of the watch (during exercise No. ……..)
A X529 @	Dummy run will now cease.

Radiotelegraph and Radiotelephone Codes, Prowords and Abbreviations

List of Radiotelegraph 'X' Codes
The Signals marked "A" are in possession of Aircraft
* Not used by Navy or Royal Air Force.   # Other Source, NOT in the B.R.266/1941.
Indicators – (NOT part of signal) ^1918, @ 1926, % 1931, ¶ 1941.

X Codes become a QUESTION when preceded by the "Interrogative" X112.
X Codes become NEGATIVE when preceded by "Negative" X114

SIGNAL	MEANING
A X530 @	W/T exercise will now cease.
A X530*%	Listen out before transmitting. You are causing unnecessary interference.
X531 @	Only message on hand is a test message. Shall I proceed to transmit it?
X532* %	Make call signs more distinctly.
X534* %	Make separative signs distinctly.
X536 %	Operator is to pay more attention.
A X538*%	"Q" was made to you by me (or by ......) during my last transmission.

FREQUENCY.(1941) ¶

A X538 ¶	Am about to shift receiver to frequency No. ....
X540*%	Send faster.
A X540 ¶	Am about to transmit on frequency No. ....
X542*%	Send more slowly.
X544 %	Senior operator is to take operator of the watch (during exercise No. ....)
A X546 %	Who (or what) is interfering with you?
X548*%	Work duplex.
A X548 ¶	Shifting to normal frequencies (freq No. ...)
A X550 %	You are (or ...... is) causing interference by inattention to order to wait.
A X552 %	You are (or ...... is) causing interference (on .... Kc/s).
A X556*%	Your morse is bad (difficult to read).
A X556 ¶	Shift to normal frequencies (or freq. No. ...)
A X558*%	Your spacing is bad.
A X660*%	You were sending at the same time as this station (or as ....)

TELEGRAMS (1931) %

X562 %	Addressee (of message time of receipt ......) not on board (or unknown)
X563 %	Cable charge to .... (is .... pence per word)
A X563 ¶	Hear you best on frequency number ....
X564 %	Charge for excess words in prepaid reply is .... Pence.
X565 %	Charges on this private telegram have been prepaid.
X566 %	Coast station charge is not applicable to this message.
X567 %	Have ...... private telegram(s) awaiting transmission to ..... (country or office of destination). Request route.
X568 %	Number of words chargeable in message .... (from ......) is .....
X569 %	Open and signal contents of private telegram for ....
X570 %	Pass following cable by deferred rate.
X571 %	Pass following lettergram. (No of words charged for is ....)
X572 %	Pass following prepaid reply to telegram for ....
X573 %	Pass following private telegram. (No of words charged for is ....)
X574 %	Pass telegram ...... words.
X575 %	Pass telegram received for .... request instructions.

INTERFERENCE and OPERATING. (1941) ¶

A X575 ¶	Interference is being experienced from ......
X576 %	Reply paid.
X577 #	Retain private telegram unopened until arrival.
A X579 ¶	Listen-out before transmitting, You are causing unnecessary interference.

TUNING (1931) %

Radiotelegraph and Radiotelephone Codes, Prowords and Abbreviations

List of Radiotelegraph 'X' Codes

The Signals marked "A" are in possession of Aircraft

* Not used by Navy or Royal Air Force.   # Other Source, NOT in the B.R.266/1941.
Indicators – (NOT part of signal) ^ 1918, @ 1926, % 1931, ¶ 1941.

X Codes become a QUESTION when preceded by the "Interrogative" X112.
X Codes become NEGATIVE when preceded by "Negative" X114

SIGNAL	MEANING
A X581*%	Am about to send call sign on my present frequency (or on .... Kc/s)
X583 %	Am about to send call sign on my present frequency (or on .... Kc/s); obtain receiving adjustments and then tune your transmitter to the same frequency by listening in.
X585*%	Am I in tune (with ....) (on .... Kc/s)?
X587 %	Decrease frequency slightly. Transmit your call sign five times on new adjustment.
X589 %	Decrease frequency very slightly to clear interference.
X589 ¶	Send faster.
X591 %	Increase frequency slightly. Transmit your call sign five times on new adjustment.
X591 ¶	Send more slowly.
X593 %	Increase frequency very slightly to clear interference.
X595*	.... Is in tune with you (or with ....)
A X597 %	Please measure my frequency.
A X597 ¶	You are (or .... is) causing interference by inattention to order to wait.
A X599*%	Please send call sign on your present frequency (or on ...... Kc/s) for one minute, or until "Q" is received.

SPARE GROUPS FOR LOCAL ALLOCATION ONLY (1926) @

X600 @	
X600 #	Rude suggestion to poor operator. (Get stuffed).
X601 %	Send in alphabetical sequence of call signs. Each station is to make its call sign once (or ...... times)
A X603 %	Tune (......) in on Divisional (or Squadron) wave.
A X605 %	Tune (......) in on Sub-divisional wave.
A X606 ¶	You were sending at the same time as this station (or as .....)
X607 %	Tune .... To my frequency (or to .... Kc/s) by reception.

TUNING (1941) ¶

A X607 ¶	Am about to send my callsign on my present frequency.
X609 %	Tune your station (or ......) to .... Kc/s.
X611*%	Your crystal is not controlling.
A X613*%	Your (or ....) frequency appears to be correct.
A X615*%	Your (or ....) frequency appears to be .... Kc/s high.
A X617*%	Your (or ....) frequency appears to be .... Kc/s low.
X619*%	Your (or ....) frequency appears to have decreased.
X621*%	Your (or ....) frequency appears to have increased.
X623*%	Your (or ....) frequency changed during last transmission.
A X623 ¶	Please measure my frequency.
A X625*%	Your (or ....) frequency has changed since last transmission (or since ....)
X626 ¶	Please send callsign on your present frequency for one minute or until "Q" is received.
A X627*%	Your (or ....) frequency is ...... Kc/s.
A X629*%	Your (or ....) frequency is steady.

WAVES (1931) %

A X631 %	Am about to shift receiver to .... Kc/s.
A X633 %	Am about to transmit on .... Kc/s.
X634 ¶	Tune your transmitter to my frequency.
X635 %	Am (or .... Is) using .... kc/s.
X637 %	Have (or has ....) shifted receiver to .... Kc/s)
A X637 ¶	Your crystal (or master oscillator) does not appear to be controlling.
X639 %	Normal frequency of this station (or of ....) is .... Kc/s.
A X639 ¶	Your (or ....) frequency is correct.
A X641 %	Shifting (or .... is shifting .... apparatus) to normal frequencies (or ...... kc/s)

Radiotelegraph and Radiotelephone Codes, Prowords and Abbreviations

List of Radiotelegraph 'X' Codes
The Signals marked "A" are in possession of Aircraft
* Not used by Navy or Royal Air Force.   # Other Source, NOT in the B.R.266/1941.
Indicators – (NOT part of signal) ^ 1918,   @ 1926,   % 1931,   ¶ 1941.

X Codes become a QUESTION when preceded by the "Interrogative" X112.
X Codes become NEGATIVE when preceded by "Negative" X114

SIGNAL	MEANING
A X641 ¶	Your (or ....) frequency is .... kc/s high.
A X643 %	Shift receiver to .... Kc/s.
A X643 ¶	Your (or ....) frequency is .... kc/s low.
A X645 %	Shift to Divisional (or Squadron) wave (or note frequency).
X647 %	Shift to Flotilla wave.
A X649 %	Shift (........ apparatus) to normal frequency (or .... Kc/s).
A X651 %	Shift to Sub-divisional wave.
A X651 ¶	Your (or ....) frequency is steady.
A X653 %	Transmit on .... Kc/s, and receive on .... Kc/s.
X654 %	Use of W/T is permitted (on .... Kc/s) (between .... Kc/s and .... Kc/s).
A X655*%	What frequency are you (or is ....) using?
X656 %	Use of W/T (on .... Kc/s) (between .... Kc/s and .... Kc/s) is permitted between .... and .... G.M.T.

D/F (1931) %

Note.– P/L Geographical references or positions by latitude and longitude are NOT to be employed with these Signals in any naval operations.

X657 %	Bearing of station which answered message from ..... was ......, class ...... or its reciprocal at ....
X659 %	Bearing of station which answered message from ..... was ......, class ... , sense determined at....
X661 %	Bearing of unknown station transmitting on ..... Kc/s was ..... or its reciprocal.
X663 %	Bearing of unknown station transmitting on ..... Kc/s was ..... , sense determined at ....
A X665 %	Bearing of you (or of .....)† was ....., class ..... , or its reciprocal, from me (or from ....) at ....
A X667 %	Bearing of you (or of .....)† was ....., class ..... , sense determined, from me (or from ....) at ....
A X669 %	Bearing should be regarded as approximate only, owing to unfavourable circumstances.
A X671 %	Cannot determine bearing of (........)
A X673 %	Cannot plot your position. You are in line (or nearly in line) with D/F station's base line.
A X675 %	Commence revolving beacon transmissions now (or at .....).
X677 %	Endeavour to obtain a D/F bearing of station now transmitting (or of .....) (on ...... Kc/s).
A X679 %	Listen out on D/F on ..... Kc/s (or between .... and .... Kc/s).
X681 %	On what frequency was D/F bearing of .... obtained (at ....).
X683 %	Pass on D/F bearing (of ......) (obtained on ...... Kc/s, or between ...... and ...... Kc/s).
A X685 %	Ready to take your bearing (or bearing of ......) on my normal wave or on .... Kc/s.
A X687 %	Send your call sign for one minute on your present frequency (or on .... Kc/s) in order that a bearing may be obtained.
A X689 %	Signal bearing as determined approximately.
A X691 %	Stand by to determine my position (or position of ......) by means of the R/A method now (or at ..) The executive signal will follow.
A X693 %	Take bearing on rotating beacons.
A X695 %	Take bearing and plot position from rotating beacon.
A X697 %	My position by rotating beacon bearings is ....
A X699 %	Your distance was approximately .... miles from me (or from .....) at ....
A X701 %	Your signals are not sufficiently strong for good determination of bearing in present unfavourable circumstances.
A X703 %	Your position was ....., class ......, by cross bearings (from ...... and ......) at ....
A X705 %	What is my D/F bearing?
A X707 %	What is my latitude and longitude position by D/F cross bearings? (See note at head of section)
A X709 %	What is my position by D/F cross bearings by gridded map (or squared chart) method?
A X711 %	What is my position by D/F cross bearings from nearest landmark? (See note at head of section)
A X713 %	What is my position by D/F from station denoted?
A X715 %	When ready (or at ....) carry out the procedure to enable your position to be fixed by R/A method.

† The identity of the message of which the bearing was taken may be inserted if known.

Radiotelegraph and Radiotelephone Codes, Prowords and Abbreviations

List of Radiotelegraph 'X' Codes

The Signals marked "A" are in possession of Aircraft
* Not used by Navy or Royal Air Force.   # Other Source, NOT in the B.R.266/1941.
Indicators – (NOT part of signal) ^ 1918,   @ 1926,   % 1931,   ¶ 1941.

X Codes become a QUESTION when preceded by the "Interrogative" X112.
X Codes become NEGATIVE when preceded by "Negative" X114

SIGNAL	MEANING

X800 – X999 %
Next page.

X800 – X999 %
GROUPS FOR SEPARATE ALLOCATION AND INTERNAL USE ONLY IN THE NAVY, ARMY, AND AIR FORCE RESPECTIVELY (1931) %
    X800 – X899   … For use in Navy only.
    X900 – X999   … For use in Army only.
    X720 – X799   … For use in Air Force only.
Further information to complete this list would be appreciated.

The following British Army Manuals, or others are sought.

OU 5301 British W/T Operating Sigs. 1923.

Royal Sigs. Sig Training Vol 5. Sig Office Org And Procedure. 1938

Radiotelegraph and Radiotelephone Codes, Prowords and Abbreviations

List of Radiotelegraph 'X' Codes

The Signals marked "A" are in possession of Aircraft
* Not used by Navy or Royal Air Force.   # Other Source, NOT in the B.R.266/1941.
Indicators – (NOT part of signal) ^ 1918,   @ 1926,   % 1931,   ¶ 1941.

X Codes become a QUESTION when preceded by the "Interrogative" X112.
X Codes become NEGATIVE when preceded by "Negative" X114

SIGNAL   MEANING

Ground Signal Codes

The British Royal Air Force also used ground codes made to pass visual instructions to overflying aircraft. These were positioned close to the airfield Watch Office in a 40 feet (12.2 metre) square marked with a white border 1 foot (305 mm) wide.
These were made of the letter "T" of panels 8ft 6in x 1ft 4in (2.6 x 0.4 m) wide and discs 1'4" diameter. They indicated 3 figure numerals which then referred to a code manual.
There are about 300 signals plus 30 misc others in the manual I have (1943) -
"R.A.F. Signal Manual Part V. Ground Signal Codes (Provisional) 1940" Air Publication 1632
    Amended to 1943.

The layout of the "T" is -

The Panel Code

A ground to air visual code using panels 6 x 2 feet (1.83m x 610mm) incorporating those in Allied Communication Publication (ACP) 136(A) was later used.

These were/are also used in search and rescue situations. "Signal Training (All Arms) Pam 1, Signalling Codes Suppl.1 The Panel Code 1962".   Superseded ditto of 1953.

Both of these are too numerous and not truly applicable to list. Below are a few of the Panel Codes.

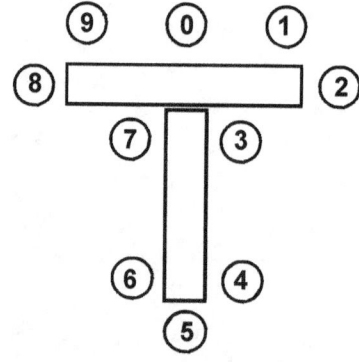

Radiotelegraph and Radiotelephone Codes, Prowords and Abbreviations

List of Military Data Transmission 'X'-Codes

These X-Codes are generally associated with "link 11" nets.
Like Q-Codes, X-Codes can be questions, commands or answers.

SIGNAL	MEANING
XAA	Transmitting primary set-up sync tone.
XAB	Synchronized with primary sync tone.
XAC	Transmitting secondary set-up sync tone.
XAD	Synchronized with secondary sync tone.
XAE	Transmitting net operations sync tone, sent by Net Control Stn (NCS).
XAF	Synchronized with net operations sync tone.
XAG	Sending data to NCS.
XAI	Synchronized for short reports with station...
XAJ	Mode 1 - transmitting mode 1 ping-pong.
	Mode 2 - transmitting mode 2 ping-pong.
	Mode 3 - transmitting mode 3 ping-pong.
XAO	Not receiving alligator data.
XAP	Receiving alligator data.
XAQ	
XAR	
XBG	Set transmitter power to maximum.
XBH	Set transmitter power to minimum.
XBL	Experiencing technical difficulties with equipment. Alligator
XBO	transmissions suspended for ...(specified time). Alligator
XBP	transmissions to recommence in ...(time specified). Mode 1 -
XBT	Mode 2 -
	Maintenance complete and ready to begin transmissions.
XBV	Transmissions stopped to carry out maintenance.
XBW	
XCB	
XCC	Change your track (track number) to my track (track number).
XCJ	Cease data transmission of track (track number).
XCK	Is your track showing my track number ...(track number)?
XCL	Identify all parameters on ...(track number).
XCP	Track full data dump transmission.
XDA	Off air for maintenance, (duration usually specified).
XDB	
XDD	Leave the net.
XJG	Transmit all available data on ...(track number).
XYI	Receiving a Mode 1 radar squawk code from track ...(track number).
XYO	I am not receiving your PU.
XYP	I am receiving your PU.

(This list is compiled from various sources, more info to complete it is requested..)

Early Line Repeater Relay c1865

Radiotelegraph and Radiotelephone Codes, Prowords and Abbreviations

Zogging

In the days of open cockpit aircraft and before inter-aircraft radio was commonly available this method was employed to communicate between aircraft.
The aircraft had to fly alongside or in easy visibility of each other.
It was also used during periods of operational radio silence.
Methods varied but Morse Code signals were sent by hand / arm movements.
A short, quick movement indicated a 'dit', a longer movement indicated a 'dash'.
Used from the early days of flying through WW2.

Method described in –
"Communications Handbook" US Navy 1944
From J. Elwood, WW7P, - MM66

The Signalling Disc or Shutter.

This ingenious device is described in the British 'Training Manual, Signalling (Provisional) 1915'

"The signalling disc consists of a wooden board fitted on the back with a handle and on the front with a metal sheet, one half of which is moveable and forms a hinged flap, which can be opened by means of a small handle at the side.

Normally the hinged flap is kept closed by means of a spring, and the metal sheet is painted so that when the hinged flap is opened, a white surface is exposed and when it is closed only black is visible.

This instrument is designed for use by a man kneeling or lying under cover, the large handle is grasped in the left hand and the base of the wooden board is rested on the ground. Signals are made by the Morse code, the hinged flap opened so as to expose the white surface for a long or short space.

It is important that the flap should always be opened fully so that it bears against the rubber stud on the lower part of the board, and for this reason signalling with this instrument must be slow and deliberate."

Signal Training (All Arms) 1938. – (**Note** – Not the 'Shutter' used with the Heliograph or Heliostat.)
"The shutter is useful for Morse signalling over short distances in the forward area.
 It is very portable and inconspicuous; trained signallers require very little practice to operate it."

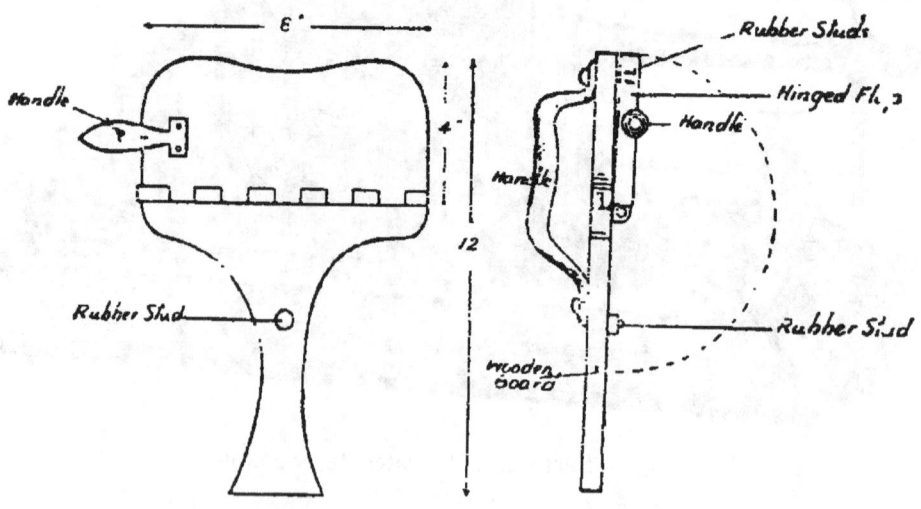

Radiotelegraph and Radiotelephone Codes, Prowords and Abbreviations

Parlez-vous Américain ? Anglais ?

American and British phraseology is slightly different.
Here is a comparative list of some of the most common ones used in WW2 service signalling.

	American		**British**
	Change		Amendment
	Cryptographed		Encoded or Encyphered
	Dispatch		Message
	GCT		GMT
	Information addressee		An addressee to whom a message is "repeated".
	Message blank		Message form
	Message centre (Army)		Signal Office (Army)
	Messages sent in strings		Batch working
	Net		Group or net
	Parenthesis		Bracket
	Period		Full stop
Prosign	**Precedence**	**Prosign**	**Priority**
Not used		OU	Most immediate
Not used		OA	Emergency enemy aircraft
O	Urgent	O	Emergency
OP	Operational priority	OP	Immediate
P R	Priority	P	Important
D	Routine	R	(No name)
	Deferred	D	Deferred
	Prosign		Procedure signal
	Quotation marks		Inverted commas
	"R" or receipt method		Direct method
	Radiotelegraph		W/T
	Radio telephone		R/T
	Slant		Oblique stroke

Types of Messages

There are two types -

1. **Plaindress -**   (address outside of the text)
   - (a) Normal (full) form
   - (b) Abbreviated form
   - (c) Procedure

2. **Codress -**   (address concealed in the text)

Radiotelegraph and Radiotelephone Codes, Prowords and Abbreviations

Summerland Amateur Radio Club
Combined Radiotelegraph Abbreviations List

References - 1896, 1902, 1907, 1912, 1917, 1924, 1933, 1942, 1956, 1960, 1972, 1979, 1985, 1987, 1995
Including 1975 listings from ITU, Geneva.

Common Abbreviations / Prosigns.

=	Equals or Double Dash - Seperates preamble, address, text, signature in radiotelegram. (1908)
?	Acknowledgment break in long message. Reply – last word +? (IWTC 1906)
+	Cross (end of transmission) 1908 also known as AR
	Stop. End of word. Not understand. (1837)
!	I will transmit on high power.
4	For.
4U	For you.
33	Signature greeting between YL operators. Orig. 1939 USA.
51	?? Latin America.
55	I wish you good success. (Sign off, esp. German and contacting stations.)
66	God bless you.
71	Sign off used by US ops working with less than one Watt transmit power.
72	Sign off used by US ops working with less than 5 Watts transmit power.
72	Wishing you a good QRP. Russian U-QRP Club.
77	Greetings. German Awards interest groups.
2U	To you.
2WD	Two Wheel Drive
4WD	Four Wheel Drive
A	Ampere. General Answer on Semaphore. Arrived. At.
A	Service telegrams or advices with urgent transmission and delivery.
B	More to follow, Byte. Bulletins and Train Register Station. Be.
B	Telegrams by Morse and sound reading devices when direct working.
B	Have you received my message?
C	Correct, Yes, Concur, Can, See, Celsius. Cents. Coaling station.
D	Diode. Important (Message Priority, 1936 >). Pence. Day telegraph station. Depart.
E	Understand. (1837) I do not understand (1878)
E	Voltage. Fraction line. East.
F	Flag station stop.
F	I am disabled; communicate with me. Am on fire, want immediate assistance.
F	Do not answer, Make no further Signals, Frequency, Farad, Farenheit.
F	FOX "F prosign" USN WW2+ Cypher broadcast to the Fleet(s), copied by all, not replied to.
G	Go on, Repeat back, Read back, Gram.
H	Move higher up or further back. (1896)
H	Henry. (unit of inductance), Hour.
H	Keep out of my way because I cannot keep out of yours.
I	Current. "Aye" (Yes)
J	Verify with originator and repeat back, Verify, Joule.
K	Standard clock, bulletins and train order station.
K	Go ahead, Invitation to transmit. over. Kelvin, Kilobyte. O'clock.
K	You should stop your ship immediately.
L	Move to left. (1896). Leave.
L	Lambert, Inductance, Stop, I have something important to send.
M	Mega. Metre
N	Negative reply to Q and Z signals; Not approved.
N	No. Night telegraph station. 9 (as in RST report) North.
O	Move closer or lower down. (1896). Of.
O	Immediate. Emergency (Precedence indicator, 1936 >).
O	Man overboard.
P	Priority (To 1936) Immediate (1936 >)
P	Private Telegram, Message prefix, Priority, Telephone.
P	Your lights are out or burning badly. Power.
P	Repeated or fig. 0 repeated - Stop your transmission.
Q	Wait. Figure of merit, (tuned circuit) Reactance. Resistance ratio.
R	Wait (1837, 1878)
R	Are, All right, OK. Receipt, Routine, Roger, Romeo, Received OK. Our. Decimal point

Radiotelegraph and Radiotelephone Codes, Prowords and Abbreviations

Combined Radiotelegraph Abbreviations List

R   The way is off my ship, you may feel your way past me.   Resistance.   For.
S   Public message. (1878)
S   Signal Service. (UK message priority. To 1936)
S   Regular station stop.   Siemens, Switch.   Second   South.
T   I understand. (1878) after each word received.
T   Telephone.   The.   Zero.
T   i. General answer on Morse.
       ii. Signal to show that a message is for retransmission.
T   Transmit to, Relay to, OK after each plain language word received.
U   You, You are standing into danger.
V   Volt, Require assistance; remain by me;   From (Navy).   From (German)
W   Go on.   Decimal point. (1837)
W   Water station.   West.
W   Word or Words, Unable to read Your message,   Have encountered ice.   Watt.
W   i. Your signals are too weak.
       ii. Used as a Procedure signal meaning "repeated" if word appears
          in the "address to" space of the message. (1936>)
X   Train will be held until order is complete.   Crossover between main tracks.
X   Interference.   Reactance.   Acknowledge.
Y   'Wye' (a Y shaped junction for turning locos) at this station.
Y   Crystal.
Z   Blocks on/off - before and after letters sent in capitals. (1896)
Z   i. Used in the "offer" of a message, showing that it is for delivery.
       ii. Used in the "address" of a message, showing that the following is a list of addresses for action.
          (c1940).
Z   Flash (highest message Priority Precedence, 1987). Impedance.   UTC time zone.

AA   Unknown station. (repeated until station responds)
AA   All after (after ? requests a repetition).
AA   Linking sign - Following letters sent separately but linked.
AB   All Before. (After ? requests a repetition).
AC   Alternating current.   Aircraft carrier flag.   Alto cumulus (Met.)
AD   Ahead,   I must abandon my vessel.
AE   I must abandon my vessel.
AF   Audio Frequency,   Affirmative flag,   Africa.,   Inverted Commas
AG   Adjutant General
AH   Ampere hour.
AI
AJ
AK
AL   All that has just been sent. (After ? requests a repetition).
AM   Amplitude Modulation.   Morning.
AN   Answer.   Answering Pendant.
AO
AP   Aeroplane flag.
AQ
AR   End of transmission, Out, Out to You, (From the American Morse for FN = Finish)
AR   Arrival Report.
AS   Wait.   Account Sales.   Alto stratus (Met.)
AT   Astern.
AU   Fractions follow.
AV   Arrive.
AW   Auf wiedersehn (German) - see you later.
AY   Any.
AZ   Azimuth.

B4   Before
BB   Blue burgee.
BC   Block clear.   Broadcast.   Battle cruiser flag.
BD   Bad, Buenos dias (Spanish) - good day (sunrise until midday).   Board.
BF   Blue flag (Navy).   Before.
BF   Aircraft is ditched in position indicated and requires immediate assistance.

Radiotelegraph and Radiotelephone Codes, Prowords and Abbreviations

Combined Radiotelegraph Abbreviations List

BG	Bearing.
BI	By.
BK	Break, Black flag. Back.
BL	Blue Pendant, above/before compass code = alter course to ......
BL	Bill(s) of Lading.
BM	Bulletin Manager.
BN	All between..... and ..... (after ? requests a repetition).
BN	Been.
BP	Black Pendant (Navy).
BQ	Announcement of reply to a request for rectification (RQ).
BS	Battleship flag.
BT	i. Long break, End of message text, Battery, Blue Pendant.
	ii. Before the "originator's number" in a cipher message.
BT	But.
BU	Bushel.
BW	Bandwidth.
BX	Squared brackets.
B4	Before.
CB	Callbook. Citizen's Band.
CB	I require immediate assistance. Citizens Band (Radio). Cumulo nimbus (Met.)
CB6	I require immediate assistance. I am on fire.
CC	Cipher groups follow. Put before and after cipher groups. (1896). Cirro cumulus (Met.)
CD	Communications Dept. (USA), ARRL Hq, Civil Defence.
CG	You should alight as near to me as possible.
CH	Church Pendant.
CI	Come in. Cirrus (Met.)
CK	Check. Figure check to follow.
CL	Call, calling, called, closing (station).
CM	Communications Manager. Complete. Came. Come.
CN	Can. Seen.
CO	Corpen (Navy). Course. Commanding Officer. Company. Care of.
CP	I am proceeding to your assistance.
CP	General call to two or more specified stations.
CQ	General call, all/any station. Call to two or more stations on circuit. Give me switch for ...(BR)
CR	Cruiser flag. Credit.Creditor. Confirmation of Delivery.
CS	Call sign, Call letters. Central Standard Time (US)
CS	Call signal (to be used to ask repetition of a call signal). Cirro stratus (Met.)
CT	Cannot. Compass Pendant, Commencing Traffic (also known as KA) Cent.
CT	Call to a known station for traffic. (IWTC 1906)
CU	See you. Cumulus (Met.)
CW	Continuous Wave, Clockwise,
CX	Capital letter (also in lower case).
CY	Copy message. Copy.
DA	Da, Yes (Russian). Day.
DB	I can't give you a bearing, you're not in my calibrated sector.
DC	The minimum of your signal is suitable for the bearing, Direct Current
DD	Position Pendant. Did. Double Deck.
DE	From.
DE	(Ger.) Deutsche Empfangsstation German receiving station.
DF	Direct line free. (1915)
DF	Your bearing at ... hrs was .... deg. Doubtful sector, error of two degrees.
DF	Direction finder. You are in communication with the called subscriber.
DG	Danger message. (Priority 1878).
DG	Advise if you note an error in the bearing given.
DH	Dead head, service message, Free or franked message.
DI	Bearing doubtful because of the bad quality of your signal.
DJ	Bearing doubtful because of interference.
DK	(Ger.) Danke - Thank you
DL	Your bearing at ... Hrs was ... deg, in the doubtful sector of this station.
DN	Down. Repeat when sending.
DO	Bearing doubtful, Ask for another later (or at ...)

Radiotelegraph and Radiotelephone Codes, Prowords and Abbreviations

Combined Radiotelegraph Abbreviations List

DP   Beyond 50 miles, possibly error can attain two degrees.
DR   Dear.   Destroyer flag.   Debit.   Doctor.   Debtor.
DS   Dispatcher.   Day's sight.
DS   Drop shutter or turn off light from your heliograph. It does not obscure. (1896)
DS   Adjust your tranmitter, your minimum signal is too broad.
DS   Danke schon (German) - Thanks.
DT   Do not.   Can't give bearing,   Your minimum signal is too broad.
DU   Hyphen.
DV   Division (Navy).
DX   Distance, Long distance, DuPlex.   Dash.
DX   I am sinking.
DY   This station is bilateral, give approx direction relative to here.
DZ   Your bearing is reciprocal.

E5   Note code.
EA   Each.
EB
ED   Your distress signals are understood.
EE   Unofficial sign off acknowlegement, WW2 service ops. Errors excepted.
EG   Emergency Coordinator.
EH   ?.
EL   Element.   Repeat the distress position.
EM   Empty.   Them.
ER   Here.
ES   And. (From the American Morse for '&' ....).   Yes.
ES   Eastern Standard Time (US)
ET   Yet.
EU   Europe.
EX   Extra train without schedule.   Express.   Excuse.
EX   Fraction separative sign (to separate a whole number from a fraction),   Express
EZ   Easy.

FA   Fanny Adams (colloquial - nothing, nil).
FB   Fine business, Excellent.
FD   Field day,   Feed,   Food.
FF   Figures finished. (1896)
FI   Numerals follow (1878), Numeral Pendant.,   Decimal Point.
FL   Filter,   Flag sign (Navy).
FM   From, Frequency modulation.
FN   (American Morse = AR International Morse) Finish, End of Transmission.
FO   Field Officer
FQ   Frequency.
FR   For,   Form (Navy),   Formation (Navy),   From
FS   First substitute (Navy).   Reforwarding at sender's request.   Fracto-stratus (Met.)
FT   Flotilla (Navy).   Foot   Fort
FU   Few.
FY   Fishery flag..

GA   Go ahead,   Resume sending.   Good Afternoon.
GA   (Ger.) Guten Abend   - Good evening.
GB   Good bye.   Close down.
GC
GD   Guard Pendants   Good day,   Good,   Guide (Navy).
GE   Good evening.
GG   Going.
GL   Good Luck. Good
GM   morning. Gone,
GN   Good night.
GP   Ground Plane, Group (word).   Poste restante delivery.
GQ   Begin new line of text. (BR)
GR   i.   Preceeds figures of a Group count.
        ii.   Separative signal.

Radiotelegraph and Radiotelephone Codes, Prowords and Abbreviations

Combined Radiotelegraph Abbreviations List

	iii. Full stop (c1940).
GS	Green Stamp. Guess.
GT	Got, Get.
GV	Give.
GW	Equal speed Pendant. Ground wire. Good Work Good Wishes.

H	Figures follow / Figure Shift (1837)
HA	Laughter. Hurry answer.
HD	Had.
HE	My ship is practically stopped but turning to starboard.
HF	High Frequency < 3-30 MHz. Half.
HH	Heil Hitler. Obligatory salutation for German ops. 1933-45. Since defunct.
HI	Laughter, from the HO of American Morse. High.
HI	My ship is practically stopped but turning to port.
HM	Him, Silence sign. (1932) Home.
HO	Horary Pendant. Laughter, American Morse.
HP	High Power, Horsepower
HQ	Headquarters. How are your signals? (1915)
HR	Here, hear, hour. Horary Pendant (Navy).
HS	Has.
HT	High tension.
HV	Have. I have collided with surface craft.
HW	How.
HX	Hyphen. Handling instructions.
HZ	Hertz (unit of frequency)

I5	Small letter or lower case.
IC	I see.
ID	Identification.
IE	Clear? That is. Request Signal Report (OE in American Morse)
IF	Figures end (1878). Intermediate Frequency.
ii	Separative sign.
IM	Him, I'm, Intermodulation.
IQ	Not through. (As – Not connected) or Switch circuit occupied.
IX	Execute to follow.
IX +(five second dash)   Executive signal.
IX	I have received serious damage in collision.

Jx	Period of retention of radiotelegrams at land stations. x = No. of days.
JA	Japan.
JJ	Amusement or laughter.
JM	If I may send, make series of dashes. To stop me, make series of dots.
JP	Justice of the Peace.
JR	Junior.

Kx	x copies in addition to the first to be delivered to addressee.
KA	Beginning of transmission. (formal)
KA	My vessel is very seriously damaged.
KC	Kilo cycle.
KD	Knocked down.
KG	Kilogram.
KK, KK	Message sent using words twice procedure. Receiver not to acknowledge, security risk. (1896)
KK	Brackets (to be signalled before and after the words concerned).
KM	Kilometre.
KN	Addressed station only transmit, Left hand bracket.
KO	Colon.
KP	Despatch to the sender of a print from the received film.
KQ	Colon quotation. Are you ready? Say when ready. (1915)
KT	Have you a line firing apparatus?
KV	Kilo volt.
KW	Know. Kilowatt.
KX	Colon dash.

Radiotelegraph and Radiotelephone Codes, Prowords and Abbreviations

Combined Radiotelegraph Abbreviations List

LB   Pound.
LC   Addressee left city.
LF   Low Frequency (30-300 KHz
LL   Land line.   Your signals are too strong (light, heliograph).
LO   Bearing Pendant.   Low.
LP   Long Path.
LQ   Wait while I am attending to counter or other instruments.
LR   Acknowledgement of receipt given at the request of the sending operator.
LS   Place for a Seal.
LT   Low tension.   Lieutenant.   Letter Telegrams.
LV   Leave.
LW   Long wave,   "Lone Wolf" (independent DXer).   Long Wire.
LX   English Pound Sterling £.   De luxe form.

MA   Milliampere.   May.
MD   Made. Month's date.
ME   Greenwich Mean Time. (1915)
MG   Motor-generator,   Emergency (Navy).
MF   Medium Frequency (300-3000 KHz).
MH   Move higher or further away (light or heliograph).
MI   My, Mile.
MK   Make, Mark.
ML   Mail.   Move left as you face me (visual signalling).
MM   Paragraph.   Code Pendant,   Millimetre,   Fraction Sign.
MN   Minute or minutes.   Preceeds the numerator of a fraction.   Exclamation mark.   Main.
MO   i. Master oscillator,   More, Moment.
       ii. Move lower or closer (visual signalling).
MP   Personal delivery.
MQ   Wait engaged. (1915)
MR   Move right as you face me (visual signalling).   Mister.   More.
MS   Message   Meteor scatter.   Month's sight.   Mountain Standard Time (US)
MT   Empty.
MX   Merry Christmas.

NA   Send KK, KK message, enemy in vicinity not safe to answer. or sun will be clouded soon. (1896)
NA   I can make no further signals.
NA   Correspondence with this subscriber is not admitted.
NA BK   Correspondence with this telegraph office is not admitted. I cut off.
NB   None Between.   Note Bene (Note Well).
NC   No connection, Normally closed,   I am in distress and require immediate assistance.
ND   Nothing doing.
NE   Nyet (Not) (Russian).
NF   Noise figure.
NF   Niederfrequenz (Ger.)   - Audio frequency.
NG   No good.
NH   Nothing heard.   Not at home.
NL   Noise limiter.
NM   No more.   Deferred (Precedence indicator)
NN   No more messages coming.,   Noon.
NO   Normally open, Negative flag,   Know, Number, Negative.
NO   But (Russian).
NP   Called party is not / no longer a subscriber. Called number not / no longer in use.
NR   Number, Near.   No record.   Indicate call number.
NS   No display of train order signal.   (ns) Nanosecond.   Nimbo stratus (Met.)
NT   Not.
NU   New. Knew.
NV   No value.
NW   I resume transmission,   Now. North West.
NX   Notice to Mariners / ... follows

OiiA   Emergency air attack (Message Precedence 1936>).

Radiotelegraph and Radiotelephone Codes, Prowords and Abbreviations

Combined Radiotelegraph Abbreviations List

OB	Old Boy, Official broadcast.
OC	Old chap. Flash (Precedence indicator). Officer Commanding.
OD	Outside diameter.
OE	Preparative flag. (American Morse = Request Signal Report. Often as IE International.)
OK	We are in agreement, White Pendant. All correct (US oll korrekt, 1840)
OL	Old lady. Optional flag. Open light. Ocean Letter.
OL	Heave to, or I will open fire on you.
OM	Old man.
OO	Official Observer.
OP	Operator. Optional flag. Operational immediate (Precedence indicator).
OR	Owner's risk.
OS	Train Order Sheet - a position report. On Schedule. Out of Station.
OS	Yellow Pendant, Colon. Union Jack in Navy List ident. (1896)
OT	Oscillation transformer, Old timer, Old top. On Time. Out.
OiiU	Most immediate (Message Precedence c1940).
OW	Old woman.
PA	Power amplifier. Pay. Per annum.
PC	Percent. Request for confirmation of delivery.
PD	Paid, Period.
PF	(pF) Picofarad.
PJ	Pilot jack.
PH	Phone, Phone number.
PM	Post Meridian Afternoon.
PN	Start parenthesis. Phase modulation.
PH	Position.
PO	Port., Post Office.
PP	Submarine port flag, Preparative. Descent through cloud.
PQ	End of message. (on some companies (BR), on others it was a very rude insult standing for 'Piss Quick'.)
PR	Pair. Position Report. Registered post delivery.
PS	Pacific Standard Time (US).
PT	R. Navy call for an unknown station.
PT	Address group or Callsign follows, point. Pendant sign (Navy). President. Pint.
PW	
PX	Boomer operator asking for the price of a meal. Press (newspaper). Prefix.
PY	End parenthesis.
QJ	End Quotation.
QK	Quick
QN	Start Quotation. Question.
QT	Quart.
QR	Quarter.
QX	Quotation within quotes. Apostrophe.
RA	Royal Artillery.
RB	Red burgee.
RC	Rag chew.
RD	When all corrections have been correctly received. (1896)
RD	Acknowledgment (1915) Read (copy), Red.
RE	Concerning. Royal Engineers.
RF	Radio frequency, Red flag (Navy). Relief.
RI	Radio Inspector.
RJ	Relief operator called so regular operator has a break.
RM	Route manager, Room.
RM	Retransmission of radiotelegram by one or two mobile stations at sender's request. (Relay)
RP	Regimental Police.
RPx	Prepaid reply. (x = amount in gold francs [1975])
RQ	After a Q-code, converts it to a question.
RQ	Correction required. Request for rectification (of error etc). Indication of request.
RR	Repeat (1860), Quotation mark. Railroad, Inverted commas.
RT	Right (1878), Radio telephony.
RU	Who are you? Are you.

Radiotelegraph and Radiotelephone Codes, Prowords and Abbreviations

Combined Radiotelegraph Abbreviations List

RW   Railway.
RX   Receiver. (Receptor – Sp.)
RY   Crew have mutinied.   Railway.

SA   Say.
SA   Announcement of name of aircraft station.
SB   Single sideband.
SC   What is the name of your ship ?   Strato cumulus (Met.)
SD   Signal displayed adding an R or Y as required.   Stop displayed.   Said.   Single deck.
SF   Announcement of name of aeronautic station.
SG   Signature.
SG fifty - Sent in long messages after every fifty words to assist counting and costing. (1896)
SI   Semicolan.
SK   Clear. End of contact or communication. (From the American Morse for 30 = End of Shift)
SK   Silent Key (Died).
SL   See you later.   Shall
SM   Some.   Submarine flag (Navy).   Same.
SN   Announcement of name of a coast station, Soon, Seen, Signal/noise.
SN   Station (Navy).
SN   Understood
SP   Important message   (Priority 1878)
SP   Short Path, Speed (Navy).   Silence Period - 3 min each 30 mins for emerg. traffic.
SP   Sailing Plan Report.   Semaphore.
SQ   End of message, another to follow.(BR)   Send quicker.   Squadron (Navy).
SR   Use the "send replies" Procedure.   Sir.
SS   Send slower.   Announcement of name of a ship station, Sweepstakes, Solid state.
SS   Second substitute (Navy).   Steamship.   Superstructure.
ST   Starboard.   Use the "straight through" Procedure.   Street.   Saint.   Paid service advice.
ST   Stratus (Met.)
SU   I'll see You.
SV   Sub-division (Navy).
SW   Short wave,   Switch.
SX   Simplex.   Dollar.

TA   Train Report (1878).   Technical advisor.
TC   Thermo couple.   Tierce.   Collation (complete repetition at sender's request).
TE   Tierce.
TF   Tariff.
TFx   Telephone delivery (x = telephone number).
TG   Telegram. (plus NR = telegram number given by sending office)
TI   Daily time signal. (1915)
TK   Take.
TL   Tack line (Navy).
TMx   Multiple addresses (x = number of addresses).
TN   Then.
TO   Action addressee(s) designator(s) follows.
TQ   Am I through?
TR   Announcement relative to the position of a mobile station. Prefix to the reply.
TR   Transit, Position, There, Transmit/receive.   Their.   Telegraph restant delivery.   Troop.
TS   Third substitute (Navy).   This.
TT   Fraction Bar (1908)
TT   That.
TU   Thank you,   Turn (Navy).
TU   Tu (Spanish) you - tu is familiar between friends. (See UD)
TV   Television.
TX   Transmit, Transmission, Transmitter, (Transmisor – Sp.)
TY   Territory.   They.

UA   You agree ?   Are we in agreement?
UD   You would, Repeat sign.
UD   Usted (Spanish) - You – usted is formal greeting, tu is familiar between friends
UJ   Underline.

Radiotelegraph and Radiotelephone Codes, Prowords and Abbreviations

Combined Radiotelegraph Abbreviations List

UK	Underline or block letters (before and after the words concerned).
UK	United Kingdom.
UL	You will.
UM	Signifies a grunt.
UN	Union flag.
UO	Negative silence signal.
UP	Upward.
UQ	Attend other circuit. (1915)
UR	Your, You're. You are.
UT	English Shillings. Fraction line. Diagonal.
UT	Church Pendant (Navy), Universal time, GMT, "Zebra / Zulu" time.
UV	Ultraviolet.
UX	Underline.
VA	i. Signing off (same as SK).
	ii. Separates messages sent to different stations in one transmission.
VE	End of message. (1896)
VE	Commencing sign, Repeated = General call. Message for you.
VL	Viel. (Ger.) - Much.
VP	Vice President.
VR	Voltage regulator.
VS	Versus.
VT	Vacuum tube.
VU	Volume unit. Dollar sign ($)
VX	Vieux (French) - Old
VY	Very.
WA	Word after (after ? to request repetition). Way.
WB	Word before (after ? to request repetition). Way bill.
WD	Would, Word.
WF	Word following., Use large white flag.
WG	Oblique Pendant.
WH	White.
WI	Why. Will. With.
WK	Weak, Week, Work.
WL	Will, Would. Well.
WN	When.
WO	Who.
WQ	I am in the middle of a message. (1878)
WR	Were. Where.
WS	Was.
WS	You should steer more to port.
WT	Wireless telegraphy, What. White. Weight.
WT	You should steer more to starboard.
WW	Wire wound.
WX	Weather, Weather report.
WZ	You should stop your vessel immediately.
XE	Oblique stroke. Fraction bar.
XO	Crystal oscillator.
XP	Paid express delivery.
XQ	Prefix indicating communication in the fixed service. Service notes.
XS	Atmospherics.
XX	Army or land party wishes to signal to navy ship. (1896)
XX	Submarine starboard flag.
YD	Yard.
YF	Wife.
YL	Young lady, Yellow Pendant (Navy).
YQ	Two or more stations. (1915)
YR	Year, Your.
YS	See your service advice.

Radiotelegraph and Radiotelephone Codes, Prowords and Abbreviations

Combined Radiotelegraph Abbreviations List

YZ	The words that follow are in plain language.
ZI	Zone of Interior (continental USA).
ZM	Weather report. (1915)
ZQ	Attend to switch. (1915)
ZT	Artillery Code Signal equivalent to verbal "Over" (1936>)
ZZ	"ZZ" Landing Procedure.
1HN	One hundred.
AAA	i. Fullstop. (1878) (Changed to iii - Amendt. 3, Feb 1936. Brit. Sig. Training (All Arms))
	ii. Break signal before "originator's no." in plain message. 1938 Now - Fullstop
AAG	Assistant Adjutant General.
ABL	Able.
ABT	About.
ABV	.Use International Abbreviations. or Repeat figures abbreviated
ADC	Aerodrome control.
ADG	Service telegrams or advices about serious interruption of telecommunication routes.
ADM	Admiral
ADR	Address (after ? to request repetition).
ADS	Address.
ADV	Advise.
ADZ	Advise.
AGN	Again.
AGT	Agent.
AHD	Ahead.
AHR	Another.
AIR	Relative to air.
AKA	Also Known As.
ALT	Radio air letter.
AMP	Ampere.
AMT	Amount.
ANH	Congestion.
ANI	Any.
ANR	Another.
ANS	Answer.
ANT	Antenna.
APP	Appreciate. Approach control.
APR	April. After (time or place).
ARQ	Automatic repeat request.
ARS	Amateur radio station.
ART	Alright.
ASC	Army Service Corps. I am ascending (to an altitude of …….. (height)).
ATC	The control referred to is Air (Sea) Traffic Control or Area Control.
ATP	At …….. (time or place).
AUF	Inverted Commas.
AVA	Before.
AVE	Avenue.
AVL	Arrival.
BAL	Balance.
BAT	Battery. Battery (Artillery)
BBL	Barrel.
BCI	Broadcast interference.
BCL	Broadcast Listener.
BCP	Beaucoup (French) - Many.
BDA	Birthday.
BDE	Brigade.
BDR	Brigadier.
BDY	Body.
BFO	Beat frequency oscillator.
BGL	Blasgodaru (Russian) - Thank you.
BIZ	Business.

Radiotelegraph and Radiotelephone Codes, Prowords and Abbreviations

Combined Radiotelegraph Abbreviations List

BJO	Bon jour (French) - Good day.
BJR	Bonjour (French) - Good day.
BKG	Breaking.
BKR	Breaker, Circuit breaker.
BLK	Black. Block.
BLV	Believe.
BND	Bound.
BOT	Bought.
BPF	Band Pass filter.
BPL	Brass pounder's league.
BPM	Buchstaben pro Minute (Ger.) - Letters per minute.
BRG	Bearing.
BRK	Break. Brake.
BRL	Barrel.
BSR	Bon soir (French) - good evening.
BTH	Both.
BTN	Between.
BTR	Better.
BTU	Back to you.
BTW	By The Way.
BUG	Vibroplex key, any auto CW key.
BUK	Book.
BWS	Bothways
C&E	Conductor and Engineer.
C&W	Coal and water.
CAF	Cancel and file our/your .....
CAV	Cavalry.
CBA	Callbook address.
CCC	Keep straight ahead.
CCT	Circuit.
CCW	Coherent CW.
CDX	Conditions.
CEN	Degrees Centigrade.
CFM	Confirm or I confirm.
CFO	Cancel Former Order.
CHF	Chief.
CHG	Charge.
CIF	Cost, Insurance and Freight.
CKT	Circuit.
CLA	Class of telegram.
CLD	Called. Could.
CLG	Calling.
CLK	Clerk.
CLR	Clear.
CMG	Coming.
CND	Commercial News Department.
CNT	Cannot.
COD	Collect on delivery.
COL	Collect, Collate or I collate. Colonel.
COM	Complete message.
COS	Because.
COY	Company.
COW	.... wagons attached to the front of train ...... (BR)
COZ	Because.
CPI	Copy.
CPO	Chief Petty Officer
CQD	Distress signal, Marconi Coy. 1904, superseded by SOS in 1906 but remained in use to 1912+.
CRA	Commander Royal Artillery
CRD	Card.
CRE	Commander Royal Engineers.
CRV	Do you / did I receive well ? How do you receive ?

Radiotelegraph and Radiotelephone Codes, Prowords and Abbreviations

Combined Radiotelegraph Abbreviations List

CSO	Chief Staff Officer
CTA	Communication of all addresses. Control area.
CTR	Control zone.
CUD	Could.
CUL	See you later.
CUM	Come.
CUZ	Because.
CWT	Hundredweight (112 lbs).
CXS	Cents.
CYS	Cycles.
DAG	Deputy Adjutant General.
DBL	Double.
DBT	Doubt.
DCN	Direction.
DCT	Direct.
DDD	Silence signal. All stations cease sending.
DDD	Identifies transmission of distress message by station not itself in distress.
DEB	Overflow position.
DEC	Decrease. December.
DES	I am descending (to an altitude of …….. (height)).
DET	Detector.
DEM	(Ger.) Deutscher Empfangsmeister- German receiving champion. Democrat.
DFS	Disregard former service.
DFT	Draft.
DIF	Different, Difference.
DIR	Direction.
DIV	Division.
DLD	Delivered.
DLY	Delivery.
DMI	Don't mention it.
DNT	Do not.
DOT	Decimal point.
DOZ	Dozen.
DPE	Dope, Information.
DPR	Day press rate.
DSB	Double sideband.
DSV	Dosvidaniya (Russian) - Good bye - (English DSW)
DSW	See you again. (Russian).
DTE	Date of handing in.
DUP	Duplicate.
DWN	Down.
EEE	Error signal.
EEK	OK
EHF	Extremely high frequency, (30-300 GHz)
EHT	Extremely high tension.
ELF	Extremely low frequency.
ELS	Elements.
EME	Earth-moon-earth (moonbounce).
EMF	Electromotive force.
EMI	Electromagnetic interference.
EMP	Electromagnetic pulse.
ENG	Engine. England.
ENI	Any.
ERB	Landing off a runway is permitted.
ERE	Here.
ERP	Effective radiated power.
E/S	Echo sounder.
ESB	(Ger.) Einseitenband - Single sideband.
ESQ	Esquire.
ESR	Yes Sir.

Radiotelegraph and Radiotelephone Codes, Prowords and Abbreviations

Combined Radiotelegraph Abbreviations List

ETA	Estimated time of arrival.
ETD	Estimated time of departure.
ETI	The information is estimated.
EVE	Evening.
EVY	Every.
EXA	Extra.
FAH	Degrees Fahrenheit.
FAX	Facsimile.
FEB	February.
FER	For.
FET	Field effect transistor.
FGA	Free of general average.
FIG	Figures.
FLD	Field, Filed.
FNA	Final approach.
FNI	Funny.
FOB	Free on board.
FOT	Units of the British system.
FPA	Free of particular average.
FRM	From.
FRT	Freight.
FSD	Full scale deflection.
FSK	Frequency shift keying.
FSR	Flight safety region.
FVR	Favour.
FVS	Fives.
FWD	Forward.
FYI	For your information.
GAA	Go ahead arrival.
GAD	Go ahead departure.
GBA	Give better address. General Baggage Agent.
GCA	Ground controlled approach.
GDO	Grid or gate dip oscillator.
GEN	General.
GEO	Geographic or true.
GES	Guess.
GFA	General Freight Agent.
GHZ	(GHz) Gigahertz (1000 MHz)
GLD	Glad.
GMT	Greenwich Mean Time. (now UTC)
GND	Ground. Relative to ground.
GNG	Going.
GOC	General Officer Commanding.
GOV	Governor.
GPA	General Passenger Agent.
GPM	Good afternoon.
GPO	General Post Office.
GPR	Registered poste restante delivery.
GQA	Get Quick Answer.
GRA	Gracias, (Spanish) thanks.
GRN	Grain.
GRS	Groups. Gracias, (Spanish) thanks.
GRT	Great.
GSA	Give some address.
GTD	Guaranteed.
GTH	Go to hell (1912)
GUD	Good.
GVG	Giving.

Radiotelegraph and Radiotelephone Codes, Prowords and Abbreviations

Combined Radiotelegraph Abbreviations List

HAM	Trainee or Student or poor operator (Railway Line Telegraphy, 19th Century)
HAM	Amateur, Brass pounder,
HDG	Heading, Antenna azimuth.
HDW	Hardware.
HED	He would.
HEE	Laughter, usually sent twice. HEE HEE
HHD	Hogshead (locomotive engineer).
HLO	Hello.
HLV	Hasta la vista (Spanish) See you later.
HMH	Unofficial Exclamation Mark (CW) postwar marine.
HND	Hundred.
HON	Honourable.
HPE	Hope.
HPG	Hoping.
HPI	Happy.
HPL	Hospital.
HPN	Happen.
HRD	Heard.
HRG	Hearing.
HRS	Hours.
HVG	Having.
HVI	Heavy
HVY	Heavy.
HWS	How is.
HX...	ARRL message handling instructions.
HXA(Followed by number)   Collect delivery within .... miles.
HXB("   ")   Cancel message if not delivered in .... hours.
HXC	Report date/time of delivery to originating station.
HXD	Report ID of receiving station, relay station, date/time, method of delivery.
HXE	Get reply from addressee and send back.
HXF(Followed by number)   Hold delivery until .... date.
HWS	How is.
HW?	How did you copy?
IAR	Intersection of air route.
ICW	i. Interrupted Carrier Wave.
	ii. Message must be encoded if liable to enemy interception. (1936).
IFR	Instrument flight rules.
IFT	Information.
III	Full stop, (1896) (R Navy 1935) (Brit. Army 1936> Written as 'dot in circle')
ILS	Instrument landing system.
IMA	Capitalise or underline
IMD	Intermodulation distortion.
IMI	Say again.
IMO	In my opinion.
IMP	Important.
INA	Initial approach.
INC	Incorporated. Increase.
IND	Answer-back code. Indiana. Indian.
INF	Subscriber temporarily unobtainable, call the information service. Infantry. Below.
INP	If not possible.
INQ	Position specialising in the handling of service notes and advices.
INS	Insurance. Inches.
INT	? Interrogative, Converts a statement into a question. e.g. INT HRD. And with Z-codes.
INV	Invoice.
IRC	International reply coupon. = One Gold Franc in 1961, One US Dollar in 1996
IRL	Intersection of range legs.
ISS	
ITL	Intelligence.
ITP	The punctuation counts.
ITO	International Telegraph Office.
IVB	If forward visibility below ....

Radiotelegraph and Radiotelephone Codes, Prowords and Abbreviations

Combined Radiotelegraph Abbreviations List

IVR	If forward flight visibility remains ……...
JAN	January.
JCT	Junction.
JFE	Office closed because of holiday.
JJJ	Report Immediate Indicator. - Alert raised when vessel is over 6 hours late reporting position.
KMH	Kilometres per Hour.
KNW	Know.
KPH	Kilometres per Hour.
KTS	Nautical Miles per Hour (Knots).
LBR	(Ger.) Lieber - Love (best wishes?) Lumber.
LDS	Loads.
LID	"Lid", a poor operator.
LIS	Licensed.
LKG	Looking.
LLL	Turn left.
LMO	Proceed to ....
LNG	Long.
LOC	Local.
LOL	
LOS	Line of Sight.
LRN	Learn.
LSB	Lower sideband.
LSN	Listen.
LTD	Limited.
LTF	Government letter telegrams.
LTR	Later, Letter.
LUK	Look.
LUP	Loop.
LVG	Leaving.
MAG	Magazine. Magnetic.
MAJ	Major. Majority.
MAR	March.
MBS	Millibars.
MCH	March. Much.
MCI	Merci (French) - thanks.
MCS	Megacycles.
MDS	Multipoint distribution, Minimum discernible (or detectable) signal.
MER	Height above sea level.
MET	Meteorological.
MFG	Manufacturing.
MFR	Manufacturer.
MGR	Manager.
MHZ	Megahertz.
MIA	Instrument Approach (SCS51/CAA).
MIL	Milliampere.
MIM	Comma. Will increase power after 30 seconds.
MIN	Minute, Minimum.
MIX	Mixer.
MKD	Marked.
MKR	Marker Radio Beacon.
MKT	Market.
MLG	Mailing.
MLN	Million.
MLS	Miles.
MMM	Seperates No. of words sent and No. of words charged for, if different. (1908)
MNG	Morning, Meaning.
MNI	Many.
MNL	Manual.

Radiotelegraph and Radiotelephone Codes, Prowords and Abbreviations

Combined Radiotelegraph Abbreviations List

MNS	Minutes.
MNY	Many.
MOD	Modulator.
MOM	Moment. Wait. Please wait. Waiting.
MOS	Months.
MPH	Statute Miles per Hour.
MRS	Misses. Mistress
MRU	Much Regret Unable (RN)
MSC	Medical Staff Corps.
MSG	Message.
MSK	Mistake.
MST	Mistake.
MTR	Matter.
MTU	Metric Units.
MUF	Maximum useable frequency.
MUT	Mutilated.
MYN	Million.
NCH	Subscriber's number changed. Number changed.
NCO	Non Commissioned Officer.
NCS	Net Control Station.
NDB	Nondirectional Radio Beacon.
NET	A group of stations operating together.
NET	Nyet (Russian) No .
NFD	National Field Day.
NIL	Nothing.
NLM	Nautical miles.
NLR	Lazy, "Nil".
NNN	Semicolon.
NOS	Knows. Numbers.
NOV	November.
NPR	Night press rate.
NSA	No such address.
NSL	Na Shledanou (Czeck / Slovak) Good Bye, CUAGN
NSN	No such number.
NSS	No such street.
NTG	Nothing.
NVR	Never.
OBS	Meteorological telegrams.
OBT	Obedient.
OCC	Subscriber is engaged. Busy.
OCT	October.
O/D	Telegraph office of destination.
OFF	Officer.
OFS	Office.
OMN	Omnirange.
O/O	Office of handing in.
OOK	On-off keying
OOO	Per mill (thousand)
OOO	Cease traffic, clear the line, very urgent message to follow. (1896)
OPC	The control indicated is Operational Control.
OPG	Operating.
OPN	Operation. Opinion.
OPR	Operator.
ORD	Order.
ORS	Official relay station.
OSD	Ordnance Store Dept.
OSO	Percent sign.
OTD	Overseas Telecommunications Division.
OTR	Other.

Radiotelegraph and Radiotelephone Codes, Prowords and Abbreviations

Combined Radiotelegraph Abbreviations List

PAM	The pleasure is all mine.
PAV	Airmail delivery. (Fr. Par Avion)
PBL	Preamble (after ? to request repetition), Probable.
PDC	Pure DC, Clean note.
PEO	People.
PEP	Peak envelope power.
PEV	Peak envelope voltage.
PFD	Preferred.
PKG	Package, Parking.
PKS	Pecks.
PIV	Peak inverse voltage.
PLS	Please.
PMO	Principal Medical Officer.
PPL	People.
PPR	Paper.
PRO	Prohibition. Public Relations Officer.
PSE	Please. Pleased.
PSD	Position.
PSN	Pointed.
PTD	Private.
PTE	Pointing.
PTG	Procedure turn.
PTN	
PTO	Permeability tuned oscillator.
PTR	
PTT	Press to talk.
PWR	Power.
	(See also Q-Codes)
QGA	May I transmit.
QHM	Tuning from high frequency to middle of band.
QLF	Try sending with left foot for a while. (Polite insult to a poor operator.)
QLM	Tuning from low frequency to middle of band.
QLZ	Operator too lazy.
QNH	Tuning from middle frequency to high frequency.
QMG	Quartermaster General.
QML	Tuning from middle frequency to low frequency.
QMN	Man made electrical noise.
QOK	Do you agree ?
QRP	Low Power, adapted from the Q Code.
QTN	Quotation.
RAB	Radio Beacon.
RAC	Rectified Alternating Current.
RAD	Glad (Russian). The control referred to is Radio Control.
RAP	Shall I call you again / back ?
RCA	Reach cruising altitude.
RCD	Received.
RCT	Telegrams concerning persons protected in time of war by the Geneva Conventions.
RDI	Ready.
RDO	Radio, Radio station.
RDY	Ready.
REB	Rebate.
RED	Submarine Contact, Port.
REF	Refers, refer to, referring to.
REG	Regular.
REL	Release.
REP	Marker beacon.
RFC	Radio frequency choke.
RFI	Radio frequency interference.
RGT	Regiment.
RIF	Reinforcements.

Radiotelegraph and Radiotelephone Codes, Prowords and Abbreviations

Combined Radiotelegraph Abbreviations List

RIG	Station equipment or set up.
RHA	Royal Horse Artillery.
RLF	Relief.
RMS	Root Mean Square.
RND	Round.
RNG	Radio range.
RPC	Request the Pleasure of your Company. (RN) Used to invite people to lunch/dinner.)
RPM	Revolutions per Minute.
RPT	Repeat, I repeat, Report.
RRR	Repeat. Turn right.
RST	Readability 1-5 Strength 1-9 Tone 1-9.
RST	Reply to paid service advices.
RTF	Radiotelephone Equipment. (Radio)
RTG	Radiotelegraphic Equipment. (Radio)
SAE	Self addressed envelope.
SAR	Search and Rescue.
SBA	Standard Beacon Approach. (British)
SBS	Send Baseball Scores.
SCM	Section Communications Manager.
SDG	Siding.
SEC	Second.
SED	Said.
SEK	Wait.
SEZ	Says.
SFB	Stay for breakfast.
SFD	Stay for dinner.
SFN	Stay for night.
SFO	See former order.
SFS	See former service.
SFT	Stay for tea.
SGD	Signed.
SGT	Sergeant.
SHD	Should.
SHF	Super high frequency (3-30 GHz)
SIA	Standard Instrument Approach.
SIG	Signature (after ? to request repetition). Signal.
SKN	Straight Key Net. No bugs or keyboards allowed.
SLD	Sledite (Russian) - Follow me (QSY?)
SLO	Slow.
SLT	Radiomaritime Letter. (Ship Letter Telegram)
SLX	A Slidex coded message follows
SM1	Someone.
SND	You have violated Russian borders. I demand that you leave Russian waters immediately. (Russia)
SNO	I demand that you leave Russian waters immediately. Unless you do so, a force of arms will be used against you. (Russian Navy)
SNO	Senior Naval Officer.
SNP	You are violating the regulations for navigating and remaining in Russian waters. I demand that you cease violations. (Russian Navy)
SNR	Despite warnings, you continue to violate the regulations for navigating and remaining in Russian waters. You are to leave them immediately. (Russian Navy)
SOE	Distress signal, (Ger), from which SOS was derived in 1906. Obsolete. General call. (Ger.) 1905
SOL	The altitude is given as height above official aerodrome level. (The abbreviation should only be used in the immediate vicinity of the aerodrome at which the aeroplane intends to land.)
SOS	Distress signal, adopted 1906.
SPK	Speak.
SPL	Special.
SPS	Spasibo (Russian) - Thanks.
SRI	Sorry.
SRS	See Our Service.
SSB	Single sideband.
SSN	Session.

Radiotelegraph and Radiotelephone Codes, Prowords and Abbreviations

Combined Radiotelegraph Abbreviations List

SSS	Finished (US 1860)	Oblique stroke. (1896)
STA	Stay. Station.	Straight-in-approach.
STK	Stock (Shares)	
STN	Station.	
STP	Stop.	
STR	Steamer.	
STX	Stock. (Shares)	
SUB	Subdivision.	
SUM	Some.	
SUN	Soon.	
SUP	Above.	
SUV	Sports Urban Vehicle. (Yuppie's 4WD)	
SVC	In-service or signals message.	
SVH	Telegrams relating to safety of life.	
SVL	Several.	
SVP	Please. (S'il vous plait - Fr.)	
SWL	Short wave listener.	
SWR	Standing wave ratio.	
SYS	Refer to your Service Telegram.	System.

TAX	What is the charge ? The charge is ....
TBL	Trouble.
TEL	Telegraph.
TFC	Traffic.
TFF	Tariff.
TFR	Transfer.
TFZ	Traffic zone.
THI	Time handed in. (Message handling procedure)
THO	Though.
THR	There, Their.
TIL	Until.
TIP	Until past .... (place).
TIS	Finishing prosign. (c1912)
TKS	Thanks.
TKU	Thank you.
TLK	Talk.
TMW	Tomorrow.
TND	Thousand.
TNG	Thing.
TNK	Think.
TNS	Tens.
TNX	Thanks.
TOD	Time of dispatch.
TOF	Try the other foot. (derogatory jibe)
TOL	Turn off extra light.
TOO	Time of origin.
TOR	Time of receipt.
TOV	Tovarich (Russian) - Comrade. (English TOW)
TOW	OM (Russian) Anglicised TOV Tovarich
TPA	Travelling Passenger Agent.
TPR	Teleprinter.
TRB	It is not necessary to keep to runways and taxiways after landing.
TRI	Try.
TRK	Track.
TRN	Train.
TRU	Through.
TRX	Transceiver.
TTS	That is.
TTT	Safety signal sent before meteorological warning ref navigation.
TTY	Teletypewriter.
TUF	Tough.
TUK	Took.
TVI	Television interference.

Radiotelegraph and Radiotelephone Codes, Prowords and Abbreviations

Combined Radiotelegraph Abbreviations List

TWX	Telegram.
TXT	Text.
UAB	Until advised by.
UFB	Ultra fine business.
UHF	Ultra high frequency. (300 MHz to 3 GHz)
UIX	Last month.
UKK	Underline
ULT	Ultimo.
UNG	Young.
URS	Yours.
USA	United States of America.
USB	Upper sideband.
UTC	Coordinated Universal Time, (formerly GMT)
VCO	Voltage controlled oscillator.
VFB	Very fine business.
VFO	Variable frequency oscillator.
VFR	Visual Flight Rules.
VHF	Very high frequency. (30 - 300 MHz)
VIA	Route to be followed. Via.
VIZ	Namely.
VJO	Viejo (Spanish) - Old man.
VLF	Very low frequency. (3 - 30 KHz)
VLN	(Ger.) Vielen - Many.
VOX	Voice operated switch.
VRI	Very.
VSA	By visual reference to the ground.
VVV	Commencement signal in Commercial use.
VXO	Variable crystal oscillator.
WAT	What.
WDS	Words.
WEA	Weather.
WEF	With effect from.
WHF	Wharf.
WID	With.
WKD	Worked.
WKG	Working.
WLD	Would.
WMP	With Much Pleasure. (RN)
WPM	Words per minute.
WRD	Word.
WRI	Worry.
WRK	Work.
WRU	Who is there ? Who are you?
WTB	Wanted to Buy.
WTG	Waiting.
WTR	Water. Weather.
WUD	Would.
WYE	Track junction, Y-shaped (delta) to enable turning around locos.
XIX	British warship or aircraft with message for British coastal station.
XMT	Exempt.
XNG	Crossing.
XTL	Crystal.
XTR	Transmitter.
XXX	Urgency signal, Urgent traffic that doesn't warrant using SOS.
XYL	Wife.
YDA	Yesterday.
YDS	Yards.

Radiotelegraph and Radiotelephone Codes, Prowords and Abbreviations

Combined Radiotelegraph Abbreviations List

YES	Yes.
YRS	Years.
ZDR	Zravstvuyte (Russian) - Hello
1TND	One thousand.
4MAN	Foreman.
ABBN	Abbreviation.
ACCT	Account.
ACCW	Alternating Current CW.
ACTN	Action.
ADRS	Address.
AFSK	Audio frequency shift keying.
AGFA	Assistant General Freight Agent.
AGPA	Assistant General Passenger Agent.
ALNG	Along.
ALRS	Admiralty List of Radio Signals.
AMTN	Ammunition.
ANUL	Delete.
AQMG	Assistant Quartermaster General.
ARTY	Artillery.
ASST	Assistant.
ATTN	Attention.
ATTY	Attorney.
AWDH	Auf Wiederhoeren (Ger.) - Until we hear (contact) again.
BABS	Beam Approach Beacon System.
BAGE	Baggage.
BAMS	Broadcast Allied Merchant Ships. WW2. Not replied to.
BATY	Battery.
BCNU	Be seeing You.
BECM	Became.
BIBI	Bye-Bye (Goodbye)
BLDG	Building.
BLNX	Blanks.
BLVD	Boulevard.
BRNG	Bearing, Heading.
BROT	Brought.
BTWN	Between.
BURO	Bureau, QSL bureau.
BUST	Destroy.
CANS	Headphones.
CAPE	Cancelled (BR)
CAPT	Captain.
CDNT	Couldn't.
CFMG	Confirming.
CHGS	Charges.
CLBK	Call book.
CLIX	Clicks.
CMUE	Communication.
CNDX	Conditions.
CNTI	County.
CNTY	County.
CNVN	Conventions
COLL	Collect.
COML	Commercial.
COMP	Complete.
CONN	Connection.
CORN	Correction.
CORP	Corporal.

Radiotelegraph and Radiotelephone Codes, Prowords and Abbreviations

Combined Radiotelegraph Abbreviations List

DAAG	Deputy Assistant Adjutant General.
DELY	Delivery.
DEPT	Department.
DETR	I am rerouting to .... / Re-route to ... / Alternative route ?
DIFF	Difference.
DINR	Dinner.
DIST	District.
DIVN	Division.
DLVD	Delivered.
DQMG	Deputy Quartermaster General.
DSNT	Doesn't.
DUPE	Duplicate quickly from origin or verify from sender, original not understood.
E&OE	Errors and omissions excepted.
EIRP	Effective isotropic radiated power.
ELEC	Election.
ENGR	Engineer.
ENUF	Enough.
ETAT	Government telegrams without request for priority.
ET AL	And others.
EXCN	Excursion train.
FFFF	Receiver not to reply or acknowledge until told by 'SR'. (Enemy intercept risk)
FILM	Delivery to the addressee of the negative film instead of the positive print.
FONE	Telephony.
FRCU	Fracto-cumulus. (Met.)
FREQ	Frequency, Frequently.
GENL	General.
GESS	Guess.
GOVT	Government.
GRNC	Groups not counted.
GTGS	Greetings.
GUFF	Gossip.
HVNT	Haven't.
IMMY	Immediately.
IMPT	Important.
INFO	Information.
INPT	Input.
IRPT	I repeat.
JOUR	Day delivery.
JUNC	Junction.
KLIX	Clicks..
KLVB	Que le vaya bien (Spanish) "That it goes well with you." Best Wishes.
LANG	Language.
LITE	Light.
MDSE	Merchandise.
MEMO	Memorandum.
MFLD	Manifold.
MFST	Manifest.
MILL	Milliampere. Typewriter as used by telegraphers, upper case only.
MILS	Milliamperes.
MITE	Might.
MNTU	My Number To You.
MSGR	Messenger.

Radiotelegraph and Radiotelephone Codes, Prowords and Abbreviations

Combined Radiotelegraph Abbreviations List

MSKN	Mistaken.
MULT	Multiplier.
NBFM	Narrow band frequency modulation.
NECY	Necessary.
NERK	All ships this broadcast (USN – unofficial call used)
NILE	Special notice received. (BR) followed by NOT - Not received.
NITE	Night.
NNNN	Answering Pendant. R. Navy answering sign, answer to a call.
NOT R	Not received.
NUIT	Night delivery.
OHMS	On His/Her Majesty's Service.
OiiA	For Emergency Air Attack. (Feb 1936>. UK- RN, RAF)
OiiS	Emergency Signal Service. (To Feb 1936. UK)
OiiU	For Most Immediate. (Feb 1936>. UK)
OMTD	Omitted.
ONLI	Only.
OTOH	On the other hand.
PARA	Paragraph.
PAVR	Registered airmail delivery.
PAYT	Payment.
PBLI	Probably.
PITA	Pain in the arse. (derogatory) nuisance, annoyance.
PONR	Point of no return
PPGN	Propagation.
PRCT	Precinct.
PRIN	Principal.
PROX	Next month.
PSBL	Possible.
PSGR	Passenger.
POSN	Position.
PUNK	Poor operator.
PYFO	Pull Your Finger Out. (Get with it, get going, do something – JWA)
QTHR	Address correct as per current Call Book.
QUAR	Quarter.
RATG	Radio Telegraphy.
RATT	Radio Teletype.
RCVD	Received.
RCVR	Receiver.
RECD	Received.
RECG	Receiving. Reclining.
RECR	Receiver.
RECT	Receipt. Correct please / I am correcting / correction ?
REFR	Refrigerator.
REGS	Regulations.
RELA	Relay.
REPN	Republican.
REPT	Repeat. Report.
RITE	Right.
RITO	Righto.
ROTE	Wrote.
RTTY	Radio teletype.
SASE	Self addressed stamped envelope.
SECN	Section train following. Section.
SECY	Secretary.
SEPT	September.
SHLD	Should.

Radiotelegraph and Radiotelephone Codes, Prowords and Abbreviations

Combined Radiotelegraph Abbreviations List

SHUD	Should.
SIGS	Signals.
SIMO	Simultaneously.
SINE	Give private or office signal.
SINE	Sign, Personal initials, Signature.
SITE	Sight.
SKED	Schedule.
SMTG	Something.
SMWR	Somewhere.
SMWT	Somewhat.
SOSO	Senior Ordnance Store Officer.
SPDT	Single pole double throw. (switch)
SPST	Single pole single throw. (switch)
SQDN	Squadron.
SSSS	Here ready for data transmission.
SSSS	Unofficial distress signal used early in WW2 but discarded. Under attack by submarine.
SUPR	Supper.
SUPT	Superintendent.
TEMP	Temperature.
TEST	Test. Contest.
THOT	Thought.
THRU	Through. You are in communication with a telex position.
TODA	Today.
TOMW	Tomorrow
TPLE	Triple word(s).
TRBL	Trouble.
TRIX	Tricks.
TTFN	Ta-Ta For Now. Jocular ending for message or traffic.
VERT	Vertical.
VSWR	Voltage standing wave ratio.
VTVM	Vacuum tube voltmeter.
WARC	World Administrative Radio Conference.
WILE	While.
WSEM	(Russian = "all") Means Russian contacts only during some contests.
XCVR	Transceiver.
XFMR	Transformer.
XMAS	Christmas.
XMTR	Transmitter.
XTAL	Crystal.
XVTR	Transverter.
YAPD	All stations this net. (USN – unofficial call used)

See also section on 5-Letter groups from the ITU 1975.

AAAAA	R. Navy erase signal.
AMVER	Automated Mutual-Assistance Vessel Rescue
ANNLD	Annulled.
ALWAS	Always.
ARFOT	Area Forecast code is being employed in English Units.
ARMET	Area Forecast code is being employed in Metric Units.
AYTNG	Anything.
BALUN	Balanced to unbalanced transformer.
BECUZ	Because.
BETWN	Between.
BRKMN	Brakeman.
CASHR	Cashier.
CLIMB	…… wagons attached in the middle of train …… (BR)

Radiotelegraph and Radiotelephone Codes, Prowords and Abbreviations

Combined Radiotelegraph Abbreviations List

CLOTH	...... wagons attached at the end of train ...... (BR)
COMBN	Combination.
COMSN	Commission.
CONDR	Conductor.
CONDX	Conditions.
CUAGN	See you again.
CUPLA	A couple of.
DAQMG	Deputy Assistant Quartermaster General.
DESPR	Despatcher.
DUNNO	I don't know.
DXPDN	Dxpedition.
ELECT	Election.
ENIHW	Anyhow.
EPIRB	Emergency Position Indicating Radio Beacon
FIVER	QSA - 5.
FONES	Telephones. Early description of Headphones.
FORGN	Foreign.
FOXES	Teleprinter test tapes.
GOTTA	I have got to, Have to, Must.
GREEN	Submarine Contact, Starboard.
HELIO	Heliograph.
HHGDS	Household goods.
KK KK	Message sent using words twice procedure. Receiver not to acknowledge, security risk. (1896)
LOTSA	Lots of.
MACHY	Machinery.
PASGR	Passenger.
PCTCS	Practices.
PHONE	Telephone.
PREST	President.
PRTBL	Portable.
PSBLI	Possibly.
RACON	Radar Beacon.
RECTS	Receipts.
ROAST	A great number.
ROFOT	Route or Flight Forecast code is being employed in English Units.
ROMET	Route or Flight Forecast code is being employed in Metric Units.
RRRRR	Receipt sign.
SENDG	Sending.
SERGT	Sergeant.
SINED	Signed.
SMTNG	Something.
SPOSE	Suppose.
TAMET	Terminal Forecast code is being employed in Metric Units.
TOGTR	Together.
TOFOT	Terminal Forecast code is being employed in English Units.
TRANS	Transmitter.
UNCHD	Unchanged.
UNDLD	Undelivered.
UNHRD	Unheard.

Radiotelegraph and Radiotelephone Codes, Prowords and Abbreviations

Combined Radiotelegraph Abbreviations List

UNLIS	Unlicensed
WATSA	What do you say ?
WILCO	Will comply with, do.
XXXXX	Error signal when using automatic error correction devices.
ZILCH	Nothing.
AA AA etc.	Call for unknown ship and general call. Continue until answered.
AAAAAA	Erase sign.
ABNDED	Abandoned.
AFTRNN	Afternoon.
ASCRTN	Ascertain.
AUSSIE	Australian amateur. (U.S.A. c 1933)
CALL NR	National call number of a Gentex office.
CANCEL	Cancel and File.
DER MOM	Bad reception, do not cut off, we are testing the line.
ECLAIR	Phototelegrams between stations with priority higher than urgent, but deliver as urgent.
ENIBDI	Anybody.
ESTRDA	Yesterday.
EXPRES	Express delivery.
GENTEX	International network (and service) with switching for the public telegraph service.
HDQTRS	Headquarters.
MANDAT	Money order telegrams and postal cheque telegrams.
MAYDAY	(Repeat 3 times) Radiotelephony distress signal. Equiv to SOS.
MEDICO	Ship without a Doctor seeking medical advice from another ship or shore station.
MOM PPR	Please wait! I have paper problem.
POSTXP	Despatch to destination by express post.
PRESSE	Press telegrams.
RPFR TM	Prepare your reperforator because of telegram with multiple addresses.
SSSDDD	Proposed distress signal (1903). Italy. Not adopted.
STRATE	Straight.
SUBFIX	We forward/submit subject to correction.
SUMBDI	Somebody.
TONITE	Tonight.
TREASR	Treasurer.
TRSMSN	Transmission.
TTTTTT etc.	Answering sign to AA AA. Continue until AA AA breaks.
UNCHGD	Unchanged.
UNDELD	Undelivered.
ZEDDER	New Zealand amateur. (U.S.A. 1933).
AURGENT	Service telegrams or advices with urgent transmission and delivery.
INSTMNT	Instrument.
INTERCO	International Code of Signals groups follow
LXDEUIL	De luxe form.
NNNNNNN	Answering sign.
PAN PAN	(Repeat 3 times) Radiotelephony Urgency signal. Equiv to XXX
RPFR TXT	Prepare your reperforator because of long or difficult text or telegrams having same text.
SUBSUNK	2nd part of automated SOS beacon indicating Submarine has sunk.
TEST MSG	Please send a test message.
EEEEEEEE	Error.
REMETTREx	Specified date of delivery. (x = date)
HM HM HM	Emergency silence imposed. Lifted by QUM.
AMPLIATION	Telegram sent a second time.

Radiotelegraph and Radiotelephone Codes, Prowords and Abbreviations

Combined Radiotelegraph Abbreviations List

CORRECTION	Cancel my last word or group, The correct word or group follows.
EEEEEEEE AR	Disregard this transmission.
EN CHIFFRES	Telegram the text of which contains only figures.
HMHMHMHMHM	Wireless silence imposed. (1938)
UOUOUOUOUO	Wireless silence lifted. Acknowledged by R. (1938)
TAXE PERCUE	Redirection charge collected.
ETATPRIORITE	Government telegrams with request for priority.
ETATPRIORITENATIONS	Telegrams relative to the application of provisions of the United Nations Charter.

Abbreviations for Months are as in the Phillips Code.
These lists are only partial and may contain errors.
Many abbreviations aren't all legally official but have been universally accepted through usage.
For the sake of space, a multitude of geographic abbreviations of places etc. for Canada, USA and Mexico have not been included. Neither have the usual abbreviations for days, months etc been included unless they were not the normal ones in daily use.
Please send additions or corrections to the Compiler. Thank you.

73, John Alcorn, VK2JWA. QTHR, Compiler. VK2JWA@sarc.org.au

Radiotelegraph and Radiotelephone Codes, Prowords and Abbreviations

Combined Radiotelegraph Abbreviations List

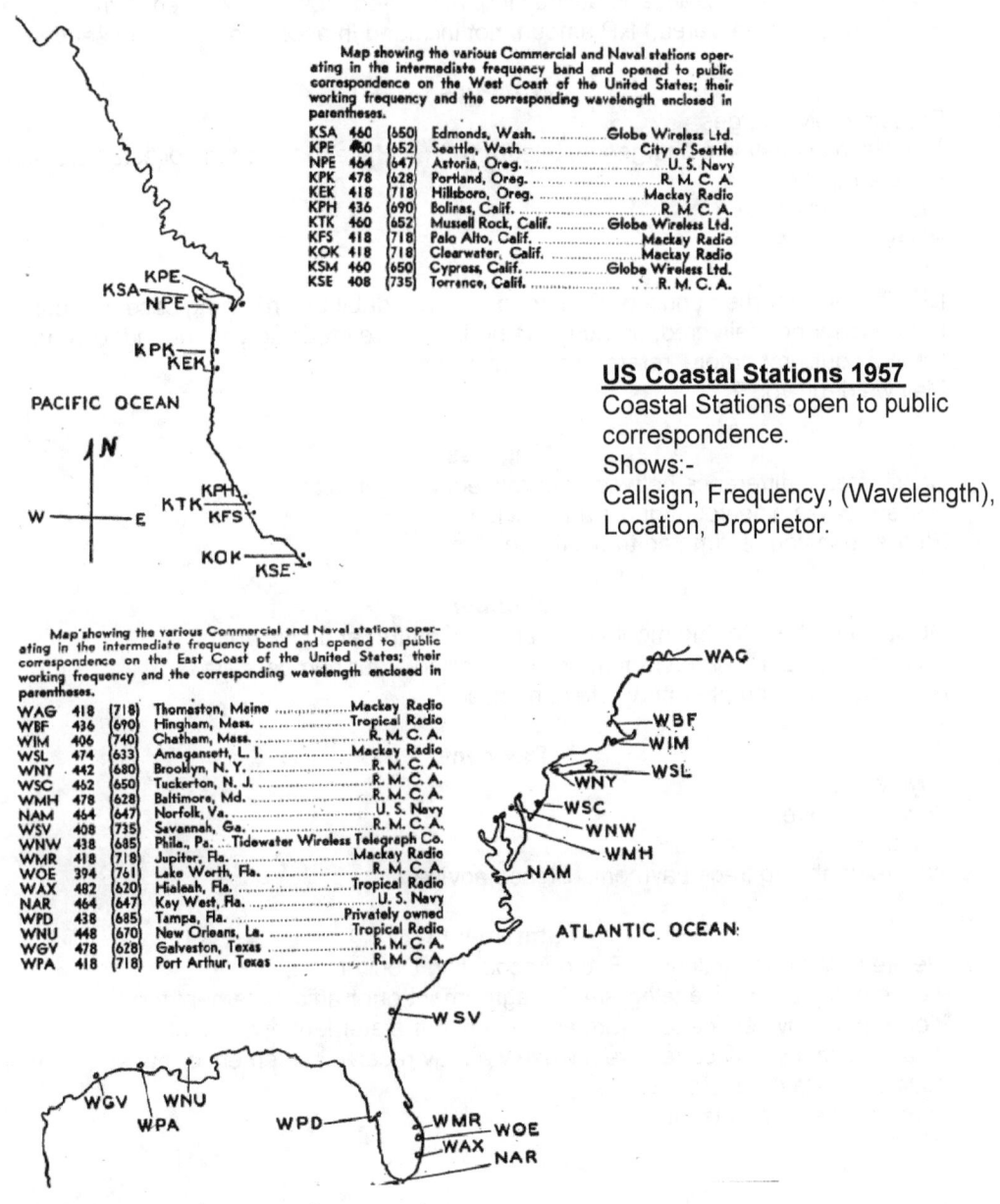

US Coastal Stations 1957
Coastal Stations open to public correspondence.
Shows:-
Callsign, Frequency, (Wavelength), Location, Proprietor.

Radiotelegraph and Radiotelephone Codes, Prowords and Abbreviations

Five Letter Code Groups - The ITU and C&W.
(Codes and Abbreviations for the use of the International Telecommunications Service - 1975)
of the C.C.I.T.T. and Cable & Wireless, not including the ICS of IMCO or the ICAO

Acceptance of Traffic

ABBAB	Can you accept traffic for .... ?
AGDEW	I cannot accept traffic for ....
AGGAS	I can accept traffic for ....
AGHUG	Traffic cannot be accepted by this route.
AKDOG	You may accept traffic for ....

Accounts

AKGAY	Account(s) payable by ....
AKHUM	Account(s) already on route to you.
AKKEY	Account(s) will be sent to you as soon as possible.
AKPEW	Account(s) debited in error. Please delete.
ALJAB	International Telephone Account.
ALKID	International Telex Account.
AMVEG	Please adjust your accounts as necessary.
APFIG	Traffic account for the month of ....
ARBEG	Your account has been debited with ....
ARDUG	Your account has been credited with ....
ARSOP	Your Radio Abstracts .... Please air copy (copies) in duplicate ....
AZWET	Cancel .... for abstract and accounting, misrouted, now reforwarded correct route.
PEDOT	RP Voucher not delivered, RP amount not included in accounts; refund to sender.

Charges

APCOB	Prepaid reply charges.
AKTUG	...... claims coast/ship charges on telegram ...... Have these been collected/credited to us?
APHAD	We are debiting you.
APJAM	We are crediting you.
APMOP	Please debit us.
APPOD	Please credit us.
PECAN	RP Voucher returned unused. Refund to sender, debit us, referring case number ....
PEFIN	RP Voucher not delivered, amount retained; We are crediting you, refund to sender.
PEHIS	Debit us our proportion, referring case number ....
PEZAC	May we debit you ?

Figures

ALBAT	Considerable difference between our respective figures on ....
AMPIP	Please re-examine your figures and advise.
AMSIN	Please rush your estimated traffic figures for ....

Numbers

AMCIS	Our last numbers for the month of ... are .... Confirm and give yours.
AMDOT	Your last numbers for the month of ... confirmed. Our numbers are ....
AMGET	Please give line number and date of message.

Payment

ALSEX	Payment is authorised.
AMBAY	Payment made.
ASBEN	We are arranging payment.
ASCOT	We are unable to trace payment. Please advise.

Statements

ALDON	We are missing the following Radio Accounting Dockets ....
AMHUT	Please notify by service telegram if in agreement our traffic statement for ....
AMKIT	Please notify by service telegram agreement our statement of account.
AMMOB	Please notify by service telegram when we may receive settlement of our statement for ....
ARFIN	Your .... statement for ....
ARPOM	Your traffic statements for ....

Radiotelegraph and Radiotelephone Codes, Prowords and Abbreviations

Five Letter Code Groups - The ITU and C&W.
(Codes and Abbreviations for the use of the International Telecommunicatiōns Service - 1975)
of the C.C.I.T.T. and Cable & Wireless, not including the ICS of IMCO or the ICAO

Addresses, addressees, destination, etc.
Address(es)

ASSUM	Cannot give better address.
ATFIX	Give full address.
ATHAS	State name and address of sender.
AXCUB	How will message be addressed ?
AXDAD	Repeat address per original copy.
AXJAY	Messages will be (are) addressed ....
AXTAB	Must be inserted in the address and charged for.
AYGUM	Please give address confirmed by sender.
AYTAG	Sender cannot give better address.
AYWEB	Sender claims good and sufficient address.
AZBIN	Sender's contact address is ....
MABAN	Sender insists message intended for ....
MAHVU	Your number ..... received addressed ...... If address on original differs notify immediately.
OLMAD	Address insufficient, we try delivery to ..... Correct if necessary.

Addresses (multiple)

AXNET	Multiple addresses (TMx) unallowed. Revise.
AZDAN	Your ... contains multiple addresses; we consider TM ..... Revise check.

Addressee / sender

ATJAW	Give name of addressee.
ATLAY	Give name of sender.
ATNED	Give names of sender and addressee.
AYDAM	Name of addressee in our copy reads ....
AYHAW	Read name of addressee ....
GAHIS	Please furnish complete address of addressee.

Telegraph office

ATBET	Destination correct, see List of Telegraph Offices.
ATCOW	Destination not in List of Telegraph Offices.
ATDAB	List of Telegraph Offices.
AYJET	Read telegraph office of destination as ....
NABRU	Telegraph office opened at ....
NEDIB	Place of destination incomplete, there are several. Advise.
NEMYD	Place of destination unknown; we forward to .... Correct if necessary.
WEJOD	Place of destination not in List of Telegraph Offices. Advise.

Administrations and Companies (1975 - ed.)

GAWOF	Associated Electrical Industries Ltd.
GEBAB	All America Cables and Radio Inc.
GEBID	American Telephone and Telegraph Company.
GEBRA	The Overseas Telecommunications Commission (Australia).
GEBYM	Régie des télégraphes et des téléphones de Belgique. (Belradio) (Belgium)
GEGUS	United Kingdom Post Office.
GEKAC	General Secretariat of the International Telecommunications Union. (ITU)
GEKFU	Cable and Wireless / Western Union International Inc.
GEKKO	Cable and Wireless (West Indies) Ltd.
GEKZA	Cable and Wireless (Mid-East) Ltd.
GELAY	Cable and Wireless.
GELIG	Canadian National Telecommunications.
GELOD	Canadian Pacific Telecommunications.
GELSU	Canadian Overseas Telecommunications Corporation.
GELXA	The Postmaster General and Director of Telecommunications. (Sri Lanka (Ceylon))
GEMAJ	The Director-General of Posts and Telegraphs, (Australia)
GEMVO	Direction générale des télécommunications. (France)
GEPAT	Compagnie français de câbles sous-marin et de radio. (France Câbles et Radio)
GEVMA	Companhia Portuguesa Rádio Marconi.
GEVYH	Raddiográfica Costarricanese S. A.

Radiotelegraph and Radiotelephone Codes, Prowords and Abbreviations

Five Letter Code Groups - The ITU and C&W.

(Codes and Abbreviations for the use of the International Telecommunications Service - 1975)
of the C.C.I.T.T. and Cable & Wireless, not including the ICS of IMCO or the ICAO

GIBCO	Commercial Cable Company.
GIFAP	Connecting Administration.
GIFID	Cyprus Telecommunications Authority.
GIFYM	Deutsch-Atlantische Telegraphengesellschaft.
GIGIS	Dirección General de Telecomunicaciones de México.
GIGRA	Swedish Telecommunications Administration.
GIGUC	Empresa Nacional de Telecomunicaciones S. A.
GIGYH	Director General of Telecommunications.
GIHOT	East African External Telecommunications Co., Ltd.
GIJAM	The Eastern Telecommunications Phillipines Inc. (ETP).
GIJEB	Eastern Telegraph Company Ltd.
GIJNO	Egyptian Telecommunications Administration.
GIJYD	Federal Republic of Germany, Telecommunications Administration.
GILEG	Great Northern Telegraph Company Ltd.
GIPAH	Overseas Telecommunications Service. (Sri Lanka (Ceylon))
GIPHO	Federal Communications Commission. (USA)
GIPLA	Ghana Department of Posts and Telecommunications.
GITAG	Italcable Servizi Cablografici, Radiotelegrafici e Radio-elettrici, Sociata per Azioni.
GIWEM	Director General Overseas Communications Service. (India)
GIWPO	Indian Telecommunications Administration.
GOBHU	Kokusai Denshin Denwa Co. Ltd.
GOBIB	Greek Telecommunications Administration.
GOBLO	German Democratic Republic, Telecommunications Administration.
GOBNE	ITT World Communications Ltd.
GOBYH	The Marconi International Marine Company Ltd.
GOCFU	Malaysian Telecommunications Administration.
GOCYC	Jamaica International Telecommunications Ltd. (Jamintel)
GODEG	Libyan Posts and Telecommunications Corporation.
GODHO	Netherlandes Antilles Government Radio and Telegraph Administration. (Landsradiodienst)
GODKA	Indonesian Telecommunications Administration.
GODOJ	Netherlands Telegraph Administration.
GODZU	Director General Post Office Headquarters. (New Zealand)
GOFDU	Nigerian External Telecommunications Ltd.
GOFEH	Official Representatives.
GOHUP	Press Wireless.
GOJJE	Radio-Austria A. G.
GOLIH	Radio Suisse, Société anonyme de télégraphie et téléphonie sans fil, Berne.
GOPAY	RCA Global Communications, Inc.
GOTAM	Radio Corporation of Cuba.
GOWON	Ras al Khaimah Telecommunications Authority. (RAKTA)
GOZAJ	Sharjah State Telecommunications Authority. (SSTA)
GOZDO	Sierra Leone Externat Telecommunications Ltd.
GOZOH	Société anonyme belge de câbles télégraphiques.
GUDIC	S.I.T.A., Société internationale de Télécommunications Aéronautiques.
GUDMO	O.G.E.R.O., ex-Société Radio-Orient.
GUDRA	Saudi Arabian Telecommunications Administration.
GUDUG	Sudan Government Department of Telecommunications.
GUDYG	South African Telecommunications Administration.
GUHHO	Trinidad and Tobago External Telecommunications Co. Ltd. (TEXTEL)
GUHMU	TRT Telecommunications Corporation.
GUJAR	Transradio Chilena, Compañia de Telecomunicaciones S. A.
GULDU	Radio Vaticana.
GULUV	West Coast of America telegraph Co. Ltd.
GULWE	Western Telegraph Company Ltd.
GUMAC	Western Union International, Inc.

Cancellations
Blanking

AZFOP	...... blank, diverted.
BACYS	Blank numbers ....

Radiotelegraph and Radiotelephone Codes, Prowords and Abbreviations

Five Letter Code Groups - The ITU and C&W.
(Codes and Abbreviations for the use of the International Telecommunications Service - 1975)
of the C.C.I.T.T. and Cable & Wireless, not including the ICS of IMCO or the ICAO

Cancellation

AZGUN	Cancel .... for abstract accounting purposes.
AZHAY	Cancel and file, sent in error.
AZJEW	Cancel, error of service.
AZKEG	Cancel our number ....
AZNIB	Cancel second message.
AZRED	Cancel, misrouted.
AZTAM	Connecting Administration / Company demands reason for cancelling.
AZWET	Cancel .... for abstract and accounting purposes, misrouted, now reforwarded correct route.
BABBA	Cancel at sender's request.
BABEC	Connecting Administration / Company informs message cancelled.
BABSO	Telegram (or service telegram / advice) number cancelled.
BADAW	Cancel and file and retain charges.
BADET	Give some reason for cancelling.
BADPO	Shall we cancel ?
JYGUS	Now cleared to ship. Cancel advice of non-delivery.
PASCA	Transmitted twice; cancel second transmission.
PYSAT	Delivered subsequently. Cancel advice of non-delivery.
CECAW	Actual number of words correct. Forward message and allow office of destination to notify by service advice office of origin concerning double words.
CEPAD	In our number ...... number of words .... correct.
CESAP	Wrong number of words .... actually received.
CIBAG	In your .... double; we check .... Confirm.
CODUN	Read number of words in .... as ....
COHOP	What is total number of words ?
COMAD	Your .... contains word counting evasions; we check ...... Confirm.

Circuit instructions (channels, routine repetition, collation, conditions, etc.)
BQs, RQs (replies, requests - ed.)

CYPAY	BQs all cleared. Advise any outstanding RQs.
CYSIN	BQs (or RQs) should be rushed, your signals becoming unreadable.
CYVOW	BQs required, following incomplete messages on hand ....
DABAY	BQs unobtainable in following messages .... Please attend.
DETNE	RQs arriving badly delayed, see .... message originally transmitted at ....
DETRU	RQs swamping us. What is reason, please ?
ROFUN	Your BQ makes no correction.
ROHUG	Your BQ unfinished, our RQ requests ....

Channels

DACOT	Can you utilise further channels ?
DAPEC	Further channel(s) not available at present.
DIWAY	Traffic conditions do not warrant additional channel(s). Please keep present outlet full.
OCJAG	Unable to transmit on ..... Advice will be forwarded via another route if direct comms unavailable.
OPBUN	... senders received advice by another route that msg undelivered. Investigate and reply quickly.

Circuit instructions

CUGIG	... and all subsequent messages on hand. Expect to be through shortly.
CUPAW	Are you checking by radio monitor ?
CYDAD	Be prepared to start .... immediately any trouble develops on ....
CYGIN	Please upstart .... dual with.
DACRU	Cease listening on ...., but keep set open for immediate reception when advised.
DACYZ	We are reading .... you may shut down .... and please upstart ....
DADAF	We are reading .... and you may shut down ....
DADIZ	We are reading .... and please upstart ....
DADNU	We are reading .... and please keep ..... on air.
DADRO	Listen to ...... and give go ahead for traffic as soon as possible.
DADXA	Cease listening on .... Acknowledge last received.
DADYC	Listen also for ...., congestion here.
DAGTU	Following traffic coming later ....
DAHPA	Circuit good only for .... words per minute. Do not request higher speed.

Radiotelegraph and Radiotelephone Codes, Prowords and Abbreviations

Five Letter Code Groups - The ITU and C&W.

(Codes and Abbreviations for the use of the International Telecommunications Service - 1975)
of the C.C.I.T.T. and Cable & Wireless, not including the ICS of IMCO or the ICAO

DALSO	.... dual with .... Observe and report.
DALUF	.... dual with .... Advise immediately you discontinue latter.
DALYJ	Adjust frequency of .... to correct allocation.
DAMAV	Total mark and space transmission of .... covering ...... Kc/s to .... Kc/s.
DAMLO	Advise frequency allocated to ....
DAMOC	Following transmitters running .... Advise which is best.
DAWAG	If communication lost, change over at ..... GMT.
DEBUM	Is .... available ? Can receive at ..... words per minute.
DEGOT	.... checks ZOA on allocation, no QRM observed here.
DEJAY	Nothing received from ..... since .... GMT. When do you expect to resume ?
DEMAT	Not working with customary speed.
DENTA	Please give our circuit preference, fading period approaching.
DEPEW	Listen now for ...... When you receive us there, discontinue listening on ....
DERSO	Observe .... and report readability.
DERZA	Please watch your speed and keep constant for both runs of ZST traffic.
DETBA	receiving nothing from ...., we listen for ......
DICOX	Shutting down.
DIDAW	Shutting down. Give last received and listen for ..... in .... minutes.
DIFIG	Shutting down till ...... GMT., we will transmit via .... Acknowledge.
DIHAF	Shutting down until traffic. Keep listening and transmit your traffic.
DILET	.... speed not up to normal. Can you improve ? Delay increasing.
DOCIR	.... unavailable. Continue listening for ....
DOCNO	.... unidentified owing to lack of callsign.
DOCUB	.... unreadable at present, will continue observe and advise later.
DOJEW	We will discontinue listening for ....., last received ....
DOLEG	..... GMT. We will now start ..... (c/s). Arrange to receive this station as soon as you hear it.
DONBO	When .... fades, listen for ....
DONNU	Will transmit from .... to .... on .... metres.
DUDAM	Your signals unreadable here. Situation .... Confirm via ....
DUDJU	Your station .... unheard. We are transmitting to you blind (twice) on .... Please advise via another route if you agree.
DUJIB	Your transmitter OK on reversals but unreadable on traffic.
LILAP	Please say what means traffic is delivered / collected to / from this customer.
OCNOR	We have breakdown in .... transmitter, you transmit to us blind (twice), but continue listening.
ONKEY	Message unacknowledged after ...... transmissions. Please advise.

Routine repetition and collation

DAFNO	Routine repetition or collation of correction herewith. Confirm and release.
DAFVE	Routine repetition or collation(s) of following omitted. Compare and rectify if necessary.
DAFYR	Routine repetition or collation of our ... incorrect; we repeat following text... Correct and confirm.
DAGER	Routine repetition or collation of our .... OK. Release.
DAGOG	Routine repetition or collation of your .... given. Advise.
DAGPO	Routine repetition or collation of the following words is different from the text which reads .... Compare and rectify if necessary.

Conditions

CUMAN	All your stations reported unheard at receiving point. Advise what trouble is via ....
CUVON	Are your conditions favourable for high speed reception ?
DACIB	Cannot receive high speed, local conditions unfavourable.
DACJE	Can only receive from ......, all other stations unreadable.
DAPUV	General fading on short waves, will advise as soon as conditions improve.
DEFYS	Signals jumping on frequency beyond receiver range.
DIWAY	Traffic conditions do not warrant additional channel(s). Please keep present outlet full.
DODAY	Variable and poor signal-to-noise ratio. To assist auto control, make keying without spaces.
DOFIN	Violent fading prevalent; single reception impossible.
DOPPA	Circuit(s) working very poorly.
DOPUD	Circuit(s) working satisfactorily.
DUDAM	Your signals unreadable here. Situation ...... Confirm via ....
DUDJU	Your station on ... unheard. we are transmitting to you blind (twice) on ....

Radiotelegraph and Radiotelephone Codes, Prowords and Abbreviations

Five Letter Code Groups - The ITU and C&W.
(Codes and Abbreviations for the use of the International Telecommunications Service - 1975)
of the C.C.I.T.T. and Cable & Wireless, not including the ICS of IMCO or the ICAO

Please advise via another route if you agree.

Interference, jamming

DAPYF	Interference from echo.
DASOB	Interference from industrial or medical machines.
DEBPA	Interference on .... appears to be due to line trouble.
DEBXU	Please endeavour to identify the jamming station.
DECOW	.... jammed by ....., unable ascertain frequency. Can you assist, please ?
DEDAN	.... jammed by ..... which is on its assigned frequency. Please check your frequency.
DEFEM	.... jamming .... Please correct to assigned frequency.
DEFIB	.... with modulation spread of plus and minus .... kc/s jamming. Please correct.
DEFUC	.... with key clicks plus and minus .... kc/s jamming .... Please remedy.
DEFWO	Parasitic radiation on .... kc/s from your transmitter ..... jamming ...... Please remedy.

Numbers

DAFEJ	Closing numbers OK. Meet again at .... GMT. Resume on ..... (stations)
DAGUT	Confirm last received, we sent you ....
DEFTU	Last numbers: transmitted .... received ....

Classes of telegrams
Classes

BIRAT	Arbitrage traffic.
BOBGU	PRESSE telegrams.
BOBKO	PRESSE telegram and URGENT PRESSE telegram with urgent transmission and delivery.
BOBOW	All classes of telegrams including press telegrams with urgent transmission and delivery.
BOCAN	Ordinary private telegram traffic.
BOHEC	Letter telegram traffic.
BOMMA	Press traffic.
BOSAD	Urgent-rate traffic.
WOCED	Service advice.

Queries and requests

BIRVO	Check class and prefix which differ.
BOFFO	..... is a letter telegram. Read serial ...... Blank ..... Amend check; service error.
BOFUP	..... is an ordinary private telegram. Read serial ...... Blank .... Amend check; service error.
BOLEH	Please give number of words in each class.
BOLJE	Prefix of message should be ....
BOSIR	What is prefix of your number .... ?
BOSOF	Your .... prefixed .... Is this correct ?

Restrictions on classes and special services

BINZA	Administration does not admit this class of traffic.
BITED	Secret language unallowed.
BOBUH	For all classes of telegrams except ....
BOJHE	No de luxe (LX) service to ....
BOJPU	No de luxe (LXDEUIL) service to ....
BORXO	Unallowed for ...... Revise class.
WOREM	Must be inserted in service instructions.

Delay (complaints of delay, capacity, filing, etc.)
Complaints (of delay)

GYGAP	Complaint has been made of ....
GYJOG	Complaint that ..... not delivered until .... Trace and advise.
GYLIL	Complaint of delay. Give time received and delivered (reforwarded) and explain any delay.
GYMAD	Complaint of delay in the delivery of traffic addressed .... Investigate and advise.
HABID	Connecting Administration / Company complains.
HAGAS	Confirm time of acceptance ......, complaint of delay.

Delay

Radiotelegraph and Radiotelephone Codes, Prowords and Abbreviations

Five Letter Code Groups - The ITU and C&W.
(Codes and Abbreviations for the use of the International Telecommunications Service - 1975)
of the C.C.I.T.T. and Cable & Wireless, not including the ICS of IMCO or the ICAO

GUTAP	A delay of .... hours.
GUTIP	...... announce delay; messages can be accepted only at "sender's risk".
GUTKA	Ask reason for delay.
GUTVU	.... complaining of delay in transmission. Please give special attention to this file.
GUYES	.... complains of delay to his (their) traffic. Investigate and reply.
HAHUM	Delay about .... hours on .... (class of traffic) from ....
HAJOT	Delay cancelled.
HAMAN	Delay continues.
HAPIG	Delay due to .....
HAYEW	.... delayed. Expedite to prevent further complaints.
HEFOG	Delayed in office of addressees.
HEGAY	Delay increasing. Can you increase speed ?
HEHUN	Delay unavoidable on account of exceptionally heavy traffic, doing best to clear.
HEPIP	Excessive delay.
HETIN	Explain delay.
HIHUT	Heavy delay.
HIZEP	Is there any delay to .... ?
HOMAT	No delay.
HOPOM	Notice of delay withdrawn.
HOZOG	Please explain delay to addressee / sender.
HUFOX	Subject to ...... delay.
HUHAG	There is delay of ...... hours to ....
HUJAM	To avoid delay.
HUMAW	Traffic addressed ..... arriving here badly delayed. Please expedite.
HYFUN	Was there any delay ?
HYGIG	We are advising .... hours delay.
HYHAM	We are advising indefinite delay.

Handing in

HEYON	Date of handing in omitted. Please supply.
HIBIN	Confirm date of handing in, received as ....
HIFOP	.... handed in .... received here ...., addressee asks reason for delay.

State of traffic

HILOG	Heavy press traffic.
HIMAR	Heavy traffic.
HITOY	Heavy Government traffic.
HOFOR	Light traffic.

Delivery (complaints of misdelivery, etc.)
Awaiting delivery

JIHAW	Delivery office closed.
JUFAR	.... is a reply to your .... Can you now deliver ?
JUMOP	Message will be called for.
JUWAY	Not registered. Delivered as trial to ..... registered for ..... and accepted. Advise if correct.
MABAN	Sender insists message intended for ....
MAHVU	Your number ..... received here addressed ..... If address on original differs notify immediately.
MEJIM	Held, radio connection not yet obtained. Ship will be called up to the ..... inclusive.
OLMAD	Address insufficient, we try to delivery to ..... Correct if necessary.
OLWAY	Address unregistered, we try delivery to ...... Correct if necessary.
ONJIG	Vessel in port ......, will hold and transmit on departure unless otherwise instructed.
ONKEY	Message unacknowledged after ...... transmissions. Please advise.
REHOW	Following radiotelegram(s) on hand, ship on route to your area. Advise when delivered.

Complaint about delivery

OMGUS	Complaint of misdelivery. Advise to whom delivered.
OMKEW	Complaint of non-delivery. Give full details of delivery and if addressee acknowledges receipt.
OMMAN	Complaint of non-delivery. Please trace forward or, if necessary, rush duplicate.
OMWEB	Complaint of non-delivery. Was it duly delivered ?

Delivered

Radiotelegraph and Radiotelephone Codes, Prowords and Abbreviations

Five Letter Code Groups - The ITU and C&W.

(Codes and Abbreviations for the use of the International Telecommunications Service - 1975)
of the C.C.I.T.T. and Cable & Wireless, not including the ICS of IMCO or the ICAO

JIBUN	Delivered on renewal of registration.
JIDEW	Delivered to and accepted by ....
JIFAG	Delivered to registered address ....
JIJAY	Duly delivered.
JIKEY	Duplicate delivered ...... Original lost over connecting Administration's / Company's system.
JOWAS	If address is the same notify sender message delivered to .... registered for ....
JUHEN	Message duly delivered, we hold signed receipt but signature is disowned by addressee.
JUJEW	Message has been called for.
JUKIT	Message received at ...... and delivered at ....
JYBAG	Now delivered, called for.
JYDOT	Now delivered to and accepted by .... (complete address)
JYGUS	Now cleared to ship. Cancel advice on non-delivery.
ONHAG	Failed in transmission on lines of connecting Administration / Company: duplicate delivered.
PYSAT	Delivered subsequently. Cancel advice of non-delivery.

Instructions for delivery

JAJAR	Can you now deliver ?
JAMEG	.... claimed good registration, messages previously sent to same address duly delivered.
JAZOG	Deliver after 24 hours.
JEBUD	Deliver after 36 hours.
JEDEN	Deliver after 48 hours.
JEFAD	Deliver on the arrival of the ship.
JEHAT	Deliver to ....
JEJAW	Deliver to registered address ....
JEKEW	Deliver to sender of ....
JERAM	Deliver to former address which had been cancelled.
JOBUT	Effect delivery at ....
JOWAS	If address is the same notify sender message delivered to ...... registered for ....
JUBAB	If unable to deliver.
JYMUD	Decode and deliver to ....
JYRIM	Please recall and deliver to ....
JYSUM	Re-tender and advise.
LILBO	Re-deliver, message will be called for.
ONMAP	Re-tender, addressee will call.

Misdelivered

JARAG	.... claims misdelivered. Give particulars of delivery.
MADPU	The message(s) was (were) misdelivered; copy (copies) have (has) been delivered to ......
MADSO	The message(s) was (were) misdelivered. Shall we deliver copy (copies) now ?
ONWET	Sender claims message misdelivered. Rush delivery with explanation, advise when done.

Queries redelivery

JOHAY	Give particulars of receipt and delivery.
JOKID	State date and time of delivery.
JOREX	Give time received and time delivered.
LILAP	Please say what means traffic is delivered/collected to/from this customer.
LILXU	Say if yet delivered.
MAHFE	.... was similarly addressed and presumably delivered.
MAHPO	Why was it not delivered ?
OHBIN	Telegraphic confirmation of delivery (CR) not received.
WEFET	Sender anxious for a reply. Confirm delivery and advise addressee.

Disposal (forwarding, etc.)
Disposal

EJJOG	No telegraph office of that name; message forwarded at "sender's risk".
EVNED	Misrouted, have forwarded message to .... under serial/reference number ....
MARSU	How did you dispose of following message(s) ....
MATIS	...... still on hand as communication not established since receipt. Message(s) will be retained for further trial unless otherwise instructed.
MATMU	Instruct us how to dispose of ....

Radiotelegraph and Radiotelephone Codes, Prowords and Abbreviations

Five Letter Code Groups - The ITU and C&W.
(Codes and Abbreviations for the use of the International Telecommunications Service - 1975)
of the C.C.I.T.T. and Cable & Wireless, not including the ICS of IMCO or the ICAO

MEFED	Messages will be forwarded by post from ....
MEGFU	Shall we forward at "sender's risk" ?
MEGLA	.... was forwarded to ...... at ....
MEJIM	Held, radio connection not yet obtained. Ship will be called up till the .... inclusive.
NEDIB	Place of destination incomplete, there are several. Advise.
NEMYD	Place of destination unknown; we forward to ..... Correct if necessary.
ONJIG	Vessel in port ....., will hold and transmit on departure
RUFUE	Advise routing originally requested by ....
WEJOD	Place of destination not in List of Telegraph Offices. Advise.

Forwarding instructions

MAJDO	Forward by cable.
MAJIG	Forward as soon as possible.
MAJOC	Forward at "sender's risk".
MAJPA	Forward by mail.
MAJUH	Forward by wireless.
MALAP	Forward immediately.
MANAG	Forwarding by mail.
MAREJ	Forward via ....
MARNE	Forwarding by mail, next post .... (date).
MARRO	.... has been forwarded with ....
MEGBO	Arrange to telephone all messages addressed .... and advise when arrangements made.
ZEKEN	Please forward all traffic via .... radio.

Diversions

EFBIN	.... diverted via you. Advise clearance times.
EFDOG	Diverting .... ordinary private telegrams via you.
EFLIL	During interruption traffic for .... will circulate via ....
EFMIX	During interruption of ...... divert via ....
EHGAG	How many messages did you divert ?
EHTAP	Message(s) diverted "ampliation" via ....
EJFOB	No telegram service to .... via .... Please advise.
EJYET	Obliged to divert .... due ....
ENDUD	Prevent diverting if possible.
ENRAM	Propose diverting ...... traffic via you. Advise if you can clear without delay.
EULOT	Shall we divert ?
EVBUD	Through which station did you divert ?
EVDUN	Through which station shall we divert ?
EVLOW	Your ...... apparently miscirculated to us, message held awaiting your instructions.
EVNED	Misrouted, have reforwarded message to .... under serial/reference number ....

Duplications (cancellations of, etc.)
Duplications

JIKEY	Duplicate delivered ...... original lost over connecting Administration / Company system.
MEROW	.... are identical.
METAB	Duplicate delivered.
MIFEN	Have you a duplicate copy of our message number .... ?
MIHYT	Message number .... is not duplicate of message number ....
MIJIB	We are mailing duplicate copies.
MIJNU	We have two different messages under number ...... Give new number.
ONHAG	Failed on transmission on lines of connecting Administration / Company; duplicate delivered.

Duplications (cancellations of)

MIDUN	Have cancelled duplicate copy (copies).
MIHOB	Message no. ... appears to have been received also under no. .... Shall we cancel latter copy ?
MIJEM	Uncertain if following message (service advice) has been sent to you before. If previously received under another number cancel this copy and report.
PASCA	Transmitted twice, cancel second transmission.

Enquiries (miscellaneous)

Radiotelegraph and Radiotelephone Codes, Prowords and Abbreviations

Five Letter Code Groups - The ITU and C&W.

(Codes and Abbreviations for the use of the International Telecommunications Service - 1975)
of the C.C.I.T.T. and Cable & Wireless, not including the ICS of IMCO or the ICAO

MIRJU	Can you enable us to answer inquiries why there is no traffic from .... ?
MIRZU	Can you explain ?
MIWON	Can you inform us ?
MOBAY	Can you trace ?
MOPYD	What is the name of the coast station ?
MORUG	What is the name of the ship station ?
MUGYA	Have you any information respecting .... ?
MUHAH	Have you anything on hand for .... ? If so, please rush.
MUHED	Have you a private wire connection ?
NACSU	Who is sender of your .... ?

Requests

MOFEW	Confirm serial and/or reference number and date of message.
MOYES	Give telegraph office of origin.
MUBED	Give particulars of message.
MUGID	Give time and date handed in.
MUGKO	Give time and date of reception.
MUSYJ	Advise present position.
MYBEG	Inquire and advise us.
MYFIG	Please explain.
MYGAY	Please obtain reply to our message number ....., customer pressing.
MYJUG	Please report present status of inquiry, we are being pressed for a reply.
MYNIP	Mail detailed list of ....
NABOC	Quote code used.

Statements

MODAB	Case now closed.
MOPOH	Following received from ....
MUJOT	No message from .... on account of ....
MUSAZ	No trace on our receiving record at time quoted.
MUSHU	Our printer record confirms.
MYPAR	Private wire connection by telegraph.
MYYEW	Private wire connection by telephone.
NABRU	telegraph office opened at ....
NACBA	We are inquiring, we will reply as soon as possible.
NACFO	...... was received at ....
NACNE	We are unable to trace.
NACOB	We have no information.
NADBO	Will inquire and report.
NADED	Regret no further details available.

Errors, mutilations, omissions
Confirmation

NEBAV	Confirmed by addressee.
NEBBO	Confirm to addressee.
NEDEJ	Connecting Administration / Company confirms following words correct ....
NODIG	Sender maintains correct.

Errors

NAFAC	Addressee claims incorrect.
NAFRO	Complaint of frequent and serious errors in messages to ..... Please give special attention.
NEBSA	Connecting Administration's / Company's error.
NEDCA	Connecting Administration / Company tracing error.
NEDYF	Error(s) made here and will be dealt with.
NEFAT	Error of service.
NEFIM	Error(s) due local circuit. Under investigation.
NEHWO	Have corrected error.
NEKEZ	In our .... insert in preamble ...., service error.
NEKGU	In our .... read at end of address ..... radio (name of coast station) as it appears in the first column of the List of Telegraph Stations.
NEKIR	Inserted in error.

Radiotelegraph and Radiotelephone Codes, Prowords and Abbreviations

Five Letter Code Groups - The ITU and C&W.
(Codes and Abbreviations for the use of the International Telecommunications Service - 1975)
of the C.C.I.T.T. and Cable & Wireless, not including the ICS of IMCO or the ICAO

NEMYD	Place of destination unknown, we forward to ... Correct if necessary.
NEPUG	Mechanical error.
NIGIF	No error our copy.
NISMA	Correct error.
NISOV	Say if any error made in transmission.
NITSU	Rectify and reply.
NODAP	Sender claims incorrect.
NODHE	Sender's error.
NOVEF	Error in telephone transmission.
NOVGO	Error in telephone transmission, read back but not challenged by sender.
NOVNU	Error(s) under investigation.
NOWFE	Words repeated still incorrect.

Mutilations

NAFNU	Claimed mutilation following words our ... Please deliver (forward) correction or confirmation.
NAFOJ	.... complains of mutilation. Say how delivered / transmitted.
NAMAH	Complaint of mutilation, say how you have it. Is your copy original or transit ? Complaint
NAMMO	traffic addressed ..... arriving badly mutilated. See ...... and report. Connecting
NEBOD	Administration regret mutilation, which occurred due to error of service their Department. Matter has been suitably noticed.
NEXFO	File threatened because of mutilation. Please give best attention.
NEHIT	Following message(s) appear(s) to have been mutilated. Investigate and reply.
NIBYP	Mutilated. Please report.
NIBZA	Mutilation alleged. Repeat from original.
NIFBO	Mutilation of signature alleged. Please confirm as follows ....
NIFEP	Mutilation of signature alleged. Rush repetition.
NIFOD	Mutilation of .... text(s) alleged. Please confirm as follows ....
NIFRA	Mutilation of .... text(s) alleged. Rush repetition.
NODGU	Sender complains of mutilation, claims text delivered reading ...., our copy reads ....
NODJO	.... senders received advice by another route of mutilation, we repeat.
NOWAV	Where did mutilation occur ?

Omissions

NAFES	Addressee complains something missing between .... and ....
NAMEV	Complaint .... text omitted, our copy reads ....
NAMIZ	Complaint that this (these) word(s) omitted. Say how delivered / transmitted.
NEDIB	Place od destination incomplete, there are several. Advise.
NEFYC	Handing in time omitted.
NRHUJ	Following omitted from ...... Correct and notify addressee.
NEKLO	Place of origin not in List of Telegraph Offices. Advise.
NIGSA	Omission occurred ....
NOWCU	Where did omission occur ?
NOWOG	Your reply omits ....

Faults
Gear faults

NUBWE	Fault suddenly developed in our transmitter. Necessary to shut down immediately. Please give last received and listen for .....
NUDIM	Gear fault here.
NUDNO	Gear fault our receiving station.
NUDOC	Gear fault our transmitting station.
OBGEM	Reversals and traffic OK, no hands signal received. Look to your key or auto switch.
OCBET	Transmitter, when on space, builds up a strong radiation forming dashes.
OCNOR	We have breakdown in .... transmitter. You transmit to us blind (twice), but continue listening.
ODBIB	Your perforator is faulty. Please remedy, see ......

Power faults

OBBEN	Power failure.
OBCUT	Power failure, all circuits affected.
OCNUR	We have breakdown in .... transmitter. You transmit to us blind (twice), but continue listening.

Radiotelegraph and Radiotelephone Codes, Prowords and Abbreviations

Five Letter Code Groups - The ITU and C&W.
(Codes and Abbreviations for the use of the International Telecommunications Service - 1975)
of the C.C.I.T.T. and Cable & Wireless, not including the ICS of IMCO or the ICAO

Other faults

NUDVE	Heavy key clicks or other similar emission between characters causing blurring.
NUFIB	Heavy lightning overhead, must earth aerial, will advise when clear.
NUFLO	.... keying bias varying from dropouts to sticks.
NUGET	Passed to authorities concerned. Advise if interference continues.
NUPES	Out of order.
OBJAB	Signals received have light dots, please remedy.
OBNOD	.... swinging bias from neutral to heavy.
OBPAT	.... swinging bias from neutral to light.
OCHOP	Unable to put you through owing to ....
OCJAG	Unable transmit on .... Further advice will be sent by another route if direct comms unavailable.
ODDAY	Your spacing wave is very strong.
ODFIX	Your spacing wave is very weak.

No faults

NUFYH	No fault traceable here.
OCPAW	We have checked our transmission on .... and find no fault. Please check reception.

Reports

NUGPU	Our receiving station reports ....
NUGUJ	Our receiving station reports .... below normal strength, other stations on same frequency are normal. Please investigate.
NUGZA	Our receiving station reports .... below normal strength, other stations on same frequency similarly affected
NUHEH	Our receiving station reports marking bias on .... Please investigate.
NUHKO	Our receiving station reports spacing bias on .... Please investigate.
NUHLA	Our receiving station reports varying frequency on .... If transmission varying please endeavour to remedy.
NUNEG	Our relay station reports(ed) our transmission.
NUNGO	Our relay station reports(ed) your transmission.

Interruptions and restorations
Interruptions

ODTOY	Advise probable period of interruption.
OFCAN	All lines interrupted; there will be delay to traffic.
OFTUG	.... cable(s) interrupted.
OGCAP	Cancel notice of interruption advised in our ....
OHJUD	Line trouble on .... will advise when restored.
OHNUT	During future interruptions ....
OHPIG	During interruption of .... divert via ....
OJGOB	Landlines between .... and .... interrupted.
OJGOT	Landlines between .... and .... interrupted, all traffic delayed, will advise when restored.
OJHUM	Landlines between .... and .... interrupted, expect to be restored shortly.
OJJAY	Landlines between .... and .... interrupted. Prospects poor.
OJPIP	Landlines between .... and .... interrupted. Prospects uncertain.
OKCAW	Lines between here and terminal station interrupted.
OKFOX	Lines to receiving station interrupted.
OKJIT	.... notifies interruption of ....
OLFUN	Unable to accept traffic during interruption.

Restorations

ODZOG	Advise prospects of restoration.
OFVAT	.... cable(s) restored.
OHFOP	Communication with .... restored.
OJWAG	Landlines between .... and .... restored; traffic normal.
OKDOT	Lines between here and terminal station restored.
OKGUM	Lines to receiving station restored.
OKKEG	.... notifies restoration of ....

Stoppage / suspension

Radiotelegraph and Radiotelephone Codes, Prowords and Abbreviations

Five Letter Code Groups - The ITU and C&W.
(Codes and Abbreviations for the use of the International Telecommunications Service - 1975)
of the C.C.I.T.T. and Cable & Wireless, not including the ICS of IMCO or the ICAO

MATIS   ..... still on hand as communication not established since receipt.
              Message(s) will be retained for further trial unless otherwise instructed.
OHDOG   Communication with ..... is suspended on account of ......
OKPOD   Please give cause of stoppage from ...... to .... GMT.
OLCIS   Stoppage from ...... to .... GMT due to ....

ITU Publications

ATBET   Destination correct, see List of Telegraph Offices.
ATCOW   Destination not in List of Telegraph Offices.
ATDAB   List of Telegraph Offices.
CTITU   Circular telegram of the ITU.
EJJOG   No telegraph office of that name; message forwarded at "sender's risk".
NABRU   Telegraph office opened at ....
NEDIB   Place of destination incomplete, there are several. Advise.
NEKLO   Place of origin not in List of Telegraph Offices. Advise.
NEMYD   Place of destination unknown; we forward to ...... Correct if necessary.
RYFAD   Destination indicator unlisted. Please advise.
SAGNE   Origin indicator unlisted. Please advise.
TCUIT   Circular telegram of the ITU. (French and Spanish texts)
UFARM   Refer to List of Indicators for the Telegram Retransmission System and
              Telex Network Identification Codes published by the ITU.
UFBUL   Refer to ITU Operational Bulletin(s) No(s) ....
UFHOB   Refer to ITU Notification(s) No(s) ....
UFITA   Refer to TA Table - Transferred Account Telegraph Service published by the ITU.
UFJAR   ITU General Secretariat notifies us ....
UFKEG   ITU General Secretariat circular No ....
UGBOB   Refer to circular telegram number .... issued from ITU.
UGDON   Refer to ITU publication
              "General information relating to the operation of the international telegraph service".
UGGET   refer to CCITT Recommendation No .... paragraph ....
UGHOG   Refer to CCIR Recommendation No .... paragraph ....
USCAN   Radio Regulations.
USDAW   Telegraph Regulations.
USFAY   See Telegraph Regulations; Article No .... number ....
USGUT   See Radio Regulations; Article No .... number ....
USHAD   See additional Radio Regulations; Article No .... number ....
UTCOD   Use the Gentex code.
VUMAT   Origin correct, see List of Telegraph Offices, Supplement no .... page ....
WEJOD   Place of destination not in List of Telegraph Offices. Advise.
WOHBA   ITU green book of
              "Codes and abbreviations for the use of the international telecommunications service".
WOHFU   Add the following to the ITU green book of
              "Codes and abbreviations for the use of the international telecommunications service".
WOLCU   Delete meaning in ITU green book of "Codes and abbreviations for the use of the
              international telecommunications service", leaving meaning in blank.

Non-delivery (misdelivery, etc.)

Complaint about delivery.

OMGUS   Complaint of misdelivery. Advise to whom delivered.
OMKEW   Complaint of non-delivery.
              Give full particulars of delivery and say if addressee acknowledges receipt.
OMMAN   Complaint of non-delivery. Please trace forward or, if necessary, rush duplicate.
OMWEB   Complaint of non-delivery. Was it duly delivered ?

Misdelivered.

JARAG   .... claims misdelivered. Give particulars of delivery.
MADPU   The message(s) was/were misdelivered; copy / copies has / have been delivered to ....
MADSO   The message(s) was/were misdelivered. Shall we deliver copy / copies now ?
ONWET   Sender claims message misdelivered.

Radiotelegraph and Radiotelephone Codes, Prowords and Abbreviations

Five Letter Code Groups - The ITU and C&W.
(Codes and Abbreviations for the use of the International Telecommunications Service - 1975)
of the C.C.I.T.T. and Cable & Wireless, not including the ICS of IMCO or the ICAO

Rush correct delivery with suitable explanation and advise when done.

Undelivered

JIHAW	Delivered office closed.
JUWAY	Not registered. delivered as trial to ..... registered for ..... and accepted. Advise if incorrect.
JYGUS	Now cleared to ship. Cancel advice of non-delivery.
OLMAD	Address insufficient, we try delivery to .... Correct if necessary.
OLWAY	Address unregistered, we try delivery to .... Correct if necessary.
ONDUN	Connecting Administration/Company claims address not registered; the message is still undelivered.
OPBUN	.... senders received advice by another route that message undelivered. Please investigate and reply quickly.
OPGAD	Still undelivered. Addressee cannot be found.
OPKID	Treat as a non-delivery.
OPSOP	Undelivered, addressee cannot be found
OPWIG	Undelivered, refused by addressee.
ORBUT	Undelivered, addressee left, present address unknown; notice mailed.
ORCOT	Undelivered, addressee left, message forwarded telegraphically to ....
ORDAD	Undelivered, addressee not on board.
ORFAN	Undelivered. Ship not in port.
ORHAS	Undelivered, secret language prohibited.
ORJOB	Undelivered. Collect redirection charges equivalent to ...... gold francs.
ORMAT	Undelivered, house closed; notice mailed.
ORSUM	Undelivered, not understood by .... (complete address)
ORWON	Undelivered owing to ....
OSBAB	Undelivered, refused by ....
OSCOW	Undelivered, refused by addressee who states sender unknown to him.
OSDAM	Undelivered, returned by agents, ship left.
OSFAR	Undelivered, returned by ......, code unknown.
OSGAP	Undelivered, returned by ......, unclaimed.
OSHAT	Undelivered, returned by postal service, unclaimed.
OSJOG	Undelivered, returned by postal service, unknown.
OSLAD	Undelivered, returned by shipping company, addressee not found.
OSMAW	Undelivered, several firms of that name.
OSRED	Undelivered, several hotels of that name.
OSSUP	Undelivered, several streets of that name, district required.
OSYES	Undelivered, ship did not touch this port.
OTGAS	Undelivered, unknown; notice mailed.
OTHAW	Undelivered, vessel has docked.
OTJOT	Undelivered, vessel in port since .... sails again ....
OTLAP	Undelivered, returned by agents, ship did not call.
OTMAY	Undelivered, no such telephone number.
OTREX	Undelivered, no such telephone exchange. Undelivered,
OTTRAB	unable to contact telephone number. Delivered
PYSAT	subsequently. Cancel advice of non-delivery. Still
RACYB	undelivered.
RAFIS	Undelivered, not called for.
RAFUJ	Undelivered, addressee absent.
RAFYZ	Undelivered, addressee left.
RAHOT	Undelivered, addressee left, forwarded by post to ......
RAJAJ	Undelivered, addressee unknown.
RAJEV	Undelivered, addressee left for ......
RAJFU	Undelivered, addressee left without leaving address.
RAJGO	Undelivered, addressee not arrived.
RAJIF	Undelivered, addressee not at hotel.
RAJSA	Undelivered, addressee has changed residence without leaving a forwarding address.
REGAD	Undelivered, several persons of the same name.
REJAB	Undelivered, ship out of range.
REKEG	Undelivered, address insufficient.
RESIN	Undelivered, address insufficient without number of the house.

Radiotelegraph and Radiotelephone Codes, Prowords and Abbreviations

Five Letter Code Groups - The ITU and C&W.
(Codes and Abbreviations for the use of the International Telecommunications Service - 1975)
of the C.C.I.T.T. and Cable & Wireless, not including the ICS of IMCO or the ICAO

RICOD	Undelivered, address no longer registered.
RIFOX	Undelivered, address insufficient without flight number.
RIHUB	Undelivered, hotel unknown.
RIJAG	Undelivered, address not registered.
RIKEN	Undelivered, place unknown.
RISOB	Undelivered, no house of the number.
ROCOG	Undelivered, place, street, road etc. unknown.
ROFAB	Undelivered, not claimed on board.
ROFER	Undelivered, ship already left.
ROFGU	Undelivered, aircraft already left.
ROFJO	Undelivered, ship did not communicate.
ROSOP	Undelivered. Several ships of the same name. Please supply nationality and/or callsign.
RUCMU	Undelivered, telephone no. in address does not correspond with the name of the addressee
RUCOS	Undelivered, hotel, house, firm etc. no longer exists.
RUCXO	Undelivered, refused, the telegram does not concern the addressee.
RUFAJ	Undelivered, ship already sailed. Could be reached by a radiotelegram.
RUFKU	Undelivered, ship not yet arrived.
RUFMO	Undelivered, addressee already disembarked from ship.

Phototelegrams
Acceptance / handed in

GAFAS	May we accept Transferred Account phototelegrams to .... from ...... valid until .... ?
GASGO	You may accept Transferred Account phototelegrams to .... from ...... valid until ....
OVFAY	.... advises received telegraphic notice of phototelegram for him (them) will be handed in by ...... at .... and wants to know when delivery can be expected.
OVLAW	Cancel phototelegram number ....
OWBAR	Can you commence phototelegram transmission sooner ?
OWCUP	..... claim phototelegram handed in ...... addressed ..... Have you any record of it ?
OXCUR	Expect phototelegram will be handed in shortly. Advise when ready.
OXFEN	Expect phototelegram will be handed in at .... GMT.
OXMIX	Has phototelegram been accepted ?
OXROB	Have you any phototelegram(s) on hand for ...... ?
OYFEW	Phototelegram(s).
OYHID	Original phototelegram lacks contrast.
OYLET	Phototelegram accepted, addressee confirms.
OYROW	Phototelegram not accepted owing to ....
OZBED	Phototelegram expected to be handed in with you by ...... addressed ..... Make inquiries and advise prospects.
OZFIB	Phototelegram handed in for ....., expect to start transmission on .... at .... GMT.
OZHIM	Phototelegram handed in size ...... addressed ...., we will use transmitter ...... Advise prospects of reception.
OZMOP	Phototelegram for ... will be handed in by .... not yet to hand.

Reception / delivery

OVMEG	Can commence phototelegram reception immediately.
OVRIB	Cannot commence phototelegram reception yet, will advise.
OVTAG	Can you commence phototelegram reception immediately ?
OVYEW	Can you commence phototelegram reception sooner ?
OWDAY	Conditions unsuitable for phototelegram reception.
OWHEN	Do you expect any phototelegrams before Monday ?
OWRIM	Negative poor, sender insists on delivery.
OXBAT	Expect phototelegram by mail from ...... Make suitable arrangements.
OZRUB	Phototelegram must be delivered before ...... GMT.
PABEG	Phototelegram number ...... fit for delivery. Please instruct us to cancel.
PACGO	Re-run of phototelegram necessary before suitable copy for delivery can be produced.
PADON	we will be ready for phototelegram reception at .... GMT.

Receipt

OHBIN	Telegraphic confirmation of delivery (CR) not received.
OMKEW	Complaint of non-delivery.

Radiotelegraph and Radiotelephone Codes, Prowords and Abbreviations

Five Letter Code Groups - The ITU and C&W.
(Codes and Abbreviations for the use of the International Telecommunications Service - 1975)
of the C.C.I.T.T. and Cable & Wireless, not including the ICS of IMCO or the ICAO

	Give full particulars of delivery and say if addressee acknowledges receipt.
ONKEY	Message unacknowledged after .... transmissions. Please advise.
PAGSO	Acknowledge receipt. Acknowledge
PAGYG	receipt of your .... Addressee
PAJAV	acknowledges receipt. Do you hold
PAJFO	good delivery receipt ?
PALAM	Get addressee's acknowledgment of receipt.
PALIL	Good delivery receipt held for....
TOPFE	Acknowledge by ....
TOPMO	Acknowledge this notification.

Refunds etc.

PEHIS	Debit us our proportion, referring case number ....
PEZES	We are refunding.
PEZIH	Refund is authorised. Refund
PEZJU	is not authorised. Telegraph
PEZVE	service not at fault.
PEZYV	refund of radio (coast and ship) charges are in order.
PIDUD	sender applies for refund of message charges. Please authorise.
YAGAC	Refund of telex charges agreed.
YAHOJ	Subscriber requests refund of telex charges due ....

RP (Reply paid) charges and vouchers

PEBEN	Addressee has returned RP voucher unused requesting the prepaid charges be refunded to the sender; refund may be made.
PECAN	Addressee has returned RP voucher unused requesting the prepaid charges be refunded to the sender. Please refund and debit us, referring to our case number ....
PEDOT	RP voucher not delivered, RP amounts not included in accounts; refund to sender.
PEFIN	RP voucher not delivered, RP amount retained in the accounts. We are crediting you for refund to sender.
PETOY	Alleged no RP voucher issued.
PIBET	Refund RP charges to sender.
PIHBU	Sender applies for refund of RP charges on grounds message was not delivered.
PIHIF	Sender applies for refund of unexpended portion of RP charges.
PILEP	Sender presents unused RP voucher and applies for refund of RP charges; we are refunding.
PILHE	Sender applies for refund of RP charges. Advise if refund is in order.
PILZU	RP voucher issued by ..... (office) number .... dated .... value .... has been lost by addressee. Please refuse RP voucher if presented at your counter, and advise us immediately.
PINED	.... unused, refund is in order.

Registered addresses

JAMEG	.... claimed good registration, messages previously sent to same address duly delivered.
JEJAW	Deliver to registered address ....
JIBUN	Delivered on renewal of registration.
JIFAG	Delivered to registered address ....
JOWAS	If address is the same notify sender message delivered to .... registered for ....
JUWAY	Not registered. Delivered as trial to ...... registered for ..... and accepted. Advise if correct.
OLWAY	Address unregistered, we try to delivery to .... Correct if necessary.
ONDUN	Connecting Administration/Company claims address not registered; message still undelivered.
ORSUM	Undelivered, not understood by .... (complete address)
PAMIV	If addressee(s) agreeable renew registration following registered addressee(s)... you collect charges.
PAMNO	.... is registered for ....
PASHO	Not registered with us.
PASUP	At request of .... please ask .... register following registered address, advise when effective.
PASZU	Please do necessary to have registration renewed and advise when done.
PATAB	Supply unpacked addressed for ....
PATHE	Supply registered address of ....
PATIN	Register following registered address ..... for .... and advise addressee.
PATOS	Registration lapsed.

Radiotelegraph and Radiotelephone Codes, Prowords and Abbreviations

Five Letter Code Groups - The ITU and C&W.

(Codes and Abbreviations for the use of the International Telecommunications Service - 1975)
of the C.C.I.T.T. and Cable & Wireless, not including the ICS of IMCO or the ICAO

PATUG   Renew registration following registered address(es) ..... advising addressee(s) quote cost for collection here.

Repetitions and corrections (indistinct writing, confirmation, etc.)
Additions

PIPJO	Add following ....
PUHOG	Insert following ....
PITUG	Sender's confirmation.
PIWAG	confirmation from sender is as follows ....
PONET	.... from confirmation copy.
PUSEZ	Message(s) received by telephone; confirmation had to be obtained when sender's office opened.
PYCAW	Original indistinctly written, sender's confirmation follows.
PYLOW	Our copy ....., confirmation from original follows.
RAPYM	The word is indistinct, we are trying to obtain confirmation.
RATUS	Unable to obtain confirmation as sender ....

Copy (copies)

POSRA	Herewith copy ....
POSUF	Herewith copy, original sent at .... GMT.

Corrections

POCAR	Connecting Administration's/Company's correction.
POFIH	correct if necessary.
POFJE	Correction follows.
POFZA	Correction has been delivered.
POHCO	Correction made by sender.
POHEG	Correct on our copy.
POMDU	Delete CTF in service instructions.
POMZO	.... forwarded "subject to correction' for ....
PONEB	Forward (or deliver) correction.
PUCWO	In our ...... erase from preamble ....
PUFOB	Is this message still "subject to correction" ?
PUSJU	Message(s) received by telephone; correction, if any, will follow when confirmation obtainable.
RABKA	Our service advice requests ......, your reply quotes .... Revise.
RAMUZ	Subject to correction.
RAPBU	.... text(s) in our number .... should read ....
ROFUN	Your BQ makes no correction.
ROKEW	Your service advice corrected and forwarded.
RONIB	Your paid service advice makes no correction.

Reference to sender / to original or to received copy

NODHE	Sender's error.
POHHU	Same our copy.
	Have referred to connecting Administration/company and will advise as soon as reply eceived.
POSAG	Consult sender.
PUCIS	How on your copy ?
PUCUD	Indistinctly written.
PUDUN	Is original copy plainly written or typed ?
PUSYR	...... on our copy, office of origin closed; will reply in morning.
PYBIN	Office of addressees closed.
PYHOP	Our copy ......, if this agrees with original consult sender.
PYNIB	Our copy is correct.
RABEM	...... on our copy, your service advice stopped.
RABUC	Plainly written on our copy.
RAFIS	Undelivered, not called for.
RAFPU	Same on our copy; endeavouring contact sender.

Repetitions

Radiotelegraph and Radiotelephone Codes, Prowords and Abbreviations

Five Letter Code Groups - The ITU and C&W.
(Codes and Abbreviations for the use of the International Telecommunications Service - 1975)
of the C.C.I.T.T. and Cable & Wireless, not including the ICS of IMCO or the ICAO

POFAZ	Connecting Administration's/company's repetition follows.
POHOC	Do not understand your service advice. Repeat references.
PUBIG	Holding your ...... which appears mutilated, apparently due indistinct writing. Please have it repeated from origin.
PUSSO	Obtain repetition quickly.
RACOP	Repeat as delivered.
RACVU	Repeat from your copy.
RACWE	Repeat your service advice commencing ....
RAFEC	Repeat your service advice concerning ....
RAPAG	Herewith repetition from our copy, confirmation follows when sender contacted.

Reply awaited / required

PIPKU	Awaiting reply from connecting ..... Administration/Company, reminders sent.
POHHU	Same our copy. Have referred to connecting Administration/Company and will advise as soon as reply received.
POMPA	First application was replied to by our ..... at .... GMT.
POSGU	Has application been forwarded ?
PUCYA	Intermediate reply not required.
PUSTA	Telegraph office closed, will reply when reopens.
RAMPO	Still awaiting connecting Administration's/Company's reply.
RATEB	Third application.
REBOB	We have made second application.
REFOR	We have made third application.
ROHOG	Your BQ unfinished, our RQ requests ....
RONCO	Your service advice stopped here.
WEDDU	Reply to our .... not received. Even if previously answered, please send a duplicate for our attention.
WEDYD	Sender advises no reply yet.
WEFET	Sender anxious for a reply. Confirm delivery and inform addressee.
WEFOM	Sender states there will be no reply.
WEFXU	Waiting reply to our service advice ....
WEHEB	Waiting reply from connecting Administration/Company.
WEHOT	Waiting reply as soon as possible.
WEHXO	Will reply as soon as possible.
WEHYJ	Will reply in morning.

Restrictions (censorship, etc.)
Censorship

BOSUV	All messages are subject to censorship.
BUCAP	Announce censorship to following countries ....
BUCOD	Cancelled by censor.
BUCVO	Censorship allows following authorised codes ....
BUCXA	Censorship calls for code used.
BUDOG	Censorship calls for explanation of texts ....
BUFAD	Censorship calls for full address.
BUHCA	Censorship calls for full signature.
BUHIR	Censorship calls for full address and signature.
BULOW	Censorship calls for plain language only.
BURIM	Censorship now allows all authorised codes.
CABUT	Have censorship restrictions been removed ?
CAGAY	Message(s) stopped by censor.

Restrictions / prohibitions

BUBUD	Announce all restrictions removed.
BUYEW	Secret language is prohibited over connecting line and/or circuit.
BYFAG	Secret language prohibited.
BYHIS	Secret language messages must carry name of code in preamble.
CAMIC	Restriction removed, secret language messages now accepted.
CAMUG	Restriction still in force.
CARUG	This restriction does not apply to ....

Radiotelegraph and Radiotelephone Codes, Prowords and Abbreviations

Five Letter Code Groups - The ITU and C&W.
(Codes and Abbreviations for the use of the International Telecommunications Service - 1975)
of the C.C.I.T.T. and Cable & Wireless, not including the ICS of IMCO or the ICAO

Routes (routing instructions, etc.)

RUFUE	Advise routing originally requested by ....
RUHUM	By what route was this message directed ?
RUKEY	By what route was this message sent ?
RUNOW	By which route did you divert ?
RUYET	By which route shall we divert ?
RYFAD	Destination indicator unlisted. Please advise
RYHUN	How shall we route traffic ?
SACOX	Message received without routing instructions
SAFAG	Message received with routing instructions via ....
SAGAH	Message was routed via ....
SAGNE	Origin indicator unlisted. Please advise.
SAGYB	Our normal route to ...... is via ....

Telex
Administrative

FOHIS	May we accept transferred account telex calls from .... to telex number .... answer-back ..... valid until .... Reply as soon as possible by service message
FOKIT	Transferred account telex calls
FONOD	We have issued I.T.U. credit card number .... to .... for telex calls to .... answer-back .... Accounts payable by .... valid until ....
FORUB	You may accept Transferred account telex calls to telex number ...... answer-back ...... Accounts payable by .... from ......until ....
YADOD	Confirm if telex message from .... received by ....
YAFAM	Please refer telex message from .... to ....
YAGAC	Refund of telex charges agreed
YAHOJ	Subscriber requests refund of telex charges due ....
YAJIJ	Telex message from .... not received by ....

Maintenance

YABOM	Following subscriber DER .... Please make further trial later.
YAGDU	Regret VF channel failure .... to ....causing DER conditions.
YAPIZ	Unable contact you on channel ....

Operational

YABAD	Can you assist with transit telex calls to ....?
YABVU	Frequent OCC condition obtained from subscriber
YABYO	If following firm a telex subscriber advise their number ....
YADAJ	Investigation shows telex call mutilated; refund of charges justified.
YADBA	Name and telex number of subscriber with answer-back ....is ....
YADDO	Advise if refund telex charges justified
YADEB	Confirm if following subscriber in working order ....
YADTU	Confirm if telex message from .... well received by monitor.
YADUF	Give chargeable minutes on telex message from ...... to ......
YADWO	Give name and telex number of subscriber with following answer-back ......
YAFCA	Please supply telex number and answer-back of ....
YAFVO	Received mutilated. Re-send on other channel ....
YAGYM	Subscribers .... found to be busy. Please make further attempts.
YAHET	Subscribers .... found to be in order. Please make further attempts.
YAHZA	Subscribers request repetition of ....
YAJJO	Telex message from .... received incomplete by .... Please reconnect.
YAJOV	Telex message from .... received mutilated by .... Please re-send.
YAJXA	Telex message from .... well received by ....
YALEG	Telex number of .... is ....
YALIM	Telex subscriber .... has now changed number which is ....
YALRU	Telex subscriber .... no longer in service.
YAPOG	We are unable to raise following telex subscriber .... Please investigate.
YAWID	We can assist with transit telex calls to ....
YAWLO	We cannot assist ....

Radiotelegraph and Radiotelephone Codes, Prowords and Abbreviations

Five Letter Code Groups - The ITU and C&W.

(Codes and Abbreviations for the use of the International Telecommunications Service - 1975)
of the C.C.I.T.T. and Cable & Wireless, not including the ICS of IMCO or the ICAO

YAWYF   Your subscriber .... frequently OCC. Do you consider telex facilities adequate? Please investigate

Transfer

TOGYS   Message duly transferred at .........G.M.T.
TOHEW   Please say time and date transferred. Please
TOHIG   say time received and transferred Received at
TOJSU   .... and transferred at .......G.M.T.
TOLIV   When and to which Administration/Company transferred ?

Transferred account (telegrams payable by addressee or third party)
Establishment of arrangements

EWLUG   Addressee refuses to pay charges. Please collect from sender.
EWRIB   Addressee will pay for telegram quoted. Please include bill with your next Transferred Account.
FOHIS   May we accept Transferred Account telex calls from ..... to telex number ..... answer-back ..... valid until .... Reply as soon as possible by service message
FOKIT   Transferred Account telex calls.
FONOD   We have issued I.T.U. credit card number ...... to for telex calls to ...... answer-back .... Accounts payable by .... valid until ....
FORUB   You may accept Transferred Account telex calls to telex number ...... answer-back ...... Accounts payable by ...... from ..... until ....
FYLAP   For telegrams payable by and addressed to ....
GABTO   ..... is authorised to send Transferred Account messages to ..... Please advise former and confirm when done
GAFAS   May we accept Transferred Account phototelegrams to ..... from ...... valid until .... ?
GAFIJ   May we accept all classes of Transferred Account messages including URGENT PRESSE from .... for .... ? Reply as soon as possible by service message.
GAFMU   May we accept Government telegrams on Transferred Account basis from ......to .... ? Reply as soon as possible by service message.
GAFPO   May we accept all classes of Transferred Account messages excluding URGENT PRESSE from ..to ..? Reply as soon as possible by service message
GAFYB   May we accept Transferred Account messages for .... from.........? Reply as soon as possible by service message.
GAGBA   May we accept ordinary press rate Transferred Account messages for .... from ......? Reply as soon as possible by service advice.
GAHIS   Please furnish complete address of addressee.
GAHNO   Please issue I.T.U. credit card to..for telegrams addressed to .... expiring .... valid .... Sender's contact address is ..... and advise number credit card issue.
GAHTU   Sender will call ...... for permit.
GAHYD   See ...... at sender's request. Please advise if addressee will pay charges of ...... If so will forward account as usual.
GAJBU   This message accepted Transferred Account. Please collect charges from addressee and report by service advice when payment obtained.
GAJCO   We have issued I.T.U. credit card number .... to .... for all classes of telegrams, including URGENT PRESSE, addressed to .... valid until ....
GAJIR   ..... want to send Transferred Account messages to .... Will latter pay?
GAJMA   We have accepted this message on Transferred Account basis addressed to .... Please ascertain if addressee will pay for it and for further messages from the sender who is ....
GANEP   ..... will communicate with ...... but in meantime will not pay for Transferred Account messages.
GANOW   ..... have requested us arrange Transferred Accounts from .... to ....
GANSA   We have issued I.T.U. credit card number ..... to ..... for telegrams addressed to ...valid until ....
GANUE   .....will pay for Transferred Account messages from .....
GAPAR   .....will pay for Transferred Account messages only at PRESSE rate from ....
GARJE   .....will not pay for Transferred Account messages from ....
GASAC   .....will pay for this message, but will not pay for future messages from ....
GASGO   You may accept Transferred Account phototelegrams addressed to ......from .....valid until .....
GASOP   You may accept all classes of Transferred Account messages including URGENT PRESSE for ...... from ...... valid until .... Please notify latter.
GASXU   You may accept PRESSE and URGENT PRESSE rate Transferred Account messages for ...... from .... valid until ....

Radiotelegraph and Radiotelephone Codes, Prowords and Abbreviations

Five Letter Code Groups - The ITU and C&W.
(Codes and Abbreviations for the use of the International Telecommunications Service - 1975)
of the C.C.I.T.T. and Cable & Wireless, not including the ICS of IMCO or the ICAO

GATES	You may accept Government telegrams on Transferred Account basis for ...... from ....
GATIG	You may accept all classes of Transferred Account messages excluding URGENT PRESSE for ...... from ...... valid until ...... Please notify latter.
GATLU	You may accept Transferred Account messages for .... from ....
GATVO	You may accept ordinary press rate Transferred Account messages for ...... from ....
GATYA	We are accepting Transferred Accounts of all classes from .... to ....
GAWAD	We are accepting Transferred Accounts of all classes to ..... from .... who holds I.T.U. credit card number ....

Cancellation of arrangements

FASAT	Cancel Transferred Accounts from .... to .... and confirm when done
FEDAM	Cancel Transferred Accounts (at addressee's request) from ...... to ....and confirm when done.
FEGIG	Cease accepting Transferred Account messages for .... from ....., addressees' credit has been stopped.
FODAW	Transferred Accounts cancelled.
FOSOB	Do not accept Transferred Account messages for .... cannot obtain guarantee of payment from addressee
FUHIT	Do not accept Transferred Account messages for ....
GALAW	We have cancelled Transferred Accounts from .... to .... at sender's request.

Accounting arrangements

EWCAR	Accounts payable by respective addressees.
FEKEY	Charges not yet paid by addressee, we are endeavouring to collect.
FENIB	Charges now collected.
FEROB	Charges to be collected your side.
FIDAN	Transferred account bill for month of ....
FIGIN	Collect at ordinary private telegram rate.
FIHIP	Collect at rate ....
FOKIT	Transferred Account telex calls.
FUWAS	Return of Transferred accounts to date omits following bill(s) ....
FYDEN	.... return of Transferred accounts includes following bill(s) ....
FYPAD	Give cost for collection here
FYWAY	Have you collected charges .... ?
GABCA	Guaranteed account bill for month of ....
GAGHE	Your ...... Transferred Account number ..... addressed to ..... Please supply line reference for telegram dated ....as we are unable to trace.
GAGRO	No trace of Transferred Account arrangements.
GAGUN	No trace of Transferred Account arrangements; charges to be collected your side, we debiting you ...... Please acknowledge.
GAGVU	Our records show following as Transferred Accounts but to date your bill not received ..... Please advise.
GANAM	.... Transferred Account item(s) untrace collection here. Please say where brought to account in your records.
GANGU	Will endeavour collect as special case. Please forward us bill as usual endorsed with reference of this service message.
GAWIP	Wish draw attention following discrepancies your Transferred Account bill ..... Please advise.

Miscellaneous

FAGEY	Advise if prepaid or Transferred Account.
FIROW	Transferred account facility exists, see our letter (service message) ....
GABIC	.... is a prepaid message.
GADEW	These telegrams should be treated on Transferred Account basis.
GAGIM	Please advise full details of your I.T.U. credit card number.
GAGYT	Please give I.T.U. credit card number and name of issuing Administration/Company.
GAHOG	Presume prepaid.
WALSA	Transferred Account case number ..... Please quote this number in reply or reference to this facility.

Unclassified

Radiotelegraph and Radiotelephone Codes, Prowords and Abbreviations

Five Letter Code Groups - The ITU and C&W.
(Codes and Abbreviations for the use of the International Telecommunications Service - 1975)
of the C.C.I.T.T. and Cable & Wireless, not including the ICS of IMCO or the ICAO

Acknowledgment confirmation

TOPFE	Acknowledge by .....
TOPMO	Acknowledge this notification
UHGEY	We confirm ......
UHHOP	Noted and confirmed
VOYEW	Confirm telegraph office of origin.

Act / arrange / attend to

TOWAY	Act according to our ....
TUBAC	Act according to your ....
TYHIM	Can you arrange ?
TYLOG	If arranged inform ....
UBBID	..... state they are unable to arrange.
UBCIS	..... state they have now arranged.
UBGAP	We are arranging
UCLOW	Give better attention
UCSEX	Give special attention
UDBIN	.... has attention
UDCOD	.... has been attended to
UDDEW	In attention serious
UDFOG	Please have it attended to immediately
UDGAY	Received and attended to
UDJAP	Will attend to it immediately

Advise / assist

TIBOH	Can you assist to ...... ?
TUBOJ	Addressee advised
TUCBO	Administration advised
TUCFE	Advise all concerned
TUCNU	Advise all offices
TUCUS	Advise if message now in order
TUFIN	Please advise your views
TUGAD	Please keep us fully advised
TUGEB	Please advise date of introduction
TUGNO	Sender advised
TUGSU	Please advise sender
TUGUZ	We are advised
TUGYD	Will advise
TUHAS	Will advise when OK
TUHIH	Please advise addressee
UBSET	Can assist to ....
UBWIG	Can not assist to ....
UFFOP	Would appreciate your help by getting in touch with the Authority concerned.

Agreement / non-agreement

TUHMA	.... is/are in agreement
TUHOD	Please ask administration (department) to agree
TUHRU	Say if in agreement
TUJUG	Subject to agreement of ....
TUNHO	We are in agreement
TUNVU	We are not in agreement
TUWEB	Administration (department) agrees

Complaints / investigations

UGJAW	Complaint has been made
UGKEN	Complaint is made by .... of ....
UGNAG	Complaint is receiving attention
UGSOP	Complaint not justified
USLEG	Case under investigation, will reply as soon as possible
USRAM	Papers with result of investigation going by next post
USTIN	Please investigate and reply as soon as possible

Copy

Radiotelegraph and Radiotelephone Codes, Prowords and Abbreviations

Five Letter Code Groups - The ITU and C&W.

(Codes and Abbreviations for the use of the International Telecommunications Service - 1975)
of the C.C.I.T.T. and Cable & Wireless, not including the ICS of IMCO or the ICAO

UHNED	Copy (copies) will be mailed to you.
UHYON	Missing ...... Please supply copy quickly
UJBOW	Please furnish copy (copies) of following message(s) for files.
UJCOX	Please furnish skeleton copy (copies) of following message(s) ....
UJDUD.	..... missing please supply copy quickly preceded by reference of this service advise.
UXLIL	Mail copies of correspondence about this case (message).

Information / Instructions

UPBAG	For your information
UPCAB	For your information only
UPDAM	For our information
UPFAR	.... has been informed
UPLAW	Instruct, instructions, give instructions
UPVOW	Following your instructions
URBAN	Instructions cancelled.
URCAD	Instructions received and noted
URFAT	Instructions will be sent
URHUT	No instructions have been received
URLAY	Waiting instructions respecting ....
URNOT	We have received instructions
URTED	We will instruct you further
USBAR	.... will not instruct

Reference / regarding

UTLET	Regarding our letter of ....
UTNUN	Regarding your letter of ....
WAJEJ	Please give prefix number or channel sequence number under which the transit telegram referred to was sent forward to its destination or next transit point.
WAJGU	Give reference
WAJHO	Please give received reference
WAJIV	Refer to following message(s)
WALAG	Reference is correct
WALEM	Reference is wrong
WALOS	Referring to our
WALPU	Referring to your
WALSA	Transferred Account case number .... Please quote this number in reply or reference to this facility.
WEJYV	Reference incorrect. Give number, date, time of handing in and say by which wire sent.

Reply

WAMIT	Reply (can you reply?)
WAMYV	Complainant(s) pressing for a reply
WAPCO	Reply direct to destination.
WAPEZ	Endeavour to get prompt reply
WAPUC	Please reply urgently
WEDAG	Pressing for a reply
WEDDU	Reply to our .... not received. Even if previously answered, please send a duplicate for our attention
WEDIJ	Sender advised, states will reply as soon as possible
WEDOB	Sender advises no reply
WEDYD	Sender advises no reply yet
WEFET	Sender anxious for a reply. Confirm delivery and inform addressee.
WEFOM	Sender states there will be no reply
WEFXU	Waiting reply to our service advice ....
WEHEB	Waiting reply from connecting Administration/Company
WEHOT	Waiting reply to our ....
WEHXO	Will reply as soon as possible
WEHYJ	Will reply in morning

Miscellaneous

Radiotelegraph and Radiotelephone Codes, Prowords and Abbreviations

Five Letter Code Groups - The ITU and C&W.
(Codes and Abbreviations for the use of the International Telecommunications Service - 1975)
of the C.C.I.T.T. and Cable & Wireless, not including the ICS of IMCO or the ICAO

UHJAY	Effective date
UJHOT	We propose to extend
UKJEW	Connecting Administration/Company replies nothing handed in with them on ....
UKKID	Connecting Administration/Company replies nothing handed in with them today for ....
UKTAB	Have you any record of such a message having been filed (received) ?
ULBUN	Nothing handed in for ....
ULCUP	Nothing handed in on ....
ULVAT	Was anything handed in for ....?
UMBUT	Will commence handing in.
UMLAD	May we follow ?
UMNIP	Please follow up
UMTAM	We are following
UNFAN	Are you holding?
UNGUM	........held at your request
UNJIM	Holding account of ....
UNLAP	Hold until further instructed
UVFEN	List will be corrected
UXBED	Please airmail as soon as possible
UXCAT	We are airmailing
UZCAW	Please advise when you mailed
UZSAP	Please make sure there is no mistake
VABEN	There is some mistake
VEBET	Please do needful
VEJAR	We will do needful
VIBIB	Until further notice
VIYET	........notifies us
VUSOB	Read telegraph office of origin
VYZEP	We follow procedure of
WAHAT	.... reported missing, OK our outgoing record
WAHIJ	Receiving record
WEJKU	Your claim was duly forwarded on the .... to appropriate authority whose reply will be sent to you on receipt.
WEKMO	Give RP in gold francs
WEPGO	...........sailed
WEPKA	...........sailed per SS ....
WEPUZ	...........sailed today
WEPYG	...........sailed yesterday
WEYAH	...........sails tomorrow
WEYNE	Sender sailed/s .... on board .... for ....
WOBAJ	Please obtain sender's name and address from the addressee
WOBMO	Sender cannot be found
WOBOB	Sender left for ...., unable to contact.
WOBUE	Sender(s) visiting .... due course
WOCED	Service advice.
WOCHU	Regret you were not advised as we were unaware of sender's itinerary.
WOCSO	Inaugurating service from .... to ....
WOREM	Must be inserted in service instructions
WORIF	Summer time
WOROT	Summer Time commences in .... and clocks advance ..... at ...... The new time will be signalled in telegrams
WORYO	Summer Time commences in .... and clocks advance ..... at ...... The new time will not be signalled in telegrams.
WOVAT	Summer Time finishes in .... and clocks retard .... at ....
WOVEJ	Understand
WOVOZ	Do not understand your ....
WOVRA	Public holiday here on
WOVYC	Not understood by ....
XEROJ	Your service advice not understood
XESCU	When and by what wire was telegram in question received ?

Radiotelegraph and Radiotelephone Codes, Prowords and Abbreviations

Special Telegraphic Service Indicators 1908-1996

Supplementary Instructions using authorised abbreviations for Radiotelegram handling.
British GPO 'Handbook for Wireless Operators' 1908, 1912-23, 1938, 1944, 1954, 1955
ITU Bulletins & Extracts 1961, 1973, 1974, 1975, 1985, 1989, 1992, 1996
From 1908 the =....= was sent before and after the Indication. i.e. =D=
(Rearranged into approx. Alphabetical Order. Italics = Obsolete. 1989)
(..* or ..x indicates insert number, amount, designator etc.)

A	Service Telegrams or Advices.
ADG	Service telegrams or advices relating to serious interruption of telecommunications routes.
ALT	Air Letter Telegram - Paid service.
AMPLIATION	Telegram sent a second time.
AURGENT	Service telegrams or advices with urgent transmission and delivery.
B	Used for Morse and sound working stations working direct.
BK	Stop transmission on Morse duplex and Wheatstone duplex instruments.
BQ	A reply to RQ.
COL	Routine repetition or collation.
CONFERENCE	Private Telegrams.
CR	Confirmation of delivery.
CTA	All addresses of a multiple address radiotelegram to be communicated to all addresses.
CTF	Correction to follow.
D	Radiotelegram to be given priority over the ordinary telegraph system.
DEVIE	Transmitted by an alternative route.
E E E	Error signal.
EN CHIFFRES	Telegram and text of which contains only figures.
Etat	Government Radiotelegram without priority..
Etat Priorité	Government Radiotelegram with priority. Also replaces EPN next.
Etat Priorité Nations	Telegram to or from the United Nations (by authorised persons only)
Exprès	Radiotelegram for express delivery, cost of delivery is to be collected from addressee.
FAX..x	Facsimile delivery.
FS	Reforwarding at sender's request.
FSDE..x	Reforwarding at sender's request from given address. (x = office of reforwarding)
GP	Radiotelegram to be called for at a Post Office. Poste restante.
GPR	Radiotelegram to be called for at a Post Office (registered).
Jour	Radiotelegram not to be delivered during the night.
Jx	Radiotelegram to be held at the disposal of the ship by the coast station for a fixed number of days. (x = no. of days)
LR......	Acknowledgment of receipt given at the request of the sending operator.
LT	Letter Telegrams.
LTF	Government Letter Telegrams.
LX	Radiotelegram, Greetings Telegram.
LXDEUIL	De luxe form of Condolence..
MANDAT	Money order telegrams and postal cheque telegrams.
MOM	Wait.
MP	Radiotelegram to be delivered to the addressee in person.
Nuit	Radiotelegram to be delivered during the night if received then.
OBS	Radiotelegram on Official Meteorological Service. (1954)
OL	Radiomaritime Ocean Letter
P (or fig 0 repeated)	Signal to stop transmission.
PAV	Radiotelegram to be delivered by air.
PAVR	Radiotelegram to be delivered by registered airmail.
PERCEVOIR	Redirection charge to be collected from the addressee.
POSTFIN	Postal financial services telegrams.

Radiotelegram of which the date and time of transmission to the ship is to be notified by the coast station -

PC	i	By Telegraph
PCP	ii	By post
PC		Request for confirmation of delivery. (1973)
Poste		Radiotelegram to be delivered by post.
PR		Radiotelegram to be posted as a registered letter.
Presse		Press Radiotelegram.
Réexpédié de x		Radiotelegram only when forwarding charge can be collected.
REEXPEDIEDE x		Redirection at the addressee's request. (1973)
Remettre x		Radiotelegram for which delivery on a specified date has been requested.

Radiotelegraph and Radiotelephone Codes, Prowords and Abbreviations

Special Telegraphic Service Indicators 1908-1996

Supplementary Instructions using authorised abbreviations for Radiotelegram handling.
British GPO 'Handbook for Wireless Operators' 1908, 1912-23, 1938, 1944, 1954, 1955
ITU Bulletins & Extracts 1961, 1973, 1974, 1985, 1989, 1992, 1996
From 1908 the =....= was sent before and after the Indication. i.e. =D=
(Rearranged into approx. Alphabetical Order.   Italics = Obsolete. 1989)
(..* or ..x   indicates insert number, amount, designator etc.)

RCT	Radiotelegram concerning persons protected in time of war.
RM	Radiotelegram to be sent through an intermediary ship / mobile station.
RP..x	Radiotelegram with reply prepaid.
RQ	Indication of a request.
RST	Reply to paid service advices.
SLT	Radiomaritime Letter (Ship Letter Telegram)
ST	Paid service advices.
SVH	Telegrams relating to safety or life.
TAXE PERCUE	Redirection charge collected.
TC	Radiotelegram to be collated, i.e. repeated from office to office throughout transmission.
TELEX..*	Radiotelegram for which delivery by Telex has been requested. (* insert 'phone no.)
TF ..*	Radiotelegram of which delivery by telephone is compulsory. (* insert telephone number)
TLX x	Radiotelegram for which delivery by Telex has been requested.
TM..*	Radiotelegram with multiple addresses. (* insert no. of addresses.)
TR	Radiotelegram to be called for at a Telegraph Office. 'Telegraphe restante'.
TTX..x	Teletex delivery.
URGENT	Urgent transmission and delivery.
VIA	Route to be followed.
XP XQ	Radiotelegram for express delivery in country of coast station, delivery prepaid.
XXXXX	Service notes.
	Error signal when using automatic error correcting devices.

From the ITU Database, Internet, Jan. 1998.

AF	Deferred Service Telegram.
BOT	Beginning of Telegram.
CLT	Code Language Telegram.
CT	Code or Cypher Telegram.
DI	Destination Indicator (Public Telegram).
DLT	Daily Letter Telegram.
GTC	Government's Telegram Code.
LT	Letter Telegram.
PBL	Preamble of Telegram.
RADD	Registered Address (public telegram)
RAIL	Railway Service Telegram at reduced rate.
RPT ALL	Repeat the whole Telegram.
RPT TG NR	Repeat Telegram Number.
SEM	Semaphore Telegram.
SLT	Social Letter Telegram.
ST	Service Telegram.
TAS	Telegram Automatic System.
TC	Telegram Collation.
TG	Telegram.
TIG	Telegram Identification Group.
TRC	Telegram Retransmission Centre.
TRS	Telegram Retransmission System.
TTBP	Telegram Retransmitted by Post.
URSIGRAM	URSI Telegram. (What is URSI ? - ed.)

37 other definitions did not have Prefix / Prosign / Service Indicator   designators.

Radiotelegraph and Radiotelephone Codes, Prowords and Abbreviations

Royal Navy Convoy Codes - WWI

Identification Codes for Convoys to Britain sailing from -

HB	Bay of Biscay.
HC	Halifax (later Quebec, troop convoys)
HD	Dakar.
HE	Mediterranean through convoys.
HG	Gibralter.
HH	Hampton Roads.
HJ	Rio de Janeiro.
HJD	Rio de Janeiro (joined HD convoys).
HJL	Rio de Janeiro (joined HL convoys).
HL	Sierre Leone.
HS	Sydney (Nova Scotia).
HX	Halifax (or New York)

Identification Codes for Convoys leaving Britain sailing from -

OB	Buncrana.
OC	Southend.
OD	Devonport.
OE	Liverpool, for Eastern Mediterranean.
OF	Falmouth.
OL	Liverpool. Liverpool (
OLB	slow). Liverpool (for
OLX	Halifax) Milford.
OM	Brest (returning US troop convoys).
OR	
OP	Quiberon. (ditto)
OV	Verdon (ditto)

Muirhead Siphon Recorder - Used on trans Atlantic and other long distance cables where a very sensitive receiver was needed to read very weak signals. Modern Electric Practice. 1907

Radiotelegraph and Radiotelephone Codes, Prowords and Abbreviations

Abbreviations — Phillips Code 1875-1945

The Phillips Code was used mainly for Press work. Here are some abbreviations it used.

AWF	Awful	AUMB	Automobile	ACX	Across		
AFN	Afternoon	AUZ	Authorise	ARJ	Around		
ASF	As follows:	AX	Ask	AXD	Asked		
BC	Because	BDA	Birthday	BDC	Broadcast		
BIT	By the	BN	Been	BNG	Bring		
BI	By	BG	Being	BGA	Began		
BGI	Begin	BGU	Begun	BTR	Better		
BV	Believe	BVD	Believed	BVG	Believing		
CA	Came	CAP	Capital	CBN	Celebration		
CBY	Celebrity	CCL	Cancel	CD	Could		
CDN	Canadian	CF	Chief	CFL	Careful		
CHG	Charge	CHGD	Charged	CHGG	Charging		
CHGS	Charges	CHH	Church	CL	Call		
CLD	Called	CLG	Calling	CLO	Close		
CLOD	Closed	CLOG	Closing	CLOS	Closes		
CLQ	Clerk	CLR	Clear	CM	Come		
CNC	Chance	CNDS	Conditions	CNTY	County		
CO	Company	CR	Care	CRD	Cared		
CRS	Cares	CT	Connect	CTY	City		

Despatch — Use concretely, as despatch an Army, or a messenger.
Dispatch — Use abstractly, as dispatch a telegram.

DAS	Days	DD	Did	DLY	Delivery		
DNG	Danger	DOLS	Dollars	DOWN	@ spell out		
DS	Discuss	DSB	Disturb	DSR	Desire		
DSV	Deserve	DT	Do not	DTH	Death		
DU	Duty	DUS	Duties	DVC	Device		
EQL	Equal	ESP	Especial	ESR	And are		
EST	And the	EXK	Expect	EXM	Examine		
EXMD	Examined	EXMG	Examining	EXQ	Excuse		
EY	Every	EYB	Everybody	EYG	Everything		
FAX	Facts	FG	Following	FGH	Photograph		
FHT	Fight	FMX	Famous	FO	For		
FOJ	Fourth of July	FS	First Few	FT	For the		
FTL	Fatal	FU	Fabulous	FVT	Favourite		
FW	Follow	FXB	Freeze	FXD	Fixed		
FXG	Fixing	FZ		FZN	Frozen		
GA	Gave	GG	Going	GF	Gulf		
GL	Girl	GN	Gone	GNI	Goodnight		
GM	Gentleman	GP	Group	GPS	Groups		
GR	Ground	GS	Guess	GV	Give		
GVG	Giving	GVN	Given	GVT	Government		
HD	Had	HEAR	@ spell out	HI	High		
HLS	Hills	HNDL	Handle	HO	Hold		
HOG	Holding	HOM	Home	HOS	Holds		
HP	Hope	HPN	Happen	HR	Hear		
HRM	Harm	HS	His	HSP	Hospital		
ICM	Income	ICP	Incorporate	ICPD	Incorporated		
ICPG	Incorporating	ICPN	Incorporation	IJ ILT	Injure		
IJD	Injured	IJG	Injuring	INXD	Illustrate		
IM	Immediately	INX	Instruct	INXS	Instructed		
INXG	Instructing	INXN	Instruction	IV	Instructs		
IP	Improve	IPO	Impose	IVT	In view		
IVA	Invade	IVG	Investigate		Invite		

Radiotelegraph and Radiotelephone Codes, Prowords and Abbreviations

Abbreviations — Phillips Code 1875-1945

The Phillips Code was used mainly for Press work. Here are some abbreviations it used.

IW	It was	IX	It is	IXN	It is not
JG	Judge	JN	Join	JND	Joined
JNG	Joining	JS	Just	JT	Joint
JU	Jury	JWY	Jewellery	JZ	Juarex
KD	Kind	KDY	Kindly	KG	King
KL	Kill	KLD	Killed	KLG	Killing
KN	Known	KNS	Knows	KP	Keep
KW	Know	KWG	Knowing	KWS	Knows
LAB	Labour	LABD	Laboured	LABG	Labouring
LABS	Labours	LAF	Laugh	LAG	Language
LAS	Last	LF	Life	LG	Long
LGL	Legal	LGR	Longer	LIT	Little
LK	Like	LN	Loan	LRJ	Large
LRN	Learn	LSN	Listen	LST	List
LTR	Letter	LUK	Look	LV	Leave
LVG	Leaving	LVS	Leaves	LW	Law
LWR	Lawyer	LX	Pounds Sterling	LYG	Lying
M	More	MD	Made	MDL	Middle
MEM	Member	MF	Manufacture	MFD	Manufactured
MFG	Manufacturing	MFR	Manufacturer	MFS	Manufactures
MFY	Manufactory	MG	Manage	MGD	Managed
MGG	Managing	MGM	Management	MGR	Manager
MGS	Manages	MIN	Minute	MIT	Might
MK	Make	ML	Mail	MMY	Memory
MNG	Morning	MNY	Many	MO	Month
MOD	Modern	MON	Money	MS	Most
MST	Must	MT	Meet	MTR	Matter
MV	Move	MYN	Million	MYS	Mystery
MYX	Mysterious	MX	Mix	MXD	Mixed
MXG	Mixing	MXR	Mixer	MXS	Mixes
N	Net	NA	Name	NAD	Named
NAG	Naming	NAL	National	NAS	Names
NBH	Neighbourhood	NBR	Neighbour	ND	Need
NF	Notify	NFD	Notified	NFG	Notifying
NI	Night	NL	Natural	NLY	Naturally
NLZ	Naturalise	NLZN	Naturalisation	NOR	Normal
NRY	Nearly	NTC	Notice	NTG	Nothing
NUS	News	NUX	Numerous	NV	Never
NX	Next	NXK	Next week	NZ	New Zealand
O	Of	OA	Of a	OAC	On account of
OB	Obtain	OBD	Obtained	OBG	Obtaining
OBO	On behalf of	OBS	Obtains	OC	O'clock
OCU	Occur	OCUD	Occurred	OCUG	Occurring
OCY	Occasionally	OD	Order	OFR	Offer
OFS	Office	OG	Organise	OGD	Organised
OGG	Organising	OGL	Original	OGN	Organisation
OGS	Organises	OJ	Object	OJD	Objected
OJG	Objecting	OJL	Objectional	OJN	Objection
OJS	Objects	OJV	Objective	OM	Omit
OMS	Omits	OMD	Omitted	OMG	Omitting
OMN	Omission	OQ	Occupy	OQD	Occupied
OQG	Occupying	OQN	Occupation	OQS	Occupies
OS	Oppose	OSD	Opposed	OSG	Opposing
OSN	Opposition	OSS	Opposes	OST	Opposite
OTR	Other	OU	Our	OWG	Owing

Radiotelegraph and Radiotelephone Codes, Prowords and Abbreviations

Abbreviations — Phillips Code 1875-1945

The Phillips Code was used mainly for Press work. Here are some abbreviations it used.

OWZ	Otherwise	OV	Over	OZ	Ounce
PAP	Paper	PB	Probable	PBY	Probably
PBM	Problem	PCD	Proceed	PCH	Purchase
PCHD	Purchased	PCHG	Purchasing	PCS	Pieces
PD	Paid	PDU	Produce	PEO	People
PF	Prefer	PFC	Preference	PFD	Preferred
PFG	Preferring	PFT	Perfect	PG	Progress
PGH	Paragraph	PGM	Program	PGR	Passenger
PH	Perhaps	PHB	Prohibit	PHBD	Prohibited
PHBG	Prohibiting	PHBN	Prohibition	PJT	Project
PKJ	Package	PL	Please	PMT	Permit
PNT	Point	POS	Possible	PPR	Prepare
PRP	Proper	PRT	Part	PS	Pass
PSD	Passed	PSG	Passing	PSJ	Passage
PSN	Person	PSS	Passes	PU	Public
PUR	Purpose	PVI	Provide	PVNT	Prevent
PVNTD	Prevented	PVNTN	Prevention	PX	Price
PXS	Prices	PVX	Previous	PW	Power
PXT	Protect	PXTD	Protected	PXTG	Protecting
PXTS	Protects	PZ	Prize	PZS	Prizes
QK	Quick	QKY	Quickly	QNY	Quantity
QOM	Quorum	QR	Quarter	QSN	Question
QSO	Quite so	QT	Quite	QTN	Quotation
QU	Quiet	QUO	Quota	QUY	Quietly
RA	Raise	RC	Receive	RCD	Received
RCG	Receiving	RCN	Reception	RCT	Receipt
RD	Read	RDG	Reading	RDN	Reduction
RDO	Radio	RDR	Reader	RDS	Reads
REPG	Repeating	REPT	Repeat	REPTN	Repetition
RF	Refer	RFU	Refuse	RG	Regular
RGD	Regard	RGDD	Regarded	RGDG	Regarding
RGDS	Regards	RH	Reach	RHT	Right
RJ	Reject	RL	Real	RLF	Relief
RLY	Really	RLZ	Realise	RM	Remain
RMD	Remained	RMG	Remaining	RTN	Return
RTND	Returned	RTNG	Returning	RTNS	Returns
RV	Remove	RVR	River	RVS	Removes
RVU	Review	RWD	Reward	RWDG	Rewarding
RWDS	Rewards	RX	Recommend	RXD	Recommending
RXG	Resulting	RXN	Recommendation	RXS	Recommends
RY	Railway	RZ	Result	RZD	Resulted
RZG	Resulting	RZS	Results	RZT	Resultant
SAL	Salary	SAP	Soon as possible	SBM	Submit
SBMD	Submitted	SBMG	Submitting	SUBN	Submission
SCA	Scare	SCB	Subscribe	SCBD	Subscribed
SCF	Sacrifice	SCFD	Sacrificed	SCFG	Sacrificing
SCG	Subscribing	SCN	Subscription	SCL	School
SD	Should	SDN	Sudden	SED	Said Says
SEG	Saying	SEN	Seen	SES	Satisfactorily
SFD	Satisfied	SFN	Satisfaction	SFLY	Satisfactory
SFR	Suffer	SFY	Satisfy	SFY	Subjected
SIM	Similar	SJ	Subject	SJD	Success
SJG	Subjecting	SJO	Subject of	SK	Scheduled
SKD	Succeed	SKJ	Schedule	SKJD	Some
SKJG	Scheduling	SLF	Self	SM	Something
SMA	Small	SMB	Somebody	SMG	Since
SMK	Smoke	SN	Soon	SNC	

Radiotelegraph and Radiotelephone Codes, Prowords and Abbreviations

Abbreviations — Phillips Code 1875-1945

The Phillips Code was used mainly for Press work. Here are some abbreviations it used.

SND	Send	SNR	Sooner	SPK	Spoke
SPKN	Spoken	SPL	Special	SPO	Suppose
SPOG	Supposing	SPQR	Speaker	SRX	Serious
SRXY	Seriously	STG	Strong	STGR	Stronger
STGY	Strongly	STY	Steady	SU	Sure
SUG	Suggest	SVC	Service	SVE	Serve
SVR	Severe	SZ	Seize	SZD	Seized
SZG	Seizing	SZN	Season	SZS	Seizes
T	The	TAN	Than	TBL	Trouble
TCH	Touch	TDE	Trade	TDG	Trading
TDY	Today	TEM	Temperature	TEY	Territory
TFK	Traffic	TFR	Transfer	TG	Thing
TGH	Telegraph	TGY	Telegraphy	TH	Those
THO	Though	THQ	Thick	THR	Their
THRU	Through	TI	Time	TK	Take
TKG	Taking	TKN	Taken	TM	Them
TMT	Transmit	TN	Then	TNK	Think
TPH	Telephone	TPN	Transportation	TPW	Typewriter
TR	There	TS	This	TSE	These
TT	That	TWD	Toward	TX	This is
TXB	This is believed	TY	They	TZ	These
UCX	Unconscious	UGT	Urgent	UK	Understand
UKD	Understood	UKG	Understanding	UKN	Unknown
UL	Usual	UN	Until	UNA	Unable
UNC	Uncertain	UND	Under	UNL	Unless
UNU	Unusual	UPN	Upon	USF	Useful
UTZ	Utilise	UV	Universe	UVY	University
VAK	Vacant	VAL	Value	VAY	Variety
VB	Valuable	VCY	Vicinity	VF	Verify
VKM	Victim	VNQ	Vanish	VNT	Violent
VO	Vote	VSB	Visible	VST	Visit
VU	View	VY	Very	VZ	Venezuela
W	With	WAT	Water	WC	Welcome
WD	Would	WDF	Wonderful	WEA	Weather
WEK	Weak	WG	Wrong	WGH	Weigh
WGT	Weight	WH	Which	WHI	While
WHL	Whole	WI	Will	WIX	Wireless
WJ	Wound	WK	Week	WN	When
WO	Who	WOS	Whose	WR	Were
WRD	Word	WRG	Writing	WRK	Work
WRN	Written	WRO	Wrote	WT	What
WUS	Worse	WX	Wait	WXD	Waited
WXG	Waiting	WXR	Waiter	WY	Why
XAC	Exact	XC	Excite	XGH	Extinguish
XGHG	Extinguishing	XGN	Legislation	XGOR	Legislator
XGR	Legislature	XGV	Legislative	XH	Exhaust
XHD	Exhausted	XHG	Exhausting	XHN	Exhausting
XHV	Exhaustive	XJ	Explain	XJD	Explained
XJG	Explaining	XJN	Explanation	XJY	Explanatory
XK	Execute	XKD	Executed	XKN	Execution
XKR	Executor	XKV	Executive	XL	Excel
XLC	Excellence	XLD	Excelled	XLG	Excelling
XLT	Excellent	XLY	Excellently	XM	Extreme
XMT	Exempt	XMTN	Exemption	XMY	Extremely
XN	Constitution	XNL	Constitutional	XBLST	
	Constitutionalist				

Radiotelegraph and Radiotelephone Codes, Prowords and Abbreviations

Abbreviations — Phillips Code 1875-1945

The Phillips Code was used mainly for Press work. Here are some abbreviations it used.

XNTY	Constitutionality	XNY	Constitutionally	XO	Exonerate
XOD	Exonerate	XCG	Exonerating	XON	Exoneration
XOY	Extraordinary	XP	Expense	XPC	Experience
XPD	Expend	XPG	Expending	XPI	Expedite
XPL	Explode	XPLD	Exploded	XPLN	Explosion
XPM	Experiment	XPN	Expedition	XPO	Expose
XPOD	Exposed	XPOG	Exposing	XPON	Exposition
XPR	Expenditure	XPS	Expense	XPT	Export
XPV	Expensive	XR	Exercise	XRD	Exercised
XRG	Exercising	XRL	External	XRN	Exertion
XRS	Exercises	XRT	Exert	XS	Exist
XSC	Existence	XSD	Existed	XSG	Existing
XSS	Exists	XT	Extent	XTD	Extend
XTG	Extending	XTN	Extension	XTV	Extensive
XTY	Extensively	XU	Exclude	XUN	Exclusion
XUV	Exclusive	XXD	Examined(cross)		
XXG	Examining(cross)	XXM	Examine(cross)	XXN	Examination(cross)
Y	Year	YA	Yesterday	YAM	Yesterday Morning
YAP	Yesterday Afternoon	YAV	Yesterday Evening	YD	Yield
YDD	Yielded	YDG	Yielding	YF	Yellow fever
YL	Yellow	YLG	Yearlings	YO	Years old
YOA	Years of age	YOHA	Years of (his or her) age		
Z	From which	ZA	Sea	ZC	Section
ZCL	Sectional	ZD	Said	ZLX	Zealous
ZM	Seem	ZN	Seen	ZNR	Senior
&	And	F	January	B	Be
4	Where	G	February	C	See
5	That the	H	March	D	In the or pence
7	That is	J	April	F	Of the From
		K	May	G	the Out of
MDA	Monday	M	June July	K	the From
TUY	Tuesday	N	August	Z	which
WDA	Wednesday	Q	September	AC	And company
THD	Thursday	U	October	AD	Adopted
FRI	Friday	V	November	CJ	Coroner's Jury
SATY	Saturday	X	December	EM	Embarrass
SDY	Sunday	Z		FB	Of the bill

This is only a short listing. A recent list received has over 6,000 entries. I shall not attempt to enter these.
A more complete listing is available from my page: http://www.nor.com.au/community/sarc/phonetic.htm
The Canadian Railways Telegraph History pages: http://web.idirect.com/~rburnet/
Also at: http://www.cris.com/~Gsraven/morse_misc/phillips.html
Also refer to Morsum Magnificat 61, Christmas 1998.
Page: http://www.qsl.net/ae0q/phillip1.htm

Radiotelegraph and Radiotelephone Codes, Prowords and Abbreviations

ARRL Fixed Text Messages - "ARL" Check.   1949

ARL   Do you have the list of ARRL-Numbered Radiograms?   Are you ready for message?   I have the list of ARRL-Numbered Radiograms.   I am ready for such a message.

Abbreviations for possible relief - emergency use - Numbers are spelt out.

ONE	All safe. Do not be concerned about disaster reports.
TWO	Coming home as soon as possible.
THREE	Am perfectly alright. Don't worry.
FOUR	Everyone safe here. Only slight property damage.
FIVE	All well here. Love to folks.
SIX	Everyone safe, writing soon.
*SEVEN	Reply by amateur radio.
EIGHT	All safe, writing soon, love.
NINE	Come home at once.
TEN	Will be home as soon as conditions permit.
ELEVEN	Cannot get home. Am perfectly alright. Will be home as soon as conditions permit.
*TWELVE	Are you safe? Anxious to hear from you.
*THIRTEEN	Is .... safe? Anxious to hear.
*FOURTEEN	Anxious to know if everything is OK, Please advise.
*FIFTEEN	Advise at once if you need help.
*SIXTEEN	Please advise your condition.
*SEVENTEEN	Kindly get in touch with us.
*EIGHTEEN	Please contact me as soon as possible (at ....)

* Not to be solicited in an emergency.
NOTE: The ARL proword must be used otherwise the number will be received as a number only.

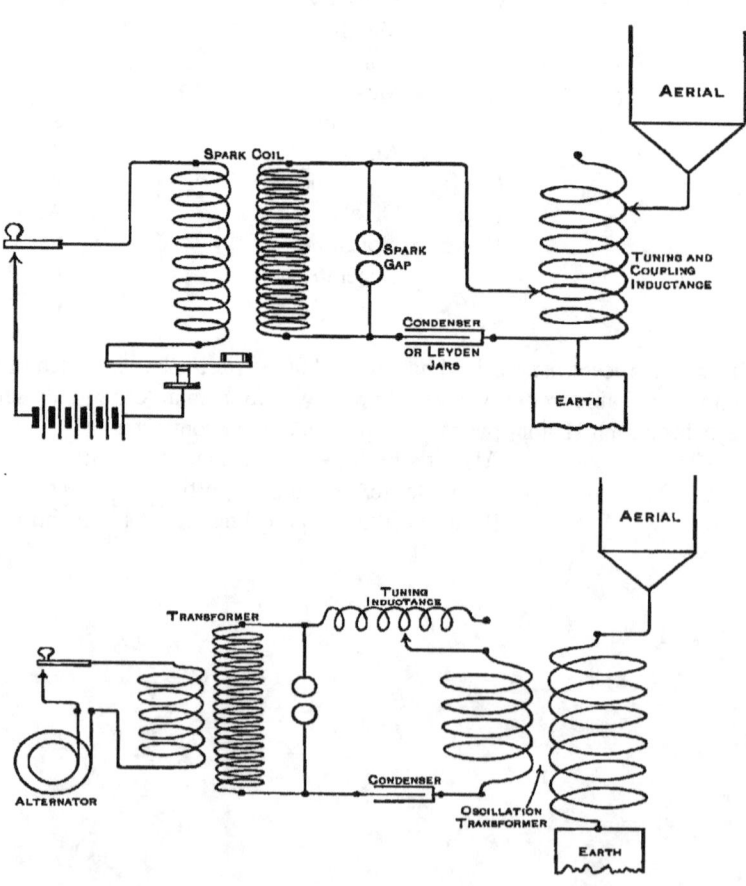

Spark Transmitter circuits using the Spark Coil and the Alternator excitation methods.
Modern Electric Practice   1907.

Radiotelegraph and Radiotelephone Codes, Prowords and Abbreviations

German Semaphore and Morse Methods and Procedures
With English translation. German from http://www.cevi.ch/buwo/pool/ubermitteln.htm

Das Semaphorsystem   The Semaphore System
Wie du bereits gesehen hast, ist dies eine Art Zeigertelegrafie. Durch verschiedene Armstellungen (Zeigerstellungen) bringst du immer einen bestimmten Buchstaben zum Ausdruck. Dieses System erfordert vom Sender und vom Empfänger mehr Genauigkeit und Konzentration als das Morsesystem, ist aber dafür bedeutend schneller (nur ein Zeichen pro Buchstabe).

The semaphore system, as already seen, is a type of visual pointer telegraph.
By different arm positions (pointer positions) you always express a certain letter.
This system requires of the Sender and of the Receiver more accuracy and concentration than the Morse system, it is however important for it is faster (only one character per letter).

Semaphoralphabet
Semaphore Alphabet

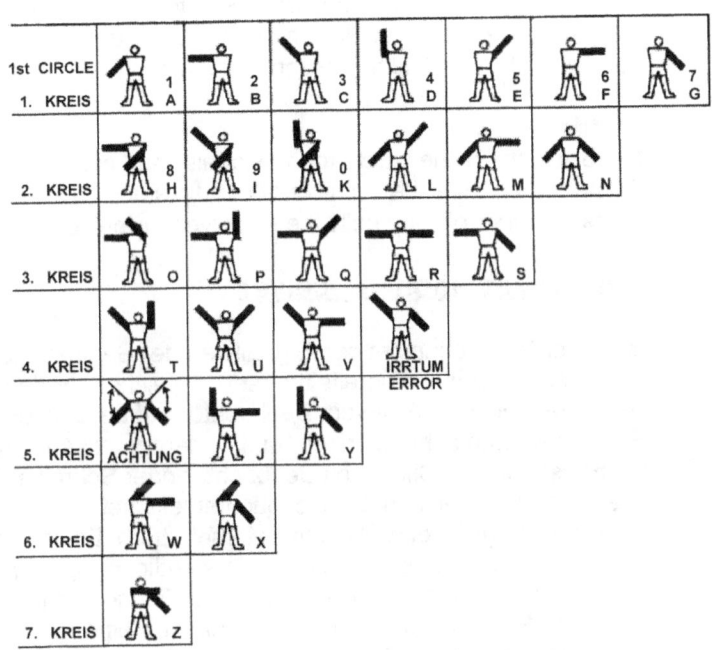

Sendemittel Transmission
Sendemittel auf ganz kurze Distanzen bis 100 m mit leeren Armen, geeigneter Hintergrund (Kontrast) auf weitere Distanz bis 500 m mit Flaggen in rechteckiger Form (etwa 25 * 60 cm), weiß bei dunklem Hintergrund, dunkel bei hellem Hintergrund bei Nacht mit Stecken, an denen je 2 Taschenlampen gebunden sind oder Stecken mit Phosphorbelag (von vorn mit Taschenlampe anstrahlen)

Transmission works on quite short distances to 100 m with plain arms, with suitable background (contrast) on a greater distance to 500 m with flags of rectangular shape (about 25 x 60 cm), light with dark background, dark with bright background, at night by using 2 flashlights or by using a fluorescent lining (illuminate from the front with a flashlight)

Verkehrsregeln Traffic Rules
Aufbau der Semaphorstationen:
1 Signalist, 1 Beobachter, 1 Schreiber.

Structure of the semaphore station:
1 Signaler, 1 Observer, 1 Recorder.
(Reader)

Morsealphabet Morse Alphabet
As in International Morse Code.

Responsibilities in a Morse station
Normal gibt es immer 2 Stationen, Sendestation und Empfangsstation, es kann aber auch eine Relaisstation (Verstärkerstation) eingebaut werden (bei grossen Distanzen, oder wenn keine direkte Sichtverbindung möglich ist).
Normally there are always 2 stations, Sender and Receiver station, a Relay station (verstaerkerstation) can be inserted (for long distances, or if no direct line of sight connection is possible).
Die Relaisstation hat die Aufgabe, die Nachricht satzweise weiterzusenden.

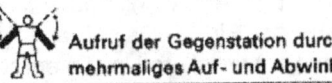

Aufruf der Gegenstation durch mehrmaliges Auf- und Abwinken

«Verstanden, bitte senden», mit dem rechten Arm 3 × kreisen

senden:
Achte darauf, dass du die Flaggen schneidig und eindeutig in Stellung bringst und dort kurze Zeit verharrst.
Wichtig: die Zeichen gelten so, wie sie die Empfangsstation sieht. Nach jedem Wort kreist die rechte Flagge 1 ×

empfangen:
Jedes Wort quittieren.
verstanden:
rechte Flagge 1 × kreisen

nicht verstanden:
1 × Irrtumzeichen

 Ende des Satzes:
2 × rechte Flagge kreisen

 Quittung Ende des Satzes:
verstanden:
2 × rechte Flagge kreisen

nicht verstanden:
2 × Irrtumzeichen

 Ende der Depesche:
3 × rechte Flagge kreisen

 Quittung Ende der Depesche:
verstanden
3 × rechte Flagge kreisen

nicht verstanden:
3 × Irrtumzeichen

 Vor Zahlen:
1 × auf und abwinken, dann Zahlen senden.

 Nach den Zahlen:
1 × rechte Flagge kreisen

Radiotelegraph and Radiotelephone Codes, Prowords and Abbreviations

German Semaphore and Morse Methods and Procedures
With English translation. German from http://www.cevi.ch/buwo/pool/ubermitteln.htm

Eine Station besteht immer aus 3 Leuten:

The relay station has the function to send on the message passage by passage.
A station always consists of 3 people:

Sendestation   Sender

Schreiber Er diktiert dem Signalisten Buchstaben um Buchstaben Kontrolliert ob der Signalist richtig sendet
Signalist Sendet die Zeichen der diktierten Buchstaben, Zahlen und Dienstzeichen
Beobachter Kontrolliert die Empfangsstation und meldet quitt, wenn diese mit . (E), quittiert oder er meldet "nicht verstanden", wenn diese mit - (T) die Buchstaben quittiert.

Sender
Reader dictates the letters to the signaler and checks whether the signaler transmits them correctly.
Signaler transmits the symbols of the dictated letters, numbers and service signals.
Observer controls and calls the Receiver's reply, being "understood" . (E), or " not understood ", — (T).

Empfangsstation   Receiver

Beobachter Beobachtet den Signalisten der Sendestation Ruft erst "quitt" oder "nicht verstanden" für den Signalisten, dann das bereits übersetzte Zeichen für den Schreiber. z.B. "quitt - e"
Schreiber Nimmt Diktat vom Beobachter auf Bei Satzende ruft er dem Signalisten zu, je nachdem ob der Satz einen Sinn hat oder nicht: "quitt" oder "nicht verstanden"
Signalist Gibt auf Diktat von Beobachter oder Schreiber "quitt" oder "nicht verstanden" mit den entsprechenden Dienstzeichen Der Beobachter ist Chef der Morsestation, er lässt die Gegenstation nie aus dem Auge und sorgt für diszipliniertem Morsebetrieb. Es soll keine unnötige Bewegung am Posten herrschen.
Der Schreiber ist für saubere und übersichtliche Aufnahme der Nachricht verantwortlich.
Der Signalist achtet auf exaktes Morsen: Flaggen schnell hochheben und einige Zeit ruhig in Stellung halten, dann Flaggen sofort senken und einige Zeit eng an den Körper angeschlossen halten. In dieser Grundstellung dürfen die Flaggen, für die Gegenstation, nicht sichtbar sein. Bei Nacht ist das Lichtzeichen bis 5* länger als mit Flaggen zu zeigen.
Damit sich das Signalmittel gut abhebt, wählst du immer einen geeigneten Hintergrund (Kontrast!).
Für die Gegenstation darf nur der Signalist sichtbar sein.
Die Nachricht, die Du übermitteln willst, soll im Telegrammstil abgefasst sein.
Also möglichst einfach und ohne unnötige Wörter.

Receiver
The **Observer** observes the signals of the Sender and calls " understood " or " not understood " for the Signaler, then reads the letter for the recorder, already received, e.g. . " I read - e "
The **Recorder** takes the dictation of the Observer to the end of the message and calls to the Signaler too, even if the message makes sense or not: " understood " or " not understood ".
The **Signaler** sends on dictation of the Observer or Recorder " understood " or " not understood " with the appropriate service signals. The Observer is in charge of the Morse station, he never looses sight of the remote station and ensures a disciplined Morse operation.
Unnecessary movement is not allowed at the post.
The Recorder is responsible for the clean and clear acquittal of the message.
The Signaler pays attention to accurate Morse: Move the flags up quickly and keep in position for some time.
Then lower the flags immediately and keep close to the body. In this home position the flags may not be visible to the remote station.
At night the light signal is made 5 times longer than that being shown with flags.
So that the signal meaning stands out well, you always select a suitable background (contrast!).
For the remote station only the signaler may be visible.
The message, which you want to transmit, should be drawn up in telegram style.
Thus made as simply as possible and without unnecessary words.

Dienstzeichen - Service Signals

E   .   Zeichen für "verstanden". Wird von der Empfangsstation nach jedem Zeichen und nach jedem

Radiotelegraph and Radiotelephone Codes, Prowords and Abbreviations

German Semaphore and Morse Methods and Procedures
With English translation. German from http://www.cevi.ch/buwo/pool/ubermitteln.htm

         Wort gegeben, wenn verstanden.
         Signal for "Understood". Given by the Receiver after each Signal and after each Word received, if understood.

T —   Zeichen für "nicht verstanden". Wird von der Empfangsstation nach jedem Wort gegeben, wenn nicht verstanden.
         Signal for "Not understood". Given by the Receiver after each word received when not understood.

Irrtum -----   Wird von der Sendestation gegeben, wenn sie ein falsches Zeichen gegeben hat: In diesem Falle wird das ganze Wort nochmals wiederholt.
Error   Sent by the Sender, when a wrong Signal has been sent: In this case the entire word is correctly repeated.

AR.—·—· "Ende der Nachricht". Wird von der Sendestation am Schluss ihrer Nachricht gegeben.
         "End of Message". Given by the Sender at the end of each message sent.

VE ···—· "Verstanden". Wird von der Empfangsstation gegeben, wenn sie die Nachricht verstanden hat.
         "Understood". Given by the Receiver, if he understood the message.

IMI ··——·· "Nicht verstanden, wiederholen". Wird von der Empfangstation gegeben, wenn sie die Nachricht nicht verstanden hat.
         "Not understood, repeat". Given by the Receiver, when the message was not understood.

QQIMI ——·——·——··——·· Wo bleibt die Quittung? Wird von der Sendestation gegeben, wenn die Empfangsstation vergisst zu quittieren. Zahlen werden falls verstanden, wiederholt, falls nicht verstanden, mit T quittiert.
         Where is your acknowledgment? Sent by the Sender, if the Receiver fails to acknowledge. If number groups, the last one understood is repeated, if not understood reply with T.

OS ———··· "Empfangenes ohne Sinn". "Message received doesn't make sense"
SL ···—·· "Signalisiert langsamer"! "Send slower"
EB ·—··· "Wartet"! Wird von der Sendestation gegeben, wenn sie die Sendung aus irgend einem Grunde unterbrechen muss.
         "Wait" Given by the Sender if it must interrupt a transmission.

RF 50 L   "Revidiert Feuer 50 Meter links", wird von der Empfangsstation gegeben und heisst: Geht 50 Meter nach links (von der Empfangsstation aus gesehen) und beginnt die Sendung von neuem!
         "Redirect light 50 metres left", Sent by the Receiver and read as: "50 metres to the left" (seen from the receiver) and begins transmission of new traffic.

BT —···— Abschnitt   — Paragraph.
ii ····   Wortende   — Break (Word end)
Abt Gr   Abteilung   — Department
Koord   Gruppe   — Group
lk   Koordinate — Coordinate
re   links   — Left
sec   rechts   — Right
min   Sekunde — Second
H   Minute   — Minute
N   Stunde (franz. heure) — Hour
S   Norden   — North
E   Süden   — South
W   Osten (franz. est) — East
             Westen — West

Notsignale Distress Signal

        Diese dürfen während Spielen und Übungen nicht verwendet werden! Nur im Ernstfall.
        Distress signals may not be used during practices or exercises! Only in case of emergency!

SOS ···———··· Notsignal (save our souls = rettet unsere Seelen)
        Distress Signal. [The above origin is incorrect, never meant Save Our Souls. – Ed, JWA]

Alpines Notsignal: Sechs gleiche Zeichen während einer Minute senden, eine Minute warten und wiederholen.
Alpine Distress Signal: Six equal signals sent during one minute, wait one minute and repeat.
Antwort: drei gleiche Zeichen während einer Minute senden, eine Minute warten und wiederholen.
Response: Three equal signals sent during one minute, wait one minute and repeat.

Flaggenstellungen Flag Positions

Radiotelegraph and Radiotelephone Codes, Prowords and Abbreviations

German Semaphore and Morse Methods and Procedures
With English translation. German from http://www.cevi.ch/buwo/pool/ubermitteln.htm

Basic 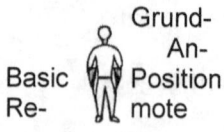 Grund-An-Position Remote  rufen  stellung der Gegen-Dot Station:  Punkt station: Dash   Strich   Calling the

Kreisen bis die Gegenstation mit Kreisen antwortet
Make a circular signal until the Remote Station replies with a circular signal.

Mit Licht: HHH Wortende   With light: HHH   Word end

Mit Licht: IIII   With light: IIII

Bei Signalisation mit Licht oder Ton:
Der Punkt ist ein kurzes Signal der Strich ist fünf mal länger   (mitzählen!)
If signalling with light or sound:
The Dot is a short signal the Dash is five times longer (take note!).

Beispiel einer Übermittlung: Example of a Transmission:
Nachricht: "Um 7 Uhr"
Message: " At 7 o'clock "

Sendestation	Sender	Empfangsstation	Receiver
- - - -	(Anruf) (Call up)		
- - - -	(Anruf) (Call up)		
- - - -	(Anruf) (Call up)	- - - -	(Antwort) (Answer)
- - —	(U)	-	(OK)
— —	(M)	—	(Nicht verstanden) (Not understood)
— —	(M [wiederhalf]) [Repeat]	-	
- - - -	(Wortende) (Word end)	-	
— — - - -	(7)	— — - - -	(7)
- - - -	(Wortende)	-	
- - -	(S [falsch > U])	-	[Wrong > U]
- - - - - - - -	(Irrtum) (Error)	-	
- - —	(U)	-	
- - - -	(H)	-	
- — -	(R)	-	
- - - -	(Wortende)	-	
- — - — -	(Ende) (AR)	- - - — -	(Verstanden) (Understood, end)

Radiotelegraph and Radiotelephone Codes, Prowords and Abbreviations

RADIO SIGNAL REPORTING CODES.

ITU Radio Regulations, Cairo, 1938.

QSA Code (Signal Strength)
- QSA 1 Hardly perceptible, unreadable.
- QSA 2 Weak, readable now and then.
- QSA 3 Fairly good, readable with difficulty.
- QSA 4 Good; Readable.
- QSA 5 Very good, perfectly readable.

QRK Code (Readability)
- R1 Unreadable
- R2 Occasional words distinguishable.
- R3 Readable with difficulty.
- R4 Readable with almost no difficulty.
- R5 Perfectly readable.

Tone Code - (Earlier Amateur Method).

- T1 Poor, 25, 50 or 60 cycle AC tone.
- T2 Rough AC Tone.
- T3 Poor rectified AC, no filter.
- T4 Fair rectified AC, small filter.
- T5 Nearly DC tone, good filter but key thumps.
- T6 Nearly DC, very good filter.
- T7 Pure DC but key thumps, back wave.
- T8 Pure DC tone.
- T9 Pure crystal controlled DC tone.

Plus in German -   x Crystal clear, stable tone.   c With chirps.   k With clicks.

ITU Radio Regulations, Geneva, 1959. - To replace "Q" and other Codes.

Overall Rating for Telegraphy.

Symbol	Mechanised Operation	Morse Operation
5 Excellent	4 Channel time division multiplex	High speed Morse
4 Good.	2 Channel time division multiplex	100 wds/min Morse
3 Fair.	Marginal, single start-stop printer	50 wds/min Morse
2 Poor	Blocks, XQ's and C/Signs readable	Blocks, XQ'S & C/S OK
1 Unusable	Unreadable	Unreadable

Overall Rating for Telephony.

Symbol	Operating Condition	Quality
5 Excellent	Signal quality unaffected	Commercial
4 Good	Signal quality slightly affected	"
3 Fair	Signal quality seriously affected Operators or Experienced Users only	Marginally Commercial
2 Poor	Channel just useable by operators	Not - Commercial
1 Unusable	Channel unusable by operators	

SINFO Signal Reporting Code for C.W.

Scale	Signal Strength	Interf (QRM)	Noise (QRN)	Fading	Overall Readably (QRK)
5	Excellent	Nil	Nil	Nil	Excellent
4	Good	Slight	Slight	Slight	Good
3	Fair	Moderate	Moderate	Moderate	Fair
2	Poor	Severe	Severe	Severe	Poor
1	Barely Audible	Extreme	Extreme	Extreme	Unusable

SINPFEMO Reports for Phone Operation.

Scale	Signal Strength	Interf (QRM)	Noise (QRN)	Propag'n disturb'n	Freq of fading	Modul'n quality	Modulation depth	Overall rating
5	Excel'nt	Nil	Nil	Nil	Nil	Excellent	Maximum	Excellent
4	Good	Slight	Slight	Slight	Slow	Good	Good	Good
3	Fair	Moderate	Moderate	Moderate	Moderate	Fair	Fair	Fair Poor
2	Poor	Severe	Severe	Severe	Fast	Poor	Poor/Nil	Unusable
1	Barely audible	Extreme	Extreme	Extreme	Very fast	Vry poor	Over Mod	

Radiotelegraph and Radiotelephone Codes, Prowords and Abbreviations

Phonetic Alphabets

Dates are for the earliest references so far found and may not be the actual dates of introduction. Corrections, Additions or earlier dates are sought.   # = from Brian Kelk's Listings.

	ca 1860 U.S. Civil War	1891 Oxford English # Dictionary	1904 Aust/Brit. Army (WW1)?	1908+? Telegraphs Tasmania (Brown's)	1914 British Post Office Telephone	1915 British Army	1917 Royal Navy
A	Ag-ainst		Ack	Authority	Apple	Ack	Apples
B	Bar-ba-ri-an	Beer	Beer	Bills	Brother	Beer	Butter
C	Cont-in-ent-al		C	Capture	Charlie	C	Charlie
D	Dah-li-a		D	Destroy	Dover	Don	Duff
E	Egg		E	Englishmen	Eastern	E	Edward
F	Fu-ri-ous-ly		F	Fractious	Father	F	Freddy
G	Gal-lant-ly		G	Galloping	George	G	George
H	Hu-mi-li-ty		H	High	Harry	H	Harry
I	I-vy		I	Invariably	India	I	Ink
J	Ju-ris-dic-tion		J	Juggling	Jack	J	Johnnie
K	Kan-ga-roo		K	Knights	King	K	King
L	Le-gis-la-tor		L	Loose	London	L	London
M	Moun-tain	Emma	Emma	Managing	Mother	Emma	Monkey
N	Nob-le		N	Never	November	N	Nuts
O	Off-ens-ive		O	Owners	October	O	Orange
P	Pho-tog-raph-er		Pip	Play	Peter	Pip	Pudding
Q	Queen-Katharine		Q	Queen	Queen	Q	Queenie
R	Re-bec-ca		R	Remarks	Robert	R	Robert
S	Se-ver-al		Esses	Support	Sugar	Esses	Sugar
T	Tea		Toc	The	Thomas	Toc	Tommy
U	Un-i-form Ve-		U	Unless	Uncle	U	Uncle
V	ry-Va-ried		Vic	Vindictive	Victoria	Vic	Vinegar
W	Wa-ter-loo		W	When	Wednesday	W	Willie
X	Ex-hi-bi-tion		X	Xpeditiously	Xmas	X	Xerxes
Y	Youth-ful-&-fair		Y	Your	Yellow	Y	Yellow
Z	2long-2short		Z	Zig zag	Zebra	Z	Zebra
			The only Phonetics. Others spoken normally.	(British origin, chart printed in Glasgow)		Add 1918	
1						Cork	
2		#				Don	
3						Eddy	
4						Ink	
5						Jug	
6						Quad	
7						Talk	
8							
9							
0							

Note: The ? indicates conflicting but apparently authentic imformation - WW1. 1920, 1940.

Radiotelegraph and Radiotelephone Codes, Prowords and Abbreviations

Phonetic Alphabets (Cont'd)

Dates are for the earliest references so far found and may not be the actual dates of introduction.
Corrections, Additions or earlier dates are sought.   # = from Brian Kelk's Listings.

	1927-41 Aust/Brit Empire Forces	1940 Aust Army (VDC) ?	1940 Aust/Brit Forces	1942-43 Royal Air # Force	1913 U.S. Navy '33 ARRL	1916 U.S. Army (Home)	1919 U.S. Army (France)
A	Ack	Ac	Ack	Apple	Able	Able	Ack
B	Beer	Beer	Beer	Beer	Boy	Boy	Boy
C	Charlie	Charlie	Charlie	Charlie	Cast	Cast	Cat
D	Don	Don	Don	Dog	Dog	Dock	Don
E	Edward	Edward	Edward	Edward	Easy	Easy	E
F	Freddie	Freddie	Freddie	Freddy	Fox	Fox	F
G	George	George	George	George	George	George	George
H	Harry	Harry/How	Harry	Harry	Have	Have	H
I	Ink	Ink Johnnie	Ink	Ink	Item	Item	I
J	Johnnie	King	Johnnie	Jug/Johnny	Jig	Jig	Jig
K	King	L	King	King Love	King	King	K
L	London	Monkey	Love	Mother	Love	Love	L
M	Monkey	N	Monkey	Nuts	Mike	Mike	Emma
N	Nuts	O Pip	Nan	Orange	Nan	Nan	N
O	Orange	Queen	Orange	Peter Queen	Oboe	Opal	O Pip
P	Pip	R	Pip	Robert/Roger	Pup	Pup	Quash
Q	Queen	Sugar	Queen	Sugar	Quack	Quack	R
R	Robert	Toc	Robert	Tommy	Rush *	Rush	Esses
S	Sugar	U Vic	Sugar	Uncle	Sail	Sail	Toc
T	Toc	William	Toc	Vic	Tare	Tare	U
U	Uncle	X	Uncle	William X-	Unit	Unit	Vic
V	Vic	Y	Vic	Ray	Vice *	Vice	W
W	William	Z	William	Yoke/Yorker	Watch *	Watch	X
X	X-Ray		X-Ray	Zebra	X-Ray	X-ray	Yoke
Y	Yorker		Yorker		Yoke	Yoke	Zed
Z	Zebra		Zebra		Zed	Zed	

* 1938 ARRL Rot Victor

Note: These two tables are not reversed. They are correct, taken from contemporary US Army Manuals.

1	Wun		Wun		William	
2	Too Thr-		Too Thr-		Zero	
3	r-ree Foer		r-ree Foer			
4	Fife		Fife			
5	Six		Six			
6	Sev-en		Seven			
7	Ate		Ate			
8	Niner		Niner			
9	Owe		Owe			
0						

Note: The ? indicates conflicting but apparently authentic imformation - WW1. 1920, 1940.

Radiotelegraph and Radiotelephone Codes, Prowords and Abbreviations

Phonetic Alphabets (Cont'd)

Dates are for the earliest references so far found and may not be the actual dates of introduction.
Corrections, Additions or earlier dates are sought.   # = from Brian Kelk's Listings.

	1922?-40 U.S. Army	1922 U.S. Navy	1938 U.S. Navy	1940 U.S. Navy	1941 U.S.A. Combined Forces	1 Jan. '43 Aust / Brit./ US Forces 1947 ICAO
A	Able	Affirmative	Afirm	Able *	Able	Able
B	Buy	Baker	Baker	Baker	Baker	Baker
C	Cast	Cast	Cast	Charlie *	Charlie	Charlie
D	Dock	Dog	Dog	Dog	Dog	Dog
E	Easy	Easy	Easy	Easy	Easy	Easy
F	Fox	Fox	Fox	Fox	Fox	Fox
G	George	George	George	George	George	Golf
H	Have	Hypo	Hypo	How *	How	How
I	Item	Interrogatory	Int	Int	Item	Item
J	Jig	Jig King	Jig	Jig	Jig	Jig King
K	King	Love	King	King	King	Love
L	Love	Mike	Love	Love	Love	Mike
M	Mike	Negative	Mike	Mike	Mike	Nan
N	Nap	Optional	Negat	Negat	Nan	Oboe
O	Opal	Preparatory	Option	Oboe *	Oboe	Peter
P	Pup	Quack	Prep	Peter *	Peter	Queen
Q	Quack	Roger Sail	Queen	Queen	Queen	Roger
R	Rush	Tare	Roger	Roger	Roger	Sugar
S	Sail	Unit	Sail	Sail	Sail	Tare
T	Tape	Vice	Tare	Tare	Tare	Uncle
U	Unit	William	Unit	Uncle *	Uncle	Victor
V	Vice	X-Ray	Victor	Victor	Victor	William
W	Watch	Yoke	William	William	William	X-Ray
X	X-Ray	Zed	Xray	Xray	X-ray	Yoke
Y	Yoke		Yoke	Yoke	Yoke	Zed
Z	Zed		Zed	Zed	Zebra	1945 Zebra
Ä						- Also -
Ö				* List		Edward
Ü				Conflicts		George
				Afirm		Tape
				Cast		
				Hypo		
				Option		
				Prep Unit		
				(Navy terms)		
1						Wun
2						Too
3						Thuh-ree
4						Fo-wer
5						Fi-yiv
6						Six
7						Seven
8						Ate
9						Niner
0						Zero

Radiotelegraph and Radiotelephone Codes, Prowords and Abbreviations

Phonetic Alphabets (Cont'd)

Dates are for the earliest references so far found and may not be the actual dates of introduction. Corrections, Additions or earlier dates are sought.   # = from Brian Kelk's Listings.

	1955 Aust / Brit./ U.S./Allied Forces	1952 I.C.A.O. International Aviation	1956 N.A.T.O. / ITU Regs Ltrs - Figs		1956-69-83+ N.A.T.O. Pronounced as	1927 Internat'l Radioteleg. Convention	1932-47-58 Internat'l Telecommun. Convention
A	Alfa	Alpha	Alpha	1	AL fah	Amsterdam	Amsterdam
B	Bravo	Bravo	Bravo	2	BRAH voh	Baltimore	Baltimore
C	Charlie	Cocoa	Charlie	3	CHAR lee	Canada	Casablanca
D	Delta	Delta	Delta	4	DELL ta	Denmark	Danemark
E	Echo	Echo	Echo	5	ECK oh	Eddystone	Edison
F	Foxtrot	Foxtrot	Foxtrot	6	FOKS trot	Francisco	Florida
G	Golf	Golf	Golf	7	Golf	Gibraltar	Gallipoli
H	Hotel	Hotel	Hotel	8	hoh TELL	Hanover	Havana
I	India	India	India	9	IN dee ah	Italy	Italia
J	Juliett	Juliet	Juliett	0	JEW lee ETT	Jerusalem	Jerusalem
K	Kilo	Kilo	Kilo	','	KEY loh	Kimberley	Kilogramme
L	Lima	Lima	Lima	'/'	LEE mah	Liverpool	Liverpool
M	Mike	Metro	Mike	'BK'	Mike	Madagascar	Madagascar
N	Nectar	Nectar	November	'.'	no VEM bah	Neufchatel	New York
O	Oscar	Oscar	Oscar		OSS kah pah	Ontario	Oslo
P	Papa	Papa	Papa		PAH	Portugal	Paris
Q	Quebec	Quebec	Quebec		keh BECK	Quebec	Quebec
R	Romeo	Romeo	Romeo		RO me oh	Rivoli	Roma
S	Sierra	Sierra	Sierra		see AIR ah	Santiago	Santiago
T	Tango	Tango	Tango		TANG go	Tokio	Tripoli
U	Uniform	Union	Uniform		YOU nee form	Uruguay	Upsala
V	Victor	Victor	Victor		VIK tah WISS	Victoria	Valencia
W	Whiskey	Whiskey	Whiskey		key ECKS ray	Washington	Washington
X	X-Ray	Extra	X-Ray		YANG key	Xantippe	Xanthippe
Y	Yankee	Yankee	Yankee		ZOO loo	Yokohama	Yokohama
Z	Zulu	Zulu	Zulu			Zululand	Zurich
			German / NATO 1949		Accent on Capitals	Slight spelling variations	Each trans- mission of figures is
			When sent as Figures precede and follow by - 'as a number'		Language variations occur. Italian > G = Giuliet.	occur between the English, French and Spanish IRC versions	preceded & followed by 'as a number' spoken twice. (1947)
1	Wun	Wun	or 'as a mark'		Wun	issued	'en nombre'
2	Too	Too	or 'en nombre'		Too	and	(French)
3	Thuh-ree	Thuh-ree	or 'en numeros'		Thuh-ree	other	'en numeros'
4	Fo-wer	Fo-wer	e.g. 38 is - "as		Fo-wer	Languages.	(Spanish)
5	Fi-yiv	Fi-yiv	a number, as a		Fi-yiv		
6	Six	Six	number		Six Se-		
7	Sev-en	Sev-en	Charlie		ven		
8	Ate	Ate	Hotel		Ate		
9	Niner	Niner	as a number,		Niner		
0	Zero	Zero	as a number"		Zero		

Radiotelegraph and Radiotelephone Codes, Prowords and Abbreviations

Phonetic Alphabets (Cont'd)

Dates are for the earliest references so far found and may not be the actual dates of introduction. Corrections, Additions or earlier dates are sought.   # = from Brian Kelk's Listings.

	1932 - 1975 Code A (French) IITS Art 40.	1932 - 1975 Code B (English) IITS Art 40.	1932 British PMG (Telecom-B)	1933 Western Union # Teleg. Co.	Pre WW2 Amateur Radio (Unofficial)	1942 British D.V. System Mnemonic
A	Amsterdam	Andrew	Andrew	Adams	Amsterdam	A.D.
B	Baltimore	Benjamin	Benjamin	Boston	Baltimore/Brazil	Buoy
C	Casablanca	Charles	Charlie	Chicago	Chile/Canada	Code
D	Denmark	David	David	Denver	Denmark	Dee
E	Edison	Edward	Edward	Edward	England/Egypt	E
F	Florida	Frederick	Frederick	Frank	France/Finland	(F)airy
G	Gallipoli	George	George	George	Geneva/Greece	Gnu
H	Havana	Harry	Harry	Henry	Hawaii	(H)ooey
I	Italia	Isaac	Isaac	Ida	Ida/Italy Japan	I.E.
J	Jerusalem	Jack	Jack	John	Kentucky/King	(J)ests
K	Kilogramme	King	King	King	Luxembourg	Kim
L	Liverpool	London	Lucy	Lincoln	Montreal	(L)ibya
M	Madagascar	Mary	Mary	Mary	Nicaragua	M.M.
N	New York	Nellie	Nellie	New York	Ontario/Ocean	No
O	Oslo	Oliver	Oliver	Ocean	Pacific/Portugal	(O)dds
P	Paris	Peter	Peter	Peter	Queen	(P)enny
Q	Quebec	Queen	Queenie	Queen	Romania/Russia	Qvid
R	Roma	Robert	Robert	Robert	Spain/Sweden	(R)ely
S	Santiago	Samuel	Sugar	Sugar	Texas/Tokio	(S)oya
T	Tripoli	Tommy	Tommy	Thomas	United/Uruguay	T
U	Upsala	Uncle	Uncle	Union	Venezuala	Uit (out)
V	Valencia	Victor	Victor	Victor	Washington	(V)aaal
W	Washington	William	William	William	X-Ray	(W)asp
X	Xanthippe	Xray	Xmas	X-Ray	Yokohama	(X)rays
Y	Yokohama	Yellow	Yellow	Young	Zanzibar	Yank
Z	Zurich	Zebra	Zebra	Zero		Zzoo
Ä			1950 Alfred			
Ö	ITU 1975	ITU 1975		-Also-	-Also-	Vowel = Dot
Ü	Codes and	Codes and	-Also-	Easy	America	Cons.= Dash
	Abbreviations	Abbreviations	Alfred	Noble	Germany	except
			Mike	Roger	Honolulu	Y = Dot
		- Also -	London	Zebra	Kilowatt	except in
		Alfred	Samuel		London	Yank.
			Xray		Mexico	Bracketed
			Also used in		Victoria	letters are
1			Collins Foreign			ignored.
2			Language			
3			Dictionaries.			
4			E.g. Dutch,			
5			French			
6			Hungarian			
7			Norwegian			
8			Polish			
9			Swedish			
10			Swiss			

Radiotelegraph and Radiotelephone Codes, Prowords and Abbreviations

Phonetic Alphabets (Cont'd)

Dates are for the earliest references so far found and may not be the actual dates of introduction. Corrections, Additions or earlier dates are sought. # = from Brian Kelk's Listings.

	1943 R.S.G.B. Britain	1945 Western Union Teleg. Co.	1955 British Radio # Engineers	1948-1957 A.R.R.L. USA	IBM Engineers	1965 Afrikaans (Phone Book) #
A	America	Arthur	Abel	Adam	Able	Andries
B	Boston	Benjamin	Bertie	Baker	Baker	Boetie
C	Canada	Charles	Charlie	Charlie Dog	Charlie	Christo
D	Denmark	David	Donald(Don)	/ David	Dog	Dawid
E	England	Edward	Edward	Edward	Easy	Eva
F	France	Frank	Freddie	Frank	Fox	Fanie
G	Germany	George	George	George	George	Gert
H	Holland	Henry	Harry	Henry	Henry	Hendrik
I	Italy	Isaac	India	Ida John	(none)	Isak
J	Japan	John King	Johnnie	King	Jack	Jan
K	Kentucky	Louis	King	Lewis	King	Karel
L	London	Mary	London	Mary	Larry	Lena
M	Mexico	Nathan	Monkey	Nancy	Mother	Marie
N	Norway	Otto Peter	Nuts	Otto	Nancy	Nellie
O	Ontario	Queen	Orange	Peter	(none)	Oom
P	Portugal	Robert	Peter (Pip)	Queen	Peter	Pieter
Q	Quebec	Samuel	Queenie	Robert	Queen	Queenie
R	Radio	Thomas	Robert	Susan	Roger	Roos
S	Santiago	Union	Sugar	Thomas	Sugar	Sannie
T	Turkey	Victor	Tommy (Toc)	Union	Tommy	Tom
U	University	William	Uncle Victory	Victor	Uncle	Unie
V	Victoria	X-Ray	William	William	Victor	Venter
W	Washington	Yellow	X-Ray	X-Ray	Whisky	Willem
X	X-Ray	Zero	Yorker	Young	X-ray	X-straal
Y	Yokohama		Zebra	Zebra	Yankee	Yster
Z	Zanzibar				Zulu	Zoeloe
Ä						
Ö	-Also-				I & O not	
Ü	Honolulu				used to	
	Kilowatt				avoid	
	Pacific				confusion	
	Spain				with	
	Tokyo				1 & 0	
	United					
0	(Unofficial)			International	Used for	
1				Unaone	HEX digits	een
2				Bissotwo	and	twee
3				Terrathree	pin	drie
4				Kartefour	positions	vier
5				Pantafive		vyf
6				Soxisix		ses
7				Setteseven		sewe
8				Oktoeight		agt
9				Novenine		nege
10				Nadazero		tien

Radiotelegraph and Radiotelephone Codes, Prowords and Abbreviations

Phonetic Alphabets (Cont'd)

Dates are for the earliest references so far found and may not be the actual dates of introduction. Corrections, Additions or earlier dates are sought. # = from Brian Kelk's Listings.

	1955 Argentina (Phone Book)	2002 Argentina Police	Austria 'Phone # Directory	1966 Azores (Phone Book)	2001 Brazil Military & Amateur etc.	Chinese Army (Romanised # Mandarin)
A	Amsterdam	Alicia	Anton	Amsterdam	Alfa	Aiya
B	Baltimore	Beatriz	Berta	Baltimore	Bravo	Boli Ciqi
C	Casablanca	Carolina	Cäsar	Casablanca	Charlie	Desheng
D	Dinamarca	Dorotea	Dora	Danemark	Delta	Egu
E	Edison	Eva	Emil	Edison	Eco	Fuzhuang
F	Florida	Francisca	Friedrich	Florida	Foca	Geming
G	Gallipoli	Guillermina	Gustav	Gallipoli	Golfe	Heping
H	Habana	Hombre	Heinrich	Havana	Hotel	Yifu
I	Italia	Ines Julieta	Ida	Itália	India	J.. Keren
J	Jerusalén	Kilo	Julius	Jerusalém	Juliete	Leguan
K	Kilogramo	Lucia	Konrad	Kilogramme	Kilo	Mofan
L	Liverpool	Maria	Ludwig	Liverpool	Lima	Nali
M	Madagascar	Natalia	Martha	Madagascar	Mike	Ouyang
N	Nueva-York	Ofelia	Nordpol	New-York	November	Polang
O	Oslo Paris	Petrona	Otto	Oslo	Oscar	Q..
P	Quebec	Quintana	Paula	Paris	Papa	Riguang
Q	Roma	Rosa	Quelle	Québec	Quebec	Sixiang
R	Santiago	Sara Teresa	Richard	Roma	Romeu	Tebie
S	Tripoli	Ursula	Siegfried	Santiago	Sierra	Weida
T	Upsala	Victoria	Theodor	Tripoli	Tango	Wudao
U	Valencia	Washington	Ulrich	Upsala	Uniforme	Wuzhuang
V	Wáshington	Xilofono	Viktor	Valencia	Victor	X..
W	Xantipo	Yolanda	Wilhelm	Washington	Wiskey	Yisheng
X	Yokoama	Zapato	Xaver	Xantippe	Xingu	Zidian
Y	Zurich	andu	Ypsilon	Yokoham	Yankee	
Z			Zürich	Zurich	Zulu	
Ä			Ärger		or Zebra	
Ö			Österreich			
Ü			Übel			
CH			Christine -Also- Norbert Xanten Zacharias Zeppelin			

		Austria			Brazil	Army - Civil
0						dong
1		ein				yao yi
2		zwei				liang èr
3		drei				san san
4		vier				sì sì
5		fünf				wû wû
6		sechs				liù liù
7		sieben				guai qi
8		acht				ba ba
9		neun				gou jiû
10		zehn				shí shí

Radiotelegraph and Radiotelephone Codes, Prowords and Abbreviations

Phonetic Alphabets (Cont'd)

Dates are for the earliest references so far found and may not be the actual dates of introduction.
Corrections, Additions or earlier dates are sought. # = from Brian Kelk's Listings.

	c1935? Czech On Field Telephone	Czech (Berlitz # Phr. Bk.)	2000 Czech (Cesky Radioklub)	2001 Czech Army 2nd HIW	Croatian #	Danish (Berlitz # Phrase Book)
A	Anna	Adam	Adam	Akat	Adria	Anna
B	Bed ich Cyril /	Božena	Božena	Blyskavice	Biokovo	Bernhard
C	en ck Daniel /	Cyril	Cyril	Cilovnici	Cavtat	Cecilia
D	ábel Ema	David	David	Dalava Erb	Dubrovnik	David
E	František	Emil	Emil	Filipiny	Europa	Erik
F	Gustav	František	František	Gronska zem	Frankopan	Frederik
G	Helena /	Gustav	Gustav	Hrachovina	Gospic	Georg
H	Ida	Helena	Helena	Ibis	Hrvatska	Hans
I	Julie	Ivan	Ivan	Jasmin bily	Istra	Ida
J	Karel	Josef	Josef	Krakora	Jadran	Johan
K	Ludvik	Karel	Karel	Lupinecek	Karlovac	Karen
L	Marie	Ludvík	Ludvík	Mava	Lika	Ludvig
M	Norbert	Marie	Marie	Nachod	Mostar	Marie
N	Ota	Norbert	Norbert	O nas pan	Novska	Nikolaj
O	Pavel	Oto	Oto (Otakar)	Papirnici	Osijek	Odin
P	Quido	Petr	Petr	Kvili orkan	Pula	Peter
Q	Rudolf / im	Quido	Quido /Kvido	Rarasek	Q Rijeka	Quintus
R	Stanislav /	Rudolf	Rudolf	Sobota	Split	Rasmus
S	Theodor /	Svatopluk	Svatopluk	Tram	Trogir	Soeren
T	U itel	Tomás	Tomáš Urban	Uceny	Ucka	Theodor
U	Václav	Urban	Václav	Vyuceny	Vukovar	Ulla
V	W-dvojite	Václav	Dvojité_vé	Wagon klad	W	Viggo
W	Xantipa	Dvojité_vé	Xaver Ypsilon	Xenokrates	X	William
X	Ypsilon	Xaver	Zuzana	Ygor mava	Y	Xerxes
Y	Zachariáš	Ypsilon	È Èenik	Znama zena	Zagreb	Yrsa
Z		Zuzana	Ï Ïáblice			Zacharias
Ä	or Žofie		CH Chrudim			Æ - Ægir
Ö		-Also-	Lubochòa			Ø - Ørsund
Ü		Dùbochña				Å - Åse
CH		Lùbochnã				
		Rehor	Ò Nina			Military use
		Š Šimon	Ø Øehoø			NATO plus
		Tèplá	Š Šimon			Æ - Ægir Ø
		Ž Žofie	Tišnov			- Ørsund Å
0			Ž Žofie			- Åse
1		jeden			jedan	én
2		dvê trî			dva tri	to
3		chtyri			cheteri	tre
4		pêt			pet	fire
5		shest			shest	fem
6		sedm			sedem	seks
7		osm			osem	syv
8		devêt			devet	otte
9		deset			deset	ni
10						ti

Radiotelegraph and Radiotelephone Codes, Prowords and Abbreviations

Phonetic Alphabets (Cont'd)

Dates are for the earliest references so far found and may not be the actual dates of introduction.
Corrections, Additions or earlier dates are sought.   # = from Brian Kelk's Listings.

	Dutch (Berlitz # Phrase Bk)	Dutch (Collins # Phrase Bk)	195? Dutch Scouts Mnemonic	1995 Esperanto	Finnish #
A	Anna	Amsterdam	An-ton	Asfalto	Aarne
B	Bernhard	Bravo	Bok-ke-wa-gen	Barbaro	Bertta
C	Cornelis	Charlie	Com-man-do-brug	Centimetro	Celsius
D	Dirk	Dirk	Dors-vle-gel	Doktoro	Daavid
E	Eduard	Edam	Eend	Elemento	Eemeli
F	Ferdinand	Freddie	Feest-ge-no-ten	Fabriko	Faarao
G	Gerard	Goed	Groot-moe-der	Gumo	Gideon
H	Hendrik	Help	Huis-be-zit-ter	Hotelo	Heikki
I	Izaak	Isaac	Ie-mand	Insekto	Iivari
J	Jan Karel	Jaap	Ja,-o-zo-mooi	Jubileo	Jussi
K	Lodewijk	Kilo	Kloos-ter-poort	Kilogramo	Kalle
L	Marie	Lasso	Lik-doorn-snij-der	Legendo	Lauri
M	Nico	Moeder	Mo-tor	Masino	Matti
N	Otto	Nico	Noor-den	Naturo	Niilo
O	Pieter	Otto	Oor-logs-vloot	Oktobro	Otto
P	Quotient	Paard	Per-mo-tor-fiets	Papero	Paavo
Q	Rudolf	Quaker	Quols-dorp-in-	* Kuo	Kuu
R	Simon	Rudolf	Re-vol-ver	Rekordo	Risto
S	Teunis	Suiker	Sein-sleu-tel	Salato	Sakari
T	Utrecht	Tafel	Toon	Triumfo	Tyyne
U	Victor	Uur	U-ni-form	Universo	Urho
V	Willem	Vogel	Va-kan-tie-oord	Vulkano	Vihtori
W	Xantippe	Wind	Waar-borg-som	* Germana_vo	Viski
X	Ypsilon	Xylofoon	Zon-der-slag-	* Ikso	Äksä
Y	Zaandam	Yankee	Yor-ker-moor-kop	* Ipsilono	Yrjö
Z	ij Ijmuiden	Zout	Zoe-loe-kaf-fer	Zinko	Tseta
Ä				Gé - Géirafo	Å - Åke
Ö			Syllables with an	Hé - Héaoso	Ä - Äiti
Ü	-Also- Quadraat		'o', 'oo' = dash, others = dot	Sé - Séilingo Also - Cefo Jurnalo	Ö - Öljy
			MM57	Omnibuso Universo_hoko	
0				* Not Esperanto letter.	
1	een	een		unu	yksi
2	twee	twee		du	kaksi
3	drie	drie		tri	kolm
4	vier	vier		kvar	nelja
5	vijf	vijf		kvin	viisi
6	zes	zes		ses	kuusi
7	zeven	zeven		sep	seitsemän
8	acht	acht		ok	kahdeksan
9	negen	negen		naû	yhdeksan
10	tien	tien		dek	kymmenen

Radiotelegraph and Radiotelephone Codes, Prowords and Abbreviations

Phonetic Alphabets (Cont'd)

Dates are for the earliest references so far found and may not be the actual dates of introduction.
Corrections, Additions or earlier dates are sought.   # = from Brian Kelk's Listings.

	Finnish (Berlitz # Phr. Book)	Flemish New Oxford Dictionary#	French #	French OUP # Vocab. book	French Langens- # cheidt	French Larousse # Busin. book
A	Anna	Arthur	Anatole	Anatole	Anatole	Arthur
B	Bertta	Brussel	Bernard	Berthe	Berthe	Bruxelles
C	Cecilia	Carolina	Cécile	César	César	Caroline
D	Daavid	Desire	Denise	Désiré	Désiré	Désiré
E	Erkki	Emiel	Émile	Eugène	Émile	Émile
F	Faarao	Frederik	François	François	François	Frédéric
G	Gabriel	Gustaaf	Gérard	Gaston	Gaston	Gustave
H	Heikki	Hendrik	Henri	Henri	Henri	Henri
I	Iivari	Isidoor	Isidore	Irma	Isidore	Isidore
J	Jaakko	Jozef	Jean	Joseph	Jean	Joseph
K	Kalle	Kilogram	Kléber	Kléber	Kléber	Kilogramme
L	Lauri	Leopold	Louis	Louis	Louis	Léopold
M	Mikko	Maria	Marcel	Marcel	Marie	Marie
N	Niilo	Napoleon	Nicole	Nicolas	Nicolas	Napoléon
O	Otto	Oscar	Oscar	Oscar	Oscar	Oscar
P	Pekka	Piano	Pierre	Pierre	Paul	Piano
Q	Quintus	Qualite	Quital	Québec	Québec	Quiévrain
R	Risto	Robert	Robert	Robert	Robert	Robert
S	Sakari	Sofie	Suzanne	Suzanne	Suzanne	Suzanne
T	Tauno	Telefoon	Thérèse	Thérèse	Théodore	Téléphone
U	Urho	Ursula	Ursule	Ursule	Ursule	Ursule
V	Väinö	Victor	Victor	Victor	Victor	Victor
W	Kaksin_V	Waterloo	Wagon	William	Wagon	Waterloo
X	Xeres	Xavier	Xavier	Xavier	Xavier	Xavier
Y	Yrjö	Yvonne	Yvonne	Yvonne	Yvonne	Yvonne
Z	Zeppelin	Zola	Zoé	Zoé	Zoé	Zéro
Ä	Äiti					
Ö	Öljy					

-Also-
Anne
Célestin
Gustave
Olga

-Morse-
Ä .—.—
Å .——.—
Ö ———.

	Finnish		French
0			
1	yksi		un
2	kaksi		deux
3	kolm		trois
4	nelja		quatre
5	viisi		cinq
6	kuusi		six
7	seitsemän		sept
8	kahdeksan		huit
9	yhdeksan		neuf
10	kymmenen		dix

Radiotelegraph and Radiotelephone Codes, Prowords and Abbreviations

Phonetic Alphabets (Cont'd)

Dates are for the earliest references so far found and may not be the actual dates of introduction. Corrections, Additions or earlier dates are sought.   # = from Brian Kelk's Listings.

	French Post # Office	1914-26 German WW1	1939 German Army, PO, Civil to 1993	1939 German Navy	German Mnemonic # Phonetics	Greek (AA Phrase Bk Gwillim Law)	
A	Anatole	Adolf	Anton	Anton	Arno	A	Aléxandros
B	Berthe	Berta	Berta	Bruno	Borvaselin	B	Vasílios
C	Célestin	Cäsar	Cäsar	Cäsar	Coburg-Gotha	G	Geórgios
D	Désiré	David	Dora	Dora	Doria	D	Demétrios
E	Eugène	Emil	Emil	Emil	Ernst	E	Eléne
F	François	Friedrich	Friedrich	Fritz	Friedrichsroda	Z	Zoe
G	Gaston	Gustav	Gustav	Gustav	Gomorrha	H	Eraklés
H	Henri	Heinrich	Heinrich	Heinz	Herrenzimmer	Q	Theódoros
I	Irma	Isidor	Ida	Ida	Ida	I	Ioánnes
J	Joseph	Jakob	Julius	Jot Karl	Jawohl_Odol		
K	Kléber	Karl	Konrad	Luci	Kolberg_Ost	K	Konstanínos
L	Louis	Ludwig	Ludwig	Max	Leonidas	L	Leonídas
M	Marcel	Moritz	Martha	Nordpol	Motor	M	Menélaos
N	Nicolas	Nathan	Nordpol	Otto	Nora	N	Nikólaos
O	Oscar	Otto	Otto	Paula	Oekonom	X	Xenofón
P	Pierre	Paula	Paula	Quelle	Per_Motorrad	O	Odusséas
Q	Québec	Quelle	Quelle	Richard	<	P	Periklés
R	Raoul	Richard	Richard	Siegfried	Revolver	R	Ródos
S	Suzanne	Siegfried	Siegfried	Toni	Sabine	S	Sotérios
T	Thérèse	Theodor	Toni	Ulrich	Tod	T	Timolón
U	Ursule	Ursula	Ulrich	Viktor	Uniform	U	Upselántes
V	Victor	Viktor	Viktor	Willi	Verbren-	Φ	Fótios
W	William	Willi	Wilhelm	Xantippe	Weltnordpol		
X	Xavier	Xantippe	Xantippe	Ypsilon	Xolabaphon	X	Chréstos
Y	Yvonne	Ypsilon	Ypsilon	Zeppelin	York_Yellowst	Y	Psáltes
Z	Zoé	Zacharias	Zeppelin		Zoroaster	W	Oméga
É	Émile	·—·—	Ä Ärger		oe Oekonomie		
		———·	Ö Ödipus		ue Ueberkonto		
	Also	··——	Ü Übel				
	Berlitz AA	————			This		
	phrase		-Also-		Alphabet		
	Larousse		1965 Karl		provides		
	Quintal		1977 Kaufman		mnemonics	(1980)	
	Rene		Samuel		for Morse	(Phonetic)	
		null	Theodore		Code.		
1		eins	Zacharias		An 'o' means	ehnah	
2		zwo	Anna		a DASH.	dheeo	
3		drei	Jakob		Other	treeah	
4		vier	Jerusalem		syllables	tehsehrah	
5		fünf	Johan		mean a	pehndeh	
6		sechs	Kaiser		DOT.	ehksee	
7		sieben	Kaufmann			ehptah	
8		acht	Sophie			okto	
9		neun	Übermut			ehnehah	
10		zehn				dhehkah	

Radiotelegraph and Radiotelephone Codes, Prowords and Abbreviations

Phonetic Alphabets (Cont'd)

Dates are for the earliest references so far found and may not be the actual dates of introduction.
Corrections, Additions or earlier dates are sought.   # = from Brian Kelk's Listings.

		Hebrew (Berlitz) # Roman Alpha-	Hebrew (Telephone)# Roman Alpha-	Hebrew # (Not Roman)	Hebrew # (Not Roman)	Hungarian (Phone # Book)	Hungarian (Amateur # Radio)
A	a	Affula	Afula	Aleph	Osnat	András	Antal
B	b	Binyamina	Binyamina	Boaz	Bela	Béla	Béla
C	c	Carmel	Karmel	Gimel	Gila	Cecil	Cecil
D	d	Dalia	Dalya	David	Dalia	Dóra	Dénes
E		Eretz	Eretz Frans	Hagar	Hagar	Elemér	Elemér
F	>	France	Gedera	Vav	Vered	Ferenc	Ferenc
G	g	Gedera	Heyfa	Zéev	Ziva	Gizella	Géza
H	h	Haifa	Yisrael	Hava	Hava	Hajnalka	Helén
I	i	Israel	Jafa Karkur	Tiach	Tova	István	Ibolya
J	j	Jaffa	Lod	Yona	Yona	János	János
K	k	Karkur	Moledet	Carmel	Carmel	Katalin	Károly
L	l	Lod	Naan Ogen	Lea	Leytal	Luca	László
M	m	Moledet	Pardes	Moshe	Miri	Mátyás	Mária
N	n	Naan	Kvin	Nesher	Nurit	Nándor	Nelli
O	o	Ogden	Rishon	Samekh	Smadar	Olga	Olga
P	p	Pardes	Sefer	Áin	Einat	Piroska	Péter
Q	q	Queen	Tverya	Pesel	Fani	Queen	Kvelle
R	r	Rishon	Urim	Tsipor	Tzila	Róbert	Róbert
S	s	Sefer	Vered	Korah	Korina	Sarolta	Sándor
T	t	Tveria	Vingeyt	Ruth	Ruth	Tímea	Tamás
U	u	Urim	Ekspres	Shamir	Sarah	Ubul	Ubul
V	v	Vered	Yavniel	Telem	Tami	Vilmos	Viktor
W	w	Wingate	Zikhron			Walter	Dupla-vé
X	x	Express				Xénia	X-es
Y	y	Yavniel				Ypsilon	Ipszilon
Z	z	Zikhron				Zoltán	Zoltán

			-Also-	-Also-		-Also-
			Tsipor	See Israeli		Cézár
			Korakh	Army in		Imre
				"Addenda"		Vilmos
	Modern					Dupla-Vilmos
	Hebrew		Yiddish			W – Viski
0			nul ein			Y – Jenki
1	àxat		tsvei		egy	
2	shtayim		drei		kettö	
3	shalosh		fier		három	
4	arba		finef		négy	
5	xamesh		seks		öt	
6	shesh		sibben		hat hét	
7	shevà		acht		nyolc	
8	shmone		nein		kilenc	
9	tesha		zehn		tiz	
10	èsha					

Radiotelegraph and Radiotelephone Codes, Prowords and Abbreviations

Phonetic Alphabets (Cont'd)

Dates are for the earliest references so far found and may not be the actual dates of introduction. Corrections, Additions or earlier dates are sought.   # = from Brian Kelk's Listings.

	Hungarian (Berlitz # Phr. Bk.)	1962 India (Bombay) #	Indonesian (Phrase Book)	1966-93 Italian (Geneva) #	Italian (E. Buie) #	Italian (Cassel) #
A	Aladár	Army	Alfa	Anna	Ancona	Ancona
B	Balázs	Brother	Bravo	Battista	Bologna	Bologna
C	Cecília	Cinema	Coca	Carlo	Como	Cagliari
D	Dénes	Doctor	Delta	Davide	Domodossola	Domodossola
E	Erzsébet	English	Echo	Ernesto	Empoli	Empoli
F	Ferenc	Father	Foxtrot	Federico	Firenze	Firenze
G	Gábor	Gold	Golf	Giovanni	Genova	Genova
H	Helén	Hotel	Hotel	Acca	Hacca	Hotel
I	Ilona	India	India	Isidoro	Imola	Imola
J	József	Jam	Juliet	i_lungo	Jolly	Jolly
K	Károly	King	Kilo	Cappa	Kappa	Kappa
L	László	Lady	Lima	Luigi	Livorno	Londra
M	Mónika	Mother	Metro	Maria	Milano	Milano
N	Nándor	Navy	Nectar	Nicola	Napoli	Napoli
O	Olga	Orange	Oscar	Olga	Otranto	Otranto
P	Péter	Paper	Papa	Pietro	Pisa/Palermo	Palermo
Q	Kú	Queen	Quebec	Quintino	Quartomiglio	Quarto
R	Róbert	Raja	Romeo	Rodolfo	Roma	Roma
S	Sándor	Sister	Siera	Susanna	Savona/Siena	Sondrio
T	Tivadar	Table	Tango	Teresa	Torino	Torino
U	Ubul	Uncle	Union	Umberto	Udine	Udine
V	Vilma	Victory	Victor	Vittorio	Venezia	Vicenza
W	Duplavé	Water	Whiskey	vu_doppia	Wagner	Vdoppio
X	Iksz	X-Ray	Extra	Ics	Xilofono	X
Y	Ipszilon	Yellow	Yankee	Ipsilon	York	Yugoslavia
Z	Zorán	Zero	Zulu	Zurigo	Zara	Zagabria

Ö - Ödön
Ü - Üröm

-Also-
Ágota
Éva

0				zero		zero
1				uno		uno
2				due		due
3				tre		tre
4				quattro		quattro
5				cinque		cinque
6				sei		sei
7				sette		sette
8				otto		otto
9				nove		nove
10				diece		diece

Radiotelegraph and Radiotelephone Codes, Prowords and Abbreviations

Phonetic Alphabets (Cont'd)

Dates are for the earliest references so far found and may not be the actual dates of introduction. Corrections, Additions or earlier dates are sought.   # = from Brian Kelk's Listings.

	Italian (BBC) #	Italian (Cassel Busin. Book)#	Italian (S. Inniami) #	Italian (Berlitz) # Phrase Book)	Italian (Collins # Phrase Book)	Italian (Collins / AA)
A	Ancona	Ancona	Ancona	Ancona	Ancona	Ancona
B	Bologna	Bologna	Bari Como	Bari Catania	Bari Catania	Bologna
C	Como	Como	Domodossola	Domodossola	Domodossola	Como
D	Domodossola	Domodossola	Empoli	Empoli	Empoli	Domodossola
E	Empoli	Empoli	Firenze	Firenze	Firenze	Empoli
F	Firenze	Firenze	Genova	Genova	Genova	Firenze
G	Genova	Genova	Acca	Hotel	Hotel	Genova
H	Hotel	Hotel Imola	Imola	Imperia	Imperia	Hotel
I	Imola	I_lunga	Jolly	I_lunga		Imola
J	Jersey	Kursaal	Cappa	Kappa		Jersey
K	Kilo	Livorno	Livorno	Livorno		Kursaal
L	Livorno	Milano	Milano	Milano	Livorno	Livorno
M	Milano	Napoli	Napoli	Napoli	Milano	Milano
N	Napoli	Otranto	Otranto	Otranto	Napoli	Napoli
O	Otranto	Padova	Palermo	Palermo	Otranto	Otranto
P	Palermo	Quarto	Quartomiglio	Cu	Palermo	Padova
Q	Quaderno	Roma	Roma Siena	Roma	Quarto	Quarto
R	Roma	Savona	Torino Udine	Sassari	Roma	Roma
S	Savona	Torino	Venezia	Torino	Savona	Savona
T	Torino	Udine	Walter	Udine	Torino	Torino
U	Udine	Venezia	Ics	Venezia	Udine	Udine
V	Venezia	Washington	York	V_doppia	Venezia	Venezia
W	Washington	Ics	Zurigo	Ix i_greca	?	Washington
X	Ics	York / Yacht		Zeta		Xeres Yacht
Y	York	Zara				Zara
Z	Zurigo				Zara	
					-also- Como	-Also- Torino

1
2
3
4
5
6
7
8
9
10

Radiotelegraph and Radiotelephone Codes, Prowords and Abbreviations

Phonetic Alphabets (Cont'd)

Dates are for the earliest references so far found and may not be the actual dates of introduction.
Corrections, Additions or earlier dates are sought.   # = from Brian Kelk's Listings.

	Italian (Pitman # Phrase Book)	Italian (Berlitz) #	Italian (Langenscheidt) #	Italian (Routledge) #	1966 Kenya - Tanzania #
A	Ancona	Ancona	Ancona	Ancona	Africa
B	Bologna	Bari Catania	Bologna	Bologna	Bombay
C	Como	Domodossola	Como	Como	Charlie
D	Domodossola	Empoli	Domodossola	Domodossola	Durban
E	Empoli	Firenze	Empoli	Empoli	England
F	Firenze / Forlì	Genova	Forli	Firenze	Freddie
G	Genova	Hotel	Genova	Genova	George
H	Acca	Imola	Hotel	Hotel	Harry
I	Imola	-	Imola	Imola	India
J	I_lunga	-	Jolanda	i lungo/Jolly	Japan
K	Cappa	Livorno	Cappa	cappa/Kennedy	Kenya
L	Livorno	Milano	Livorno	Livorno	London
M	Milano	Napoli	Milano	Milano	Mombasa
N	Napoli	Otranto	Napoli	Napoli	Nairobi
O	Otranto	Palermo	Otranto	Otranto	Orange
P	Palermo	Quarto	Pisa	Palermo	Peter
Q	Cu	Roma	Quattro	cu/quaranto *	Queen
R	Roma	Sassari	Roma	Roma	Robert
S	Savona	Torino	Salerno	Salerno	Sugar
T	Torino	Udine	Torino	Torino	Tanga
U	Udine	Venezia	Udine	Udine	Uganda
V	Venezia	-	Venezia	Venezia	Victory
W	Washington	-	Washington	Washington	William
X	Ics	-	Ics Ypsilon	Ics	X-Ray
Y	Ipsilon	-	Zeta	Ypsilon	Yellow
Z	Zara			Zeta/Zara	Zanzibar

* Quarto

1	uno
2	due
3	tre
4	quattro
5	cinque
6	sei
7	sette
8	otto
9	nove
10	diece

Radiotelegraph and Radiotelephone Codes, Prowords and Abbreviations

Phonetic Alphabets (Cont'd)

Dates are for the earliest references so far found and may not be the actual dates of introduction.
Corrections, Additions or earlier dates are sought.   # = from Brian Kelk's Listings.

	Kenya Analogy Alphabet	Kwanyama (SW Bantu, Nth Namibia)#	Latin America # (Langenscheidt)	Latin America (Berlitz) #	Latin America (AA Phr bk) #
A	Alfred	Anna	Antonio	Amalia	Ana
B	Benjamin	Beata	Bogotá	Beatriz	Bueno
C	Charlie	Cesilia	Carmen	Carmen	Carlos
D	David	David	Dora	Domingo	Dedo
E	Edward	Eva	Enrique	Enrique	Eduardo
F	Frederick	Feni	Francisco	Federico	Francia
G	George	Gerson	Gibraltar	Guatemala	Gato
H	Harry	Hosea	Historia	Honduras	Historia
I	Isaac	Immanuel	Inés	Ida	Inés
J	Jack	Johanna	José Kilo	José	José
K	King	Kayosho	Lorenzo	Kilo	Kilo
L	London	Lamek	Mexico	Lima	Luis
M	Mary	Maria	Nicaragua	México	Madrid
N	Nellie	Nande	Océano	Nicaragua	Norma
O	Oliver	Otto	Paraguay	Olimpo	Omar
P	Peter	Pauli	Querido	Pablo	Pedro
Q	Queen	Quini	Ramón	Quito	Querido
R	Robert	Rauha	Sábado	Rafael	Ramón
S	Samuel	Simon	Tomás	Santiago	Sábado
T	Tommy	Tuuli	Ulises	Teresa	Teresa
U	Uncle	Ulania	Venezuela	Uruguay	Ulises
V	Victor	Vilho	Washington	Venezuela	Victor
W	William	Wilkka	Xiquena	Washington	Washington
X	X-Ray	Xokulu	Yegua	Xilófono	Xiquena
Y	-	Yoleni	Zaragoza	Yucatán	I_griega
Z	Zebra	Zola		Zorro	Zaragoza
				LL - Lave	
			- also -	Ñ - Ñoño	- also -
			Chocolate		Chocolate
			Ll Llobregat		Ll Llanes
			Ñ Ñoño		Ñ Ñoño

				(Spanish)	
1				uno	
2				dos	
3				tres	
4				cuatro	
5				cinco	
6				seis	
7				siete	
8				ocho	
9				nueve	
10				diez	

Radiotelegraph and Radiotelephone Codes, Prowords and Abbreviations

Phonetic Alphabets (Cont'd)

Dates are for the earliest references so far found and may not be the actual dates of introduction. Corrections, Additions or earlier dates are sought.   # = from Brian Kelk's Listings.

	1964 Malaya 'Phone Directory #	Ndonga (SW Bantu, Nth Namibia#	1965 Norwegian ('Phone Book) #	Polish (Phone Book) #	Polish (Amateur Radio) #
A	Australia	Anna	Anna	Adam	Adam
B	Bombay	Beata	Bernhard	Barbara	Bozena
C	China	Cesilia	Caesar	Celina	Celina
D	Denmark	David	David	Danuta	Dawid
E	England	Eva	Edith	Ewa	Ewa
F	Fiji	Feni	Fredrik	Franciszek	Franek
G	Ghana	Gerson	Gustav	Genowefa	Grazyna
H	Hongkong	Hosea	Harald	Henryk	Henryk
I	India	Immanuel	Ivar	Irena	Irena
J	Japan	Johanna	Johan	Jadwiga	Janusz
K	Kedah	Kayoso	Karin	Karol	Kilo
L	London	Lamek	Ludvig	Leon	Ludwik
M	Malacca	Maria	Martin	Maria	Maria
N	Norway	Nande	Nils	Natalia	Natalia
O	Osaka	Otto Pauli	Olivia	Olga	Olga
P	Penang	Quini	Petter	Pawel	Pawel
Q	Queensland	Rauha	Quintus		Quido
R	Russia	Simon	Rikard	Roman	Roman
S	Singapore	Tuuliki	Sigrid	Stanislaw	Stefan
T	Turkey	Ulania	Teodor	Tadeusz	Tomasz
U	Uganda	Vilho	Ulrik	Urszula	Urban
V	Victoria	Wilika	Enkelt-V		Violeta
W	Wales	Xerxes	Dobbelt-V	Wladyslaw	Wanda
X	X'Ray	Yoleni	Xerxes	Xantypa	Xawer
Y	Yokohama	Zola	Yngling	Ygrek	Y-Grek
Z	Zanzibar		Zakarias	Zygmunt	Zygmunt
			Æ - Ælig		
			Ø - Østen		
			Å - Åse	-Also-	
				Lukasz	
			-Also-		
			W - Dobbelt-V		
			V - Enkel-V Æ		
			- Aeleg		
			Ø - Øern		
1			en	jeden	
2			to -Note-	dwa trzy	
3			tre Ynling	cztery	
4			fire Aerleg	piec	
5			fem are	szesc	
6			seks considered	siedem	
7			sju incorrect	oisem	
8			åtte	dziewiec	
9			ni	dziesiec	
10			ti		

Radiotelegraph and Radiotelephone Codes, Prowords and Abbreviations

Phonetic Alphabets (Cont'd)

Dates are for the earliest references so far found and may not be the actual dates of introduction. Corrections, Additions or earlier dates are sought.   # = from Brian Kelk's Listings.

	Polish (Berlitz # Phr. Bk.)	Polish (Collins Dictionary)	2001 Polish Survival Page	Portuguese Berlitz #	Portuguese Collins #	Portuguese (AA # Phrase book)
A	Adam	Adam	A-zot	Aviero	Alexandre	América
B	Barbara	Barbara	Bo-ta-ni-ka	Braga	Banana	Bernardo
C	Celina	Cecylia	Co-raz-moc-niej	Coimbra	Carlos	Colónia
D	Dorota	Dorota	Do-li-na	Dafundo	Daniel	Dinamarca
E	Ewa	Ewa	Ełk	Évora	Eduardo	Espanha
F	Franciszek	Franciszek	Fi-lan-tro-pia	Faro	França	França
G	Grazyna	Genowefa	Go-spo-da	Guarda	Gabriel	Gabriel
H	Henryk	Henryk	Ha-la-bar-da	Horta	Holanda	Holanda
I	Iwona	Irena	I-gła	Itália	Itália	Irlanda
J	Jan	Jadwiga	Jed-no-kon-no	José	José	Japão
K	Karol	Karol	Ko-la-no	Kodak		Kremlin
L	Leon	Leon	Le-o-ni-das	Lisboa	Lisboa	Londres
M	Maria	Maria	Mo-tor	Maria	Maria	Madrid
N	Natalia	Natalia	No-ga	Nazaré	Nicolau	Nápoles
O	Olga	Olga	O-pocz-no	Ovar	Óscar	Oslo
P	Piotr	Pawel	Pe-lo-po-nez	Porto	Paris	Portugal
Q	Quiz	Quebec	-	Queluz	Quarto	Quilo
R	Roman	Roman	Re-tor-ta	Rossio	Ricardo	Rússia
S	Stanislaw	S'wiatowid	Sa-ha-ra	Setúbal	Susana	Suécia
T	Tadeusz	Tadeusz	Tom	Tavira	Teresa	Turquia
U	Urszula	Urszula	Ur-sy-nów	Unidade	Ulisses	Uruguai
V	Violeta	Violetta	-	Vidago	Venezuela	Vitória
W	Waclaw	Waclaw	Wi-no-ro l	Waldemar		Washington
X	Xymena	Xantypa	-	Xavier	Xangai	Xangai
Y	Ypsylon	Ypsylon	-	York		-
Z	Zenon	Zygmunt	Zlo-to-li-te	Zulmira	Zebra	Zurique
	-Also-	-Also-		-Also-	-Also-	-Also-
	Lukasz	Lukasz		1966 Bragança Kilograma Wilson (Ph Bk Azores)	Bastos	Grécia
1				um	um	
2				dois	dois	
3				três	três	
4				quatro	quatro	
5				cinco	cinco	
6				seis	seis	
7				sete	sete	
8				oito	oito	
9				nove	nove	
10				dez	dez	

Radiotelegraph and Radiotelephone Codes, Prowords and Abbreviations

Phonetic Alphabets (Cont'd)

Dates are for the earliest references so far found and may not be the actual dates of introduction.
Corrections, Additions or earlier dates are sought.   # = from Brian Kelk's Listings.

	Portuguese (Collins) #	Romanian (Berlitz # Phr. Bk.)	Romansch (Rumansh # Rumantsh etc.)	1983 Russian (Roman) Alphabet	Russian As Spoken Alphabet
A	Antônio	Ana	Anna	Anna	ah
B	Beatriz	Barbu	Berta	Boris	beh
C	Carlos	Constantin	Carla	Centrali	veh
D	Dado	Dumitru	Dora	Dima	gueh
E	Eliane	Elena	Emil	Elena	deh
F	Francisco	Florea	Flurin	Feeder	yeh / yoh
G	Gomes	Gheorghe	Guido	Grigory	zheh zeh
H	Henrique	Haralambie	Hugo	Hariton	ee
I	Irene	Ion	Ida	Ivan	yeey
J	José	Jiu	Judit	Ivan Krosky	kah
K	Kátia	Kilogram	Kilo	Kostya Luba	ehl
L	Lúcia	Lazăr	Luisa	Maria	ehm
M	Maria	Maria	Maria	Nickoli Olga	ehn
N	Nair	Nicolae	Nesa	Parvel, Payo	oh
O	Osvaldo	Olga	Otto	Shoogar	peh
P	Pedro	Petre	Paula	Roman	ehr
Q	Quintela	Qu Radu	Quirin	Segay	es
R	Roberto	Sandoo	Rita	Tatjana	teh
S	Sandra	Tudor	Silvia	Oolyana	oo
T	Tereza	Udrea	Toni	Zook Vasily	ef
U	Úrsula	Vasile	Ursin	Znak Eegrek	khah
V	Vera	Dublu_V	Victor	Zeena	tseh
W	William	Xenia	Willi	(Spelling is	cheh
X	Xavier	I_Grec	Xaver	a phonetic	shah
Y	Yolanda	Zahăr	Yvonne	interpretation)	shchah
Z	Zebra		Zita		tvyordy znak
					yh
					myagkiy znak
		- Also -			eh
		Luca			yuh
		Jean		10 Dyeset	yah
		Tară		15 Pitnatsat	
		Zamfir		20 Dvatsat	
				30 Tridsat	
				100 Sto	
0		un		Null	0 Nula
1		doi		Odin	1 Yedinitsa
2		trei		Dva	2 Dvoyka
3		patru		Tree	3 Troika
4		cinci		Chiterya	4 Tchetvyorka
5		s,ase		Pyat	5 Pyatyorka
6		s,apte		Shest	6 Shestyorka
7		opt		Sye-em	7 Sedmyorka
8		nouâ		Vosyem	8 Vasmyorka
9		zece		Dyevit	9 Devyatyorka

Radiotelegraph and Radiotelephone Codes, Prowords and Abbreviations

Phonetic Alphabets (Cont'd)

Dates are for the earliest references so far found and may not be the actual dates of introduction.
Corrections, Additions or earlier dates are sought. # = from Brian Kelk's Listings.

Russian (AA # Phr. Bk.)	1996 Russian (Cyrillic Alphabet) #	1996 Russian (Amateur Radio) #	1996 Russian (Informal) #	Serbo-Croat (Berlitz # Phr. Bk.)
Anna	Aleksej	Anna, Anton		Avala
Boris	Boris	Boris	Borya	Beograd
Viktor	Vasilij	Vasiliy	Vasya	Cetijne
Grigoriy	Grigorij	Galina, Grigoriy	Grisha / Galya	Dubrovnik
Dmitriy	Dmitrij	Dmitriy	Dima	Europa
, Elena, Yolka	, Elena	Yelena, Yozh, Yolka		Focàa
Zhenya	Zhenja	Zhuk, Zhenya		Gorica
Zoya	Zoya	Zinaida, Zoya Ivan,	Zina	Hercegovina
Irina Yod	Ivan	Irina, Igor		Istra Jadran
Konstantin	Ivan_Kratkij	Ivan_Kratkiy, Yot		Kosovo Lika
Liza	Kilowatt	Konstantin, Kilowatt	Kostya, Kolya	Mostar
Mariya	Leonid	Leonid, Lyubov	Lyonya, Lyuba	Niš
Natasha	Maria	Maria, Mikhail	Misha / Masha	Osijek
Olga	Nikolai	Nikolay, Nadezhda, Nina	Nadya	Pirot
	Olga	Olga, Oleg		Kvadrat
Pyotr	Pavel	Pavel, Polina	Pasha	Rijeka
Ruslan	Roman	Roman, Radio	Roma	Skopje
Semyon	Sergej	Sergey, Semyon	Sasha	Titograd
Tatyana	Tatjana	Tamara, Tatyana	Tanya	Uroševac
Ukraina	Uljana	Ul'yana		Valjevo
Fyodor	Fjodor	Fyodor	Fedya	Duplo_V
Khar'kov	Hariton	Hariton Tsentr,		Iks
Tsaritsa	Zaplja	Tsaplya		Ipsilon
Chekhov	Chelovek	Chelovek		Zagreb
Shura	Shura Schuka	Shura		
Schuka	Tviordiy_Znak	Shchyuka Tvyordy_Znak,		
Tviordiy_Znak	Igrek	Znak, Iks Yery, Igrek		
	Miagkiy_Znak	Myagkiy_Znak, Znak, Iks		-Also-
Miagkiy_Znak	Emilija	Ekho		Cóacàak
Erik	Yuri	Yuliana		C$uprija
Yuriy		Yakov	Yulya	Djakovo
Yana	! Jakow		Yasha	Dzàamija
				Njegoš
				Šïbenik
				Zôôïrnovnica
				1 jedan
				2 dva
				3 tri
				4 chetiri
				5 pet
				6 shest
				7 sedam
				8 osam
				9 devet
				10 deset

ENGLISH, RUSSIAN & MORSE ALPHABETS

A	· —	L	· — · ·	W	· — —			
B	— · · ·	M	— —	X	— · · —			
C	— · — ·	N	— ·	Y	— · — —			
D	— · ·	O	— — —	Z	— — · ·			
E	·	P	· — — ·	—	— — — — —			
F	· · — ·	Q	— — · —	—	· — — — —			
G	— — ·	R	· — ·	—	· · — — —			
H	· · · ·	S	· · ·	!	· — · — ·			
I	· ·	T	—	—	· · · · —			
J	· — — —	U	· · —	—	— — — · ·			
K	— · —	V	· · · —					

Radiotelegraph and Radiotelephone Codes, Prowords and Abbreviations

Phonetic Alphabets (Cont'd)

Dates are for the earliest references so far found and may not be the actual dates of introduction.
Corrections, Additions or earlier dates are sought. # = from Brian Kelk's Listings.

	Slovak ('Phone Book) #	Slovenian de P. Peterlin #	1965 South Africa # (Johannesburg)	1960 Spanish Madrid #	Spanish BBC, Collins Berlitz #	Spanish Telephonist's #
A	Adam	Ankaran	Arthur	Alicante	Antonio	Antonio
B	Bozàena	Bled	Betty	Bilbao	Barcelona	Barcelona
C	Cyril	Celje Crnomelj	Charlie	Cádiz	Carmen	Carmen
D	Dávid	Drava Evropa	David	Dinamarca	Dolores	Domingo
E	Emil	Fala	Edward	España	Enrique	España
F	František	Gorica	Frederick	Francia	Francia	Francia
G	Gustáv	Hrastnik	George	Girona	Gerona	Gerona
H	Helena	Izola	Harry	Huelva	Historia	Historia
I	Ivan	Jadran	Isaac	Italia	Inés	Italia
J		Kamnik	Jane	Jaén Kilo	José Kilo	José Kilo
K	Karol	Ljubljana	Kate	Lugo	Lorenzo	Lérida/Llave
L	Ludvík	Maribor	Lucy	Madrid	Madrid	Madrid
M	Mária	Nanos	Mary	Navarra	Navarra	Navarra
N	Norbert	Ormroz	Nellie	Oviedo	Oviedo	Oviedo
O	Oto	Piran	Olive	Portugal	Parìs	Portugal/Parìs
P	Peter	Ku	Peter	Queso	Querido	Queso
Q	Quido	Ravne Soca,	Queen	Roma	Ramón	Ramón/Roma
R	Rudolf	Smarie	Robert	Sevilla	Sábado	Sevilla
S	Svätopluk	Triglav	Simon	Toledo	Tarragona	Tarragona
T	Tomás	Unec	Thomas	Único	Ulises	Ursula/Ubeda
U	Urban	Velenje	Union	Valencia	Valencia	Valencia
V	Václav	Dvojni-V	Violet	UveDoble	Washington	Washington
W	Dvojité_vé	Iks	William	Equis	Xiquena	Xilofòn
X	Xaver	Ipsilon	X-Ray	Yugoslavia	Yegua	Yegua
Y	Ypsilon		York	Zaragoza	Zaragoza	Zaragoza
Z	Zuzana	Zalog, Zalec	Zero			
	-Also-			-Also-	-Also-	-Also-
	Cãdca			LL - LLamar	Israel	Ñ - Ñando
	CH - Chrudim				Ñ - Ñoño	Enrique
	Ñ - Nitra				Chocolate	I - iLatina
	N~ - Teplá				Llobregat	Jaen
	Zôofia				Quebec	Toledo
					Uruguay	
0				0 cero		
1	jeden			uno		
2	dva tri			dos		
3	shtyri			tres		
4	pät			cuatro		
5	shest			cinco		
6	sedem			seis		
7	osem			sette		
8	devät			ocho		
9	desat			nueve		
10				diez		

Radiotelegraph and Radiotelephone Codes, Prowords and Abbreviations

Phonetic Alphabets (Cont'd)

Dates are for the earliest references so far found and may not be the actual dates of introduction. Corrections, Additions or earlier dates are sought.   # = from Brian Kelk's Listings.

	Spanish (Langenscheidt)	Spanish (Berlitz) # Latin Amer.	Spanish (AA Ph Bk) # Latin Amer.	Spanish (F.Anedragnes)	Swahili (Berlitz # Phr. Bk.)	Swahili (Later # edition)
A	Antonio	Amalia	Ana	Alicia	Aali	Ali
B	Bogotá	Beatriz	bueno	Beatriz	Bibi	Banda
C	Carmen *	Carmen	Carlos *	Carolina	Cyprus	Chakechake
D	Dora	Domingo	dedo	Dorotea	Daniel	Dodoma
E	Enrique	Enrique	Eduardo	Eva	Elfu	Entebe
F	Francisco	Federico	Francia	Federico	Fiwi	Fumba
G	Gibraltar	Guatemala	gato	Guillermina	Gombe	Gogo
H	Historia	Honduras	historia	Hombre	Henry	Homa
I	Italia *	Ida	Inés	Ines	Ida	Imba
J	José *	José	José	Josefina	Jinja	Jambo
K	Kilo	Kilo Lima /	Kilo	Kilo	Kenya	Kenya
L	Lorenzo *	Llave	Luis / Llanes	Lola *	Leso	Lala
M	México	México	Madrid Norma	Maria	Mtu	Mama
N	Nicaragua *	Nicaragua *	/ Ñoño Omar	Natalia / Ñandu	Nairobi	Nakuru
O	Océano	Olimpo	Pedro	Ofelia Pandora	Olga	Ona
P	Paraguay	Pablo	querido	Quintana Rosa	Paul	Punda
Q	Querido	Quito	Ramón	Sara Teresa	Quebec	Kyela
R	Ramón	Rafael	sábado	Ursula	Robert	Rangi
S	Sábado	Santiago	Teresa	Veronica	Sana	Simu
T	Tomás	Teresa	Ulises	Washington	Tanga	Tatu
U	Ulises	Uruguay	Victor	Xilofon	Unga	Uganda
V	Venezuela	Venezuela	Washington	Yolanda	Victor	Vitu
W	Washington	Washington	Xiquena	Zapato	William	Wali
X	Xiquena	Xilófono	i_griega		Xavier	Eksrei
Y	Yegua	Yucatán	Zaragoza		Yatima	Yai
Z	Zaragoza	Zorro			Zanzibar	Zanzibar
	* Chocolate	* Ñoño	* chocolate	* Doble_Lola		
	* i_latina					
	* Jaen					
	* Llobregat					
	* Ñoño					
	* In s					

1		moja
2		mbili
3		tatu
4		nne
5		tano
6		sita
7		saba
8		nane
9		tisa
0		kumi

Radiotelegraph and Radiotelephone Codes, Prowords and Abbreviations

Phonetic Alphabets (Cont'd)

Dates are for the earliest references so far found and may not be the actual dates of introduction.
Corrections, Additions or earlier dates are sought.   # = from Brian Kelk's Listings.

	Swedish (Also in Finland)	Swedish (Early 20th Century) #	1993 Swiss - French 'Phone Directory	1966-1993 Swiss -German 'Phone Directory	1966-1993 Swiss-Italian 'Phone Directory	Swiss-Romansh (Roumansh)
A	Adam	Aron	Anna	Anna	Anna	Anna
B	Bertil	Bertil	Berthe	Bertha	Battista	Berta
C	Cesar	Cesar	Cécile	Cäsar	Carlo	Carla
D	David	David	Daniel	Daniel	Davide	Dora
E	Erik	Emanuel	Emile	Emil	Ernesto	Emil
F	Filip	Frans	François	Friedrich	Federico	Flurin
G	Gustav	Gustaf	Gustave	Gustav	Giovanni	Guido
H	Helge	Harald	Henri	Heinrich	Acca	Hugo
I	Ivar	Ivar	Ida	Ida	Isidoro	Ida
J	Johan	Johan	Jeanne	Jakob	I lungo	Judit
K	Kalle	Kalle	Kilo	Kaiser	Cappa	Kilo
L	Ludvig	Lars	Louise	Leopold	Luigi	Luisa
M	Martin	Martin	Marie	Marie	Maria	Maria
N	Niklas	Niklas	Nicolas	Niklaus	Nicola	Nesa
O	Olof	Olof	Olga	Otto	Olga	Otto
P	Petter	Petter	Paul	Peter	Pietro	Paula
Q	Quintus	Qvintas	Quittance	Quelle	Quintino	Quirin
R	Rudolf	Rudolf	Robert	Rosa	Rodolfo	Rita
S	Sigurd	Sigurd	Suzanne	Sophie	Susanna	Silvia
T	Tore	Teodore	Thérèse	Theodor	Teresa	Toni
U	Urban	Urban	Ulysse	Ulrich	Umberto	Ursin
V	Viktor	Viktor	Victor	Viktor	Vittorio	Victor
W	Wilhelm	Wilhelm	William	Wilhelm	Vu doppia	Willi
X	Xerxes	Xenofon	Xavier	Xaver	Ics Ipsilon	Xaver
Y	Yngve	Yngve	Yvonne	Yverdon	Zurigo	Yvonne
Z	Zäta	Zakarias	Zurich	Zürich		Zita
Å - Åke	Å - Åke					
Ä - Ärlig	Ä - Ärlig					
Ö - Östen	Ö - Öern					

	-Also- Fredrik Olle Rikard	Old Phonetics For digits 0-9		
	nolla	Julia	zéro	null
1	ett Stockholm	Anna	un	eins
2	tvåa Police	Beda	deux	zwei
3	trea X = Kryss	Cecilia	trois	drei
4	fyra	Dora	quatre	vier
5	femma	Ebba	cinq	fünf
6	sexa	Fina	six	sechs
7	sjua	Greta	sept	sieben
8	åtta	Hedda	huit	acht
9	nia	Ida	neuf	neun
0	tio		dix	zehn

Radiotelegraph and Radiotelephone Codes, Prowords and Abbreviations

Phonetic Alphabets (Cont'd)

Dates are for the earliest references so far found and may not be the actual dates of introduction.
Corrections, Additions or earlier dates are sought.   # = from Brian Kelk's Listings.

	Turkish (G. Cetin) #	Turkish (Berlitz # Phrase Book)	1982 Turkish for # Telephone	Turkish (AA Phrase Bk Gwillim Law)	Turkish # (kadefile@cmpe.boun.edu.tr)	Ukrainian (Amateur # Radio)
A	Ankara	Adana	Ankara	Adana	adana	Andriy
B	Bursa	Balikesir	Bursa	Bursa	bursa	Bogdan
C	Ceyhan	Ceyhan	Ceyhan	Cide	ceyhan	Vasil' (W)
D	Denizli	Diyarbakir	Denizli	Denizli	denizile	Grigory
E	Edirne	Edirne	Edirne	Edirne	edirne	Dmitro
F	Fatsa	Fatsa	Fatih	Fethiye	fatih	Yenei (E)
G	Giresun	Giresun	Giresun	Giresun	giresun	Zhuk (V)
H	Hopa	Hatay	Hakkâri	Hatay	hatay	Zenoviy (Z)
I	Izmir	Istanbul	Izmir	Izmir	izmir	Igrek (Y)
J	Jale	Jandarma	Japonya		jale	Ivan (I)
K	Kayseri	Kastamonu	Kayseri		kayseri	Izhak (I)
L	Lüleburgaz	Lüleburgaz	Lüleburgaz	Lüleburgaz	lUleburgaz	Yosip (J)
M	Manisa	Manisa	Malatya	Malatya	malatya	Kilovat
N	Nazilli	Nazilli	Nevs¦ehir	Nevsehir	nevSehir	Levko
O	Ordu	Ordu	Ordu	Ordu	ordu	Mariya
P	Pazar	Pazar	Polatli	Pamukkale	polatlI	Natalka
Q		Quebek				Olga
R	Rize	Rize	Rize	Rize	rize	Pavlo
S	Samsun	Samsun	Sivas	Sinop	samsun	Roman
T	Trabzon	Trabzon	Trabzon	Tokat	trabzon	Stepan
U	Urfa	Urla	Us¦ak u_nye	Urfa	urfa	Taras
V	Van	Van	Van	Van	van	Ukraina
W		Dubel_V				Fedir
X		Xavier				Khristina (H)
Y	Yalova	Yozgat	Yozgat	Yozgat	yozgat	Tsentr (C)
Z	Zonguldak	Zonguldak	Zonguldak	Zonguldat	zonguldak	Cholovik
						Shura
	-Also-	-Also-	-Also-	-Also-	-Also-	Shchuka (Q)
	Çankiri	Çorum	Çanakkale	Çanakkale	Canakkale	Znak (X)
	Isparta	Irmak	Ilgaz	Isparta	yumuSak ge	Yuri
	Sarköy	Ödemis	Ödemis	Ören	Isparta	Yakiv
		Ünye	S¦ile uS¦ak	Sirvan	OdemiS	
				Uskup	Sile	Also used
					Unye	for Roman
						alphabet,
1	bir					as the above
2	iki üç					tries to
3	dört					indicate.
4	bes¦					
5	alti					
6	yedi					
7	sekiz					
8	dokuz					
9	on					
0						

Radiotelegraph and Radiotelephone Codes, Prowords and Abbreviations

Phonetic Alphabets (Cont'd)

Dates are for the earliest references so far found and may not be the actual dates of introduction. Corrections, Additions or earlier dates are sought.   # = from Brian Kelk's Listings.

	1996 U.S.A. Police California	1996 U.S.A. Police Pittsburgh
A	Adam	Apple
B	Boy	Boy
C	Charles	Charles
D	David	David
E	Edward	Edward
F	Frank	Fox
G	George	Gary
H	Henry	Harry
I	Ida	Indigo
J	John	John
K	King	Kevin
L	Lincoln	Lincoln
M	Mary	Mary
N	Nora	Nancy
O	Ocean	Ocean
P	Paul	Paul
Q	Queen	Queen
R	Robert	Robert
S	Sam	Sam
T	Tom	Tom
U	Union	Uniform
V	Victor	Victor
W	William	William
X	Xray	X-ray
Y	Yellow	Yellow
Z	Zebra	Zebra
	-Also-	-Also-
	Peter	Adam
		Albert
	Also used with	Frank
	slight variations	Ford
	by Police of -	George
	Hutchison, KA	Henry
	Nassau Cy. NY	James
1	Clark Coy. WA	King
2		Larry
3		October
4	Every US	Unit
5	authority	Yankee
6	seems to have	Young
7	its own	
8	version.	
9		
0		

1793 – 1911 Chappe and others – Visual Telegraph Tower showing signalling arms.

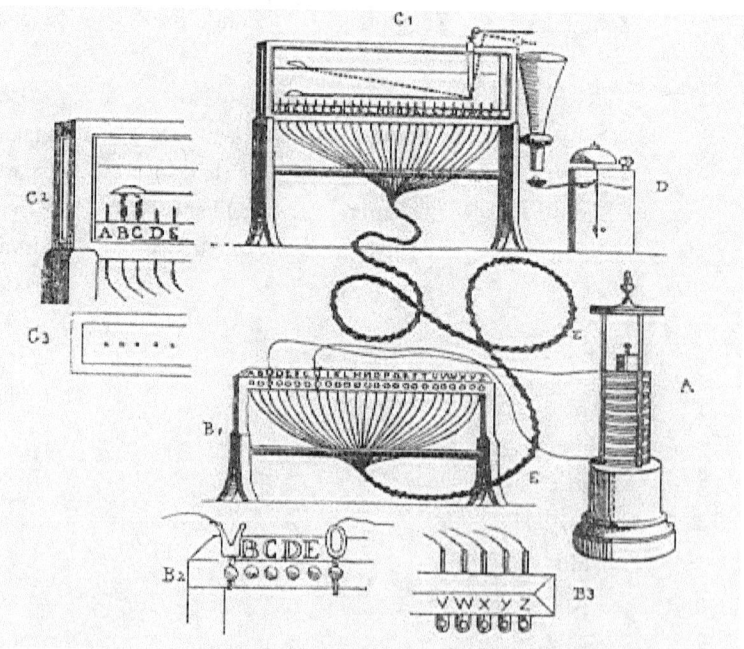

1807 Dr. Von Soemmering, Chemical Telegraph – Electric current created bubbles at the Receiver letter in circuit from the Sender

Radiotelegraph and Radiotelephone Codes, Prowords and Abbreviations

Phonetic Alphabets (Cont'd)

Dates are for the earliest references so far found and may not be the actual dates of introduction.
Corrections, Additions or earlier dates are sought.

Japanese Phonetics - 1999, de Atsu Taniguchi JE1TRV, JARL A1 Club. Email: je1trv@jarl.com
From a Japanese radio operator's text book.   Page: http://member.nifty.ne.jp/je1trv/index_e.html
The Japanese alphabet consists of 50 basic Characters and 25 variations in pronunciation.
Popular and simple words are applied for the phonetic codes.

Eg. TO = "Tokyo no TO"   means   "TO for Tokyo"
     O = "Osaka no O"   means   " O for Osaka"
     FU = "Fujisan no FU" means   "FU for Fuji-yama",
etc.

Dakuten is shown as ˝.
eg. か(KA) ni dakuten shows が(GA)
き(KI) ni dakuten shows ぎ(GI)

Han-dakuten is shown as °.
eg. は(HA) ni han-dakuten shows ぱ(PA)
ひ(HI) ni han-dakuten shows ぴ(PI)

A - Asahi no A
I – Iroha no I
U – Ueno no U
E – Eigo no E
O – Osaka no O
KA – Kawase no KA,   GA – Kawase no KA ni dakuten
KI – Kitte no KI,   GI – Kitte no KI ni dakuten
KU – Kurabu no KU,   GU – Kurabu no KU ni dakuten
KE – Keshiki no KE,   GE – Keshiki no KE ni dakuten
KO – Kodomo no KO,   GO – Kodomo no KO ni dakuten
SA – Sakura no SA,   ZA – Sakura no SA ni dakuten
SI(SHI) – Shinbun no SI(SHI),   ZI(JI) – Shinbun no SI ni dakuten
SU – Suzume no SU,   ZU – Suzume no SU ni dakuten
SE – Sekai no SE,   ZE – Sekai no SE ni dakuten
SO – Soroban no SO,   ZO – Soroban no SO ni dakuten
TA – Tabako no TA,   DA – Tabako no TA ni dakuten
TI(CHI) -Chidori no TI(CHI),   DI – Chidori no TI ni dakuten
TU(TSU) – Tsurukame no TU(TSU), DU – Tsurukame no TU ni dakuten
TE – Tegami no TE,   DE – Tegami no TE ni dakuten
TO - Tokyo no TO,   DO – Tokyo no TO ni dakuten
NA – Nagoya no NA
NI – Nippon no NI
NU – Numazu no NU
NE – Nezumi no NE
NO – Nohara no NO
HA – Hagaki no HA,   BA – Hagaki no HA ni dakuten,   PA – Hagaki no HA ni handakuten
HI- Hikouki no HI,   BI – Hikouki no HI ni dakuten,   PI - Hikoukino HI ni handakuten
HU(FU)- Fujisan no FU, BU – Fujisan no FU ni dakuten,   PU - Fujisan no FU ni handakuten
HE – Heiwa no HE,   BE – Heiwa no HE ni dakuten,   PE - Heiwa no HE ni handakuten
HO – Hoken no HO,   BO – Hoken no HO ni dakuten,   PO - Hoken no HO ni handakuten
MA – Match no MA
MI – Mikasa no MI
MU – Musen no MU
ME – Meiji no ME
MO – Momiji no MO
YA – Yamato no YA
YI – Ido no YI
YU – Yumiya no YU
YE – Kaginoaru YE
YO – Yoshino no YO   0 – Suuji no Maru   4 – Suuji no Yon   8 – Suuji no Hachi
WA – Warabi no WA   1 – Suuji no Hito   5 – Suuji no Go   9 – Suuji no Kyu
WO – Wowari no WO   2 – Suuji no Ni   6 – Suuji no Roku   . – Kugiriten
N – Oshimai no N   3 – Suuji no San   7 – Suuji no Nana

Radiotelegraph and Radiotelephone Codes, Prowords and Abbreviations

Phonetic Alphabets (Cont'd)
Letter and Figure Spelling Tables
From the International Code of Signals. 1987. (pp18-19)

FIGURES: Note: Each syllable should be equally emphasised. The second component of each code word is the code word used in the Aeronautical Mobile Service.

Letter	Code Word	English	French
A	Alpha	ALFAH	ALFAH
B	Bravo	BRAHVOH	BRAVO
C	Charlie	CHARLEE*	TCHAHLI*
D	Delta	DELLTAH	DELTAH
E	Echo	ECKOH	EKO
F	Foxtrot	FOKSTROT	FOXTROTT
G	Golf	GOLF	GOLF
H	Hotel	HOHTELL	HOTÈLL
I	India	INDEEAH	INDIAH
J	Juliett	JEWLEEETT	DJOULIÈTT
K	Kilo	KEYLOH	KILO
L	Lima	LEEMAH	LIMAH MAÏK
M	Mike	MIKE	NOVÈMMBER
N	November	NOVEMBER	OSSKAR
O	Oscar	OSSCAH	PAHPAH
P	Papa	PAHPAH	KÉBÈK
Q	Quebec	KEHBECK	ROMIO
R	Romeo	ROWMEOH	SIÈRRAH
S	Sierra	SEEAIRRAH	TANGGO
T	Tango	TANGGO	YOUNIFORM*
U	Uniform	YOUNEEFORM*	VIKTAR
V	Victor	VIKTAH	OUISSKI
W	Whiskey	WISSKEY	ÈKSSRÉ
X	X-Ray	ECKSRAY	YANGKI
Y	Yankee	YANGKEY	ZOULOU
Z	Zulu	ZOOLOO	

		*or	*ou
		SHARLLEE	CHARLI
		OONEEFORM	OUNIFORM
		Note: The bold syllables	are emphasised.

0	Nadazero	NAH-DAH-ZAY-ROH	NA-DA-ZE-RO
1	Unaone	OO-NA-WUN	OUNA-OUANN
2	Bissotwo	BEES-SOH-TOO	BIS-SO-TOU
3	Terrathree	TAY-RAH-TREE	TÉ-RA-TRI
4	Kartefour	KAR-TAY-FOWER	KAR-TÉ-FO-EUR
5	Pantafive	PAN-TAH-FIVE	PANN-TA-FAIF
6	Soxisix	SOK-SEE-SIX	SO-XI-SICKS
7	Setteseven	SAY-TAY-SEVEN	SÉT-TEÉ-SEV'N
8	Oktoeight	OK-TOH-AIT	OK-TO-EIT
9	Novenine	NO-VAY-NINER	NO-VÉ-NAI-NEU
.	Decimal Point	DAY-SEE-MAL	DÉ-SI-MAL
.	Stop	STOP	STOP

Radiotelegraph and Radiotelephone Codes, Prowords and Abbreviations

New International Code of Signals
Updated to September 1986.

Extracted from the International Code of Signals. 1987. Adopted 1965 - 1986
The new Operating Signals have been simplified and replace previous ICS and Q etc. signals.
Only signals relative to Communications and Emergencies have been extracted.
The bracketed chapter and page numbers (p54) refer to the ICS 1987 which has over 180 pages.
Definitions have been abbreviated .... to save space, for more detail refer to ICS 1987.
Generally chapter endnotes etc. have NOT been reprinted.

(Chapter III)
(p4)
Methods of Signalling

1 The methods of signalling which may be used are:-
  .1 Flag signalling, the flags used being those shown on (page 165).
  .2 Flashing light signalling, using the Morse symbols shown on (p17).
  .3 Sound signalling using the Morse symbols shown on (p17).
  .4 Voice over a loud hailer.
  .5 Radiotelegraphy.
  .6 Radiotelephony.
  .7 Morse signalling by hand-flags or arms.

  (The use of a machine gun [1941 instruction] seems to have been dropped. HI HI - Ed.)

2 **Flag Signalling.**
  A set of signal flags ..... Instructions as in (chapter V.)

3 **Flashing light and sound signalling.**
  .1 Use Morse symbols representing letters, numerals etc. .....
  .2 .... make the dots rather shorter in proportion to the dashes to be plainer.
  .... The standard rate of signalling by flashing light can be as forty letters per minute.
  Detailed instructions are given in (chapters VI and VII).

4 **Voice over a loud hailer.**
  Use plain language but in difficulties use the ICS using the phonetic spelling tables.

5 **Radiotelegraphy and Radiotelephony.**
  Comply with the Radio Regulations and ITU regulations then in force. (See chapter VIII).

(Chapter IV)
(p5)
General Instructions.

1 **Originator and addressee of message.**
  ...... To be from the master of the vessel of origin to the master of the vessel of destination.

2 **Identification of ships and aircraft.**
  ...... Use identity signals as per the international allocation or national supplement to the Code.

3 **Use of identity signals.**
  ...... Used to speak to, or call, of, or indicate a station. e.g.
  YP LABC = "I wish to communicate with vessel LABC by ... (Compliments Table 1)."
  HY 1 LABC = "The vessel LABC with which I have been in collision has resumed her voyage."

4 **Names of vessels and places.**
  Names of vessels and places are to be spelt out. (Especially in difficult working.) e.g.
  RV Gibraltar = Romeo Victor Golf India Bravo ... etc. "You should proceed to Gibraltar."

5 **How to signal numbers.**
5.1.1 Flag signalling: by the numeral pendants of the Code.
  .2 Flashing light or sound: by numerals in Morse Code or they may be spelt out phonetically.
  .3 Radiotelephony or loud hailer: by the code words of the figure-spelling table. e.g.
5.2 **DI 20** = "I require boats for 20 persons."
  FJ 2 = "Position of accident (or survival craft) is marked by sea marker."

Radiotelegraph and Radiotelephone Codes, Prowords and Abbreviations

New International Code of Signals
Updated to September 1986.
Extracted from the International Code of Signals. 1987.

5.3 A decimal point between numerals is to be signalled as follows:
    .1 Flag signalling: by inserting the answering pendant where the decimal point is needed.
    .2 Flashing light and sound signalling: by "decimal point" signal AAA.
    .3 Voice: by use of the word "**DECIMAL**" as indicated in the figure-spelling table. p87 (p19)

5.4 Indicating depths, the figures are followed by: "**F**" for Feet, "**M**" for Metres.

6   Azimuth or bearing.   (p6)

6.1 Three figures denoting true degrees 000 to 359 clockwise. If in doubt, precede by "**A**". e.g.
    LW 005   = "I receive your transmission on bearing 005° ".
    LT A120 T1540 = "Your bearing from me is 120° at (local time) 1540".

7   Course.

7.1 Three figures denoting true degrees 000 to 359 clockwise. If in doubt, precede by "**C**". e.g.
    MD 025   = "My course is 025° ".
    GR C240 S18   = "Vessel coming to your rescue is steering course 240°, speed 18 knots".

8   Date.

8.1 By two, four or six figures preceded by letter "**D**"
    Two figures indicate day of transmitted month. e.g. **D15** = 15th day of transmitted month.
    Four figures indicate day and month meant. e.g. **D1504** = "15 April".
    Six figures indicate the year if necessary   e.g. **D181083** = "18 October 1983".

9   Latitude.

9.1 Four figures preceded by letter "**L**". First two denote degrees, second two denote minutes.
    Letters "**N**" (North) or "**S**" (South) follow if needed but may be omitted if no risk of confusion.

9.2 Example: **L3740S** = "Latitude 37° 40′ S".

10   Longitude.

10.1 By four or five figures preceded by letter "**G**". The first two (or three) denote degrees and the last two minutes. If over 99° the hundreds can be omitted if there is no risk of confusion. The letters "**E**" (East) or "**W**" (West) follow if needed but may be omitted if no risk. e.g.
    G13925E = Longitude 139° 25′ E".

11   Distance.

11.1 Figures preceded by the letter "**R**" indicate the distance in Nautical Miles.
11.2 **OV A080 R10** = "Mine(s) is (are) believed to be bearing 080° from me, distance 10 miles."
    The letter "**R**" may be omitted if there is no possibility of confusion.

12   Speed.

12.1 Speed is indicated by figures preceded by:
    .1 the letter "**S**" to denote speed in knots: or
    .2 the letter "**V**" to denote speed in kilometres per hour. e.g.
    BQ S300   = "The speed of my aircraft in relation to the surface of the Earth is 300 knots."
    BQ V300   = "The speed of my aircraft in relation to the surface of the Earth is 300 KPH."

13   Time.

13.1 Four figures, the first two denote the hour, 00 to 23, the second two the minutes 00 to 59.
    .1 preceded by letter "**T**" indicating "Local Time": or
    .2 preceded by letter "**Z**" indicating "Coordinated Universal Time (UTC)".   e.g.
    BH T1045 L2015N G3849W C125 = I sighted an aircraft at local time 1045 in lat 20° 15′ N
                                    long 38° 40′ W flying on course 125° ".
    RX Z0830 = "You should proceed at UTC 0830".

14   Time of Origin. (TOO)

Add at end of message. Indicates originating time and is a convenient reference number.

15   Communication by local signal codes.

If using a local code, the signal "**YV 1**" should precede the local code groups.

Radiotelegraph and Radiotelephone Codes, Prowords and Abbreviations

New International Code of Signals
Updated to September 1986.
Extracted from the International Code of Signals. 1987.

(Chapter VIII)
(p13)
Radiotelephony

Only those procedures which are new or have changed have been extracted.
Chapter / Page / Paragraph numbers are those of the International Code of Signals. 1987.

1   With language difficulties the spelling tables and codes are to be used according to the Radio Regulations and the International Telecommunications Union.

2   When coast and ship stations are called, the identity signals (callsigns) or names shall be used.

3   **Method of calling**
3.1 The call consists of:
- the call sign or name of the station called, not more than three times at each call.
- the group **DE** (DELTA ECHO):
- the call sign or name of the calling station, not more than three times at each call.

3.2 Difficult names or calls should be spelt.
After contact has been made, the callsign or name need not be sent more than once.

4   **Form of reply to calls**
The reply to calls consists of:
- the call sign or name of the calling station, not more than three times.
- the group **DE** (DELTA ECHO):
- the call sign or name of the station called, not more than three times.

5   **Calling all stations in the vicinity**
5.1 The group **CQ** (CHARLIE QUEBEC) shall be used, but not more than three times each call.

6   When groups of the ICS are following, **INTERCO** is to be inserted before them.
When plain language words such as names or places are amongst the groups the group **YZ** is to be inserted if necessary.

7   If unable to accept traffic immediately, reply **AS**, wait, adding time in minutes of delay.

8   The receipt of a transmission is indicated by the signal **R** (ROMEO).

9   If a repeat is requested the signal **RPT** is used supplemented as necessary by -
AA, AB, BN, WA, WB etc. as required.

10   The end of a transmission is indicated by the signal **AR** (ALPHA ROMEO).

Dummy Key and Sounder.
Used for Training and Practice. c1881

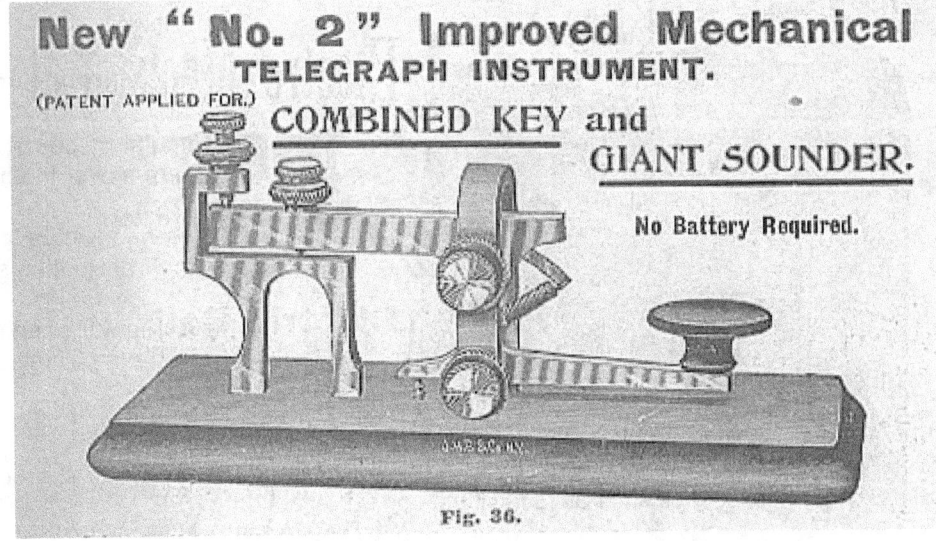

Fig. 36.

Radiotelegraph and Radiotelephone Codes, Prowords and Abbreviations

New International Code of Signals
Updated to September 1986.
Extracted from the International Code of Signals. 1987.

(Chapter IX)
(p15)

Morse Signalling by Hand Flags or Arms.

1. To open, make to other station **K1** or the call signal **AA AA AA** instead.

2. The receiver answers with the signal **YS1**.

3. The sender and receiver use the call signal **AA AA AA** and **T** respectively.

4. Normally both arms should be used but if not possible, one arm may be used.

5. All signals will end with the ending signal **AR**.

TABLE OF MORSE SIGNALLING BY HAND-FLAGS OR ARMS

1. Raising both hand-flags or arms.

Dot

2. Spreading out both hand-flags or arms at shoulder level.

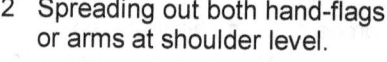

Dash

3. Hand-flags or arms brought before the chest.

Separation of dots and/or dashes

4. Hand-flags or arms kept at 45° away from the body downwards.

Separation of letters groups or words

5. Circular motion of hand-flags or arms over the head.

- **erase signals**, if made by the transmitting station.

- **request for repetition** if made by the receiving station.

<u>Note:</u> The space of time between dots and dashes and between letters, groups or words should be such as to facilitate correct reception.

Radiotelegraph and Radiotelephone Codes, Prowords and Abbreviations

New International Code of Signals
Updated to September 1986.
Extracted from the International Code of Signals. 1987.

Procedure Signals
(p20)

Note: Many signals have a bar over the letters to denote that they should be sent as one symbol. Unfortunately I have not yet been able to find a font with this overline. - JWA.

1. **Signals for voice transmissions (radiotelephony or loud hailer).**

   Pronunciation

Signal	ENGLISH	FRENCH	Meaning
Interco	IN-TER-CO	IN-TER-CO	International Code groups follow.
Stop	STOP	STOP	Full stop
Decimal	DAY-SEE-MAL	DÉ-SI-MAL	Decimal point
Correction	KOR REK SHUN	KOR-REK-CHEUNE	Cancel my last word or group. The correct word or group follows

2. **Signals for flashing-light transmission.**

AA AA AA etc.	Call for unknown station or general call
EEEEEE etc.	Erase signal
AAA	Full stop or decimal point
TTTT etc.	Answering signal
T	Word or group received

3. **Signals for flags, radiotelephony and radiotelegraphy transmissions.**

   CQ Call for unknown station(s) or general call to all stations
   Note: When this signal is used in voice transmission, it should be pronounced in accordance with the letter-spelling table.

4. **Signals for use where appropriate in all forms of transmission.**

   AA "All after ..." (Used after the repeat signal (RPT)) means "Repeat all after...."

   AB "all before...." (Used after the repeat signal (RPT)) means "Repeat all before...."

   AR Ending signal or End of Transmission or Signal.

   AS Waiting signal for period.

   BN "All between... and ..." (Used after the repeat signal (RPT)) means "Repeat all between .... and ....."

   C Affirmative -YES or "The significance of the previous group should be read in the affirmative".

   CS "What is the name or identity signal of your ship (or station) ?"

   DE "From ...." (used to precede the name or identity signal of the calling station).

   K "I wish to communicate with you" or "Invitation to transmit".

   NO Negative -NO or "The significance of the previous group should be read in the negative". When used in a voice transmission the pronunciation should be "NO".

   OK Acknowledging a correct repetition or "It is correct".

Radiotelegraph and Radiotelephone Codes, Prowords and Abbreviations

New International Code of Signals
Updated to September 1986.
Extracted from the International Code of Signals. 1987.

RQ Interrogative, or, "The significance of the previous group should be read as a question".

R "Received" or "I have received your last signal".

RPT Repeat signal "I repeat" or "Repeat what you have sent / received".

WA "Word or group after..."(Used after the repeat signal (RPT)) = "Repeat word etc. after".

WB "Word or group before..." (Used after the repeat signal (RPT)) = "Repeat word etc. before".

1. The procedure signals "C", "N", or "NO" and "RO" cannot be used in conjunction with single-letter signals.
2. Signals on COMMUNICATIONS appear on pages (103-106)
3. When these signals are used by voice use the letter-spelling table, except "NO" which should be pronounced "NO".

(Chapter XI)

(p22)

Single-Letter Signals

May be made by any method of signalling

A I have a diver down; keep well clear at slow speed.

B I am taking in, or discharging, or carrying dangerous goods.

C Yes (affirmative or "The significance of the previous group should be read in the affirmative".)

D Keep clear of me; I am manoeuvring with difficulty.

E I am altering my course to starboard.

F I am disabled; communicate with me.

G I require a pilot. When made by fishing vessels operating in close proximity on the fishing grounds it means: "I am hauling nets".

H I have a pilot on board.

I I am altering my course to port.

J Keep well clear of me. I am on fire and have dangerous cargo on board or I am leaking dangerous cargo.

K I wish to communicate with you.

L You should stop your vessel instantly.

M My vessel is stopped and making no way through the water.

N No (negative or "The significance of the previous group should be read in the negative".) Visual or sound signal only, when used by voice or transmission by radio the pronunciation should be "NO".

O Man overboard.

P **In Harbour.** All persons should report on board as the vessel is about to proceed to sea.
At sea. It may also be used as a sound signal to mean: "I Require a pilot".
At sea. It may be used by fishing vessels to mean: "My nets have come fast upon an obstruction".

Q My vessel is "healthy" and I request free pratique.

S I am operating astern propulsion.

Radiotelegraph and Radiotelephone Codes, Prowords and Abbreviations

New International Code of Signals
Updated to September 1986.
Extracted from the International Code of Signals. 1987.

T   Keep clear of me: I am engaged in pair trawling.

U   You are running into danger.

V   I require assistance.

W   I require medical assistance.

X   Stop carrying out your intentions and watch for my signals.

Y   I am dragging my anchor.

Z   I require a tug. When made by fishing vessels operating in close proximity on the fishing grounds it means: "I am shooting nets".

Note: 1   Sound signals "**G**" and "**Z**" may continue to be used by fishing vessels in close proximity to other fishing vessels.

        2   Signals "**K**" and "**S**" have special meanings as landing signals for small boats with crews or persons in distress. (ICSLS, 1974, ch. V, reg. 16).

(Chapter XIII)
(p25)

Single-Letter Signals Between Ice-Breaker and Assisted Vessels

The following single-letter signals, when made between an ice-breaker and assisted vessels, have only the significations given in this table and are only to be made by sound, visual or radiotephony signals.

WM   Ice-breaker support is now commencing. Use special ice-breaker support signals and keep continuous watch for sound, visual or radiotelephony signals.

WO   Ice-breaker support is finished. Proceed to your destination.

Code letters or figures	Ice breaker	Assisted vessel(s)
A .—	Go ahead (proceed along the ice channel)	I am going ahead (I am proceeding along the ice channel)
G ——.	I am going ahead; follow me.	I am going ahead; I am following you.
J .———	Do not follow me (proceed along the ice channel)	I will not follow you (I will proceed along the ice channel)
P .——.	Slow down	I am slowing down
N —.	Stop your engines	I am stopping my engines
H	Reverse your engines	I am reversing my engines
L .—..	You should stop your vessel instantly	I am stopping my vessel
4 ....—	Stop. I am ice-bound	Stop. I am ice-bound
Q ——.—	Shorten the distance between vessels	I am shortening the distance
B —...	Increase the distance between vessels	I am increasing the distance
5	Attention	Attention
Y —.——	Be ready to take (or cast off) the towline	I am ready to take (or cast off) the towline

Radiotelegraph and Radiotelephone Codes, Prowords and Abbreviations

New International Code of Signals
Updated to September 1986.
Extracted from the International Code of Signals. 1987.

DISTRESS

New Code	Meaning	Old Code
	DZ-EG Vessel / aircraft in distress	
	I am in distress and require immediate assistance.	NC
DZ	Vessel (or aircraft) indicated appears to be in distress	
	DZ 1 Is vessel (or aircraft) indicated in distress ?	
	DZ 2 What is the name (or identity signal) of vessel in distress ?	
EA	Have you sighted or heard of a vessel in distress ?	
	(Approximate position lat ... long ... or bearing .... from place indicated.	
	EA 1 Have you any news of vessel/aircraft reported missing or in distress in this area ?	
	I am (or vessel indicated is) in distress in lat ... long ... (or bearing ... from place indicated, distance ...) and require immediate assistance. Complements Table II if required.	CC
EB	There is a vessel (or aircraft) in distress in lat ... long ... (or bearing ... distance ... from me, or Complements Table III).	
EC	A vessel which has suffered a nuclear accident is in distress in lat ... etc.	

Distress signals

ED	Your distress signals are understood.	
	ED 1 Your distress signals are understood; the nearest life-saving station is being informed.	
EF	SOS/MAYDAY has been cancelled.	
	EF 1 Has the SOS/MAYDAY been cancelled ?	
	I have intercepted SOS/MAYDAY from vessel (name or identity signal) (or aircraft) in position lat ... long ... at time indicated.	FF
EG	Did you hear SOS/MAYDAY given at time indicated.	
	EG 1 Will you listen on 2182 kHz for signals of emergency position-indicating radio beacons ?	
	EG 2 I am listening on 2182 kHz for signals of emergency position-indicating radio beacons ?	
	EG 3 Have you received the signal of an emergency position-indicating radio beacon on 2182 kHz ?	
	EG 4 I have received the signal of an emergency position-indicating radio beacon on 2182 kHz .	
	EG 5 Will you listen on ... MHz for signals of emergency position-indicating radio beacons ?	
	EG 6 I am listening on ... MHz for signals of emergency position-indicating radio beacons ?	
	EG 7 Have you received the signal of an emergency position-indicating radio beacon on ... MHz ?	
	EG 8 I have received the signal of an emergency position-indicating radio beacon on ... MHz.	

Radiotelegraph and Radiotelephone Codes, Prowords and Abbreviations

New International Code of Signals
Updated to September 1986.
Extracted from the International Code of Signals. 1987.

New Code	Meaning	Old Code
EJ	I have received distress signal transmitted by coast station indicated.	
EJ 1	Have you received distress signal transmitted by coast station indicated ?	
EK	I have sighted distress signal in lat ...long ...	
EK 1	An explosion was seen or heard. (position or direction and time to be indicated).	
EK 2	Have you heard or seen distress signal from survival craft ?	

Position of distress

EL	Repeat the distress position.	
EL 1	What is the position of vessel in distress ?	
	Position given with SOS/MAYDAY from vessel (or aircraft (was lat ... long ... (or bearing ... from place indicated, distance ... (.	FG
	What was the position given with SOS/MAYDAY from vessel (or aircraft) ?	FG 1
	Position given with SOS/MAYDAY is wrong. The correct position is lat ... long ...	FH
	Position given with SOS/MAYDAY by vessel is wrong. I have her bearing by radio direction-finder and can exchange bearings with any other vessel.	FI
	Survival craft are believed to be in the vicinity of lat ... long ...	GI
EM	Are there other vessels/aircraft in the vicinity of vessel/aircraft in distress ?	

Contact or Locate

EN	You should try to contact vessel/aircraft in distress.	
EO	I am unable to locate vessel/aircraft in distress because of poor visibility.	
EP	I have lost sight of you.	
	I have located (or found) wreckage from the vessel/aircraft in distress (position to be indicated if necessary by lat ... long ... or by bearing ... from specified place, and distance ...).	GL
EQ	I expect to be at the position of vessel/aircraft in distress at time indicated.	
EQ 1	Indicate estimated time of your arrival at position of vessel/aircraft in distress.	
	I am flying to likely position of vessel in distress.	BI
	One or more vessels are assisting the vessel in distress.	CM
	Vessel/aircraft reported in distress is receiving assistance.	CM 1
	I am proceeding to the assistance of vessel/aircraft in distress in lat ... long ...	CR
	I have found vessel/aircraft in distress in lat ... long ...	GF

Radiotelegraph and Radiotelephone Codes, Prowords and Abbreviations

New International Code of Signals
Updated to September 1986.
Extracted from the International Code of Signals. 1987.

New Code　　　　　　　　　　　**Meaning**　　　　　　　　　　　**Old Code**

POSITION

ER	You should indicate your position at time indicated.
ET	My position at time indicated was lat ... long ...
EU	My present position is lat ... long ... (or bearing from place indicated, distance ...).
EU 1	What is your present position ?
EV	My position, course and speed are lat ... long ..., ... knots....
EV 1	What are your present position, course and speed ?
EW	My position is ascertained by dead reckoning.
EW 1	My position is ascertained by visual bearings.
EW 2	My position is ascertained by astronomical observations.
EW 3	My position is ascertained by radio beacons.
EW 4	My position is ascertained by radar.
EW 5	My position is ascertained by electronic position-fixing system.
EX	My position is doubtful.
EY	I am confident as to my position.
EY 1	Are you confident as to your position ?
EZ	Your position according to bearings taken by radio direction-finding stations which I control is lat ... long ... (at time indicated).
EZ 1	Will you give me my position according to bearings taken by radio direction-finding stations which you control ?
FA	Will you give me my position ?
FB	Will vessels in my immediate vicinity (or in the vicinity of lat ... long ...) please indicate position, course and speed ?

Position of distress

FC	You should indicate your position by visual or sound signals.
FC 1	You should indicate your position by rockets or flares.
FC 2	You should indicate your position by visual signals.
FC 3	You should indicate your position by sound signals.
FC 4	You should indicate your position by searchlight.
FC 5	You should indicate your position by smoke signal.
FD	My position is indicated by visual or sound signals.
FD 1	My position is indicated by rockets or flares.
FD 2	My position is indicated by visual signals.
FD 3	My position is indicated by sound signals.
FD 4	My position is indicated by searchlight.

Radiotelegraph and Radiotelephone Codes, Prowords and Abbreviations

New International Code of Signals
Updated to September 1986.
Extracted from the International Code of Signals. 1987.

New Code	Meaning	Old Code
FD 5	My position is indicated by smoke signal.	
	I expect to be at the position of vessel/aircraft in distress at time indicated.	EQ
	Indicate estimated time of your arrival at position of vessel/aircraft in distress.	EQ 1
	Position given with SOS/MAYDAY from vessel (or aircraft) was lat ... long ... (or bearing ... from place indicated, distance ...).	FG
	What was position given with SOS/MAYDAY from vessel (or aircraft) ?	FG 1
	Position given with SOS/MAYDAY is wrong. The correct position is lat ... long ...	FH
	Position given with SOS/MAYDAY by vessel is wrong. I have her bearing by radio direction-finder and can exchange bearings with any other vessel.	FI
	Position of accident (or survival craft) is marked.	FJ
	Position of accident (or survival craft) is marked by flame or smoke float.	FJ 1
	Position of accident (or survival craft) is marked by sea marker.	FJ 2
	Position of accident (or survival craft) is marked by sea marker dye.	FJ 3
	Position of accident (or survival craft) is marked by radio beacon.	FJ 4
	Position of accident (or survival craft) is marked by wreckage.	FJ 5
	Is position of accident (or survival craft) marked ?	FK
	You should transmit your identification and series of long dashes or your carrier frequency to home vessel (or aircraft) to your position.	FQ
	Shall I home vessel (or aircraft) to my position ?	FQ 1
	You should indicate position of survivors by throwing pyrotechnic signals	HT

SEARCH AND RESCUE

(p46)

Assistance, Proceeding to

New Code	Meaning	Old Code
	I am proceeding to the assistance of vessel/aircraft in distress (lat... long ...).	CR
FE	I am proceeding to the position of accident at full speed. Expect to arrive at time indicated.	
FE 1	Are you proceeding to the position of accident ? If so, when do you expect to arrive ?	
	I am unable to give assistance.	CV
	Can you assist ?	CV 4

Position of distress or accident

New Code	Meaning	Old Code
FF	I have intercepted SOS/MAYDAY from vessel (name or identity signal) (or aircraft) in position lat ... long ... at time indicated.	

Radiotelegraph and Radiotelephone Codes, Prowords and Abbreviations

New International Code of Signals
Updated to September 1986.
Extracted from the International Code of Signals. 1987.

New Code	Meaning	Old Code
FF 1	I have intercepted SOS/MAYDAY from vessel (name or identity signal) (or aircraft) in position lat ... long ... at time indicated; I have heard nothing since.	
FG	Position given with SOS/MAYDAY from vessel (or aircraft) was lat ... long ... (or bearing ... from place indicated, distance ...).	
FG 1	What was position given with SOS/MAYDAY from vessel (or aircraft) ?	
FH	Position given with SOS/MAYDAY is wrong. The correct position is lat ... long ...	
FI	Position given with SOS/MAYDAY by vessel is wrong. I have her bearing by radio direction-finder and can exchange bearings with any other vessel.	
FJ	Position of accident (or survival craft) is marked.	
FJ 1	Position of accident (or survival craft) is marked by flame or smoke float.	
FJ 2	Position of accident (or survival craft) is marked by sea marker.	
FJ 3	Position of accident (or survival craft) is marked by sea marker dye.	
FJ 4	Position of accident (or survival craft) is marked by radio beacon.	
FJ 5	Position of accident (or survival craft) is marked by wreckage.	
FK	Is position of accident (or survival craft) is marked ?	

Information - Instructions

New Code	Meaning	Old Code
FL	You should steer course ... (or follow me) to reach position of accident.	
	Course to reach me is	MF
	What is the course to reach you ?	MF 1
FM	Visual contact with vessel is not continuous.	
FN	I have lost all contact with vessel.	
	I have lost sight of you.	EP
FO	I will keep close to you.	
FO 1	I will keep close to you during the night.	
FP	Estimated set and drift of survival craft is ... degrees and ... knots.	
FP 1	What is the estimated set and drift of survival craft ?	
FQ	You should transmit your identification and series of long dashes or your carrier frequency to home vessel (or aircraft) to your position.	
FQ 1	Shall I home vessel (or aircraft) to my position ?	

Radiotelegraph and Radiotelephone Codes, Prowords and Abbreviations

New International Code of Signals
Updated to September 1986.
Extracted from the International Code of Signals. 1987.

New Code	Meaning	Old Code

Search

FR	I am (or vessel indicated is) in charge of co-ordinating search.	
*FR 1	Carry out search pattern ... starting at ... hours. Initial course ... search speed ... knots.	
*FR 2	Carry out radar search, ships proceeding in loose line abreast at intervals between ships ... miles. Initial course ... search speed ... knots.	
*FR 3	Vessel indicated (call sign or identity signal) is allocated track number ...	
*FR 4	Vessel(s) indicated adjust interval between ships to ... miles.	
*FR 5	Adjust track spacing to ... miles.	
*FR 6	Search speed will now be ... knots.	
*FR 7	Alter course as necessary to next leg of track now (or at time indicated).	

* These signals are intended for use in connection with the Merchant Ship Search and Rescue Manual (MERSAR).

FS	Please take charge of search in sector stretching between bearings ... and ... from vessel in distress.	
FT	Please take charge of search in sector between lat ... and long ... and ...	
FV	Search by aircraft/helicopter will be discontinued because of unfavourable conditions.	
FW	You should search in the vicinity of lat ... long ...	
FX	Shall I search in the vicinity of lat ... long ... ?	
FY	I am in the search area.	
FY 1	Are you in the search area ?	
	Aircraft is coming to participate in search. Expected arrive over the area of accident at time indicated.	BP
FZ	You should continue search according to instructions and until further notice.	
FZ 1	I am continuing to search.	
FZ 2	Are you continuing to search ?	
FZ 3	Do you want me to continue to search ?	
GA	I cannot continue to search.	
GB	You should stop search and return to base or continue your voyage.	

Results of search
(p49)

GC	Report results of search.	
GC 1	Results of search negative. I am continuing to search.	
GC 2	I have searched area of accident but have found no trace of derilect or survivors.	

Radiotelegraph and Radiotelephone Codes, Prowords and Abbreviations

New International Code of Signals
Updated to September 1986.
Extracted from the International Code of Signals. 1987.

New Code	Meaning	Old Code
GC 3	I have noted patches of oil at likely position of accident.	
GD	Vessel/aircraft missing or being looked for has not been heard of since.	
GD 1	Have you anything to report on vessel/aircraft missing or being looked for?	
GD 2	Have you seen wreckage or derelict?	
GE	Vessel/aircraft has been located at lat ... long	
GF	I have found vessel/aircraft in distress in lat ... long ...	
GG	Vessel/aircraft was last reported at time indicated in lat ... long ... steering course.	
GH	I have sighted survival craft in lat ... long ... (or bearing ... distance ... from me).	
GI	Survival craft are believed to be in the vicinity of lat ... long ...	
GJ	Wreckage is reported in lat ... long ...	
GJ 1	Wreckage is reported in lat ... long ... No survivors appear to be in the vicinity.	
GK	Aircraft wreckage is found in lat ... long ...	
GL	I have located (or found) wreckage from the vessel/aircraft in distress (position to be indicated if necessary by lat ... long ... or by bearing from specified place or distance ...)	

Rescue
(p50)

GM	I cannot save my vessel.	
GM 1	I cannot save my vessel; keep as close as possible.	
GN	You should take off persons.	
GN 1	I wish some persons taken off. Skeleton crew will remain on board.	
GN 2	I will take off persons.	
GN 3	Can you take off persons?	
GO	I cannot take off persons.	
GP	You should proceed to the rescue of vessel (or ditched aircraft) in lat ... long ...	
GQ	I cannot proceed to the rescue owing to weather. You should do all you can.	
GR	Vessel coming to your rescue (or to the rescue of vessel or aircraft indicated) is steering course ... speed ... knots.	
GR 1	You should indicate course and speed of vessel coming to my rescue (or to the rescue of vessel or aircraft indicated)	
GS	I will attempt rescue with whip and breeches buoy.	
GT	I will endeavour to connect with line-throwing apparatus.	
GT 1	Look out for rocket line.	
GU	It is not safe to fire a rocket.	

Radiotelegraph and Radiotelephone Codes, Prowords and Abbreviations

New International Code of Signals
Updated to September 1986.
Extracted from the International Code of Signals. 1987.

New Code	Meaning	Old Code
GV	You should endeavour to send me a line.	
GV 1	Have you a line-throwing apparatus ?	
GV 2	Can you connect with line throwing apparatus ?	
GV 3	I have not a line-throwing apparatus.	
GW	Man overboard. Please take action to pick him up. (Position to be indicated if necessary).	
	Man overboard.	O
GX	Report results of rescue.	
GX 1	What have you (or rescue vessel/aircraft) picked up ?	
GY	I (or rescue vessel/aircraft) have picked up wreckage.	
GZ	All persons saved.	
GZ 1	All persons lost.	
HA	I (or rescue vessel/aircraft) have rescued ... (number) injured persons.	
HB	I (or rescue vessel/aircraft) have rescued ... (number) survivors.	
HC	I (or rescue vessel/aircraft) have picked up ... (number) bodies.	
HD	Can I transfer rescued persons to you ?	

SURVIVORS

(p51)

HF	I have located survivors in water, lat ... long ... (or bearing ... from place indicated, distance ...).	
HG	I have located survivors in survival craft, lat ... long ... (or bearing ... from place indicated, distance ...).	
HJ	I have located survivors in on drifting ice, lat ... long ...	
HK	I have located bodies in lat ... long ... (or bearing ... from place indicated, distance ...).	
HL	Survivors not yet located.	
HL 1	I am still looking for survivors.	
HL 2	Have you located survivors ? If so, in what position ?	
HM	Survivors are in bad condition. Medical assistance is urgently required.	
HM 1	Survivors are in bad condition.	
HM 2	Survivors are in good condition.	
HM 3	Condition of survivors not ascertained.	
HM 4	What is condition of survivors ?	
HN	You should proceed to lat ... long ... to pick up survivors.	

Radiotelegraph and Radiotelephone Codes, Prowords and Abbreviations

New International Code of Signals
Updated to September 1986.
Extracted from the International Code of Signals. 1987.

(Chapter VIII)
COMMUNICATIONS
(p103)

ACKNOWLEDGE - ANSWER

New Code	Meaning	Old Code
YH	I have received the following from ... (name or identity signal of vessel or station).	
YI	I have received the safety signal sent by ... (name or identity signal).	
YJ	Have you received the safety signal sent by ...(name or identity signal)?	
YK	I am unable to answer your question.	
	Received. or I have received your last signal.	R

CALLING

YL	I will call you again at ... hours (on ... kHz or MHz).	
YM	Who is calling me ?	

CANCEL

YN	Cancel my last signal/message.	
	My last signal was incorrect. I will repeat it correctly.	ZP

COMMUNICATE

	I wish to communicate with you by ... (CT I)	K (with one numeral)
	I wish to communicate with you.	K
YO	I am going to communicate by .... (CT I)	
YP	I wish to communicate with vessel or coast station (identity signal)(CT I)	
YQ	I wish to communicate by ... (CT I) with vessel bearing ... from me.	
YR	Can you communicate by ... (CT I) ?	
YS	I am unable to communicate by ... (CT I).	
YT	I cannot read your ... (CT I).	
YU	I am going to communicate with your station by means of the ICS.	
YV	The groups that follow are from the International Code of Signals.	
	YV 1 The groups that follow are from the local code.	
YW	I wish to communicate by radiotelegraphy on frequency indicated.	
YX	I wish to communicate by radiotelephony on frequency indicated.	

Radiotelegraph and Radiotelephone Codes, Prowords and Abbreviations

New International Code of Signals
Updated to September 1986.
Extracted from the International Code of Signals. 1987.

New Code	Meaning	Old Code
YY	I wish to communicate by VHF radiotelephony on frequency indicated.	
YZ	The word that follow are in plain language.	
ZA	I wish to communicate with you in ... (language indicated by following complements)	
	0 Dutch	
	1 English	
	2 French	
	3 German	
	4 Greek	
	5 Italian	
	6 Japanese	
	7 Norwegian	
	8 Russian	
	9 Spanish	
ZB	I can communicate with you in language indicated. (complements as above)	
ZC	Can you communicate with me in language indicated. (complements as above)	
ZD	Please communicate the following to all shipping in the vicinity.	
	ZD 1 Please report me to Coast Guard New York	
	ZD 2 Please report me to Lloyd's London.	
	ZD 3 Please report me to Minmorflot Moscow.	
	ZD 4 Please report me to M S A Tokyo.	
ZE	You should come within visual signal distance.	
	You should keep within visual signal distance from me (or vessel indicated).	PR 2
	I have established visual communications with the aircraft in distress on 2182 kHz.	BC
	Can you communicate with the aircraft ?	BC 1
	I have established communications with the aircraft in distress on ... kHz.	BD
	I have established communications with the aircraft in distress on ... MHz.	BE

EXERCISE

ZF	I wish to exercise signals with you by .... (Complements Table I)	
ZG	It is not convenient to exercise signals.	
ZH	Exercise has been completed.	

Radiotelegraph and Radiotelephone Codes, Prowords and Abbreviations

New International Code of Signals
Updated to September 1986.
Extracted from the International Code of Signals. 1987.

New Code	Meaning	Old Code

RECEPTION - TRANSMISSION

ZI   I can receive but not transmit by ... (Complements Table I)

ZJ   I can transmit but not receive by ... (CT I)

ZK   I cannot distinguish your signal. Please repeat it by ... (CT I)

ZL   Your signal has been received but not understood. I cannot read your ...   (CT I)

ZM   You should send (or speak) more slowly.

    ZM 1   Shall I send (or speak) more slowly ?

ZN   You should send each word or group twice.

ZO   You should stop sending.

    ZO 1   Shall I stop sending ?

REPEAT

ZP   My last signal was incorrect. I will repeat it correctly.

ZQ   Your signal appears incorrectly coded.
You should check and repeat the whole.

ZR   Repeat the signal now being made to me by vessel (or coast station)
... (name or identity signal).

(Chapter IX)

INTERNATIONAL HEALTH REGULATIONS

(p107)

PRATIQUE MESSAGES

ZS   My vessel is "healthy" and I request free pratique.   Q

     * I require health clearance.   (* Show red over white light.)   QQ

ZT   My Maritime Declaration of Health has negative answers to the six health questions.

ZU   My Maritime Declaration of Health has positive answers to question(s) ...
(indicated by complements 1 - 6).

ZV   I believe I have been in an infected area during the last thirty days.

ZW   I require Port Medical Officer.

    ZW 1   Port Medical Officer will be available at (time indicated).

ZX   You should make the appropriate pratique signal.

ZY   You have pratique.

ZZ   You should proceed to anchorage for health clearance
    (at place indicated)

    ZZ 1   Where is the anchorage for health clearance ?

I have a doctor on board.   AL

Have you a doctor ?   AM

New International Code of Signals
Updated to September 1986.
Extracted from the International Code of Signals. 1987.

TABLES OF COMPLEMENTS
(p 108)

Table I.

1. Morse signalling by hand-flags or arms
2. Loud hailer (megaphone)
3. Morse signalling lamp
4. Sound signals

Table II.

0. Water
1. Provisions
2. Fuel
3. Pumping equipment
4. Fire-fighting equipment
5. Medical assistance
6. Towing
7. Survival craft
8. Vessel to stand by
9. Ice-breaker

Table III.

0. Direction unknown (or calm)
1. North-east
2. East
3. South-east
4. South
5. South-west
6. West
7. North-west
8. North
9. All directions (or confused or variable)

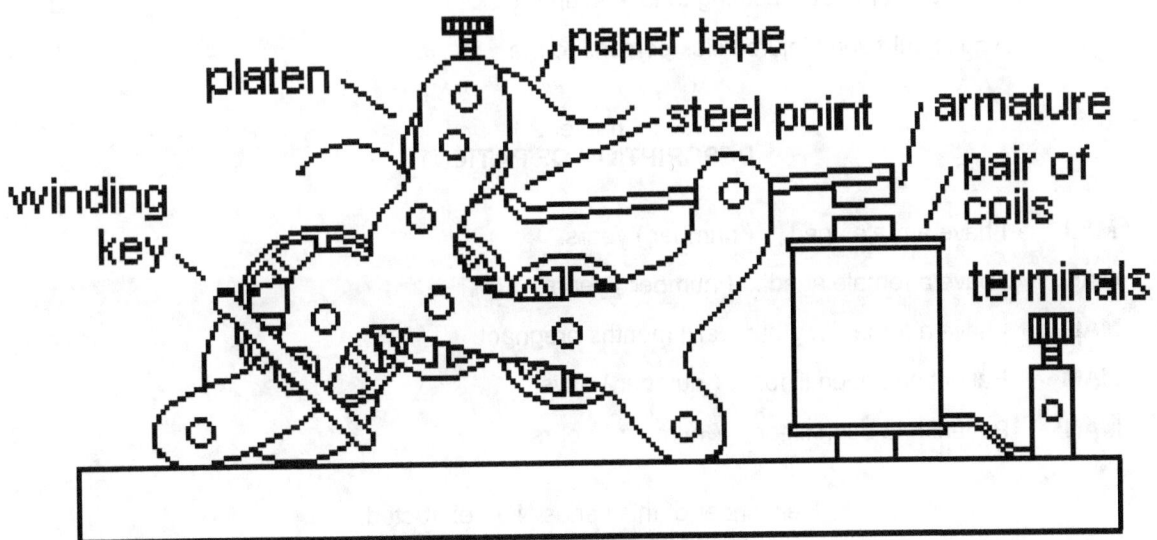

Morse Register

Radiotelegraph and Radiotelephone Codes, Prowords and Abbreviations

New International Code of Signals
Updated to September 1986.
Extracted from the International Code of Signals. 1987.

New Code	Meaning	Old Code
	(Chapter 1) **REQUEST FOR MEDICAL ASSISTANCE** (p 115) **REQUEST GENERAL INFORMATION**	
MAA	I request urgent medical advice.	
MAB	I request you to make rendez-vous in position indicated.	
MAC	I request you to arrange hospital admission.	
MAD	I am ... (indicate number) hours from nearest port.	
MAE	I am converging on nearest port.	
MAF	I am moving away from nearest port.	
	I require medical assistance.	W
	I have a doctor on board.	AL
	Have you a doctor ?	AM
	I need a doctor.	AN
	I need a doctor. I have severe burns	AN 1
	I need a doctor. I have radiation casualties.	AN 2
	I require a helicopter urgently with a doctor.	BR 2
	I require a helicopter urgently to pick up injured/sick person.	BR 3
	Helicopter is coming to you now (or at time indicated) with a doctor.	BT 2
	Helicopter is coming to you now (or at time indicated) to pick up injured/sick person.	BT 3
	I have injured/sick person (or number of persons indicated) to be taken off urgently	AQ
	You should send a helicopter/boat with a stretcher.	BS
	A helicopter/boat is coming to take injured/sick.	BU
	You should send injured/sick persons to me.	AT

(Chapter 2)
DESCRIPTION OF PATIENT

New Code	Meaning	
MAJ	I have a male aged ... (number) years.	
MAK	I have a female aged ... (number) years.	
MAL	I have a female ... (number) months pregnant.	
MAM	Patient has been ill for ... (number) days.	
MAN	Patient has been ill for ... (number) hours.	

Remainder of this series NOT extracted.
Extends to **MVU** describing illnesses.

Radiotelegraph and Radiotelephone Codes, Prowords and Abbreviations

International Code of Signals
SUPPLEMENT - 1995.
Standard Signals to Make Innocent Passage through the Territorial Sea or Freedom of Navigation.

Signal	Meaning
UV 1*	I am conducting innocent passage in the territorial sea.
UV 2*	Your course leads into an area of the territorial sea in which the right of innocent passage is temporarily suspended.
UV 3*	You should leave the area of the territorial sea in which the right of innocent passage is temporarily suspended.
UV 4* (...)	You are violating the conditions of innocent passage through the territorial sea (as indicated in the table of complements below). Request you comply with the conditions of innocent passage through the territorial sea.
UV 5* (...)	I am not violating the conditions of innocent passage through the territorial sea (as indicated in the table of complements below).
UV 6* (...)	I have ceased violating the conditions of innocent passage through the territorial sea (as indicated in the table of complements below).
UV 7*	Having disregarded our request for compliance with the conditions of innocent passage through the territorial sea, you are required to leave the territorial sea immediately.
UV 8*	I am conducting transit passage through an international Strait.
UV 9*	I am exercising freedom of navigation.

* Signals UV 1 - UV 9 are not mandatory. Use of these signals is not a precondition to the exercise of the right of innocent passage or freedom of navigation.

TABLE OF COMPLEMENTS
Conditions of innocent passage.

Signal	Meaning
0	By threatening or using force against our/your sovereignty, territorial integrity, or political independence.
1	By exercising or practising with weapons.
2	By engaging in acts aimed at collecting information to the prejudice of our/your defence or security.
3	By engaging in acts of propaganda aimed at affecting our/your defence or security.
4	By engaging in the launching, landing or taking on board of aircraft or a military device.
5	By engaging in the loading or unloading of a commodity, currency or person contrary to the customs, fiscal, immigration or sanitary laws or regulations of our/your country.
6	By engaging in wilful and serious pollution.
7	By engaging in fishing activities.
8	By engaging in research or survey activities.
9	By engaging in acts aimed at interfering with our/your systems of communication or other facilities or installations.

Other additional signals.

Signal	Meaning
UW 2	Welcome !
UW 3	Welcome home !

Radiotelegraph and Radiotelephone Codes, Prowords and Abbreviations

International Code of Signals
US/Russia Supplementary Signals for Naval Vessels
United States Edition, 1969 (Revised 1999).

IR 1	I am engaged in oceanographic operations.
IR 2	I am streaming/towing hydrographic survey equipment.
IR 3	I am recovering hydrographic survey equipment.
IR 4	I am conducting salvage operations.
JH 1	I am attempting to recover a grounded vessel.
MH 1	Request you not to cross my course ahead of me.
NB 1	I have my unattached hydrographic survey equipment bearing in direction from me as indicated .... (Table 3 of ICS).
PJ 1	I am unable to alter course to my starboard.
PJ 2	I am unable to alter course to my port.
PJ 3	Caution, I have a steering casualty.
PP 8	Dangerous operations in progress. Request you remain clear of the hazard which is in the direction from me as indicated ...... (Table 3 of ICS).
QF 1	Caution, I have stopped engines.
QS 6	I am proceeding to anchorage on course ....
QV 2	I am in a fixed multiple leg moor using two or more anchors or buoys fore and aft. Request you remain clear.
QV 3	I am anchored in deep water with hydrographic survey equipment streamed.
RT 2	I intend to pass you on your port side.
RT 3	I intend to pass you on your starboard side.
RT 4	I will overtake you on your port side.
RT 5	I will overtake you on your starboard side.
RT 6	I am / Formation is manoeuvring. Request you remain clear of the hazard which is in the direction from me as indicated ..... (Table 3 of ICS).
RT 7	I shall approach your ship on starboard side to a distance of .... 100's of metres (yards).
RT 8	I shall approach your ship on port side to a distance of .... 100's of metres (yards).
RT 9	I shall cross astern at a distance of .... 100's of metres (yards).
RU2	I am beginning a port turn in approximately ..... minutes.
RU3	I am beginning a starboard turn in approximately ..... minutes.
RU4	The formation is preparing to alter course to port.
RU5	The formation is preparing to alter course to starboard.
RU6	I am engaged in manoeuvring exercises. It is dangerous to be inside the formation.
RU7	I am preparing to submerge.
RU8	A submarine will surface within two miles of me within 30 minutes. Request you remain clear.
TX 1	I am engaged in fisheries patrol.
SL 2	Request your course, speed and passing intention.
UY 1	I am preparing to launch / recover aircraft on course ....
UY 2	I am preparing to conduct missile exercises. Request you remain clear of the hazard which is in the direction from me as indicated ..... (Table 3 of ICS).
UY 3	I am preparing to conduct gunnery exercises. Request you remain clear of the hazard which is in the direction from me as indicated ..... (Table 3 of ICS).
UY 4	I am preparing to conduct /am conducting operations employing explosive charges.
UY 5	I am manoeuvring in preparation for torpedo launching exercises. Request you remain clear of the hazard which is in the direction from me as indicated ..... (Table 3 of ICS).
UY 6	I am preparing to conduct /am conducting underway replenishment on course.. Request you remain clear
UY 7	I am preparing to conduct extensive small boat and ship to shore amphibious training operations.
UY 8	I am manoeuvring to launch / recover landing craft / boats.
UY 9	I am preparing to conduct /am conducting helicopter operations over my stern.
UY 10	I am testing my gun systems.
UY 11	I am testing my missile systems.
UY 12	I am preparing to conduct /am conducting gunnery / bombing exercises from aircraft on a towed target. Request you remain clear of the hazard which is in the direction from me as indicated .. (Table 3 of ICS).
ZL 1	I have received and understood your message.
ZL 2	Do you understand? Request acknowledgment.

NOTE: The current Edition (1999) of the International Code of Signals may be downloaded from US National Imaging and Mapping Agency site: http://164.214.2.59/

Radiotelegraph and Radiotelephone Codes, Prowords and Abbreviations

Numeral Code used in the USA Line Telegraphy.

This time saving code was established at the Telegraph Convention held in 1857.

* Some are modern usages not original.

WIRE Preference over everything except 95.

1	Wait a minute.
2	Important business.
3	What is the correct time?
4	Where shall I start / resume in message?
5	Have you anything for me?
6	I am ready. Also - I have something for you; are you ready?
7	Are you ready?
8	Close your key; circuit is busy you are breaking.
9	Attention, or clear the wire. (Wire test - preference over 25 and 55. - 1902) (Train order complete)
10	Keep this circuit closed. (Low. - 1902.)
12	Do you understand? I (Circuit is yours. - 1902.)
13	do not understand. Also - I understand. (Understand? - 1902)
14	What is the weather?
15	For you and others to copy. (Have you any orders? - 1902.)
16	
17	Daily weather report. Also - Lightning here. Following for all stations on the line.
18	What is the trouble?
19	Form 19 Train Order. - Picked up without the train stopping using a loop and hook.
20	
21	Stop for meal. Also - This message has precedence. Emergency
22	Wire test. Also - Busy on other wire. and - Love and Kisses
23	All copy. Also - Accident or Death Message.
24	Repeat this back.
25	Busy on another circuit. Also - Time reports of passenger trains. Preference over ordinary and 55.
26	Put on ground wire.
27	Priority, very important.
28	Do you get my writing?
29	This message is private, and must be delivered in a sealed envelope. Also - Train Orders.
30	End of Traffic; Finished. (American Morse for 30, = 30 min past the hour. i.e. end of shift.)
31	Form 31 Train Order. - Train stopped and order signed for.
32	I understand that I am to ....
33	Car report. Also - Answer is paid for.
34	Message for all officers.
35	You may use my signals to answer this.
36	
37	Diversion. Also - Inform all interested.
39	Sleep Car report. Also - Important, with priority on through wire.
44	Answer promptly by wire.
47	Display Signals.
48	Signals are Displayed.
51	Handshake, Greetings. * 'God bless you' - Latin America.
55	This message is of great importance.
72	* Sign off by QRP (low power, under 10 watts) operators
73	Accept my compliments. (Now - Best Regards.)
77	I have a message for you. * Greetings – German oprs.
82	Warning signal for yard reports in terminal areas.
88	Love and Kisses. (Note: The opposite of 22, possibly the response)
91	Superintendant's signal.
92	Deliver promptly.
92D	Delivered.
93	Vice President's and General Manager's signal.
94	Superintendent's business only signal.
95	Following is very urgent. President's signal.
97	Urgent stock market info (1928 Associated Press)
99	Keep Out.
100	
134	Who is at the key?

Usage varied with different companies.   Additions required to complete this List would be appreciated.

From the Morse Telegraph Club Inc.

Weather Reporting Code used by Train Dispatchers. (US Railroads)

Radiotelegraph and Radiotelephone Codes, Prowords and Abbreviations

Numeral Code used in the USA Line Telegraphy.

This time saving code was established at the Telegraph Convention held in 1857.

A	Light Snow	B	Heavy Snow.	C	Drifting Snow.	D	Light Fog.
F	Heavy Fog.	G	Light Rain.	H	Heavy Rain.	J	Heavy Wind.
K	Calm.	N	Sleeting.	Q	Clear.	R	Cloudy.

Telegraphic Numerals. "Wood's Plan of Telegraphic Instruction 1864" -

1	Wait a moment.	2	Give precise standard time.
3	Get immediate answer from	4	Where shall I go ahead?
5	Keep Still.	6	I am ready.
7	Don't know.	8	Busy on other line.
9	Get answer, sure and quick.	10	Has ... train reached your station?
11	Did you get my last?	12	What time did .... train leave your station?
13	Report when ..... train leaves your station.	14	Write more firmly.
15	Separate words more.	16	What is the weather?
17	Very important ...... hurry up.	18	What is the trouble?
19	How many cars has ..... train?	20	I will see.
21	Collect special messenger's charges for delivery, which are guaranteed.		
22	Paid here.	23	Message for all offices.
24	Have you anything for me?	25	Write dots.
26	Write alphabets.	27	Take off ground wire.
28	Do you get me?	29	Report special messenger's charges to be paid here.
30	Finish.	31	How do you understand my last message?
32	I understand that	33	Deliver this only to whom addressed.
34	If statement ready, go ahead.	35	Connect wires through straight.
36	Require correspondent to prepay answer.	37	If corresp. will prepay answer, it will be paid here.
43	Answer will be paid here.	73	Compliments to ....

Railroad Manual Block System Communicating Code - Association of American Railroads, April 25, 1900.

1	Display Stop Signal. Answer by SD or 5.	2	Block clear. Answer by 13.
3	Block wanted. Answer by 2 or 5.	4	Train has entered block. Answer by 13.
5	Block is not clear.	7	Train following.
8	Opening Block Station. Answer by Nos. of trains in extended block with time each train entered block.		
9	Closing Block Station. Answer by "13" after receiving transfer of the records of trains in the extended block.		
13	I understand.	71	Train following. Display Stop Signal. Answer by SD.

Amendments adopted 1909.

1	Display Stop Signal	2	Block clear.
3	Block wanted for other than passenger train.	4	Train other than passenger has entered block.
5	Block is not clear of train other than passenger.	7	Train Following.
8	Opening Block Station. Answer by record of trains in the extended block.		
13	I understand.	17	Display Stop Signal - Train following.
36	Block wanted for passenger train.	46	Passenger train has entered block.
56	Block is not clear of passenger train.		

Train Order Abbreviations - Chicago & Alton RR. 1909.

C&E	For Conductors and Enginemen.		Com	Complete.
Dispr	Dispatcher.		Eng	Engine.
Frt	Freight.		Jct	Junction.
Mins	Minutes.		No	Number.
Opr	Operator.		OS	Train Report.
Pagr	Passenger.		Sec	Section.
SD	Stop Displayed.		X	Train will be held until order is made complete.

31 or 19 To clear the line for Train Orders and for Operators to ask for Train Orders.

Variations occurred between different companies and periods. There is no standardised list.

Radiotelegraph and Radiotelephone Codes, Prowords and Abbreviations

The following Radiotelephony Codes are included because of the general interest in them and their use by CB operators.

Official 10-Code of the Associated Police Communication Officers, Inc. (USA). Postwar USA to 2002.

	Original	Alternative	Alternative
10-0	Use Caution		
10-1	Unable to copy, Change location.	Call command (NYPD)	
10-2	Signals Good.	Return to command (")	
10-3	Stop Transmitting.	Call dispatcher. (NYPD)	
10-4	Acknowledgment.		
10-5	Relay.	Repeat. (NYPD)	
10-6	Busy - stand by unless urgent.	Change channel. (Calif.)	
10-7	Out of service. (Give location and or Telephone Number)		Verify address. (NYPD)
10-8	In service.		
10-9	Repeat.		
10-10	Fight in Progress.	Negative	Out of service
10-11	Dog case.	.... on duty	Dispatching too rapidly
10-12	Stand by. (stop)		Visitors present.
10-13	Weather and Road Report.	Officer in danger. (NYPD)	
10-14	Report of Prowler.	Message / information	Convoy / Escort
10-15	Civil Disturbance.	Message delivered	Prisoner in Custody.
10-16	Domestic Trouble.	Reply to message.	Daily Reports
10-17	Meet Complainant.	Enroute.	Pick up Papers.
10-18	Complete assignment quickly.	Urgent.	Equip. exchange. (Calif.)
10-19	Return to	(in) contact.	Returning to Stn. (Calif.)
10-20	Location.	Robbery done. (NYPD)	
10-21	Call .... by telephone.	Burglary done. (NYPD)	
10-22	Disregard.	Larceny done. (NYPD)	Report in person to ......
10-23	Arrived at scene. Assignment	Bomb threat. (NYPD)	Standby. (Calif.)
10-24	completed. Report in person	Assault done. (NYPD)	Car to car traffic. (Calif.)
10-25	to ...... Detaining suspect,	Do you have contact with ... ?	
10-26	expedite. Drivers Licence	Estimated arrival time	Clear. (Calif.)
10-27	information.	Any answer our #??	I am moving to channel ....
10-28	Vehicle Registration information.	Please identify your station.	
10-29	Check records for wanted / stolen.	Other crime. (NYPD)	Your air-time limit is up.
10-30	Illegal use of Radio.	Robbery in progress. (NYPD)	Danger / caution.
10-31	Crime in Progress.	Burglary in progress. (NYPD)	Pick up ......
10-32	Man with gun.	Units needed specify / number / type.	Is drunkometer available?
10-33	EMERGENCY.	Bomb threat in progress. (NYPD)	Help me quick.
10-34	Riot.	Trouble at station.	Time.
10-35	Major crime alert.	Interdiction	Confidential information.
10-36	Correct time.	Security check.	Confid. info. (Calif.)
10-37	Investigate suspicious vehicle.	Gang activity.	Theft/shoplifting. (Ottawa)
10-38	Stopping suspicious vehicle. (Give complete description first.)		Computer down.
10-39	Urgent - use light and siren.	Assist Officer ..... at	Can .. come to radio? (Calf)
10-40	Silent run - no light or siren.	Do not Divulge Location.	Is .. aval. for phone? (Calif)
10-41	Beginning tour of duty.	Switch to Alternate Channel.	Break-in. (Ottawa)
10-42	Ending tour of duty.	Call Home.	Holdup, viol. robbery. (")
10-43	Information.	Shuttle.	Sexual assault. (Ottawa)
10-44	Request Permission to leave patrol for	Have msg for you.	Murder/suicide. (Ottawa)
10-45	Animal carcass in ...... lane at	What condit. patient? (Calif.)	Check for Driver's Licence.
10-46	Assist motorist.	Fish & Game Violation Check.	Sex assault. (Canada)
10-47	Emergency road repairs needed at	Investigate Vehicle.	Urinalysis Report
10-48	Traffic standard needs repairs.	Disturbing the Peace.	Blood Alcohol Report.
10-49	Traffic light out.	Proceed to .... (Calif.)	Threat/Obscene call. (Can.)
10-50	Traffic Accident - Fatality, Person Injured, Property Damage.		Disorderly person. (NYPD)
10-51	Wrecker needed.	Roving Band. (NYPD)	Subject drunk. (Calif.)
10-52	Ambulance needed.	Dispute. (NYPD)	Resuscitator needed (Calif.)
10-53	Road blocked.	Traffic Control.	Pers injured, Amb. reqd.
10-54	Livestock on highway.	Change to Channel #.	Fatality.
10-55	Intoxicated driver.	EMS Call, PD not needed (NYPD)	Funeral for ....
10-56	Intoxicated Pedestrian.	Verify EMS needed. (NYPD)	Suicide. (Calif.)

Radiotelegraph and Radiotelephone Codes, Prowords and Abbreviations

U.S. Police 10 Codes Continued.

10-57	Hit and run - Fatality, Person Injured, Property Damage.
10-58	Direct traffic.
10-59	Convoy or escort.
10-60	Squad in vicinity.
10-61	Personnel in area.
10-62	Reply to message....
10-63	Prepare to make written copy.
10-64	Message for local delivery.
10-65	Net message assignment.
10-66	Message cancellation.
10-67	Clear to read net message....
10-68	Dispatch information.
10-69	Message received.
10-70	Fire alarm.
10-71	Advise nature of fire. (size, type and content of building).
10-72	Report progress on fire.
10-73	Smoke report.
10-74	Negative.
10-75	In contact with ...
10-76	En route.
10-77	Estimated Time of Arrival (ETA).
10-78	Need assistance.
10-79	Notify coroner.
10-80	Chase in Progress.
10-81	At station (or substation)
10-82	Reserve lodging.
10-83	Confidential Information.
10-84	Are you going to meet .... Advise ETA.
10-85	Victim's Condition. -
	A - Fair
	B - Poor
	C - Critical
	D - Possible Fatality
	E - Obvious Fatality
10-86	Crime in Progress.
10-87	Pick up cheques for distribution.
10-88	Advise telephone number to contact.
10-89	Bomb Threat.
10-90	Bank alarm at .....
10-91	Unnecessary use of radio.
10-92	Theft.
10-93	Blockade.
10-94	Drag racing.
10-95	Prisoner in custody. Out at Home.
10-96	Mental subject.
10-97	Arriving at Assignment.
10-98	Prison or Gaol break.
10-99	Records indicate wanted or stolen.
10-100	Police needed.
10-101	Shots fired.
10-102	Shooting.
10-103	Homicide.
10-104	Fight in progress.
10-105	Dead person.
10-106	Suspicious person.
10-107	Check residence
10-108	Hit and run accident.
10-109	Unfounded call.
10-110	Person in custody, en route to detention.
10-111	Stolen auto to report.
10-112	Missing person to report.
10-113	Target vehicle.

Additional meanings (middle column):

- Airplane Crash.
- Reckless Driver
- Out of car, on violator. Veh. Id. No. Inspection Request permission car to car. Net Directed.
- Net Free.
- Clear for next assignment.
- Unusual incident. (NYPD)
- Traffic/Parking prob. (NYPD)
- Repeat Dispatch.
- Missing Person.
- Confirmed Wanted / Stolen.
- Dead Person.
- Rape.
- Civil Disturbance.
- Domestic Problem.
- Meet / See Complainant.
- Return to ....
- Back up Unit.
- Cancel. (NYPD).
- Breathalyser.
- Prisoner in Custody.
- Report to be filed. (NYPD)
- Visitor Present.
- Will be late. / Delayed by ....
- Need additional units. (NYPD)
- Abduction/Kidnap   (Canada)
- Tow truck req'd. (Calif.)
- Delayed due to ... (US Nat Pks)
- Violent dom. disp. (Suffolk Co.)
- Transporting female. (NYPD)
- Abandoned Vehicle.
- Man with Gun.
- Other interim status. (NYPD)
- -N Situation normal. (NYPD)
- Burglary.
- Action taken. C-Court (NYPD)
- Report prepared. (NYPD)
- Done previously. (NYPD)
- Refer to another agency. (")
- Summons served . (NYPD)
- Test Signal.
- Assignment completed
- Emergency.
- Radio Silence (Drug Enf. Agency)

Additional meanings (right column):

- EMS second call. (NYPD)
- Req. to talk to car ##.
- Complete.
- What is next item?
- Clear for Assignment.
- En Route to Assignment.
- Check out on Assignment.
- Vandalism.
- Juvenile Problem.
- Major Crime Alert.
- Person calling help. (Calif.)
- Runaway Juvenile.
- Drug Call.
- Prowler.   (Calif.)
- Attempted Suicide.
- Fire- prog. report. (USNPS)
- Abandoned Car.
- Theft.
- Juvenile Trouble.
- Prowler.
- Ambulance run, Sick Call.
- Domestic Trouble.
- Sex Offense.
- Adt or Bank Alarm.
- Burglary.
- Disturbance.
- Fight.
- Knifing.
- Hold up.
- Shooting.
- Officer Needs Help.
- Homicide.
- Tower Light Check.
- Disregard Further Help.
- Reserve room for .....
- Unnecessary use of Radio.
- Contact your Home.
- Test W/Normal Module.
- CD "Alert"
- CD "Evacuate"
- CD "Take Cover"
- CD "Test"

Radiotelegraph and Radiotelephone Codes, Prowords and Abbreviations

U.S. Police 10 Codes Continued.

'11 - Codes' as used by San Francisco / California Police.   Some are -

11-7	Prowler.		
11-10	Take a report	11-24	Abandoned auto.
11-25	Traffic Hazard	11-26	Abandoned bicycle.
11-27	10-27 + driver held.	11-28	10-28 + driver held.
11-29	Clear, no warrants.	11-30	Missing person.
11-40	Advise if Ambulance needed.	11-41	An Ambulance needed.
11-42	No Ambulance needed.	11-44	Fatality.
11-45	Suicide.	11-48	Furnish transportation.
11-50	Field interrogation.	11-51	Escort / Security check.
11-52	Funeral detail.	11-54	Suspicious vehicle.
11-55	Being followed by automobile.		
11-56	Followed by auto containing dangerous persons.		
11-57	An unidentified auto appeared at the scene of the assignment.		
11-58	Radio is being monitored. Phone all non-routine messages.		
11-59	Give intensive attention to high hazard / business areas.		
11-60	Attack in a high hazard area.	11-65	Signal light is out.
11-66	Defective traffic light.	11-71	Fire.
11-78	Aircraft accident.	11-79	Accident - ambulance has been sent.
11-80	Accident - major injuries.	11-81	Accident - minor injuries.
11-82	Accident - no injuries.	11-83	Accident - no details.
11-84	Direct traffic.	11-85	Tow truck required.
11-86	Special assignment.	11-94	Pedestrian stop.
11-95	Routine traffic stop.	11-96	Checking suspicious vehicle.
11-97	Time/security check on patrol vehicles.		
11-98	Meet Officer	11-99	Officer needs help.

'12 - Codes' as used by Douglas County Sheriffs.

12-1	In service.	12-2	Out of service.
12-3	Return to Station.	12-4	Telephone.
12-5	Repeat.	12-6	Contact.
12-7	Vehicle registration.	12-9	Location.
12-10	Driver's Licence check.	12-12	Bad radio reception, change location.
12-16	Non injury accident.	12-17	Injury accident.
12-20	Check for Wants or Warrants.	12-21	No Wants or Warrants.
12-25	Clear for Confidential radio traffic.	12-26	Off Duty.
12-28	Suspicious.	12-29	Disturbance.
12-31	Intoxicated driver.	12-32	Intoxicated person.
12-33	Clear for Emergency traffic.	12-34	Resume normal traffic.
12-35	Abandoned vehicle.	12-39	Out of car/outside speaker.
12-40	Standby.	12-41	Go ahead.
12-43	Disregard.	12-44	Time.
12-45	Service Equipment.	12-49	Out of car/Paper service.
12-50	Back up request.	12-56	Clear for assignment.

Usage varies over different states and administrations. I think every US Police Force uses a different version.

Radiotelegraph and Radiotelephone Codes, Prowords and Abbreviations

Modified 10-Code adopted by CB Operators in the USA and Australia.

10-1	Receiving poorly.
10-2	Receiving well.
10-3	Stop transmitting.
10-4	OK, message received.
10-5	Relay message.
10-6	Busy, stand by.
10-7	Out of service, leaving air.
10-8	In service, subject to call.
10-9	Repeat message.
10-10	Transmission completed, standing by.
10-11	Talking too rapidly.
10-12	Visitors present.
10-13	Advise weather / road conditions.
10-14	Time by the clock.
10-16	Make pick up at ...
10-17	Urgent business.
10-18	Anything for us?
10-19	Nothing for you, return to base.
10-20	My location is ...
10-21	Call by telephone.
10-22	Report in person to ...
10-23	Stand by.
10-24	Completed last assignment.
10-25	Can you contact ... ?
10-26	Disregard last information.
10-27	I am moving to channel ....
10-28	Identify your station.
10-29	Time is up for contact.
10-30	Does not conform to ACA (FCC) rules.
10-31	No longer breaking rules or regulations.
10-32	I will give you a radio check.
10-33	Emergency traffic at this station.
10-34	Trouble at this station, help needed.
10-35	Confidential information.
10-36	Correct time is ...
10-37	Wrecker needed at ...
10-38	Ambulance needed it ...
10-39	Your message delivered.
10-40	Change to pre-arranged channel at this time.
10-41	Please tune to channel ...
10-42	Traffic accident at ...
10-43	Traffic tie-up at ...
10-44	I have a message for you (or ......)
10-45	All units within range please report.
10-46	Assist motorist.
10-47	
10-48	
10-49	
10-50	Break channel.
10-51	
10-52	
10-53	
10-54	
10-55	Intoxicated driver (DUI).
10-56	
10-57	
10-58	
10-59	
10-60	What is next message ?
10-61	

Radiotelegraph and Radiotelephone Codes, Prowords and Abbreviations

Modified 10-and 11Codes adopted by CB Operators in the USA and Australia.

10-62	Unable to copy, use phone.
10-62sl	Unable to copy on AM, use Sideband Lower.
10-62su	Unable to copy on AM, use Sideband Upper.
10-63	Net directed to ......
10-64	Not clear or understood. Net clear.
10-65	Awaiting your next message assignment.
10-66	Cancel message.
10-67	All units comply.
10-68	Repeat message.
10-69	Message received.
10-70	Fire at ....
10-71	Proceed with transmission in sequence.
10-72	
10-73	Speed trap at. Goodbye, ending conversation
10-74	Negative.
10-75	You are causing interference.
10-76	
10-77	Negative contact.
10-78	
10-80	
10-81	Reserve hotel room for ....
10-82	Reserve room for ...
10-83	Work school crossing. (Emerg)
10-84	My telephone number is: ...
10-85	My address is ...
10-86	Officer / operator on duty.
10-87	
10-88	Advise phone number of ......
10-89	Radio repairman needed at ...
10-90	I have TVI,
10-91	Too soft, talk closer to mike.
10-92	Too loud, talk further from mike. Your transmitter is out of adjustment.
10-93	Check my frequency on this channel.
10-94	Please give me a long count.
10-95	Transmit dead carrier for 5 seconds.
10-96	
10-97	Check test signal.
10-98	
10-99	Mission completed, all units secure. (US)
10-99	Unable to receive your signals (10-1). (Aust)
10-100	Restroom stop.
10-101	
10-102	Have a beer / drink.
10-200	Police needed at ....

Citizen's Band 11 Code.

GENERAL STATION OPERATION.
- 11-1 Receiving poorly.
- 11-2 Receiving well. Stop
- 11-3 transmitting. OK,
- 11-4 Acknowledged.
- 11-5 Identify your station by correct callsign.
- 11-8 This station is standing by on ch. ....
- 11-9 On which other channels can you transmit and receive?
- 11-10 Switch to channel ....
- 11-11 Unable to copy you because of ....
- 11-12 Please repeat your last message.
- 11-13 Trouble at station because of ....
- 11-20 What is your location? (My location is ....)

MESSAGES AND TRAFFIC HANDLING.
- 11-30 Does not conform to operating rules and regulations.

Radiotelegraph and Radiotelephone Codes, Prowords and Abbreviations

CB Operators' 11-Code and 12-Code

11-31	Stand by! (Order).
11-33	Please relay message ……
11-35	Confidential information.
11-36	Correct local time.
11-37	Please call this station by telephone.
11-38	Visitors present.
11-41	Do you have any messages for this station?
11-45	Your reply is satisfactory.
11-46	I have an urgent message for ……….
11-47	Please clarify your message.
11-48	What is the next message?
11-49	Please confirm …..
11-50	Telephone ………….! (Order).
11-51	Can you contact …………. ?
11-52	I have an urgent message for ……….. (NOT for emergency use)

MOBILE AND EN ROUTE.

11-61	Can you recommend a good local restaurant?
11-62	Can you recommend a good local hotel or motel?
11-63	Please advise weather / road conditions.
11-64	What is the highway or best route to ……….. ?
11-65	What is the location of the nearest service station/

COMMERCIAL.

11-70	Rush – quick action desired.
11-71	Return to base.
11-72	Assignment completed.
11-73	Report in person to ………….

MARINE.

11-80	Please advise sea conditions at ……….. ?
11-81	Do you have dockside moorings available for ………….. (boat type)?
11-82	Do you have dockside fuel available?
11-83	I will monitor marine channel ………… (9 or 13) while under way.

EMERGENCY.

11-90	Send police to ……………
11-91	Send ambulance to ………….
11-92	Send fire dept. to ……………
11-95	Personal injury due to accident at ………………
11-96	Please summon Doctor to your station to give emergency first aid by radio.
11-99	Emergency conditions no longer exist.
11-100	I have emergency traffic regarding the safety of life and property. Will all stations give me priority use of this channel until the emergency traffic is completed.

Trucker's 12-Code. (1976)

12-1	One in every crowd.
12-2	Get your own towel, mine's already wet.
12-3	I can't believe I ate the whole thing.
12-24	A pill a day keeps the doctor away.
12-25	Quit chewing the rag.
12-35	Ride on.
12-37	You're jiving me.
12-38	Get off my back.
12-39	Beats the hell out of me.
12-45	Big deal.
12-46	Here we are fellas, Miss America.
12-47	Beautiful, just beautiful.
12-48	Today's just not my day.
12-49	So much for you and the horse
12-50	If you got it, a truck brought it.

Radiotelegraph and Radiotelephone Codes, Prowords and Abbreviations

CB Operators' 12 and 13-Code

12-61	Bull.
12-62	You can't fight City Hall.
12-65	Screwed up like Hogan's goat.
12-69	Excuse please, couldn't find my way.
12-72	You have me confused with someone who cares.
12-73	A terrific screwing up is in progress.
12-74	That figures.
12-75	Here I am, Mr.Terrific.
12-76	Situation normal and all screwed up.
12-77	Want me to call a chaplain.
12-78	Oh my God, now he thinks he's a cop.
12-83	Who, me?
12-84	I can't receive you, a bird messed on my antenna.
12-85	Let's be careful and let someone else do it.
12-86	I think you have problems, stupid!
12-94	Mobile, you have motor oil in your mouth.
12-96	CB maniacs of America, unite.
12-100	Just another cotton picking truck driver.
12-200	Don't mess with me.

Further information to complete these lists would be appreciated.

13-Code used by US CB Operators.

GENERAL.

13-1	All units can copy you and think you are an idiot.
13-2	Yes, I copy you, but I'm ignoring you.
13-3	You're beautiful when you're angry.
13-4	Sorry 'bout that, Big Fella.
13-5	Same to you, Mack !
13-6	OK, so I goofed, none of us are human.
13-7	If you can't copy me it must be your fault because I'm running 3,000 watts.

OPERATORS.

13-20	Is your mike clicking or are your uppers loose again?
13-21	Good grief, are you being paid by the word?
13-22	Lady, is that your voice or did you install a steam whistle ?
13-23	If you had spoken for another 30 seconds you would have been eligible for a Broadcast Station licence.
13-24	You know, you made more sense last time when you were smashed.
13-25	Some of the local operators and I have chipped in to purchase your rig from you. Have you considered stamp collecting?
13-26	Next time you eat garlic would you talk farther from the mike?

TECHNICAL.

13-40	Your signal sounds great, now shut off the set and give me a landline so I can find out what you want.
13-41	Either my receiver is out of alignment or you're on channel 28.
13-42	Either my speaker cone is ripped or you better try it again when you sober up a little.
13-43	That was a beautiful 10, try it with your mike connected.
13-44	I love the way your new rig sounds, now I know why the manufacturer discontinued that model so fast.
13-45	Your transmitter must have a short circuit because there's smoke coming from my speaker.
13-46	That's a new antenna? Could get a better signal out of a 6-inch piece of damp string.
13-47	What a fantastic signal - give me a few minutes to bring the mobile unit to your driveway so I can copy your message.

SIDEBANDERS.

13-50	Say fella, can you slide that thing down 250 KHz?
13-51	You've tried the upper sideband, you've tried the lower side, you've even tried both sides, hope you're satisfied. Now will you go QRT so we can use the centre slot?
13-52	Good thing about hearing you on Single Sideband is that with only one sideband you're only half as offensive as you were on AM !

Radiotelegraph and Radiotelephone Codes, Prowords and Abbreviations

CB Operators' 13-Code

13-53   Attention AM station on centre slot: Just because they won't talk to you on your own channels what makes you think we'll talk to you here?

Further information to complete these lists would be appreciated.

British Police Radio Codes – Restricted. 1972

- 10-1   On watch, beginning of shift.
- 10-2   Contact Station.
- 10-3   Return to station.
- 10-4   Off watch. Followed by contact location.
- 10-5   Off watch. No contact location.
- 10-6   Any message? Back on watch after 10-4 or 10-5.
- 10-7   Bad reception, please repeat.
- 10-8   Confidential message. Turn off loudspeaker and use handset.
- 10-9   Followed by location and callsign, Officer in personal danger – HELP.
- 10-10   End of shift – off watch

Fig. 3. THE BATTERY

THE BATTERY consists of a number of Leyden Jars whose inside surfaces can be connected by metal rods, bars and chains as required. The outside surfaces are connected through the metal bottom of the box and a wire leading from it.
Using these wires etc. any number of jars can be charged or discharged at will.
                                                         Encyclopaedia Britannica   1771.

Radiotelegraph and Radiotelephone Codes, Prowords and Abbreviations

Standard Marine Navigational Vocabulary

Common words in use by the International Maritime Organisation as extracted in the 'Handbook for Radiotelephone Ship Station Operators' RIB 175 (Jun '96) SMA, Australia.

PROWORD	MEANING
"Question"	Indicates the following message is of interrogative character.
"Answer"	Indicates that the following message is the reply to a previous question.
"Request"	Indicates that the contents of the following message is asking for action with respect to the ship.
"Information"	Indicates that the following message is restricted to observed facts.
"Intention"	Indicates that the following informs others about immediate navigational actions intended to be taken.
"Warning"	Indicates that the following message informs other traffic participants about dangers.
"Advice"	Indicates that the following message implies the intention of the sender to influence the recipient(s) by a recommendation.
"Instruction"	Indicates that the following message implies the intention of the sender to influence the recipient(s) by a regulation.
Responses	Where the answer to a question is in the affirmative, say "Yes" followed by the appropriate phrase in full.
	Where the answer to a question is in the negative, say "No" followed by the appropriate phrase in full.
	Where the information is not immediately available, but soon will be, say: "Stand by".
	Where the information cannot be obtained, say: "No information".
	Where the message is not properly heard, say: "Say again".
	Where a message is not understood, say: "Message not understood".

Miscellaneous phrases: What is your name (and call sign)?

How do you read me ?

I read you ...... /1   bad
 /2   poor
 /3   fair
 /4   good
 /5   excellent

Stand by on channel .....

Change to channel ......

I cannot read you (pass your message through .... / Advise try channel ....)

PROWORD	MEANING

Radiotelegraph and Radiotelephone Codes, Prowords and Abbreviations

Standard Marine Navigational Vocabulary

	I cannot understand you. Please use the Standard Marine Vocabulary or International Code of Signals.
	I am passing a message for vessel ......
Correction	I am ready/not ready to receive your message.
	I do not have channel ..... Please use channel .....
Repetition	If any parts of the message are considered sufficiently important to need particular emphasis, use the word "repeat". e.g. "Do not, repeat, do not ..."
Position	When latitude and longitude are used, these should be expressed in degrees and minutes (and decimals of minutes) north or south of the Equator and east or west of Greenwich.
	When the position is related to a mark, the mark shall be a well defined charted object. The bearing shall be in the 360-degree notation from true north and shall be that of the position from the mark.
Courses	Courses should always be expressed in the 360-degree notation from true north (unless otherwise stated). Whether this is to, or from a mark can be stated.
Bearings	The bearing of the mark or vessel concerned is the bearing in the 360-degree notation from true north (unless otherwise stated), except in the case of relative bearings. Bearings may be either from the mark or from the vessel.
Distances	Distances should be expressed in nautical miles or cables (tenths of a nautical mile), otherwise in kilometres or metres. The unit should always be stated.
Speed	Speed should be expressed in knots (without further notation meaning speed through the water). "Ground speed" meaning speed over ground.
Numbers	Numbers should be transmitted by speaking each digit separately. e.g. one five zero for 150.
Geographical Names	Place names should be those on the chart or Sailing Directions in use. Should these not be understood, latitude and longitude should be used.
Time	Time should be expressed in the 24-hour notation indicating whether UTC, zone time or local shoretime is being used.

Camelback key – c1848 – 1881

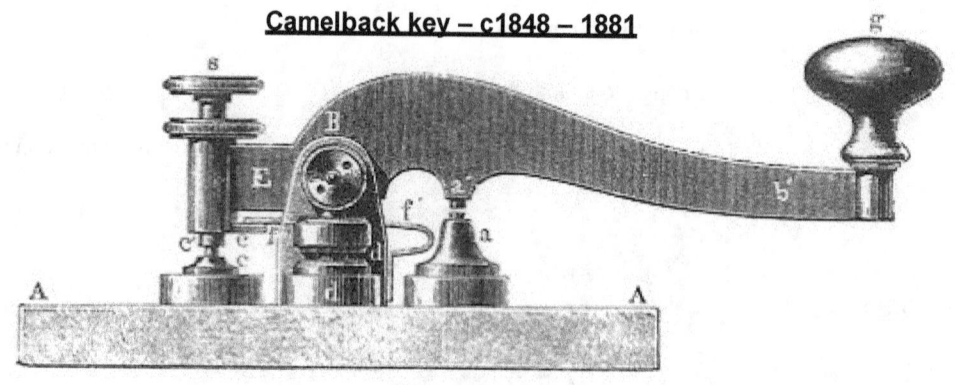

Radiotelegraph and Radiotelephone Codes, Prowords and Abbreviations

Telegraph Transmission Codes

It was not originally intended to include these Codes. The compilation of the disjointed lists of Q etc Codes being the aim. However this research inevitably resulted in accumulating much information about these Codes.
No inclusion will be made of the technical, legal, political or financial history and difficulties of the various inventors of the codes. This would take volumes and has been written and rewritten many times.
Sufficient chronology, as is known, will be included to put them into context.

Static and Needle Telegraph codes are not included although Needle Telegraphs were still used into the 1940's.

The surprising thing out of this research has been how many of the early and special codes survived and overlapped each other into this century. The International or Continental Code was formalised in 1851 but was not universally in use until long after WW2. The ending dates of the codes (except the US Navy Code) are approximates only. They did not suddenly stop but gradually fell into disuse.

Code Chronology

The '?' indicates an approximation derived from the literature, a firm date not yet found.

From ancient Greek times two element codes were used for signalling using hooded lights, semaphore etc.

1084 BC		Fall of Troy signalled 500 miles by line-of-sight beacon fires by King Agamemnon.
586 BC		Babylonian Jewish priests signal religious timings to Jerusalem by signal fires.
300 BC		Polybius reports a method of signalling the 24 letter Greek alphabet.
1340		"Black Book of the Admiralty" describes early English naval signal codes.
1543		"Book of War by Sea and by Land" by Jehan Bythorne contains signals references.
1605		Francis Bacon (England) devises a binary code for messages.
1649		Jesuit Priest predicts electric signalling. He and students work on it for 50 years.
1727		S.Gray, London, sends electrification over 700 feet of wire. 10,000 ft 20 years later.
1747		W.Watson (England) demonstrates the earth return telegraph circuit.
1753		C.Morrison, (Scotland) publishes proposal for an electrostatic telegraph.
1774		G.L. Le Sage (France) constructs 24 wire electric telegraph.
1787		Lomond (Switzerland) devises a two bit code. Betancourt also proposes a system.
1793		Chappe (France) his semaphore system first to be described as a ' Telegraph '.
1798		D.F.Salva (Spain) operates spark discharge telegraph over 40 Kms.
1816		Sir Francis Rolands (England) constructs a static discharge telegraph.
1820		A.M.Ampere constructs the first Needle Telegraph system.
1825		Schilling (Russia) devises a code for the Needle Telegraph at St Petersburg.
1826		H.Dyar (USA) constructs first telegraph to use dots and dashes. 13 Kms, earth return.
1827		Sydney, Australia, Visual Telegraph from South Head to Fort Phillip, marine traffic.
1829 - 1841		C.F.Gauss, W.Weber, Sir W.F.Cooke, Sir C.Wheatstone, bros. H. & E. Highton - make improved Needle Telegraphs.
1831		J.Henry (USA) constructs the first electromagnetic telegraph over 1.6 Km.
1832 - 1837		Morse's original code.
1833		C.F.Gaus, W.E.Weber (Germany) Needle teleg. 2.3 Kms. Improved to 1836.
1835		J.Henry invents the 'relay' and uses an earth return telegraph circuit.
1837 - 1844		Morse Code (some attribute to A.Vail)
1838		A.Vail invents the hand key.
1839		W.F.Cooke and C.Wheatstone - Needle telegraph Paddington to W Drayton, 21 Kms.
1842, 6th April		Albany Evening Journal (England) - The word 'Telegram' first used.
1842 - 1924?		Bain Code - More accurate than Morse when sent by fast machine.
1844 - 1982+		American Code, derived from the Morse Code, USA, Canada, Latin America, Australia.
1851 - Now		Continental or International Code, an improved version of the Morse Code.
1854		Australia's first telegraph line - Melbourne to Williamstown to Geelong.
1857		Tasmania, Australia, Electric Telegraph lines in operation.
1858		Melbourne to Sydney Telegraph line in operation.
1860 - 16 Nov 1912		US Army/Navy Code (General Service Code, Myer Code)
1875? - 1930's?		Phillips Code - Less dashes, 5% faster than Morse. Press use, sent by machine.
1879 - 1900		Heliograph service Rottnest Is. - Fremantle, W Aust. 18 Km (11 Mi.)
1880		Tasmania, Australia, Last Visual Telegraph closed down.
1917		Curacao - Last known Visual Telegraph ceases.
1991		AT&T closes down its last telegraph service.
1994		Afghans still using Heliographs in their war against the Russians.

Radiotelegraph and Radiotelephone Codes, Prowords and Abbreviations

Early Machine Codes

1833 - 1837		Morse's first sender and receiver actually a mechanical telegraph. The hand key came later.
1837		A.Vail designed a printing telegraphy system but not developed.
1846		E.House patented a printing telegraphy system.
1848		A. Bain Chemical System achieves 1,000 WPM in New York demonstration.
1853		W.Gintl devises the Duplex working system.
1855 - 1930's	D.E.Hughes	Originally sent by hand, adapted to machine. App 42-60 WPM.
1858 - 1900's		Wheatstone System - 70 WPM improved to 300 - 400 WPM by early 1900's
1865		US Navy Observatory send out Noon time signals over the Western Union Telegraph system.
1865		Caselli's Pantelegraph from Paris to Lyon. London - Liverpool. St. Petersburg - Moscow.
1866 - 19??		S.S.Laws (Western Union Telegraph Co.) Ticker Tape stock market report machines 60 wpm.
1874		T.A.Edison (Western Union Telegraph Co.) establishes Quadruplex working.
1875		Muirhead System - Duplex working on Submarine Cables to about 90 WPM.
1875 - 19??		Phelps
1874 - 1920's		J.M.E.Baudot - 5 unit code, originally sent by hand, adapted to machine to Murray Code.
1902 - Now		Murray Code - 7 unit code. From the codes of J.B.Moore and H.C.A. Van Duuren.
1968 - Now		ASCII Code

Wireless Telegraphy / Telephony

1795	Salva proposes a through water (Majorca to Alicanti, Spain. 300 Kms) communications experiment.
1811	Sommerring, Munich, conducts such a through water experiment.
1838	Steinheil rediscovers and uses the earth return telegraph system.
1842	J. Henry magnetises a needle by transmission from a lightning strike 13 Kms away.
1842	Morse demonstrates first practical wireless telegraph about 1.6 Km through water, N.Y. harbour.
1845	M.Faraday (UK) states his 'Electromagnetic origin of light' in his experiments and lectures.
1864	Maxwell (UK) mathematically proves Faraday's theories.
1866	Dolbear (USA) demonstrates an electrostatic telegraph between stations over 800 metres apart.
1866	Dr. M Loomis transmits messages 15 miles using kite antennae. Patent granted 1872. Inventor of wireless.
1876	Alexander G.Bell invents the Telephone.
1882	Dolbear does wireless telephony experiments using induction coils, highly elevated wires and detectors.
1886	Onesti observed that loose metal filings tend to cohere when an electrified wire or coil is discharged.
1887	H.Hertz (Ger.) demonstrates the electromagnetic radiation of Hertzian Waves.
1890	Branley observes the same effect as Onesti caused by Hertzian waves. Invents the Branley coherer.
1891	Lodge (UK) demonstrates the Branley coherer as a very sensitive detector for wireless telegraphy.
1891	Edison and Phelps patent an induction telegraph. Used between moving trains to ground stations.
1896	G. Marconi (Italy) introduces his radio system practically combining the inventions made to date.
1896	A. Popov, Russia, transmits radio signals. St. Petersburg University.
1896	G.W. Selby, Victoria, experiments with WT transmissions, built first X-ray machine in Aust.
1897	First radio transmission in Australia - Adelaide University demonstration over 200 metres.
1899	First Aust. radio telegraph link from Adelaide Observatory to Henly Beach, about 9 Kms.
1899	Radio experiments, Swan R., W.Aust. for proposed service to Rottnest Is. 1.2 Km.
1900	A number of wireless experimenters known to be active in Australia.
1901	First Aust. Services radio use - Melbourne - HMS Juno - HMS Ophir, about 30 Kms.
1901	Marconi makes his historic trans-Atlantic radio telegraphy link.
1902	Fessenden - First radiotelephony (voice) transmission using Alexanderson alternator.
1903	First radio use in manoeuvres, Qld Naval Brigade HQ to Gunboat 'Gayundah' traffic for several days.
1904	Dr A. Fleming invents the diode valve utilising the 'Edison effect, 1883' as a detector.
1906	L. De Forest invents the triode valve. Improved by Western Electric in 1913 as an amplifier.
1906	Fessenden - First broadcast of voice and music using Alexanderson alternator on 42 Khz.
1910	Wireless Institute of Aust. (WIA) formed. The first Amateur radio society in the world.
1910	First Aust. military use of radio at Heathcote at annual camp. Assisted by three WIA members.
1910	G.A. Taylor, Melbourne, demonstrates that pictures could be sent by wireless.
1911	D.J. Garland - Qld's first experimenter. Spark transmissions heard 50 Kms.
1914	XQA M. Brimms's (Qld) now dismantled spark station the oldest still existing (1985).
1914	The following 'locals' are listed in the first Australian call book -

	XBD	P. Crook, Coffs Harbour Jetty.	XABD	A.V. Costelow, Dorrigo.
	XHH	H. Hawker, Grafton.	XABO	E. Mc Pherson, Grafton.
	XIF	J.A. Eagles, Jiggi.	XADF	C.S. Mackay. Coffs Harbour Jetty.
	XIX	P.L. Grimwood, Germanton (now Empire Vale).		
	XAAZ	F.W. Kimpton, Grafton.	XAEG	H. Tuson, North Coast.

Totals were NSW - 166, Vic. - 180, Qld. - 10, SA. - 20, WA - 12, Tas. - 10 = 398. (3,800 in USA).

Radiotelegraph and Radiotelephone Codes, Prowords and Abbreviations

Information Sought

There are many discrepancies, errors and omissions in the information presented.
Additional information and corrections are requested for all sections of the book but clarification of the following particular points would be appreciated.

1. Fill in missing Q, X and Z Codes etc.

2. When the Phelps Code was first devised and adopted.

3. The complete list of the 1857, 1859 etc. US Line Telegraph abbreviations.

4. The completion of the US Police and CB Ten Codes etc.

5. The missing numerals for the various 'Morse' Codes.

6. The differences between the Phonetic Alphabets used by Aust / British forces between WW1 and WW2.
   Apparently authentic information contradicts as to the use of a partial or full phonetic alphabets.

7. More info on the Cairns - Coffs Harbour heliograph system during WW2.

8. Introduction / Application Dates for various Alphabets and Codes.

9. 1923 edition of – OU 5371 'British Army W/T Operating Signals. X-Codes'.

This book is being produced in very small runs to allow the inclusion of additions and corrections as soon as possible after being received.
My thanks go to anyone providing these amendments which will contribute to a more complete publication.

73,

   John W. Alcorn, Compiler.

Wireless or Radio ?

Definition (1917): Wireless Telegraphy - Any system of telegraphy which successfully substitutes some medium other than wire for the connecting conductors.

Such systems are -   1. Conduction.
                     2. Induction, Electrostatic or Electromagnetic.
                     3. Radiation.

Radio Telegraphy is only the third of these, Radiation using Hertzian Waves.

Morse and Other Telegraph Codes.

The following Tables of various Codes are included for historical and general interest.
Most are obsolete.
Research indicates that Vail probably was more responsible for the code improvements and for inventing the Morse key.
His contract with Morse meant that these were all patented and credited to Morse.
Morse's code was not original in that many elements are the same or similar to earlier codes by Cooke, Wheatstone, Schilling, Steinheil, Gauss and Weber.
Morse was not greatly aware of these systems and nothing indicates that he took from them.
However Morse's code, with the assistance of his partners, was promoted, marketed and improved to become the Morse Code of 1844 and amended by others to the Continental Code in 1851 to 1854.

Radiotelegraph and Radiotelephone Codes, Prowords and Abbreviations

French Method of Semaphoring by Hand Flags - 1911

From Brown's Signalling - 1911. How long did France use this method? Information is Requested.				The 'Number Sign' is given at the beginning and end of Numerical Signals to indicate both the start and finish of Numbers in a message.		
SIGNS						
Alphabetical Signification	A	B	C	D	E	F
Numerical Signification	1	2	3	4	5	6
SIGNS						
Alphabetical Signification	G	H	I	J	K	L
Numerical Signification	7	8	9	0		
SIGNS						
Alphabetical Signification	M	N	O	P	Q	R
SIGNS						
Alphabetical Signification	S	T	U	V W is V sent twice.	X	Y
SIGNS						
Signification	Z		DO NOT UNDERSTAND	NUMBERS	ATTENTION	END OF WORK OR PAUSE

Radiotelegraph and Radiotelephone Codes, Prowords and Abbreviations

The Semaphore Alphabet
International Code of Signals 1931 (British Navy – Pasley 1866)

CHARACTERS	HAND FLAGS	CHARACTERS	HAND FLAGS	CHARACTERS	HAND FLAGS	CHARACTERS	HAND FLAGS
A 1		H 8		O		V	
B 2		I 9		P		W	
C ANSWERING SIGN 3		J LETTERS		Q		X	
D 4		K 0		R		Y	
E 5		L		S		Z	
F 6		M		T		ATTENTION	
G 7		N		U		BREAK	

Morse Flags
Dot is a-b
Dash is a-c
Move left or right dependant on wind and background.

Flag Positions -
NOTE: -
Error = 'E' repeated.
Annul = Pos 3 & 7.
Numerical = 4 & 5.

209

Radiotelegraph and Radiotelephone Codes, Prowords and Abbreviations

US Army General Service Code 1860 - 1912

This Code is better known outside the USA as the US Navy Code because foreign operators usually encountered it in marine use. Inside the USA it is also known as the Army / Navy Code and the Myer Code.
It was used by the US Army, Navy and Coast Guard until 16 November 1912 when the International Code was adopted.

Albert J. Myer (1828 - 1880) was the founder of the US Signal Corps. While studying medicine he worked in a Bain Telegraph office. He devised a variation of the Bain Code to communicate with the deaf by tapping on their cheek or hand etc. He joined the US Army in 1854 as an Assistant Surgeon. Posted to Texas he developed a flag signalling code based on the above. This was the "wig wag" system needing only one flag not two as in Semaphore. His persistence resulted in the creation of the US Army Signal Corps in 1860.

Used from 1860, the Navy adopted it in 1862 and the first Handbook was published in 1864.
When electric telegraphy was adopted the services simply applied dots to the Myer Code.
"1" was a "dot" and "2" was "2 dots". It remained in service until 1912 when it was dropped. Operators complained of having to learn three codes, Myer for the services, Morse for line telegraphy and Continental for cable and foreign radio work. The "wig wag" system was applied to Morse Code after 1912.

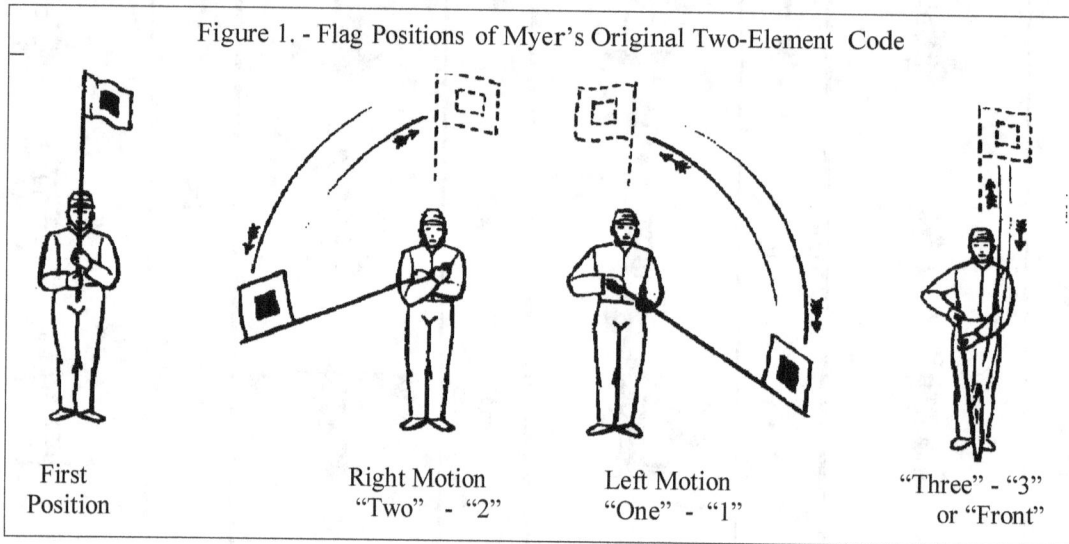

Figure 1. - Flag Positions of Myer's Original Two-Element Code

| First Position | Right Motion "Two" - "2" | Left Motion "One" - "1" | "Three" - "3" or "Front" |

(These motions were reversed soon after the introduction of the Code.) 'Getting the Message Through'
Figure 2. The General Service Code
(Below) 'Manual of Military Telegraphy' - Signal Service - US Army 1872

Alphabet	Flag	Telegraph	Alphabet	Flag	Telegraph
A	22	. . . .	U	112	. . . .
B	2112	. . . . . .	V	1222	. . . . . .
C	121	. . . .	W	1121	. . . . .
D	222	. . . . .	X	2122	. . . . . .
E	12	. . .	Y	111	. . .
F	2221	. . . . . .	Z	2222	. . . .
G	2211	. . . . . .	ing	2212	. . . . . .
H	122	. . . .	tion	1112	. . . . .
I	1	.	&	1111	. . . .
J	1122	. . . . . .	Fullstop	.	. . .
K	2121	. . . . . .	1	21112	. . . .
L	221	. . . . .	2	12221	. . . .
M	1221	. . . . . .	3	22122	. . . .
N	11	. .	4	22212	. . . .
O	21	. . .	5	22221	. . . .
P	1212	. . . . . .	6	12222	. . . .
Q	1211	. . . . .	7	11222	. . . .
R	211	. . . .	8	11112	. . . .
S	212	. . . .	9	11211	. . . .
T	2	. .	0	22222	. . . .

Known as the 'Dot Code' on Telegraph.
The General Service (or Myer) Code was applied to the electric telegraph as shown in the table.

The receiving instrument in use was the sounder.

This made a 'click' 'clack' sound when the key was closed and opened.

The timing and interval between these movements made up the American or Morse Code.

In the GS Code '1' was a single working of the key - "click-clack".

A '2' was a double operation of the key quickly - 'click-clack click-clack'.

In the Telegraph table each 'dot' indicates a single operation of the key.

So a 'K' would be heard as - 2121 - 'click-clack click-clack' 'click-clack' 'click-clack click-clack' 'click-clack'.

Radiotelegraph and Radiotelephone Codes, Prowords and Abbreviations

US Army General Service Code 1860 - 1912

The following prosigns were not included here but did appear in Myer's first manual, the 1864 issue - 'A Manual of Signals: for the Use of Signal Officers in the Field'.
- **3** end of word.
- **33** end of sentence.
- **333** end of message.

These were in use as they appear in later lists (1912).

The 1864 manual did not list the numerals but in the 1872 table they are denoted by five-letter groups. Numerals were later reduced to four letter groups and so were the same as some letters.
They were indicated by the prosign:
- **XX3** 'numerals follow' or 'numerals end'

The Numerals changed and were listed in 1912 as:-

1 1111		6 2211
2 2222		7 1222
3 1112		8 2111
4 2221		9 1221
5 1122		0 2112

Procedures and Abbreviations - Myer Code c 1912

Aye "I understand"	22, 22, 3	Cease Signalling	22, 22, 22, 333
Repeat Last Word ...	121, 121, 3	Repeat Last Message ...	121, 121, 121, 3
Error	12, 12, 3	Move to the right......	211, 211, 3
Wait a Moment	1111, 3	Move to Left	221, 221, 3
Signal Faster	2212, 3	Repeat after (word) ..	121, 121, 3, 22, 3 (word)

Abbreviations

A .. After	H .. Have	T .. The	W .. Word	XX3 .. "Numerals Follow"
B .. Before	N .. Not	U .. You	WI .. With	or "Numerals End"
C .. Can	R .. Are	UR .. Your	Y .. Why	SIG 3 .. Signature

Code Calls

ASU	Action Signals Use		CBU	Cipher "B" Use etc.
ICU	International Code Use.		GLU	Geographical List Use.
TDU	Telegraph Dictionary Use.		NLU	Navy List Use.
GSU	General Signals Use.		VNU	Vessel's Numbers Use.
CAU	Cipher "A" Use.			

Flag Usage With American Morse Code.

The dot is a sender's RIGHT motion, a dash a LEFT and space a FRONT motion.
So spaced characters (C,O,R,Y,Z,&.) were -

C - R,R,F,R.	O - R,F,R.	R - R,F,R,R.
Y - R,R,F,R,R.	Z - R,R,R,F,R.	& - R,F,R,R,R.

L and Zero (long dashes) distinguished from 'T' by a slight pause at the low point of dip.

Radiotelegraph and Radiotelephone Codes, Prowords and Abbreviations

US Army General Service Code 1860 - 1912 and Others

USA - Conventional Signals for Heliograph or Flash Lantern 1912.

To call a station, make a steady flash until acknowledged by a steady flash. Adjust beams and then break the flash. Continue with message. Other signals the same as above. Telegraph signals are the same except the break is done by opening the key.

USA - Conventional Signals for Flag or Torch, 1912.

'A' repeated - To call a station, repeat until acknowledged.
'III' - To acknowledge a calling station.
'A' repeated - To break or stop signals. Repeat until acknowledged.
'GA' + Last word received - Sender to resume message after break. If nothing received -
'RR' - Sender will repeat all message.
(- - - - - - -) Seven Dots - Error in sending. Sender resumes with last word correctly sent.
(- - — — - -) End of Address.
'SIG' - Signature follows.
'OK' - Acknowledge receipt of message.

USA - Conventional Signals for Heliograph or Flash Lantern 1912.

To call a station, make a steady flash until acknowledged by a steady flash. Adjust beams and then break the flash. Continue with message. Other signals the same as above. Telegraph signals are the same except the break is done by opening the key.

1903 ed. "Instructions for the Use of Wireless-Telegraph Apparatus"

This lists a code proposed by Niblack in 1892 for the Navy light signals which used Myer letters but different numerals. (See p 220). Probably introduced in 1897 as Telephotos. It was in use in 1903 as a wireless code but not known for how long.

1909 ed. International Code of Signals - American Edition.

"United States Army and Navy Signal Code." (ICS p545)
"Communications may be had by this code with the United States Army, Navy, Revenue Cutter and Life-Saving services."
The Myer code is described using the 1-2-3 notation.

For fog signals or fog horns, ... one (1) toot, about one-half second will be "one" ... of the Myer alphabet. Two toots in quick succession will be "two" and a blast about two seconds long will be "three". The ear not the watch is to be relied upon for the intervals.
For signalling with flash lantern, heliograph or search-light shutter, same as in fog signals; substitute "short flash" for "toot", and "long steady flash" for "blast".
The elements of a letter should be slightly longer.
In the use of any other appliance, such as a bell, by which a blast can not be given, three strokes in quick succession will be given in place of the blast to indicate '3'. "

"Morse Signal Code" (ICS p547)
International Morse is described, American Morse is not included.

"Flag Waving"
One flag, short & long arc method for Morse. (See p. 209)

Light and Sound Signals. According to Colomb's Flashing Signals System. (ICS p547)

Radiotelegraph and Radiotelephone Codes, Prowords and Abbreviations

US Army General Service Code 1860 - 1912 and Others

Short flash/sound =   1 second,
Long flash/sound = 3 seconds,
Interval   =   1 second.
Answer or "I understand"   —-—--—-— etc.

SIGNALS

You are standing into danger   --—   I want assistance; remain by me   ----—
Have encountered ice   -—-   Your lights are out (or want trimming) -——-
The way is off my ship; you may feel your way past me.   -—-
Stop, or, heave too; I have something important to communicate.   -—--
Am disabled; communicate with me.   --—-

Vessel under tow to towing vessel or tug -
Steer more to starboard -   Steer more to port   --   Cast off hawsers   ----

1912 ed. "American Telegraphy & Encyclopedia of the Telegraph"
p362-366 states (abbrev)

"In flag and torch signalling as well as in heliographic and lantern signalling the American Morse Code .....
is used by the US war department, when a dot and dash alphabet is to be availed of.

The US Army and Navy Code, known as the Myer Wigwag Alphabet, and extracts......., and also for the use of Morse code in wigwagging, etc., are given below. -"
It then describes the **Myer code** and all its procedures etc.

The article transcribes dots and dashes for L & R etc inferring the use of both codes for all modes.
It also describes -

"Sound signals with fog whistle, fog horn or bugle." Same as for fog horn etc. above.

"It may be added that the foregoing conventional signals, for flag and torch signalling, are practically similar to those employed in commercial telegraphy in the United States and Canada."

1915 ed. International Code of Signals - American Edition.

"United States Army and Navy Signal Code." (p545)
Lists the International (Continental) Morse Code.
Lists then current Conventional Signals but adds "Secondary Meanings" -

"Used only in flag hoists, Ardois, Semaphore, Very, or in transmitting Navy Flag Code by other systems.

(The use of Navy Flag Code is indicated by   "Signals Follow"   --——)

Negative (K)   —-—
Preparatory (L)   -—--
Annulling (N)   —-
Interrogatory (O) ———
Affirmative (P)   -—— -

HOWEVER! When describing the Wigwag System, it describes the Myer method.

  90deg arc to right of sender   = 'dot'
  90deg arc to left of sender   = 'dash'
  To ground, to front of sender   = 'interval'   "applied to the dot dash code"

Same applied to lights, sound, bells (1, 2, 3. strikes) as in 1909.

Radiotelegraph and Radiotelephone Codes, Prowords and Abbreviations

Other US Services Codes 1900 - 1915

"Ardois System"

Although described as "Ardois", this was replaced by "Telephotos" in 1897 but Navy light codes were often misnamed Ardois for a long time.

As in dot dash code, except numerals.   Red light (R) = 'dot',   White (W) = 'dash'
The following have secondary meaning when the upper light is pulsated.

A (RW)	Error.	Q (WWRW)	One	W (RWW)		Seven	
K (WRW)	Negative	R (RWR)	Two	X (WRRW)		Eight	
L (RWRR)	Preparatory	S (RRR)	Three	Y (WRWW)		Nine	
N (WR)	Annulling	T (W)	Four	Z (WWRR)		Zero	
O (WWW)	Interrogatory	U (RRW)	Five	Interval (RWRW) Designator			
P (RWWR)	Affirmative	V (RRRW)	Six	IX (Twice) Execute			

"Very System" - [Pronounced ' Veirie' - JWA, Ed]

Based on the dot dash code.   Red star = 'dot',   Green star = 'dash'.

Only signals that may be sent by Navy flag code may be sent by this system.
Conventional signals are limited to the following -

General call:	Rocket and green star.
Answering (acknowledgment):	Red star.
Repeat:	Green star (-)
Interval (separating the alphabet letters of a signal):	{Red, Green star} Fired at same time.
Double interval (separating code groups):	Two intervals, one after the other.
Triple interval (end of message):	Three intervals.
Execute:	Rocket and red star.
Distress or danger:	Red star several times.
Numerals follow (or end) Rocket:	{Red & Green star} Rocket.

The preparatory, affirmative, negative, interrogatory, and annulling are as in flag signalling, L, P, K, O and N.

"Semaphore"

Two arm semaphore as in usual published methods. However -

'Interval' =	one chop-chop. (Arms horizontal, wave up and down.)
'Double Interval' =	two chop-chops
'Triple Interval' =	three chop-chops.
Error =	"A" Chopped.
Interrogatory =	"O" Chopped.

Those of five or six elements can not be made and must be spelled out.

Problems using Three Codes – Morse, Myer (GS) and International.

In US Services the three codes were used simultaneously by electric telegraphists to the end, when the Myer code was discontinued on the 16th Nov. 1912.
There was an obvious problem of operator training and expense to learn three codes and there had been compatibility problems with some marine emergencies on the American seaboard.
The US Navy and Coastguard used Myer which was not understood by foreign operators using International and vice versa.

According to the history of the US Signal Corps, "Getting the Message Through", operators complained of having to use three codes. American for telegraph and land use, Myer for Army/Navy and Coastguard, and International for maritime and foreign cable services.

Following the "Titanic" disaster international conferences were held in London to improve things.
This resulted, among many things, in the Q code being established and the US dropped the Myer code.
The US then applied the Wig Wag system to International Morse which was used for all external traffic.
American Morse continued to be used on landline traffic for over another 50 years.

Radiotelegraph and Radiotelephone Codes, Prowords and Abbreviations

Needle Telegraph Codes

These developed many years before the Morse type codes but overlapped and continued in use for many years especially in England. Railways with working systems simply kept them.
Last believed to be in use on the Doncaster, UK, line to 1979.

Signalman John Hinson believes he did the last Needle Telegraph course for British Railways in 1971.
See his excellent pages: http://www.trainweb.com/signalbox/branches/jh/telegraph.htm

Needle Codes are listed here for historical interest and continuity into the later methods.
Simultaneously direct reading instruments were designed. Wheatstone's 5-needle one was the most popular. It did not need a code but needed six wires so was too expensive to build and maintain.
From it developed the Single and then the Double Needle Systems.

Illustrated are some direct reading instruments.
The Steinheil code (Germany 1837) was originally a printing code with dots printed L/R on paper tape.
On Needle Instruments, the long line deflections are done first, then the short ones.

NOTE: On the Needle Instrument, because the handles hang down, the bottom of the needle indicates the direction of movement. The far right indicator below is / \ - Left Right.

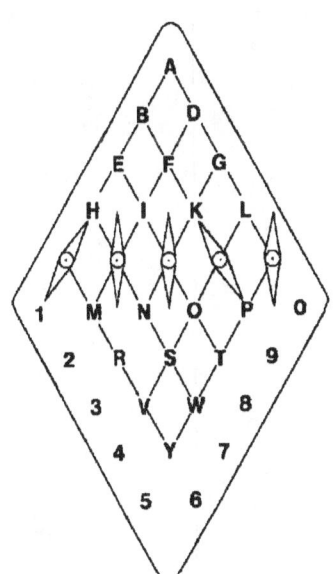

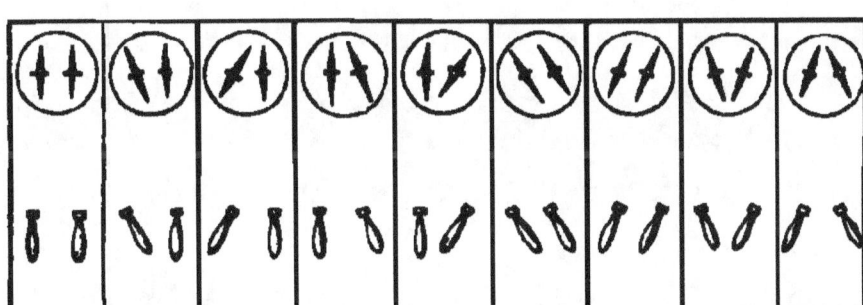

Handle and Needle positions of the Two Needle Telegraph. (above and right).

(Left) Wheatstone's Five Needle Telegraph. The first practical electric telegraph. Shows "B". Superseded by the Single and Double Needle instruments.

Many direct reading telegraphs were also developed.

Needle telegraphs remained in use long after Morse came along even into the 20th century until 1979.

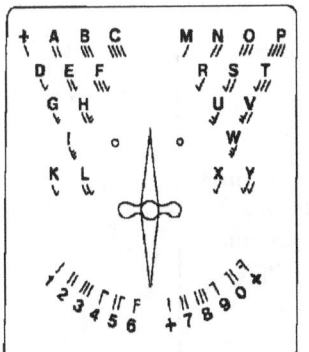

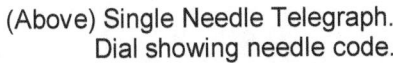

(Above) Single Needle Telegraph. Dial showing needle code.

(Right) Direct Indicating Dial Telegraph - Receiver, left. Manipulator (Sender), right.

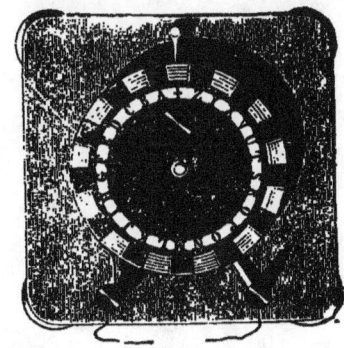

Radiotelegraph and Radiotelephone Codes, Prowords and Abbreviations

Needle Telegraph Codes

	1820 Schilling Austria	1833 Gauss & Weber	Single 1837 Steinheil - Germany	1837 Cooke & Wheatstone	1878-1979 British Railways	1836 Double Cooke & Wheatstone Left	1836 Double Cooke & Wheatstone Right	Needle 1836 De La Rive Left	Needle 1836 De La Rive Right
A	\/	\	/\/	\\	\/	\		//	
B	\\\	//	/\\/	\\\	/\\\	/		///	
C	\//	\\\	//\	\\\\	/\/\		\	\/	
D	\\/	\\/	\/	/\	/\\		/	/\	
E	\	/	/	/\\	\	\	\	\	(understood
F	\\\\	\/\	/\\	/\\	\\/\	/	/	\\	(yes)
G	////	/\\	\\/	/\	/\\	\\		\\\	
H	\///	///	\\\\	/\\	\\\\	//			/
I	\\	\\	\	///\	\\		\\		// (as
J	\\//	—	—	—	\///		\\	\\\	G)
K	\\\/	\\\	//\	\/\	/\/		//		///
L	/\\\	//\	\//	/\/\	\/\\	\\	\\		\/
M	/\/	/\/	\\\	/	//	//	//		/\
N	/\/	\\	\\	//	/\	\/			\
O	\/\	\/	///	///	///	/\			\\
P	//\\	\\\\	\//\	////	\//\		\/		\\\
Q	///\	—	—	\//\	//\/		/\	(as K)	///
R	/\\	\\\/	//	\/	\/\	\/	\/	/ (wait)	/
S	//	\\/\	/\\	\//	\\\	/\	/\	//	//
T	/	\/\\	/\	\///	/	//\		///	///
U	//\	/\	\/	\\/	\\/	\//		\/	\/
V	///	\/\	\/\	\\//	\\//		\\	/\	/\
W	\/\/	/\\\	\/\/	\\\\	\//		\//	\ (go on)	\
X	/\/\	—	—	/\/	/\\/		\//	\\\	\\
Y	\//\	—	—	\/\/	/\//	\\/	/\\	\\\	\\\
Z	\/\\	\\//	\\//	/\\/	//\\ This	\//	\//	// (as S) //
&	\\/\			Stop ( ) \	Equates to			/ Stop( ) Not underst'd
1	\/\/\	\/\\	/\\\	/	Internat'l	Note:		\/	
2	\\/\\	/\\/	\/\\	//	Morse.	The bottom of the		/\	
3	\//\\	/\\/	\\/\	///	\ = Dot	Needle indicated the		\	
4	/\\\\	/\\\	\\\/	\/	/ = Dash	direction of movement.			/
5	/\\//	///\	\//\	\//	From 1878	/\ = Left Right.			\/
6	/\/\/	/\\/	/\/\	\\/	or 1864??				/\
7	\\/\	/\/\	//\\	\\	<-<-<-				\
8	\//\\	\///\	///\	\\\	End Figs			/	/
9	//\/\	////	\\/	/\	\//			\/	\/
0	/\\\	\/\\	///	/\\				/\	/\

Radiotelegraph and Radiotelephone Codes, Prowords and Abbreviations

Needle Telegraph Codes

	Double 1852 Needle Wilson – UK.	
	Left	Right
A	/	
B	//	
C	///	
D	////	
E	/	\
F	/	\\
G	/	\\\
H	//	\
I	//	\\
J	//	\\\
K	///	\
L	///	\\
M	////	\
	Right	Left
N	\	
O	\\	
P	\\\	
Q	\\\\	
R	\	/
S	\\	/
T	\\\	/
U	\	//
V	\\	//
W	\\\	//
X	\	///
Y	\\	///
Z	\	////

Note:

The bottom of the Needle indicated the direction of movement.
/ \ = Left Right.

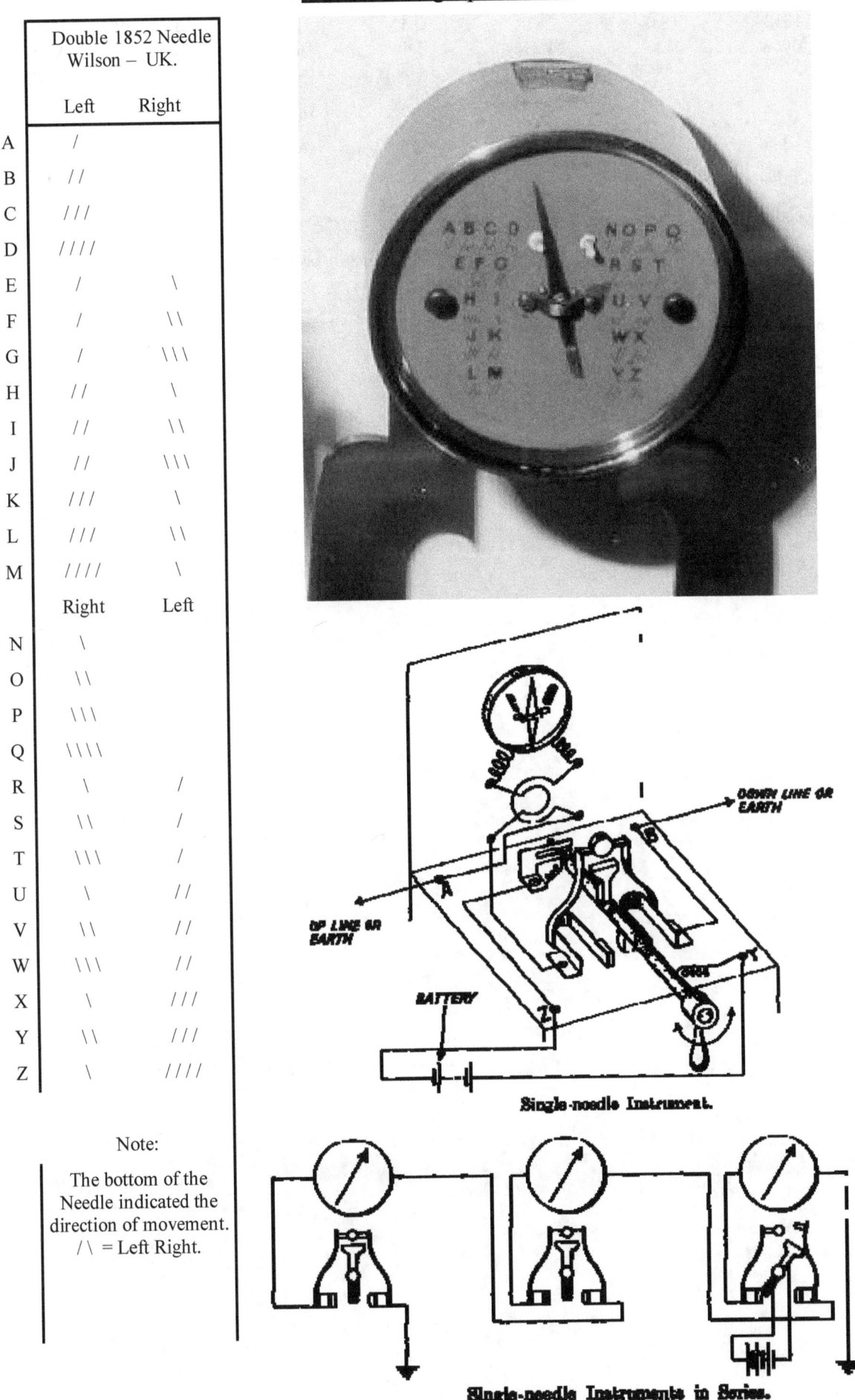

Single-needle Instrument.

Single-needle Instruments in Series.

From - http://www.samhallas.co.uk/railway/single_needle.htm

Radiotelegraph and Radiotelephone Codes, Prowords and Abbreviations

Morse and Other Telegraph Codes

	1832 Morse	1837 Morse Caveat	1838 Morse / Vail	1842 Bain (UK)	1852 Boston Fire Dept.	1844 - 1982+ Morse / American	1851 Austro-German
A		· —	· —	· —	Alphabet	· —	· —
B	The	— · ·	— · · ·	— · — ·	As by	— · · ·	— · · ·
C	original	· · ·	· · ·	· ·	Bain.	· · ·	— · — ·
D	code	— · ·	— · ·	— · —		— · ·	— · ·
E	had no	·	·	·	Districts	·	·
F	letters,	· — · ·	· — ·	· — — —	1 ·	· — ·	· · — ·
G	a Number	— — ·	— — ·	— · — —	2 · ·	— — ·	— — ·
H	code only	· · · ·	· · · ·	· — —	3 · · ·	· · · ·	· · · ·
I	using a	· —	· —	· ·	4 · · · ·	· ·	· ·
J	Code book	— · — ·	— · — ·	· — — —	5 · · · · ·	— · — ·	none
K	for	— · —	— · —	· — — ·	6 · · · · · ·	— · —	— · —
L	coding.	— — —	— — —	· · · ·		—	· — · ·
M		— · ·	— · ·	— — ·		— —	— —
N		— ·	— ·	— — · ·		— ·	— ·
O		· ·	· ·	—		· ·	— — —
P		· · · · ·	· · · · ·	· — — ·		· · · · ·	· — — ·
Q		· · — ·	· · — ·	— · — ·		· · — ·	— — · —
R		· ·	· ·	· — ·		· · ·	· — ·
S		· — ·	· — ·	· · ·		· · ·	· · ·
T		— — ·	— — ·	—		—	—
U		· — —	· — —	— · ·		· · —	· · —
V		—	—	· · · — ·		· · · —	· · · —
W		· — —	· — —	— — ·		· — —	· — —
X		— —	— —	· — · ·		· — · ·	— · · —
Y		· —	· —	— —		· · · ·	— · — —
Z		· — ·	· — ·	— — —		· · · ·	— — · ·
&				— — — —	Stations	· — · · ·	
1	·			· — — — —		· — — ·	· — — — —
2	· ·			· · — — —	· —	· · — · ·	· · — — —
3	· · ·			· · · — —	— · ·	· · · — ·	· · · — —
4	· · · ·			· · · · —	· — ·	· · · · —	· · · · —
5	· · · · ·			· · · · ·	· · —	— — —	· · · · ·
6	· — —			— · · · ·	· — ·	· · · · · ·	— · · · ·
7	· · — —			— — · · ·	· · — ·	— — · ·	— — · · ·
8	· · · — —			— — — · ·	· — · ·	— · · · ·	— — — · ·
9	· · · · — —			— — — — ·	— · · ·	— · · —	— — — — ·
0	· · · · · — —			— — — — · ·	10 — · —	— — — — —	— — — — —

Radiotelegraph and Radiotelephone Codes, Prowords and Abbreviations

Morse and Other Telegraph Codes

	1854 Continental / International	1860 Myer 1864, '72 list	1860 - 16 Nov 1912 Myer	1869 WATCo. Western Australia	1875 Phillips
A	·—	——	——	Letters as International Code	Letters and Numerals the same as US Morse Code. Different Punctuation and Special Characters.
B	—···	—···	—···		
C	—·—·	···	·· ·	, —···—	
D	—··	—··	—··		
E	·	·	·	; ···—·—·	
F	··—·	—··—·	——·—·	. ·····	
G	——·	—···	——··	? ··—···	
H	····	··—·	··—·	' ·————·	
I	··	·	·	" ·——··—·	
J	·———	—·—·	—·—·	(·——·—·	
K	—·—	—·—·	—·—·	= ···—··—·	
L	·—··	——·	——·	7 8 ·——··——·	
M	——	——··	—·——·	> 8 —··—··	
N	—·	··	··	! ·—··—·	, ·——·—·
O	———	· ·	· ·		: —··— ··
P	·——·	··—··	·····	? ·····	:- ·—··— ·—··
Q	——·—	··—·	··—·	⅛ ·······	; ··· ··
R	·—·	· ··	· ··	! ·—··—·	, ·—··
S	···	···	···	! ·—··—·	? ··—····
T	—	—	—	4 ———··—·	! ———·
U	··—	··—	··—	, # ·—···—	·
V	···—	·—·—	·—·—	− @ = ·······	··— ·—··
W	·——	·——	·——	− # ———	···· ·—··
X	—··—	·—··	·—··	= ···—··—	' ···— ·—··
Y	—·——	· · ·	· · ·	⅛ ·—····	$ ···· ·—··
Z	——··	———·	———·	, ·——··—·	···· ——
&		Fullstop ···	& ·—···	··—·	——·
1	·————	·——·	····	·——·	——··
2	··———	··—··	——·—	··—··	! ··—·—··
3	···——	———·	···—	···—	:" —·— —·—·
4	····—	———·	————	····	·· ·
5	·····	———	———	·····	———
6	—····	·———·	—····	————·	————
7	——···	——··	—·——	———··	= ·—· ·—··
8	———··	—····—	—····	—————	"·" ······ again
9	————·	—··—·	——··—	—····	( ) ···· ·—··
0	—————	————	·——	——————	% ——·——·

Radiotelegraph and Radiotelephone Codes, Prowords and Abbreviations

Morse and Other Telegraph Codes

	1902 Buckingham (Machine Code)	1902?+ Barclay (Machine Code)	1903 US Navy Code Wireless	1911? Anderson (Chemical Telg.)	1914 Phillips American	1920 US Navy Bugle Code
A	—··	— ···	— —	·—	·—	·
B	—·—	·—··	—···	—···	—···	·—··
C	—·—	—···	·—·	—·—··	·—··—·*	·—·—
D	—··	— ··	—··	—··	—··	·—·
E	·—·	·—··	·	·	·	—
F	—·—	—····	——··	——··	·—··	·——··
G	··—	··——	——··	——··	——·	——
H	·——	·——	·——	····	····	·——··
I	··—	····	·	··	··	·——
J	·——	·——	·——·	·——·	·——·	·——··
K	——	——·	—·—	—·—	—·—	·—··
L	·—·	·——	——·	——	·······*	—··
M	——	—·—	—·—·	——	——	···
N	·—·	·—··	··	—·	—·	—··
O	···	··· ·	—·	——·	——·*	——
P	·——	·——	·····	·····	·····	····
Q	———	—·——	··—·	·—·—	·—·—	·————
R	·—·	·—·	——·	·——	——·*	—·——
S	——·	! ····	—·—	···	···	·—
T	··	" ···	—	—	—	··
U	···	# ···	·——	··—	··—	——·
V	——·	$ ——·	·——	···—	···—	··—··
W	·—·	% ·—·	·····	·——	·——	·——··
X	··—	& ··—	————	——··	——··	——··
Y	—··	' ·—··	···	—·——	·——·*	——··
Z	—·—	) ·—·	————	·—···	·—··—*	——·—
&	———	+·——			·———	
1	,·——	,·———	····	·——·	* Proposed	····—
2	·—·—	+· ···	————	··—··	substitute	······
3	——·—	/○ ·——	···—	···—·	for US	·———
4	1 ·——	2 3 ———	———·	·····—	Morse	—————
5	+· ···	4 5 ·——	·—·—	———	characters	·····
6	>> /	8	——··	······		—····
7	/	-	——·——	——··	MM61	——···
8	A ½ B	-	—···	—····		———··
9	Long space		·———	—··—		—————
0	= 3 Units		··—··	——		

Radiotelegraph and Radiotelephone Codes, Prowords and Abbreviations

Morse and Other Telegraph Codes - Punctuation

	1965 US POW's Vietnam	2001 Polish Survival Page		1844 Morse	1851 Continental International	1860 Myer US Army GS	1938 I.R.C. Cairo
A	· ·	As for	.	·· — — ··	·· — ·· — ··	· · ·	· — · — · —
B	· · ·	International	,	· — — ·	— ·· — —		— — ·· — —
C	· · · ·	Code plus	?	— ·· — ·	·· — — ··		·· — — ··
D	· — · · · ·	Specials	-	— — — · — —	— ···· —		— ···· —
E	· — — — — —	· — · —	-	· — — ·	— ···· —		
F	·· ·	· — · — ·	(	·· — · — ·	— · — — ·		— · — — · —
G	·· ··	·· — · —	)	— ···· — ··	— · — — · —		— · — — · —
H	·· · · ·	Ch — — — —	"	· — · · — ·	· — ··· — ·		
I	·· · · · ·	Ł · — ··	"	· — · · — ··	· — ··· — ·		
J	·· · ·	— — · —	$	··· · — ··			
K	· · · ·	Ó — — — ·	.	spell "dot"			
L	··· ·	··· — ··	Cap	·· — · — ··			
M	··· ··	— — ·· —	( )	— · · — —	— ···· — —		
N	··· · · ·	— — · — ·	:	— ·· — ·· —	— — — ···		— — — ···
O	··· ·· ·		;	· · · — ·	— · — · — ·		
P	··· ··· ·	. ······	_	··· — ···	·· — — · —		
Q	···· ·	, · — · — · —	_	··· — ···	·· — — · —		
R	···· ··	; — · — · —	:-	··· — — —	— · — ··		
S	···· ···	: — — — ···	:"	· · — · · —			
T	···· ····	! — — ·· — —	!	— — — —	— — ·· — —		None
U	···· ·····	? ·· — — ··	/	·	— ·· — ·		— ·· — ·
V	····· ·	= — ··· —	¶	— — —			
W	····· ··	+ · — · — ·	£	····· · — ···			
X	····· ···	- — ·· — —	/-	· — — —			
Y	····· ····		=		— ··· —		— ··· —
Z	····· ·····		+		· — · — ·		· — · — ·
&	0		&	· ···		····	
1							
2							
3							
4							
5							
6	C 6	!					
7	+ A '.						
8	+ A '						
9	B						
0		#					

Radiotelegraph and Radiotelephone Codes, Prowords and Abbreviations

(1943)

INTERNATIONAL MORSE

THE ALPHABET

A ·—	N —·
B —···	O ———
C —·—·	P ·——·
D —··	Q ——·—
E ·	R ·—·
F ··—·	S ···
G ——·	T —
H ····	U ··—
I ··	V ···—
J ·———	W ·——
K —·—	X —··—
L ·—··	Y —·——
M ——	Z ——··

NUMERALS

1 ·————	6 —····
2 ··———	7 ——···
3 ···——	8 ———··
4 ····—	9 ————·
5 ·····	0 —————

ABBREVIATED NUMERALS

1 ·—	6 —····
2 ··—	7 —···
3 ···—	8 —··
4 ····—	9 —·
5 ·····	0 —

USEFUL PUNCTUATION & OTHER SIGNS

FULL STOP (.)	·—·—·—
COMMA (,)	——··——
COLON (:)	———···
HYPHEN OR DASH (-)	—····—
FRACTION BAR (/)	—··—·
SEPARATION SIGN (BETWEEN WHOLE NUMBER & FRACTION)	·—··—
BRACKETS (())	—·——·—
BREAK OR DOUBLE DASH (=)	—···—
INTERROGATION MARK (?)	··——··
ERASE (OR ERROR)	········
STARTING SIGNAL	—·—·—
END OF MESSAGE	·—·—·
CLOSING DOWN	···—·—
INTERVAL (WAIT)	·—···
MESSAGE RECEIVED	·—·
READY TO RECEIVE	—·—
DISTRESS CALL OR SOS	···———···

ACCENTED LETTERS

Ä	·—·—	Ñ	——·——
Á OR Å	·——·—	Ö	———·
CH	————	Ü	··——
É	··—··		

U.S.A. MORSE

LETTERS

A ·—	O ··
B —···	P ·····
C ·· ·	Q ··—·
D —··	R · ··
E ·	S ···
F ·—·	T —
G ——·	U ··—
H ····	V ···—
I ··	W ·——
J —·—·	X ·—··
K —·—	Y ·· ··
L —	Z ··· ·
M ——	& · ···
N —·	

NUMERALS

1 ——·—	6 ······
2 ··—··	7 ——··
3 ···—·	8 —·····
4 ····—	9 —··—
5 ———	0 —

PUNCTUATION MARKS ETC.

PARENTHESIS	····· —· ····· ·· ··
QUOTATION	··—· ·—·
END OF QUOTATION	··—· —·—·
COLON DASH	—·— —···
CAPITALIZED LETTER	·· · ·—··
SMALL LETTER	··——
COLON FOLLOWED BY QUOTATION	—·— ——·—
QUESTION MARK	—··—·
EXCLAMATION MARK	———
COLON	—·— ··
SEMICOLON	··· ··
PARAGRAPH	————
APOSTROPHE	··—· ·—··
DOLLAR	··· ·—··
CENTS	·· ·
POUND STERLING	— ·—··
SHILLING	··— —
PERCENT	·· ·· ··
PERIOD	··—·—·
COMMA	·—·—
HYPHEN	—·· ·—··

ARABIC MORSE

PRONUN-CIATION	ARABIC LETTER	MORSE SYMBOL
ALIF	ا	·—
BA	ب	—···
TA	ت	—
THA	ث	—·—·
JEEM	ج	·———
HA	ح	····
KHA	خ	———
DAL	د	—··
DHAL	ذ	——··
RA	ر	·—·
ZAY	ز	———·
SEEN	س	···
SHEEN	ش	————
SAD	ص	—··—
DAD	ض	···—·
TA	ط	··—
ZA	ظ	—·——
AIN	ع	·—·—
CHAIN	غ	——·—
FA	ف	··—·
QAF	ق	——·—
KAF	ك	—·—
LAM	ل	·—··
MEEM	م	——
NOON	ن	—·
WAW	و	·——
HE	ه	····—
YA	ي	··
LAM-ALIF	لا	·—···—

Radiotelegraph and Radiotelephone Codes, Prowords and Abbreviations

(1943)

GREEK MORSE

English Name	Greek Letter	Morse Symbol
ALPHA	A	·−
BETA	B	−···
GAMMA	Γ	−−·
DELTA	Δ	−··
EPSILON	E	·
ZETA	Z	−−··
ETA	H	····
THETA	Θ	−·−·
IOTA	I	··
KAPPA	K	−·−
LAMBDA	Λ	·−··
MU	M	−−
NU	N	−·
XI	Ξ	−··· ·
OMICRON	O	−−−
PI	Π	·−−·
RHO	P	·−·
SIGMA	Σ	···
TAU	T	−
YPSILON	Y	−·−−
PHI	Φ	··−·
CHI	X	−−−−
PSI	Ψ	−−·−
OMEGA	Ω	·−−
ETA YPSILON	HY	···−
YPSILON IOTA	YI	·−−−
OMICRON YPSILON	OY	··−
ALPHA IOTA	AI	·−·−
ALPHA YPSILON	AY	··−−
EPSILON YPSILON	EY	−−−·
OMICRON IOTA	OI	−−−··

RUSSIAN MORSE

Russian Letter	Nearest Equivalent English Letter	Morse Symbol
А	A	·−
Б	B	−···
В	V	·−−
Г	G	−−·
Д	D	−··
Е,Э	E	·
Ж	J	···−
З	Z	−−··
И	I	··
Й	Y	·−−−
К	K	−·−
Л	L	·−··
М	M	−−
Н	N	−·
О	O	−−−
П	P	·−−·
Р	R	·−·
С	S	···
Т	T	−
У	U	··−
Ф	F	··−·
Х	KH	····
Ц	TS	−·−·
Ч	CH	−−−·
Ш	SH	−−−−
Щ	SHCH	−−·−
ъ,ь	MUTE	−··−·
Ы	I	−·−−
Ю	YU	··−−
Я	YA	·−·−

TURKISH MORSE

Letter	Morse Symbol
A	·−
B	−···
C	−·−·
Ç	−·−··
D	−··
E	·
F	··−·
G	−−·
H	····
I	··
J	·−−−
K	−·−
L	·−··
M	−−
N	−·
O	−−−
Ö	−−−·
P	·−−·
R	·−·
S	···
Ş	−−−−
T	−
U	··−
Ü	··−−
V	···−
Y	−·−−
Z	−−··

JAPANESE MORSE (KNOWN AS KATA KANA RADIO CODE)

A ·−	ア	HA −···	ハ	KA ·−··	カ	MA −··−	マ	NA ·−·	ナ	RA ···	ラ	SA −·−·−	サ	TA −·	タ	WA −·−	ワ	YA ·−−	ヤ
E −·−−·	エ	HE ·	ヘ	KE −·−−	ケ	ME −···−	メ	NE −−·−	ネ	RE −−−	レ	SE ·−−−·	セ	TE ·−·−−	テ	(W)E ·−−··	ヱ	(Y)E −·−−··	エ
I ·−	イ	HI −−··−	ヒ	KI −·−··	キ	MI ··−·−	ミ	NI −·−·	ニ	RI −−·	リ	SI −−·−·	シ	TI ··−·	チ	(W)I ·−··−	ヰ	(Y)I ·−	イ
O ·−	オ	HO −··	ホ	KO −−−−	コ	MO −··−·	モ	NO ··−−	ノ	RO ·−·−	ロ	SO −−−·	ソ	TO ··−··	ト	WO ·−−−	ヲ	YO −−	ヨ
U ··−	ウ	HU −−··	フ	KU ···−	ク	MU −	ム	NU ·−·−·	ヌ	RU −·−−·	ル	SU −−−·−	ス	TU ·−−·	ツ	(W)U ··	ウ	YU −··−−	ユ

	Symbol
N	·−·−· ン
NAN NIGORI	··
PERIOD	·−·−·−
QUOTES	·−··−·
BRACKETS ( )	−·−−·−
QUESTION MARK ?	··−−··
PARAGRAPH ¶	·−·−··
NIGORI	··
HYPHEN	−····−

Radiotelegraph and Radiotelephone Codes, Prowords and Abbreviations

Japanese Morse or Katakana Radio Code

Refer to the previous page for the table of the Katakana Radio Code.

Japan adopted Chinese characters in about the 4th century AD. There are about 50,000 characters. After WW2 the Education Ministry modified and reduced the commonly used ones to 2,000.
The average Japanese learns about 900.

Unlike Chinese, the Japanese adopted a phonetic usage of the characters. There are 50 phonetics in both high 'Hiragana' and low 'Katakana' Japanese. The 'inferior' Katakana was relegated to women and foreign usage etc. Morse Code fell into this category.

In DX contests, contacts and QSO's the Japanese usually use International Morse and abbreviations. Operators are also keen to practise English as this is the most popular foreign language in Japan.

In QSO's etc the Japanese use International Morse for opening and closing calls and for callsigns or foreign references within the QSO but may use Katakana Code, "wabun" in Japanese, for general language and surnames. Given names, RST and QTH are often in International Morse.

The following procedure characters are used -

The start of "wabun" characters   —··———   The end of "wabun" characters   ···—·
"Wabun" QSO wanted   CQ   —··———
Parentheses are used to include International Morse within a message.
         Japanese (—·—·—·
         Japanese)   ·—··—·   (also meant Quote " .. " - 1943)

Cardinal Numbers -

0   ray   REI
1   each   ICHI   6   rock   ROKU
2   knee   NI   7   hitch   SHICHI
3   sun   SAN   8   hatch   HACHI
4   she   SHI   9   q   KYU
5   go   GO   10   jew   JYU

Japanese Amateur Licence Morse requirements are (1997) -
   1st Class -   12 wpm   International   2nd Class -   9 wpm International
                10 wpm   Katakana   3rd Class -   5 wpm International

In 1997 the Japanese Amateur Radio League introduced a Morse Receiving Award in both Katakana and International Morse as follows -

The traditional Judo / Karate method of ranking is used.

Class	WPM	Exam Length
Master	36	5 minutes
5th Dan	32	5 minutes
4th Dan	28	5 minutes
3rd Dan	24	5 minutes
2nd Dan	22	5 minutes
Shodan	18	3 minutes
1st Kyu	12	3 minutes
2nd Kyu	9	2 minutes
3rd Kyu	5	2 minutes

de "Amateur Radio" Jan. 1989. p 13.
    "Morsum Magnificat #51", WY5I Report, 1997 and other sources.

Radiotelegraph and Radiotelephone Codes, Prowords and Abbreviations

Chinese Morse

The problems in sending the Chinese language by telegraph are considerable. Although there are many different dialects spoken in China, the written language is the same throughout the country.
There are over 50,000 ideograms of which about 7,000 are commonly used. They must be learnt by heart.
The Chinese Govt. considered using the Pantelegraph (France, 1865, the first fax machine) which could send the ideograms but this was not proceeded with. Telegrams were translated into a European language, transmitted and retranslated at the destination. This was clumsy, produced errors and depended on a translating capability at each end, not always possible.

The Danish Great Northern Telegraph Co. planned to set up telegraph systems in China.
From 1868-9, after contacts with a Chinese delegation, the GNT asked a Dane, Hans Schjellerup to devise a method. He was a University Professor, technician, astronomer and specialist in Arabic and Chinese.
He produced a draft of two pages of 260 Chinese ideograms coded by numbers by 19 April 1870.
The ideograms were arranged in the same order as the current Chinese dictionaries and were allocated a number. The numbers were transmitted and could be transcribed at the destination.
The dictionary was to include 5454 ideograms based on 214 special radical Chinese characters.
The draft was sent to Shanghai on 1 August 1870 to be completed in China.

However a Frenchman, Captain of the Port of Shanghai, M.S.A. Viguier was also working on a similar system based on the same 214 characters. He arranged his characters in a table format using the numbers as a vertical and horizontal co-ordinate system.
After consideration of both methods, Schjellerup's numbering system was used but in Viguier's table format for clarity. Viguier worked on it and devised boxes of stamps with the Schjellerup number on one end and the Chinese ideogram on the other. By turning them, coding and decoding was done.

The GNT opened the Hong Kong - Shanghai line in April 1871 and the method was successfully tried.
In 1871 GNT printed copies of the dictionary and Chinese telegraphists soon got so familiar with it that the clumsy stamp box device was discarded.
Subsequent issues of the dictionary expanded to over 7,000 characters. Viguier claimed credit for the system and argued with GNT over payments. This was settled in 1876 but Schjellerup's part was not credited until the GNT's Jubilee Publication in 1894.

This method is still used for Morse in Chinese. (Year 2000)

Exert from a page of a later edition of the Chinese Telegraph Dictionary.

Sometimes also called the Chinese Telegraph Code (CTC).

This system continued into the computer era when Schjellerup's number system formed the basis for devising the DOS for Chinese computers.

More powerful, modern computers use more direct methods of constructing Chinese ideograms which have also been rationalised (A later example next page)

de - 'Morsum Magnificat'

Radiotelegraph and Radiotelephone Codes, Prowords and Abbreviations

Chinese Morse

Explanatory Notes

1. The Standard Code Book contains code expressions in groups of four figures, each representing a Chinese character.

2. The code expressions are arranged horizontally from left to right, 100 to a page, e.g., Page 1 from 0000 to 0099, Page 2 from 0100 to 0199, and so on.

3. To code a telegram for transmission, first ascertain the radical of the character and the index of the radical, then look for the codeword of the relevant character. For instance, the radical for the character "中" is "丨", whose index is "00", and a short search on page 1 will yield the code expression "0022" for "中".

4. Characters and marks not available in the Standard Code Book proper may be found in one of the appendices named below:

   1) For simplified characters, refer to "Code for Simplified Chinese Characters";

Chinese Telegraphic Code Book, with a specimen page showing the affinity between the radicals (0354, 0360, etc) and the characters following them

Above are pages from a later issue of the CTC Book containing 10,000 characters.
This included an alphabetic reference as well for those preferring this.
The alpha code used three units against four in the numerical code for each character.
This commercial code was used widely in both China and Japan and was used during WW2 for characters not found in the military code books.

Great   North-

Radiotelegraph and Radiotelephone Codes, Prowords and Abbreviations

The Heliograph

This section has been included because the Heliograph was a very important signalling equipment in use for about 80 years in major armies and another 50 years in minor theatres of war. Yet this instrument is very little known amongst conventional telegraphers.

The use of mirrors to reflect the sun has been used from ancient times but on an ad hoc basis with no specific signalling instrument devised. Codes used were clumsy, temporary and mostly forgotten.
Charles Babbage, of computer fame, was given a surveying task in 1827. To facilitate this he invented the Heliotrope (also attributed to Gauss). This instrument used sunlight in a similar way that modern surveyors use laser beams. Using mirrors it projected a beam from one survey point to another. A clockwork driver mirror tracked the sun. There was at this time no need for a sunlight signalling device.

Chronic bad weather in Europe, unstability of ships made solar signalling devices not in popular demand. Babbage was aware of of the signalling possibility as he wrote to The Times, 16 July 1855,
"On the Possible Use of the Occulting Telegraph at Sebastapol" (Crimean War).

Railway construction and military needs caused the British to undertake a mapping survey of India.

A huge task for the time. The Heliotrope was used as well as many other instruments designed for the purpose. India's mountainous terrain and finer weather favoured solar optical devices.

The British Army used signaller/soldiers in the Crimean War 1854-6. The School of Signals being opened at Chatham in 1865.
An officer, H.C. Mance was interested in signalling by sunlight and was aware of the use of the Heliotrope in India. Although not proven, it is surmised that pre-arranged signals might have been passed using this.
He designed the Mance Heliograph which remained in use for over 130 years and is probably still in use now.

The Heliograph is a simple instrument using one or two mirrors to direct a beam of sunlight (or moonlight) at the target. A finger knob is moved to tilt the mirror allowing Morse Code to be sent.
The knob is rotated on a screw to adjust the alignment as the sun progressed.

The Heliograph was a late starter in telegraphy. There were three reasons for its development.

1. Need. Wars and surveys in finer climates of India, the Middle East, Africa, South West USA outside the poor weather of Europe. Distances were great, roads and telegraph lines were few.
2. The invention of the Silvered Glass Mirror in 1840 made them cheaper and better to make.
3. The Morse Code which was practical, easy to use and universally accepted.

The Mance Heliograph 5 inch Mk. V (Aust) 1942
(Author's Collection)

It was first used by the British Army in battle in the Zulu War of 1879 then by both sides in the Boer War. Its use continued in the desert campaigns of WW1 and WW2.

In 1879 a Heliograph service was introduced between Rottnest Island and Fremantle, Western Australia. A distance of 18 Km (11 Miles) the only regular Heliograph service in the Australian Telegraph System. It was replaced by a cable in 1900 following radio experiments in 1899 that were not taken up.

Radiotelegraph and Radiotelephone Codes, Prowords and Abbreviations

The Heliograph

The U.S. Army Signal Corps was established on 21 June 1860. Knowing of the British use of Heliographs in India, in 1877 some British instruments were obtained and tested. In 1878 the US adopted a Heliograph which used louvre shutters instead of the tilting mirror to interrupt the signal.
Used during the Indian Wars, its demonstration to Geronimo was a factor causing his surrender.
A World distance record of 183 miles (294 Kms) was achieved in 1894 in Colarado.

The Australian Army used Heliographs into WW2. During the Egyptian campaign Capt. F.A. Carruthers (VK2PF), from Lismore, and section claimed a moonlight Heliograph record of 25 miles (40 Kms).

At home (1 Bn VDC, Lismore) during 1942 while on net exercises L/Cpl A.Webb (VK2UC) and crew worked from Mt. Warning to Coffs Harbour (Bonville Peak ??) a distance of 216 Kms (133 miles).
The crew were Sgt R. Carr, Cpl A.Axtens and L/Cpl A.Webb. This was part of a chain of Heliograph stations which existed as a backup comms system in the event of a Japanese landing. It went from Cairns, Nth. Queensland to Coffs Harbour, NSW. a distance of about 1,793 Kms (1,114 miles).

Each group was responsible only for their particular leg of the system. Lismore covered Kyogle - Mt Boorabee - Goonellabah - Lismore - Parrot's Nest - Casino. Casino passed traffic south to Grafton to Coffs Harbour. Kyogle had a path north through the Ranges to the Tweed thence further North Operators were not told of details of paths outside their own areas.

Lismore operated an eastern link, Lismore - Goonellabah - Wollongbar - Newrybar (near Cape Byron) 77 Kms (48 Miles). This was to report Japanese submarine and other marine traffic off the coast. Other than operational traffic, these nets were exercised fortnightly for verification and operator training.

Aldis Lamps and Flag signalling (wig-wag and Semaphore) was also used. Using binoculars the range achieved, dependent on weather, was about the same, 5 miles (8 Kms). These systems were kept up, on a reducing degree of readiness, throughout the war period.   (Info Mr. A Webb, VK2UC, now 96yo)
More information on this system is sought and welcomed.

As late as 1994 the Afghans used Heliographs in their war against the Russians. They are simple, rugged, need minimum maintenance and no electricity but could not be monitored by Russian satellites like the radio could. They are probably still using them.

Australian 8th Light Horse Signallers with the Heliograph at Tiberias, Palestine. 1918.

Radiotelegraph and Radiotelephone Codes, Prowords and Abbreviations

WORLD MAP OF TIME ZONES

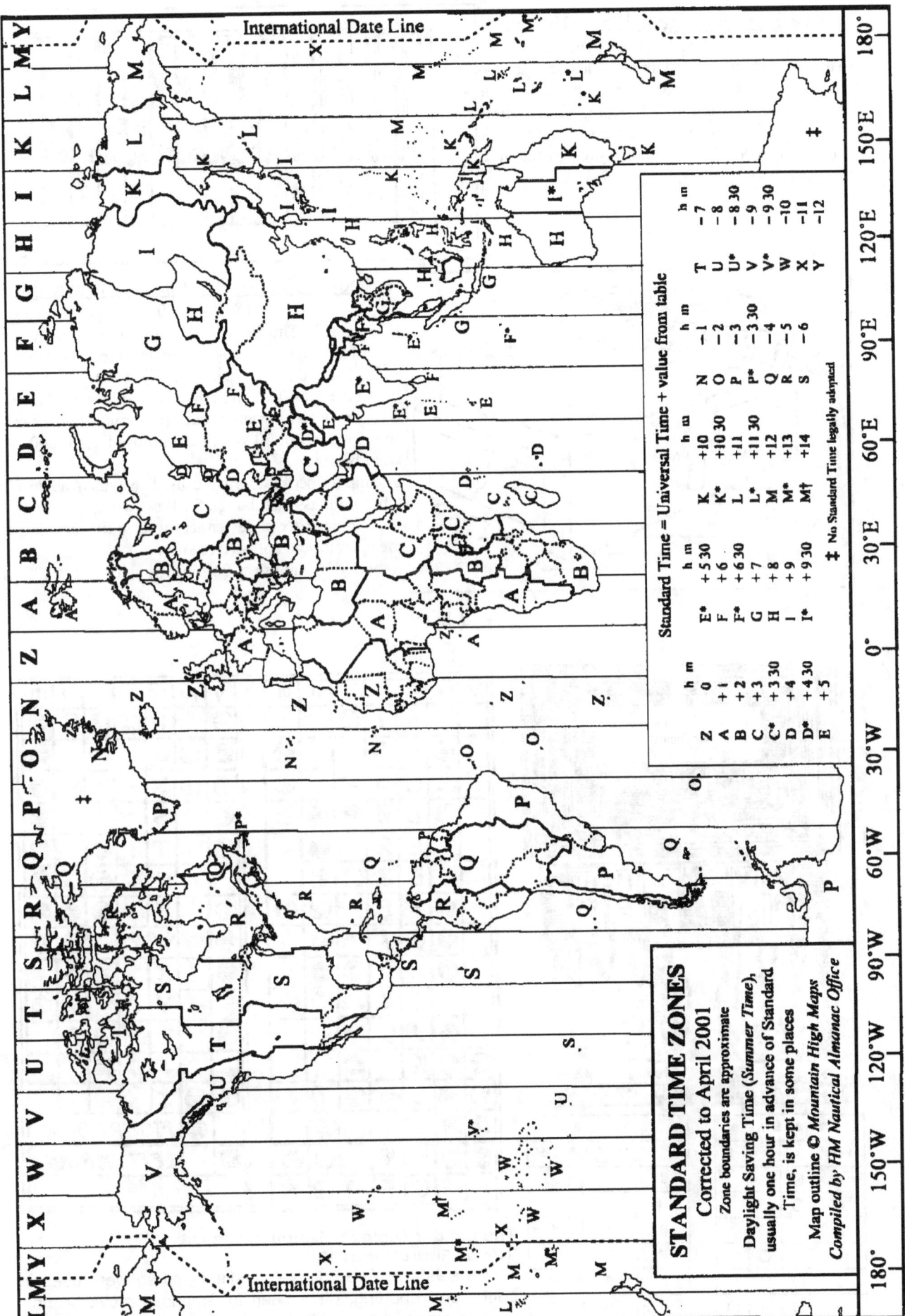

Radiotelegraph and Radiotelephone Codes, Prowords and Abbreviations

Popular Telegraph Systems

The Baudot System - 1877 to 1980's+

The Hughes System 1855 - 1930's?

The Hughes Keyboard (right)
The message was typed in, encoded and sent as timed pulses to a receiver which printed out in normal text. Capable of 140 wpm, normal speed was from 42 to 60 wpm. Operators do not need to know any code but machine synchronisation is necessary.

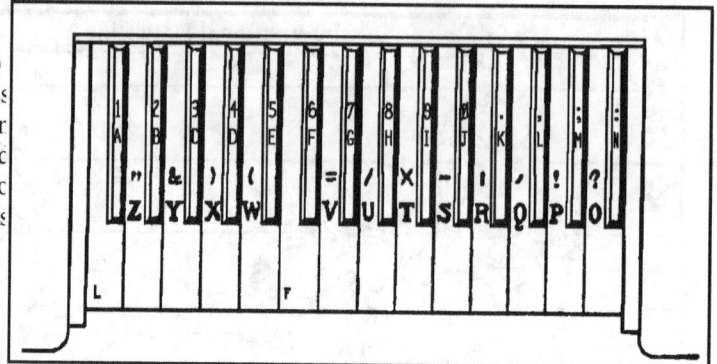

The Wheatstone Automatic Telegraph
1858 - 1950's?

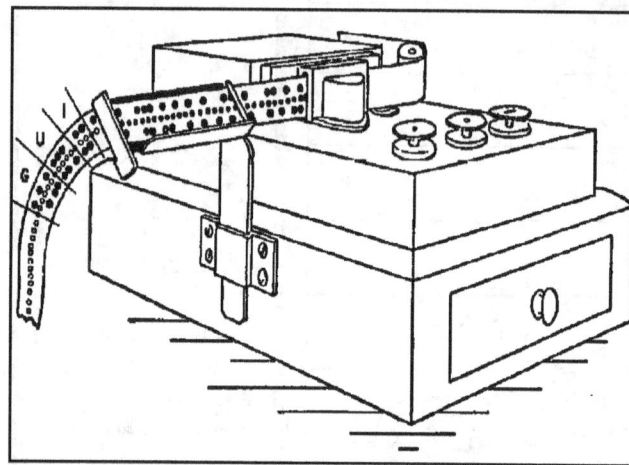

(Figure left) The Perforator, the three operating keys (top front) manually perforated the tape. They were - Left - Dot, Centre - Space and Right - Dash.
The tape was fed through a transmitter to line to a receiver which printed out in normal text. Normal speed was about 70 wpm but improved up to 300 - 400 wpm by 1900.
Pneumatic perforators were used to punch up to eight tapes for mass distribution for Press work.
Later typewriter style senders were built meaning that the operator did not need to know any code.
Reported still in use at Burnie, Tasmania in the 1950's

(below)

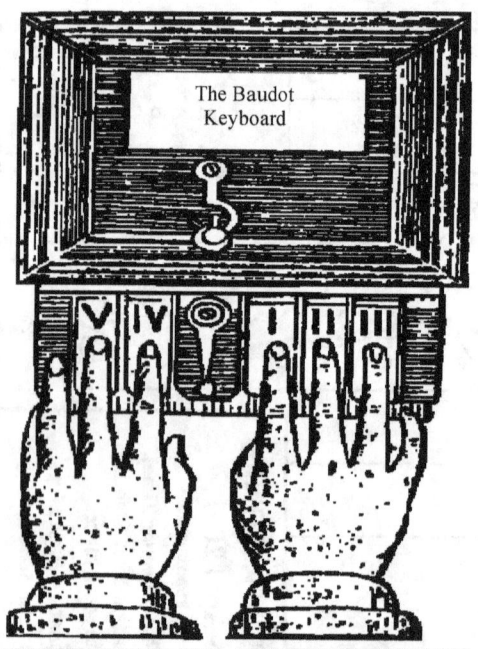

TABLE A			
KEYS	1	2	3
A	O		
É	O	O	
E		O	
I		O	O
O	O	O	O
U	O		O
Y			O

TABLE B		
WITH KEY 4	WITH KEYS 4 AND 5	WITH KEY 5
J	K	t̲
H	L	Z
G	M	X
F	N	W
D	P	V
C	Q	T
B	R	S

The Baudot Table of Manipulations
('Modern Electric Practice' 1907)
These senders were completely silent and so were used in courtroom reporting, often seen in American movies, until modern times when replaced by tape recording systems

Radiotelegraph and Radiotelephone Codes, Prowords and Abbreviations

Addenda
Material received after printing of main texts.
'Q' and 'Z' Codes 1949. JANAP 131(A) and others.

CODE	QUESTION	ANSWER or NOTICE
QFK	Send up landing/taxiing/etc signals by lamp.	Watch tower for landing/taxiing/take off signals by lamp.
QTD		Word count you are confirming is accepted.
QTK		True bearing relative to me is …… degrees.
QTL		Sending signals to permit bearing, with respect to the radio beacon.
QTN		Cannot take bearing of your station.
QTS		True bearing of my station relative to you is ……. degrees.
ZES		The following multiple address or book message tape is in abbreviated form.
ZNI		This is an unparaphrased literal text of a cipher message and is to be handled accordingly. (NOTE: This signal will be used only on approved line (wire) circuits.)
ZNJ		Do not forward this message by radio or nonapproved circuit.
ZNM		Check encipherment (cryptographing) of message …. (or portions indicated) and repeat.
ZNN	Am unable to decipher message …… Will you check decipherment and repeat correct indicators?	Correct indicators (of message ….) are ……..
ZOA		Relay this message (or message ……) by visual (to …..)
ZOC		Station(s) called relay this message to addressees for whom you are responsible.
ZOD		Act as radio link (relaying station) between me and …. (or between ….. and …..).
ZOE	Can you accept message for ……?	Give me your message. I will dispose of it.
ZOF		Relay (pass) this message (or message ….) to …. now (or at ….).
ZOG	Transmit (pass) this message (or message ….) to ….. (for ….) (1. Action; 2. Information.).	
ZOH		Send message for …. on ….kcs (or mcs) (by …. method).
ZOI		Pass this method to the nearest (or ….) weather central.
ZOJ	Unable to relay message …. in present form …. (1. Call signs not encrypted; 2. Text not encrypted.).	
ZOK		Relay this message via …..
ZOL		I will relay your call sign to SOPA, whose call sign is ……..
ZON	Place this message (or message ….) on primary FOX indicated by numerals following …… (1. NSS; 2. NPG; 3. NPM; 4. NBA; 5. NPN.).	
ZOO	Place this message on MERFOX indicated by numerals following …. (1. NSS; 2. NPM; 3. NBA; 4. NPG; 5. NPN.).	
ZOP	This message has been delivered to the following areas: Ø. All other areas; 1. NPN area; 2. NPM area; 3. NPG area; 4. NBA area; 5. NSS area; 12. NPN and NPM area; 23. NPM and NPG area, etc.	
ZOQ	Deliver this message to the following areas only: Ø. All other areas; 1. NPN area; 2. NPM area; 3. NPG area; 4. NBA area; 5. NSS area; 12. NPN and NPM area; 23. NPM and NPG area, etc.	
ZOR		Route traffic for …. via ….. area broadcast.
ZOS	Request area routing for radiotelegram for ….	Route for radiotelegram for ….. is area ………
ZOU	How should traffic for …… be routed?	Route traffic for ….. through ….. (on …. kcs (or mcs)).
ZSG	May I make an approach using the facility indicated?	You may approach using the facility indicated.
ZSH	What is …. (1. The date of the Rekoh Card you are using; 2. The date of the Bomber Card` you are using; 3. The date of the Aircraft Reporting Card you are using; 4. The Indicator number of your Alametco (request) Card; 5. The date of the (….) Meteorological Card you are using.)?	I am using …. (1. Rekoh Card for the …. day of the month; 2. Bomber Code Card for the …… day of the month; 3. Aircraft Reporting Card for the …. day of the month; 4. Alametco (request) Card numbered …… 5. The (….) Meteorological Card for the …. day of the month.).
ZTG		…. (1. Radiotelgraph; 2. Modulated Radiotelegraph; 3. Radiotelephone; 4. Radiotele-typewriter; 5. Radio Direction Finder.)
ZTH		…. (1. Frequency modulation; 2. Amplitude modulation; 3. Pulse modulation; 4. Frequency shift (…. Cycle shift); 5. SCFM.).
ZUD		Until further orders (or until …….).
ZZB		Indicate name of ….. (1. Operator on watch; 2. Senior rating on watch.).
ZZC		The following is to be taken as applying to ratings on watch only.
ZZD	Carry out communication …. V/S Exercise No. … at … Sr. Officer (or …) is to conduct.	
ZZE		Voluntary exercise (No. ….) may be carried out now (or at ….).
ZZI		Answer last question (or question ….).
ZZJ	Stations are to answer …. Taking the following duties … A, … B, ….C, etc.	
ZZK		Following is answer to last question (or question …).
ZZL	Correct answer to last question (or question ….) is …. (or will be found in …..).	

Radiotelegraph and Radiotelephone Codes, Prowords and Abbreviations

Addenda
Material received after printing of main texts.
'Q' and 'Z' Codes 1949. JANAP 131(A) and others.

CODE	QUESTION	ANSWER or NOTICE
ZZM		Correct version of the part of the last message (or message ...) which was sent incorrectly is .... (or will be found in).
ZZN#		Following message (or question, or exercise) is for the exercise of ..... (1. Junior operators; 2. Sr. operators; 3. Ratings on watch now.).
ZZO#		A Junior operator is to carry out ..... (1. A standard flashing procedure; 2. A standard semaphore procedure; 3. A standard W/T transmitting exercise; 4. A standard W/T receiving exercise.).

Line Codes used by 19th Century British Railways. Others are already included in Abbreviations Lists.
- GQ   Begin new line of text.
- LQ   Wait while I am attending to counter or other instruments.
- PQ   End of message. (On some companies, on others it was a very rude insult, meaning 'Piss Quick')
- SQ   End of message, another to follow.

ABBREVIATIONS

G	(Sp.)	Adelante = Go Ahead.
R	(Sp.)	OK, QSL, received.
, ,	(Sp.)	Two commas out of traffic text = considered an insult (Son-of-a-bitch etc.)
BN	(Sp.)	Buenas noches = Good night, since the sky is dark, not used as 'Until tomorrow'.
BT	(Sp.)	Buenas tardes = Good afternoon, from midday until sunset.
CA	(Sp.)	Corriente alterna = Alternating current.
CP	(Sp.)	Codigo postal = ZIP, Postcode.
DR	(Sp.)	Doctor, estimado = Doctor, dear.
HH		Error in sending. Transmission continues with last word correctly sent.
HX		Handling Instructions.
I I	(Sp.)	- - - - Error during traffic text etc.
IM	(Sp.)	Informe meteorologico = QAM on the rail network.
HL	(Sp.)	Hasta luego = See you later.
HM	(Sp.)	Hasta maña = See you tomorrow, till tomorrow.
MB	(Sp.)	Muy bien = Well done, very good.
PF	(Sp.)	Por favor = Please.
SR	(Sp.)	Señor = Mister.
SS		Superstructure.
UD	(Sp.)	Usted = You. UDS = You (Plural).
BNA – BNO	(Sp.)	Buena, Bueno = Good, well.
CSE		Course.
FTE	(Sp.)	Fuerte = Strong.
FTG		Fuck the Guard. Derogatory comment by US Coast Guard oprs on unpopular postings.
GRS	(Sp.)	Gracias = TNX Thanks.
HXG		Delivery by mail or toll call not required. If expense involved, cancel and service sending station.
ITV	(Sp.)	Interferencia en TV = TVI.
POB		Persons on board.
QRA	(Sp.)	Phone oprs use for 'name'.
QRJ	(Sp.)	Enfermo = Sick, ill.
SRA	(Sp.)	Señora = Missis, Mrs.
STA	(Sp.)	Señorita = Miss.
UDS	(Sp.)	Ustedes = You (plural).
ULV		You leave vessel.
ABZO	(Sp.)	Abrazo = Embrace.
ADEE		Addressee.
ABZO		Embrace (Spanish, S.America)
IMHO		In my honest opinion.
JA JA	(Sp.)	Risas = Laughter, HI HI
MATE	(Sp.)	Mate (locally used infusion).
MGRS	(Sp.)	Muchas gracias = Many TNX.
NOME	(Sp.)	from Portuguese, also NAME from English = Name.

Radiotelegraph and Radiotelephone Codes, Prowords and Abbreviations

Addenda
Material received after printing of main texts.

PIBA	(Sp.) Adolescente = Missy, female teenager.
PIBE	(Sp.) Adolescente = Male teenager.
SEEU	See you, I will see you.
SIIK	Stuffed if I know.
TEMP	(Sp.) Temperatura = Temperature, WX and QAM are generally used too.
FUBAR	Fouled up beyond any repair.
PROFE	(Sp.) Profesor, maestro = Teacher.
SNAFU	Situation normal, all fouled up. - or similar.
TARFU	Things are really fouled up.
TAKE P	Piss break (American Morse P = - - - - -) When female operators arrived this became - "Take 5", the same in International Morse. The origin of this saying.
TRONCO	(Sp.) Tronco, malo = Bad operator, LID. (Perhaps origin of "Drongo" ?? - JWA)
OPNOTE	Operator's Note. Marginal note or comment in log book etc.

Phonetic Alphabets

2002 U.S.A. Patriot Militias		2002 Israeli Army 1996			
		Letter	Sound	Code Word	Number Equiv
A	America	a	Alef	-	Alef	1
B	Bible	b	Bet (Vet)	B (V)	Boaz	2
C	Concord	g	Gimel	G	Gimel	3
D	Dakota	d	Dalet	D	David	4
E	Eagle	h	Hey	H	Hagar	5
F	Freedom	v	Vav	V	Vav	6
G	Gunfight	z	Zain	Z	Ze'ev	7
H	Hamburger	x	kHet	kH	Khana	8
I	Idaho	u	Tet	T	Tit	9
J	Jazz	y	Yud, Yod	Y	Yoria	10
K	Kansas	K [	Kaf (Haf)	K (H)	Carmel	20
L	Lexington	l	Lamed	L	Le'a	30
M	Musket	m	Mem	M	Moshe	40
N	Nuke	n	Nun	N	Nesher	50
O	Outlaw	,	Sameh	S	Sameh	60
P	Puma	i	Ain	-	Ain	70
Q	Question	P [	Pey (Fey)	P (F)	Pesel	80
R	Rebel	J /	Tzadi	Tz	Tzipor	90
S	Samson	q	Kuf	K	Koreah	100
T	Tomahawk	r	Reish	R	Rut	200
U	Underdog	s	Shin (Sin)	Sh (S)	Shamir	300
V	Victory	t	Tav	T	Telem	400
W	Waco					
X	X-Men					
Y	Yorktown					
Z	Zippo					

Radiotelegraph and Radiotelephone Codes, Prowords and Abbreviations

Addenda
Material received after printing of main texts.

1918, 1942
US Army, WW1 and WW2
Indian Code Speakers
Not really a Phonetic, but unusual and very successful.

	Navajo	English		Navajo	English
A	Wol-La Chee	Ant	L	Dibeh-Yazzie	Lamb
	Be-La-Sana	Apple		Ah-Jad	Leg
	Tse-Nill	Axe		Nash-Doie-Tso	Lion
B	Na-Hash-Chid	Badger	M	Tsin-Tliti	Match
	Shush	Bear		Be-Tas-Tni	Mirror
	Toish-Jeh	Barrel		Na-As-Tso-Si	Mouse
C	Moasi	Cat	N	Tsah	Needle
	Tla-Gin	Coal		A-Chin	Nose
	Ba-Goshi	Cow		Nesh-Chee	Nut
D	Be	Deer	O	A-Kha Tlo-Chin	Oil
	Chindi	Devil		Tlo-Chin	Onion
	Lha-Cha-Eh	Dog		Ne-Ahs-Jah	Owl
E	Ah-Jah	Ear	P	Cla-Gi-Aih	Pant
	Dzeh	Elk		Bi-So-Dih	Pig
	Ah-Nah	Eye		Ne-Zhoni	Pretty
F	Chuo	Fir	Q	Ca-Yeilth	Quiver
	Tsa-E-Donin-Ee	Fly	R	Gah	Rabbit
	Ma-E	Fox		Dah-Nes-Tsa	Ram
G	Ah-Tad	Girl		Ah-Losz	Rice
	Klizzie	Goat	S	Dibeh	Sheep
	Jeha	Gum		Klesh	Snake
H	Tse-Gah	Hair	T	D-Ah	Tea
	Cha	Hat		A-Woh	Tooth
	Lin	Horse		Than-Zie	Turkey
I	Tkin	Ice	U	Shi-Da	Uncle
	Yeh-Hes	Itch		No-Da-Ih	Ute V
	A-Chi	Intestine		A-Keh-Di-Glini	Victor
J	Tkele-Cho-Gi	Jackass	W	Gloe-Ih	Weasel
	Ah-Ya-Tsinne	Jaw	X	Al-Na-As-Dzoh	Cross
	Yil-Doi	Jerk	Y	Tsah-Ah-Dzoh	Yucca
K	Jad-Ho-Loni	Kettle	Z	Besh-Do-Tliz	Zinc
	Ba-Ha-Ne-Di-	Key			
	Klizzie-Yazzie	Kid			

This is the WW2 code, the WW1 code not yet found.

An extensive word codebook was also used.

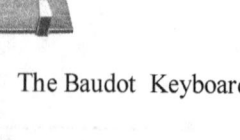

The Baudot Keyboard

The Baudot Transmitter / Sender.
Modern Electric Practice, 1907

Radiotelegraph and Radiotelephone Codes, Prowords and Abbreviations

Bibliography and References

1771	Encyclopaedia Britannica - Priestly, Franklin, Watson et al. - Electric transmission, 3.5 Kms. etc.
1857	Chamber's Information for the People - Volta, Morse, Bain, Wheatstone - Telegraphs.
1860	Guide to Scientific Knowledge of Things Familiar, Dr Brewer - Needle Telegraph & Lightning.
1866	History. Theory and Practice of the Electric Telegraph. G.G. Prescott. Reprint 1972. Needle & Bain codes.
1872	Manual of Military Telegraphy - Signal Service, US Army. General Service (Myer) Code application.
1878	The Popular Educator - Early history of Telegraphs - Semaphore to Morse.
1880	The Royal Treasure House of Knowledge - Static, Needle, Morse, Indicating and Chemical Telegraphs.
1884, 1889, 1902	US Army Soldier's Handbook. – Changing Signals modes and procedures. CD.
1885	Telegraphic Code to Insure Secrecy in the Transmission of Telegrams - US War Dept., Secretary of War.
1885	The Universal Self-Instructor - History and progress of the Telegraph.
1896	Signalling Instructions - British War Office, HMSO. Army Visual and Morse signalling and procedures.
1899, 1906	Electrical and Signal Dept. Rules and Regulations. L&NWR. Needle, Time, Abbrevs etc.
1901, 1911, 1917	The Telegraph Instructor - G.M. Dodge. Codes and Abbreviations.
1902	Telegraphy Self Taught, A Complete Manual of Instruction. - T.A. Edison.- Number Codes and Abbreviations.
1903	Instructions for the Use of Wireless-Telegraph Apparatus. - USN, - Wireless Telegraph Navy Code. (MM64)
1907	'Training Manual (Signalling)' - British Army - Phonetics.
1907	British Signal Manual - Admiralty, HMSO. Marine Procedure and Z-Codes
1907	Modern Electric Practice, Vol VI, - pp 31, 64, Morse, Baudot and Murray Telegraphic Codes.
1908	Handbook for Wireless Telegraph Operators - British Post Office. Abbr, Proc, RA-SF Codes.(BT Archives)
1908	Morse Code Made Easy - Chart at Low Head Pilot Station, Tasmania - Morse and Phonetics.
1909	Handbook for Wireless Telegraph Operators - British Post Office. Abbr, Proc, QRA-QSJ Codes
1909, 1915	International Code of Signals, American Edit. - US Army & Navy Code etc. (USN)
1911	Brown's Signalling - 12th ed. British, Marine Visual and Morse signalling and procedures.
1911	Infantry Training - British Army. Machine gun Fire Observation Semaphore Signals.
1911	Outdoor Signalling – E.Wells. – General Service (Myer) Code. Methods, Variants, Abbrevs. Etc.
1912	Handbook for Wireless Telegraph Operators - Repr 1923 - British PO. Q Codes, abbrevs. procedures.
1912	American Telegraphy & Encyclopedia of the Telegraph - Repr 1997 - Buckingham, Barclay Codes.
1913, 1917, 1922, 1938, 1940, 1943, 1950	The Bluejacket's Manual, US Navy - Phonetics, Codes, Procedures. (USN)
1914	Signalling - Imperial Army Series - UK - (Training Manual - Signalling Pt II, 1914) Codes and Procedures.
1914	Signal Book US Army – War Dept. Procedures, Methods, Eqpt. Codes, flags, semaphores, Ardois, Very, gas lamps etc.
1914	Telephone Trouble – Evening News for British Post Office - Telephone procedures and Phonetic Alphabet.
1914	Twentieth Century Manual of Railway Commercial and Wireless Telegraphy. F.L.Meyer Procedures etc.
1914 – 1917	Field Service Regulations - US Army - Procedures and Signals.
1915	Training Manual – Signalling (Provisional) - British Army. Abbrevs, Phonetics, Prosigns, Time.
1915	Hawkins Electrical Guide No. 9. – pp 2201-2262 Telegraph. 2263-2338 Wireless Telegraphy.
1916	Signalling Handbook for Australian Military Forces. - Codes, Methods and Procedures.
1916	Signal Book, United States Army. War Dept. Doc. 500. - Phonetics etc. - de David W. Gaddy.
1917	Hawkin's Electrical Guide No. 8 - pp 2270 - 2272, Five early codes and procedures, 1912 Q Codes.
1918	Australian Comforts Funds Gift Diary - A.I.F. Phonetics, Codes and Procedures etc.
1918	Signal Training. Part VI. Procedure. British Army. - Phonetics, Brit. & German Morse Procedures, X Codes.
1919	Signal Communications for All Arms (AEF No. 2-R) American Expedit. Force, France. - Phonetics - de D.W. Gaddy.
1924	The Radio Handbook - pp 406 -421 Morse, Phillips, International Codes, Q Codes.
1925	Australian Meteorological Observer's Handbook. - Codes and Abbreviations.
1926	British W/T Operating Signals – O.U. 5371/1926. - X=Codes.
1927, 1932, 1938, 1947, 1958-9	ITC / IRC / ITU Regs - Abbrevs., Phonetics, Procedures. (de ITU 1996)
1931	Drake's Radio Encyclopedia - Code, Morse.
1931	British W/T Operating Signals – O.U. 5371/1931. - X=Codes.
1931	International Code of Signals, and 1950 Supplement. Code changes.
1931	Naval Operations, vol. V, Royal Navy Convoy Codes.
1932	Manual of Seamanship, Vol I. Admiralty. Morse procedures, prosigns etc.
1932	Signal Training (All Arms) Suppl. 1934, Amendt. to 1937 - British Army - Phonetics and Procedures.
1935	Practical Radio Communication - pp 739 - 744 - Q Codes, International Morse Code.
1936	Cavalry Signal Communications – US Cavalry Weapons and Materiel, Pt 9, Procedures.
1938	Signal Training (All Arms) - British Army. Phonetics, Abbreviations.
1938	ITU Radio Manual - pp 976 - 985, 1054 - 1089 - Various codes.
1938	Magnetism and Electricity - pp 251-278 Electric telegraphy and telephony.
1938, 1944	Handbook for Wireless Telegraph Operators - UK GPO -Rg67 - ITU Codes etc. Madrid 1932, Cairo 1938.
1939	Nicholls's Seamanship and Nautical Knowledge - Semaphore, Codes, Morse and Procedures.
1941	VDC Instructions, Mr A Webb, VK2UC - Heliograph, Phonetics and Abbreviations etc.
1941	R/T Signal Procedure 1941.- British – Canadian Army aide-memoire. Phonetics and procedures.
1941	Wireless Transmission - pp 132 - 139 - Various codes.
1941	Army Wireless Operating Signals, B.R.266/1941 - British, X Codes, de Ken E. Brown, G0PSW.
1942	Rev 1949 Signal Card (RAN) ABR 232 - Semaphore, Flag, Morse and various Procedures.
1942	The Radio Amateur's Handbook - ARRL - Various Codes, Abbreviations and Procedures.
1942	The Morse Alphabet - How to Learn it Quickly - D.V., London. Mnemonic phonetics (MM53).
1942	Signal Communications FM 24-5 - US Army – Procedures, Codes and Phonetics.
1943	War Diary, 41st Battalion, 2nd AIF. - Phonetic Alphabet intro. 1 Jan 1943.
1943	McElroy Chart of Codes and Signals - Q and Z codes etc. de Rich Dailey, KA8OKH.
1943	The Amateur Radio Handbook - RSGB - Various Codes, Abbreviations and Procedures.
1943	"Signalcards", International. USA, Flags, Codes, Procedures.
1943	Signal Training (All Arms). Pam 5 Signal Procedure Pt 1. HMSO. Phonetic Alphabet..
1943	The Service Aircrew. Pt 4: W.A.G.'s RCAF CAP12. Wireless Air Gunners. - Q Codes, Procedures etc.
1943	Combined Operating Signals. UK, AM. Air Publ. 3026. Q Codes + amendments & addits.
1944	Exerpts from the International Code of Signals – Signals, Codes, 1 2 3 & 4 Letter Abbreviations, Flags.
1945	The Phillips Code – TCR Edition – Abbrevs, Q, Z Codes, Greek, Turkish, Arab, Russian, Jap, US etc Morse Codes.
1945	Radio Reference Book, No 45 - Greek, Turkish, Arab, Russian, Jap, US etc Morse Codes.
1949	Joint Communication Instructions, App 1, Operating Signals. JANAP 131(A) - US Joint Services. Q, Z Codes, Groups.
1949	The Radio Amateur's Handbook - ARRL - "ARL" Code and QRRR Procedure.

Radiotelegraph and Radiotelephone Codes, Prowords and Abbreviations

Bibliography and References

1952	Minor Landing Craft and Boat's Signal Book. B.R. 98 (3) Admiralty. - Codes and Procedures.
1952	Signal Training - Signalling Codes - (Aust. Army) Phonetics, Morse and Semaphore.
1954	Handbook for Wireless Operators - British PMG. HMSO Rg 67. Codes, Abbrevs. etc. 1947.
195?	Communications Procedure - Aust. Civil Defence - undated - Phonetics and Procedures.
1955	Radio Engineer's Pocketbook - pp 10,11. 68 - 71 - Various codes and abbreviations.
1955	Signal Training, Pam 7 - Voice Procedure. - (Brit./Aust Army) Various Codes and Procedures.
1955	Allied Communications Publication 131B (ACP-131B) Q and Z Codes. de B. Bradfield, W5CGH.
1959	Ham Radio Handbook - Q Codes and Phonetics.
1961	Manual for Use by the Mobile Services - ITU Regulations.
1961	Encyclopaedia Britannica - Various references.
1962	Signal Training - The Panel Code - Ground to Air Visual Signals, usually in Emergencies.
1963	Signal Training (All Arms) Pam 7 - Voice Procedure - (Aust Army) Phonetics and procedures.
1964	Codes and Ciphers - J.Laffin. - Bacon binary code, various codes.,
1965	Operating Aid No. 9a - ARRL Comms Dept. - Codes, Abbreviations and Procedures.
1966	Inside SOE - Brit. Special Operations Executive - WW2 agents in Europe, Signals procedures.
1967	Radio Telegraph Procedure – Vol IV, Pam 4. British Army. Procedures and Codes etc.
1968	Handbook for Radio Operators - British PMG. HMSO Rg 67. Codes, Abbrevs. etc. 1959-67.
1969	Signal Training - Radiotelephone Procedure. - (Aust. Army) Various Codes and Procedures.
1970	Secret Writing - J.E.Barry - Various codes and ciphers etc.
1972	Signal Training - Radiotelegraphy Procedure. - (Aust. Army) Various Codes and Procedures.
1973	The Semaphore Telegraph System of Van Diemen's Land (1939 notes) - Low Head Morse.
1973	SOS The Story of Radio Communication. - Early Radio and important events.
1973, 1974, 1985, 1989, 1992, 1996, 1998	Extracts from ITU Bulletins and Manuals - Teleg. indicators. de ITU 1998
1975	Codes and Abbreviations for the use of the International Telecommunications Service. ITU, de Ted Bastow VK2WL.
1976	'Secret Language' - Various codes and cyphers. Facsimile edition.
1976	Official CB Dictionary. Terms, definitions, jargon, CB and Police 10-Codes. FCC Rules.
1976	Big Dummy's Guide to C.B. Radio - CB Ten Code.
1976	Signal Card (RAN) ABR 232 (2)- Semaphore, Flag, Morse and various Procedures.
1978	Technical Guide to Aust. CB Radio. T.B.Floyd ISBN 855668725 - 10 Codes, Q Codes etc.
1979	The Radio Bulletin, Nov. p 15 - Abbreviations.
1980	European Phrase Book - Berlitz - Various Phonetics and Numerals.
1980	Annual Summary of Aust. Notices to Mariners - Prosigns and Abbreviations.
1980	Signalling and Communicating at Sea - Woods - Arno Press - Phonetic alphabets, derivation.
1983	MLW Signal Training - Radiotelephone Procedure (Aust Army) Phonetics and Procedures etc.
1983	MLW Signal Training - Radiotelegraph Procedure (Aust Army) Telegraph Procedure etc.
1985	Amateur Radio, Jan. - p 13 The Origin of 73 - G.M.Hull, VK3ZS.
1985	Amateur Radio, Mar. - p 37 A History of SOS - G.M.Hull, VK3ZS, Derivation of SOS.
1985	Amateur Radio, Aug. - pp 10-11 - The 1914 Experimenter's Call list and other items.
1986	List of Q Codes - Dept. of Civil Aviation.
1987	'Morsum Magnificat' - Q and Z Codes.
1987	Signals - RA Corps of Signals - pp5,6 Tasmanian Telegraphs 1858
1987	Great Days of the Heliograph – Lewis Coe. Heliograph history and usage.
1987	Herr Adolf Ehni DL1SX, Inspector of Signals, Europe, Wehrmacht, WW2. - German Codes.
1987	International Code of Signals - New Universal Comms Codes, Sound, Visual, Light, Radio.
1988	Ham Radio, Sept. - p 82 - Radiotelegraph Codes.
1989	US PMG's Historian - Letter - History of Morse and telegraphy early USA Govt. involvement.
1989	Amateur Radio - Jan. p13. Hints on using Japanese Morse.
1989	Amateur Radio - pp 16-20 Morse Code is a Myth, Mervyn Eunson VK4SO - Early Codes.
1989	Amateur Radio, Sep. - pp 24 - 29 L.Butler, VK5BR - Early Telegraph Codes 1837 - 1968.
1989	Amateur Radio Action, Jan, Vol 11, No 10 - Morse, American and International Codes.
1990	Amateur Radio, Mar. - p 44 Pounding Brass - G.Griffith, VK3GC - American Morse etc.
1991	Railroad Telegrapher's Handbook - T. French - Railroad, Numerical Codes etc circa 1900.
1993	The Telegraph – A history of Morse's Invention and its Predecessors in the United States – Lewis Coe.
1993	**The Native American Almanac - A Portrait of Native America Today – Navajo Speakers ROs – US Army.**
1994	Amateur Radio, Mar. - p 47 Pounding Brass - S.P.Smith, VK2SPS - 5 Early codes 1832 - 1851.
1995	Supplement to ICS 1987. - Innocent passage, freedom of navigation signals etc.
1996	Amateur Radio, Feb. - p 43 Pounding Brass - S.P.Smith, VK2SPS - Bain Chemical Telegraph.
1996	US Dept of the Navy, Naval Historical Center - Codes & Phonetics and other extracts 1875 - 1956
1996	ITU Geneva, Terrestial Services Dept.- Abbrev. Phonetics IRC 1927,1947. English, French, Spanish.
1996	'Getting the Message Through' - History of the US Army Signal Corps. - US Army, Ft. Gordon GA. (USSC)
1996	'Handbook for Radiotelephone Ship Station Operators' RIB 175, SMA, Australia.
1996 - 2002	Internet - esp Brian Kelk, Cambridge, UK. and many others. Phonetic Alphabets.
1996	Internet - Morsum Magnificat. various issues and many others - Various extracts.
1996	Canadian Railway Telegraph History - R. Burnet - 1860 Phonetics, 1920,1965 Codes etc.
1997	Internet - The Early History of Data Networks - Visual Telegraphs.
1997	The Phonetic Dilemma - QST, April, Lee Aurick, W1SE, US Phonetic Alphabet 1941.
1999	Internet - JARL A1 Club. Atsu Taniguchi, JE1TRV, Japanese Morse and Phonetics.
2000	Internet - Morse Telegraph Club inc. - Wood's Telegraph codes, 1864. Morse's Telegraphic Institute, Syracuse NY.
2002	Internet – Israeli Army – Phonetic Alphabet.

Thanks to all other persons, sources or references inadvertently omitted or overlooked. - JWA.

Radiotelegraph and Radiotelephone Codes, Prowords and Abbreviations

The Baudot Keyboard

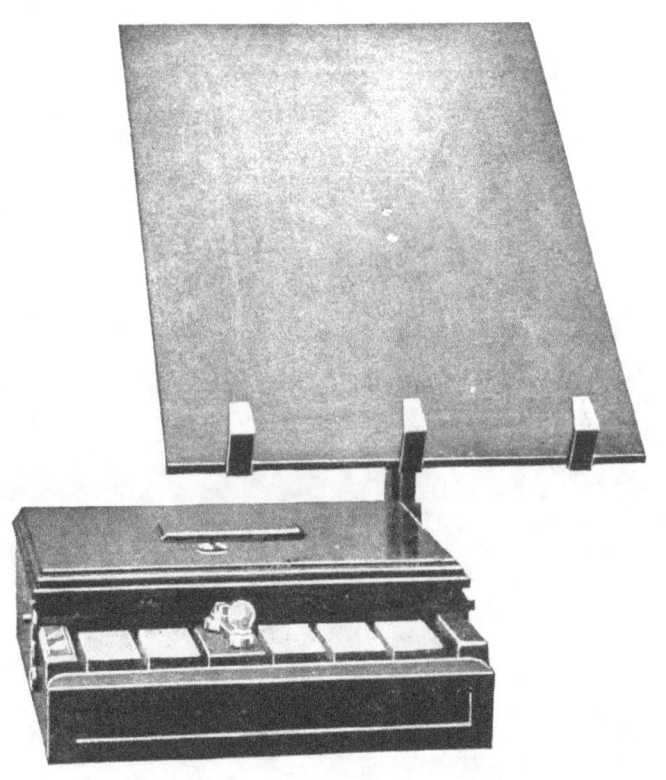

The Baudot Transmitter / Sender.
Modern Electric Practice, 1907

www.ingramcontent.com/pod-product-compliance
Lightning Source LLC
Chambersburg PA
CBHW080054200426
43197CB00053B/2717